STREET ANGEL

ANGEL

volume one:

THE PRINCESS OF POVERTY

created and written
Jim Rugg *and* **Brian Ma**

drawn by
Jim Rugg

Published by SLG Publishing
Dan Vado, *President and Publisher*
Jennifer de Guzman, *Editor-in-Chief*

SLG Publishing
P.O. Box 26427
San Jose, CA 95159

www.slgcomic.com
www.streetangelcomics.com

ISBN 978-1-59362-012-7
Second Printing: September 2009

Introduction
by Evan Dorkin

My first encounter with Street Angel was when I saw the solicitation for the first issue in the pages of Diamond Previews (which, for you blissfully unaware readers out there, is a depressingly mind-numbing monthly catalogue of upcoming comic book releases that may or may not one day appear on the dusty shelves of the few comic shops left in America).

The cover to Street Angel #1 featured an unkempt scientist looking up past the logo at the legs of a girl on a skateboard sailing overhead, set against a background of magnetic, eyeball-yanking pink. The title of the book also begged attention. Looked good. Sounded good. Two for two. And there was that cover. Pink is a ballsy color choice for a comic book cover, only readers of shoujo manga or Betty and Veronica can withstand pink without breaking out into a confused rash. I made a mental note to keep an eye out for the book, and then promptly forgot because I have a lousy memory. But eventually Street Angel #1 hit my local shop, and I flipped through it, and I took it home, and I read it, and it made me a believer.

Street Angel might not be the kind of comic (excuse me, "graphic novel") that the New York Times is writing up these days. But it's a hell of a lot more fun than those books are. I like fun comics that knock me on my ass. That's why I like Street Angel. Rugg and Maruca handle comic book and action genre tropes, pop culture kitsch, superhero parody and other beaten horses with aplomb. Yes, that's right, I said aplomb. I've been saving that word for twenty years now just to use it here.

I'm reminded of a handful of comics I've enjoyed since my Marvel fanboy days that comfortably straddled the fence between superhero adventure and alternative quirk: Mike Baron and Steve Rude's early run on Nexus, Scott McCloud's Zot, Mike Mignola's Hellboy and The Amazing Screw-On Head and Paul Grist's Jack Staff. While there are recognizable genre influences and tropes on display in all of these comics, they are uniquely tweaked and fine-tuned by the creator's personal vision, imagination and style. There is also a playfulness to these works, in the stories and the way the stories are told. Finally, the creators don't seem to take themselves too seriously. They take the medium seriously, and they take their work seriously, and that's clearly reflected in the books. And I think Street Angel shares these qualities, and that's probably why I enjoy it so much.

Here's what I also appreciate:

Nothing is rammed down the reader's throat. There are no lengthy explanations of who everyone is and what they do and how they do it and why they do it and where they learned eagle claw or snake fist. No didactic fanboy world-creating nonsense. The stories get in fast, get going even faster, and twenty-four pages later Jesse skates off, passes out or scratches her unwashed head in utter confusion. Street Angel is bullshit-free, concentrating on the good stuff.

Street Angel is also thankfully bullshit-free when it comes to the folks who write and draw it. No smug sense of accomplishment saturates these pages, no self-satisfaction, no grandstanding. Rugg and Maruca are not the stars of Street Angel, Jesse Sanchez is, and if anything threatens to upstage their character it's the work itself, not the personalities of the creators.

So, what can I say? I love a comic book about a girl on a skateboard who fights crime. Jesse Sanchez walks softly and carries a big skateboard and kicks reams of evil, ungodly ass.

Bless you, kind reader, for giving this little book about a homeless little kung-fu skateboarder who fights crime a good home. If you like Jesse Sanchez as much as I do, you'll buy another copy for someone unfamiliar with her exploits. That way we might get to see her kick some more ninja ass up and down the dirty black and white streets of Wilkesborough.

Evan Dorkin
Friday the 13th, 2005

I'm the best there is at what I do.
But what I do isn't very nice.

- WOLVERINE, 1982

Dr. Pangea's Continental Conundrum

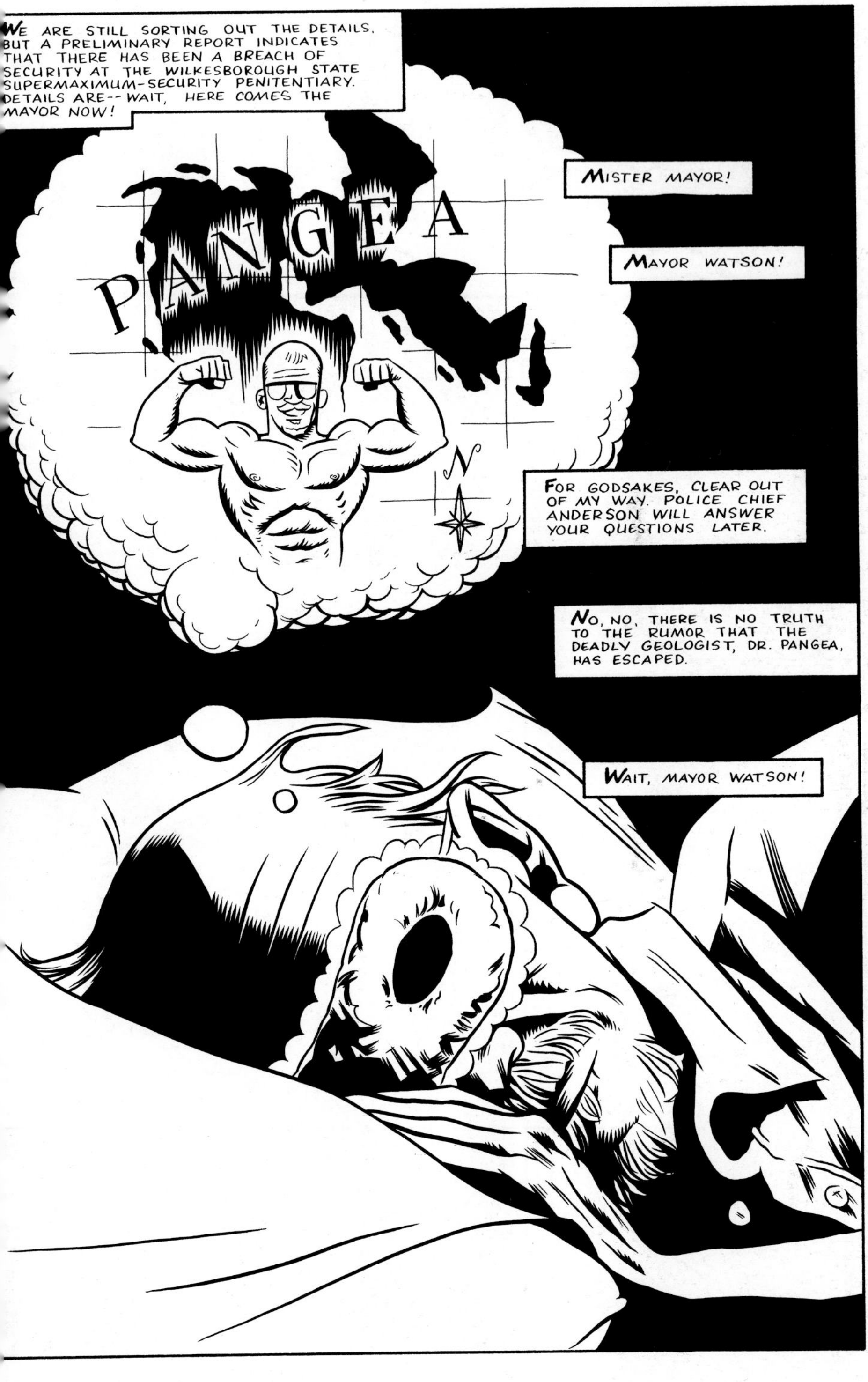
WE ARE STILL SORTING OUT THE DETAILS, BUT A PRELIMINARY REPORT INDICATES THAT THERE HAS BEEN A BREACH OF SECURITY AT THE WILKESBOROUGH STATE SUPERMAXIMUM-SECURITY PENITENTIARY. DETAILS ARE-- WAIT, HERE COMES THE MAYOR NOW!
PANGEA
N
MISTER MAYOR!
MAYOR WATSON!
FOR GODSAKES, CLEAR OUT OF MY WAY. POLICE CHIEF ANDERSON WILL ANSWER YOUR QUESTIONS LATER.
NO, NO, THERE IS NO TRUTH TO THE RUMOR THAT THE DEADLY GEOLOGIST, DR. PANGEA, HAS ESCAPED.
WAIT, MAYOR WATSON!

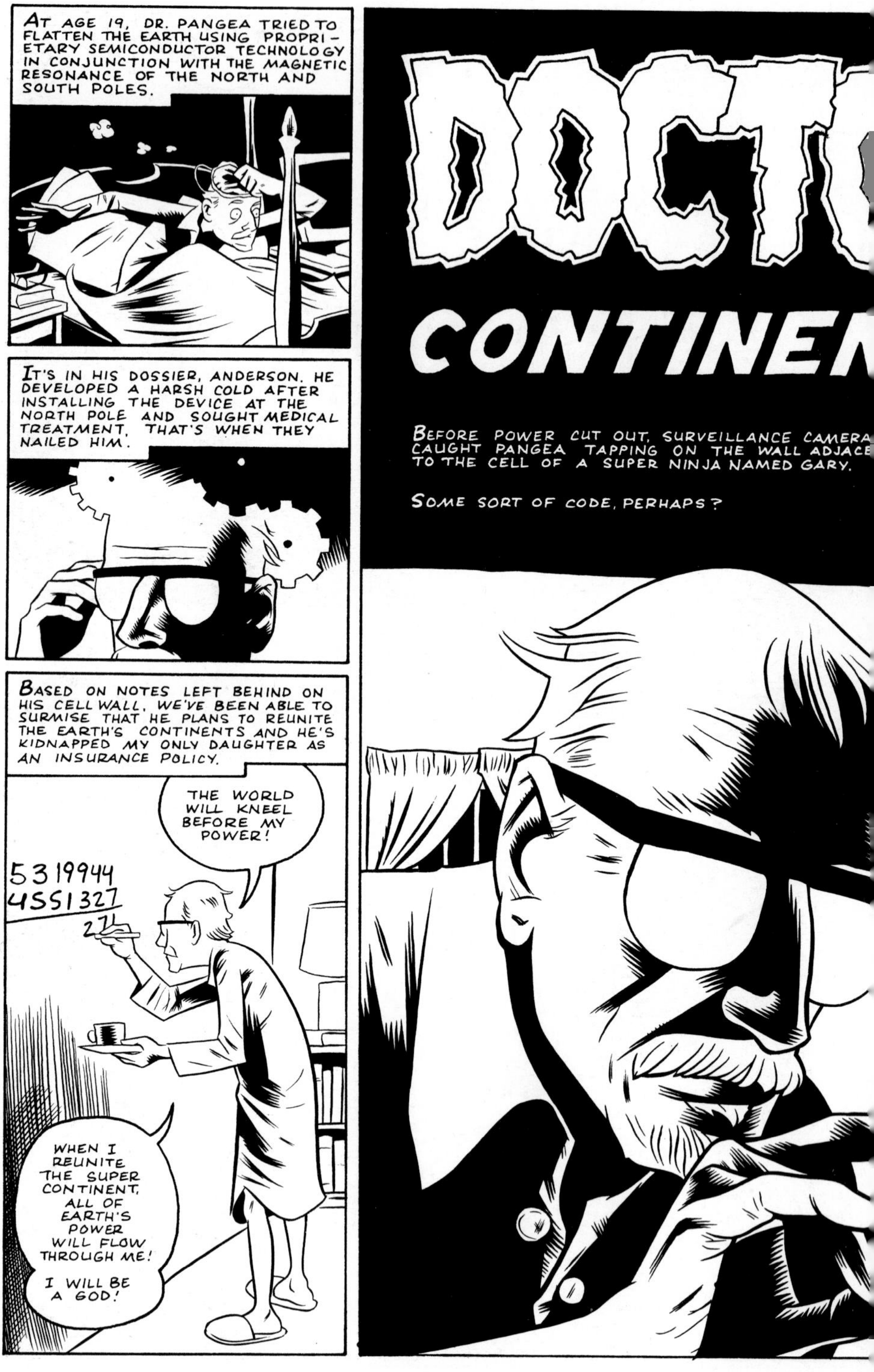

AT AGE 19, DR. PANGEA TRIED TO FLATTEN THE EARTH USING PROPRIETARY SEMICONDUCTOR TECHNOLOGY IN CONJUNCTION WITH THE MAGNETIC RESONANCE OF THE NORTH AND SOUTH POLES.
IT'S IN HIS DOSSIER, ANDERSON. HE DEVELOPED A HARSH COLD AFTER INSTALLING THE DEVICE AT THE NORTH POLE AND SOUGHT MEDICAL TREATMENT. THAT'S WHEN THEY NAILED HIM.
BASED ON NOTES LEFT BEHIND ON HIS CELL WALL, WE'VE BEEN ABLE TO SURMISE THAT HE PLANS TO REUNITE THE EARTH'S CONTINENTS AND HE'S KIDNAPPED MY ONLY DAUGHTER AS AN INSURANCE POLICY.
THE WORLD WILL KNEEL BEFORE MY POWER!
5319944
4551327
271
WHEN I REUNITE THE SUPER CONTINENT, ALL OF EARTH'S POWER WILL FLOW THROUGH ME!
I WILL BE A GOD!
DOCT
CONTINEN
BEFORE POWER CUT OUT, SURVEILLANCE CAMERA CAUGHT PANGEA TAPPING ON THE WALL ADJACE TO THE CELL OF A SUPER NINJA NAMED GARY.
SOME SORT OF CODE, PERHAPS?

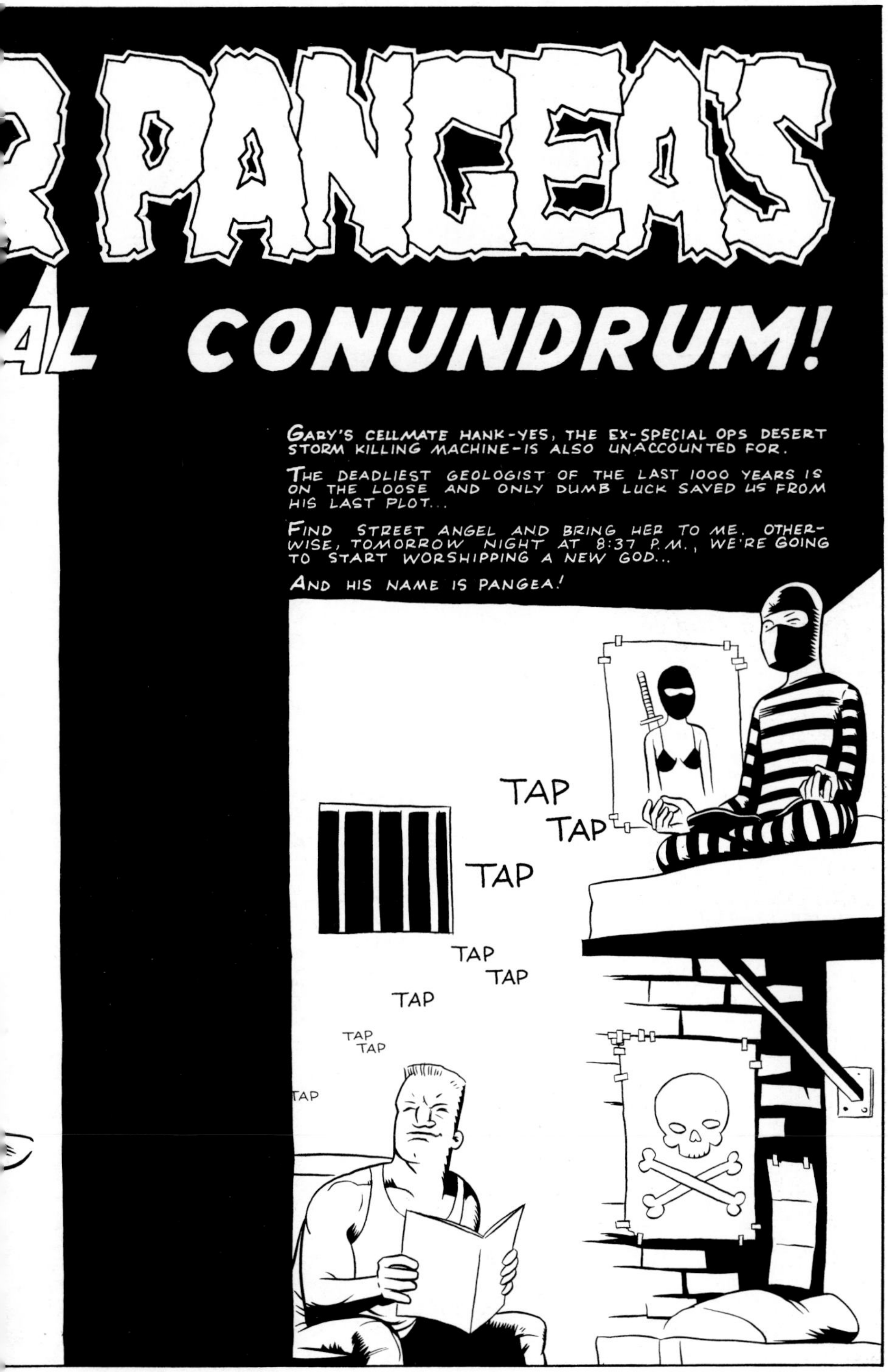
R PANGEA'S
AL CONUNDRUM!
GARY'S CELLMATE HANK-YES, THE EX-SPECIAL OPS DESERT STORM KILLING MACHINE-IS ALSO UNACCOUNTED FOR.
THE DEADLIEST GEOLOGIST OF THE LAST 1000 YEARS IS ON THE LOOSE AND ONLY DUMB LUCK SAVED US FROM HIS LAST PLOT...
FIND STREET ANGEL AND BRING HER TO ME. OTHERWISE, TOMORROW NIGHT AT 8:37 P.M., WE'RE GOING TO START WORSHIPPING A NEW GOD...
AND HIS NAME IS PANGEA!
TAP
TAP
TAP
TAP
TAP
TAP
TAP
TAP
TAP

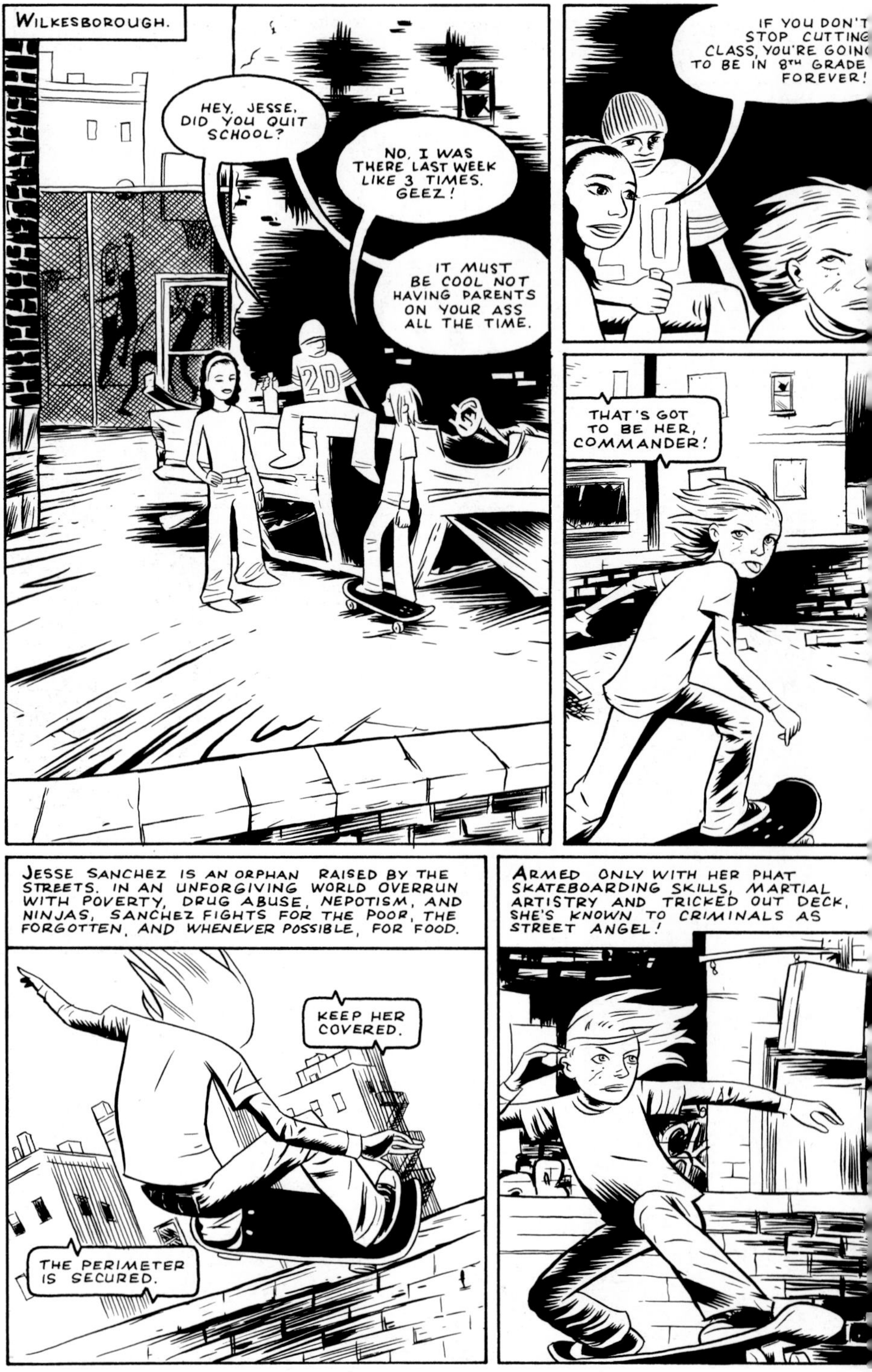
WILKESBOROUGH.
HEY, JESSE, DID YOU QUIT SCHOOL?
NO, I WAS THERE LAST WEEK LIKE 3 TIMES. GEEZ!
IT MUST BE COOL NOT HAVING PARENTS ON YOUR ASS ALL THE TIME.
IF YOU DON'T STOP CUTTING CLASS, YOU'RE GOING TO BE IN 8TH GRADE FOREVER!
THAT'S GOT TO BE HER, COMMANDER!
JESSE SANCHEZ IS AN ORPHAN RAISED BY THE STREETS. IN AN UNFORGIVING WORLD OVERRUN WITH POVERTY, DRUG ABUSE, NEPOTISM, AND NINJAS, SANCHEZ FIGHTS FOR THE POOR, THE FORGOTTEN, AND WHENEVER POSSIBLE, FOR FOOD.
KEEP HER COVERED.
THE PERIMETER IS SECURED.
ARMED ONLY WITH HER PHAT SKATEBOARDING SKILLS, MARTIAL ARTISTRY AND TRICKED OUT DECK, SHE'S KNOWN TO CRIMINALS AS STREET ANGEL!

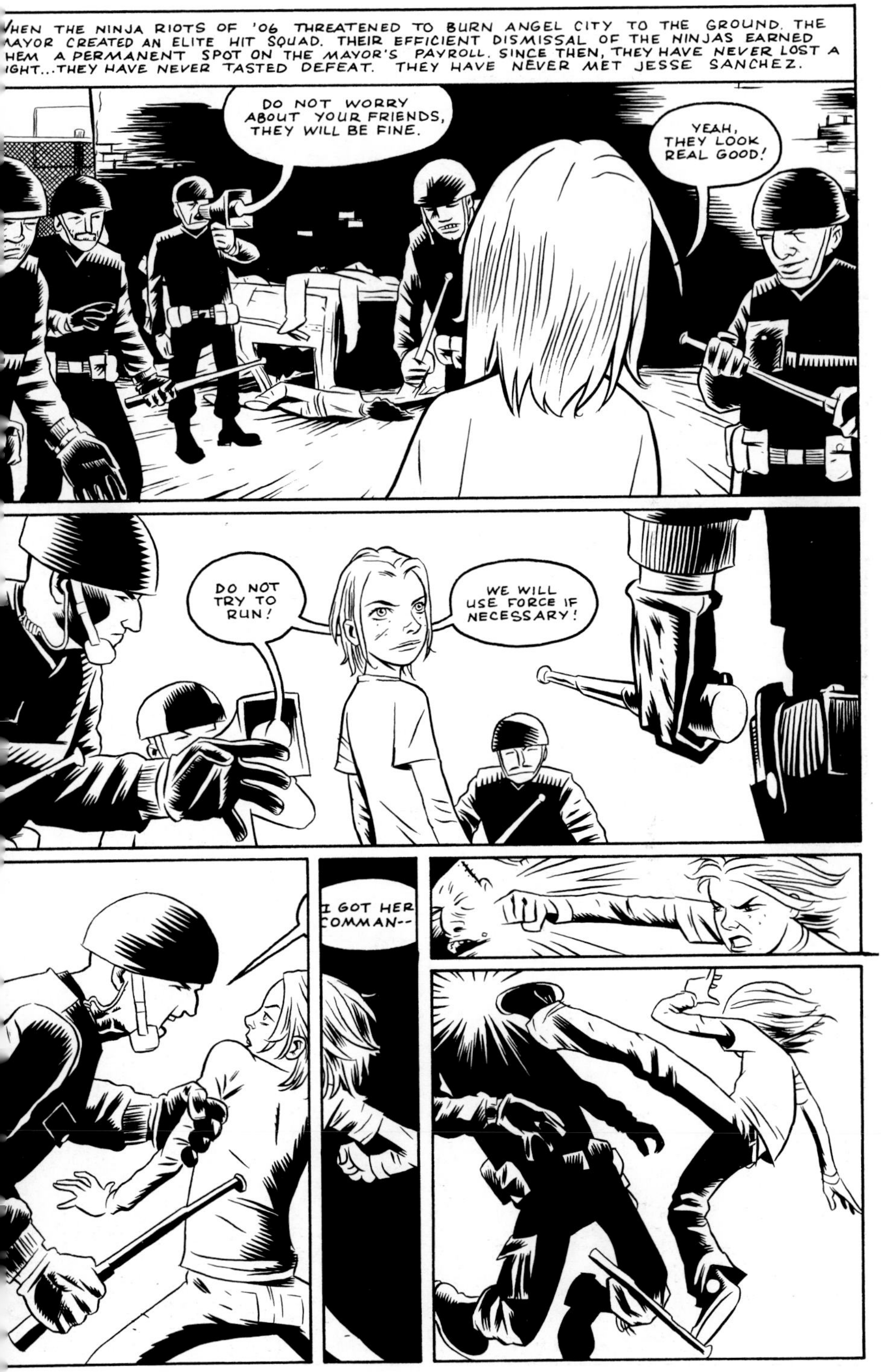
WHEN THE NINJA RIOTS OF '06 THREATENED TO BURN ANGEL CITY TO THE GROUND, THE MAYOR CREATED AN ELITE HIT SQUAD. THEIR EFFICIENT DISMISSAL OF THE NINJAS EARNED THEM A PERMANENT SPOT ON THE MAYOR'S PAYROLL. SINCE THEN, THEY HAVE NEVER LOST A FIGHT... THEY HAVE NEVER TASTED DEFEAT. THEY HAVE NEVER MET JESSE SANCHEZ.
DO NOT WORRY ABOUT YOUR FRIENDS, THEY WILL BE FINE.
YEAH, THEY LOOK REAL GOOD!
DO NOT TRY TO RUN!
WE WILL USE FORCE IF NECESSARY!
I GOT HER COMMAN--

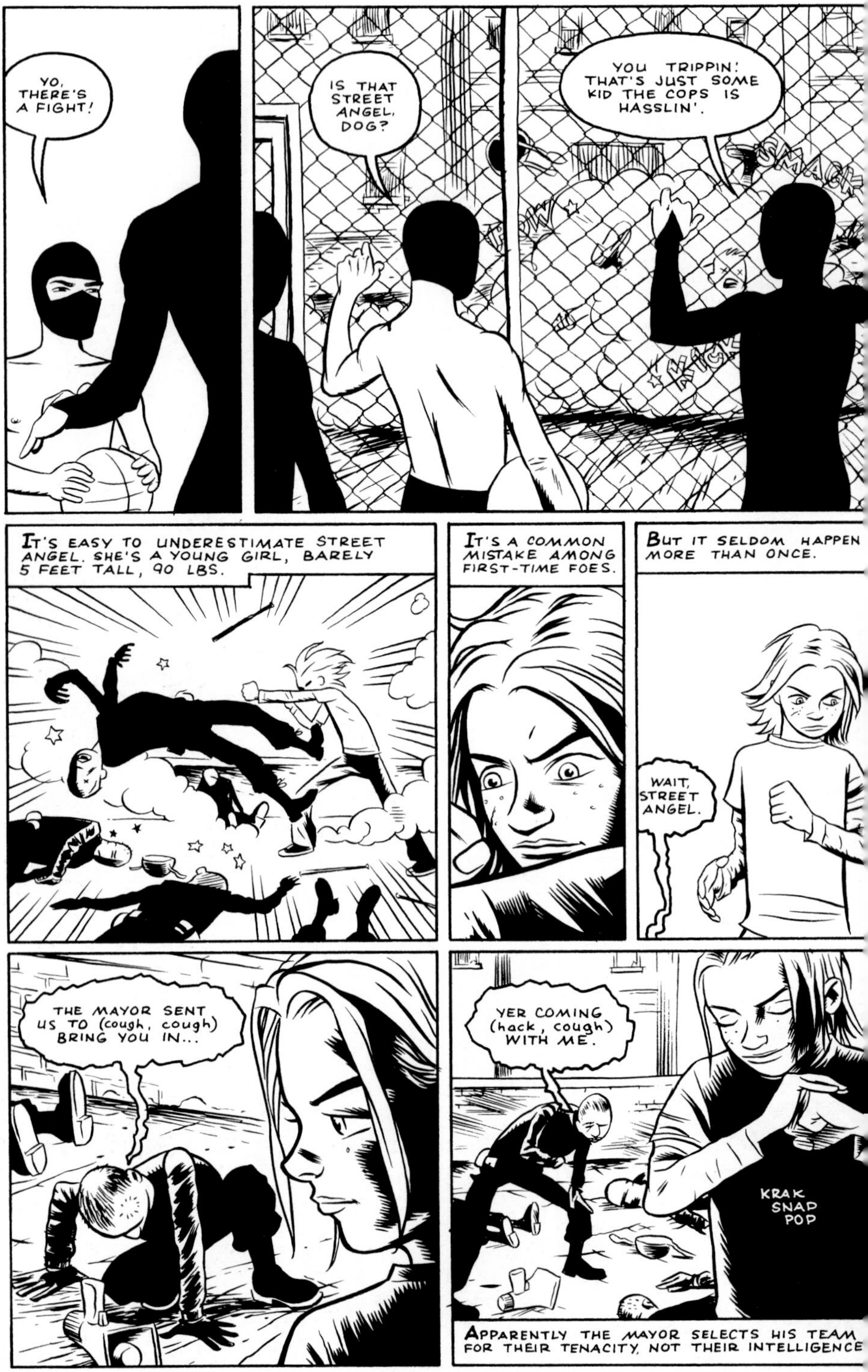
YO, THERE'S A FIGHT!
IS THAT STREET ANGEL, DOG?
YOU TRIPPIN'! THAT'S JUST SOME KID THE COPS IS HASSLIN'.
SMACK
POW
KICK
IT'S EASY TO UNDERESTIMATE STREET ANGEL. SHE'S A YOUNG GIRL, BARELY 5 FEET TALL, 90 LBS.
IT'S A COMMON MISTAKE AMONG FIRST-TIME FOES.
BUT IT SELDOM HAPPEN MORE THAN ONCE.
WAIT, STREET ANGEL.
THE MAYOR SENT US TO (cough, cough) BRING YOU IN...
YER COMING (hack, cough) WITH ME.
KRAK SNAP POP
APPARENTLY THE MAYOR SELECTS HIS TEAM FOR THEIR TENACITY, NOT THEIR INTELLIGENCE

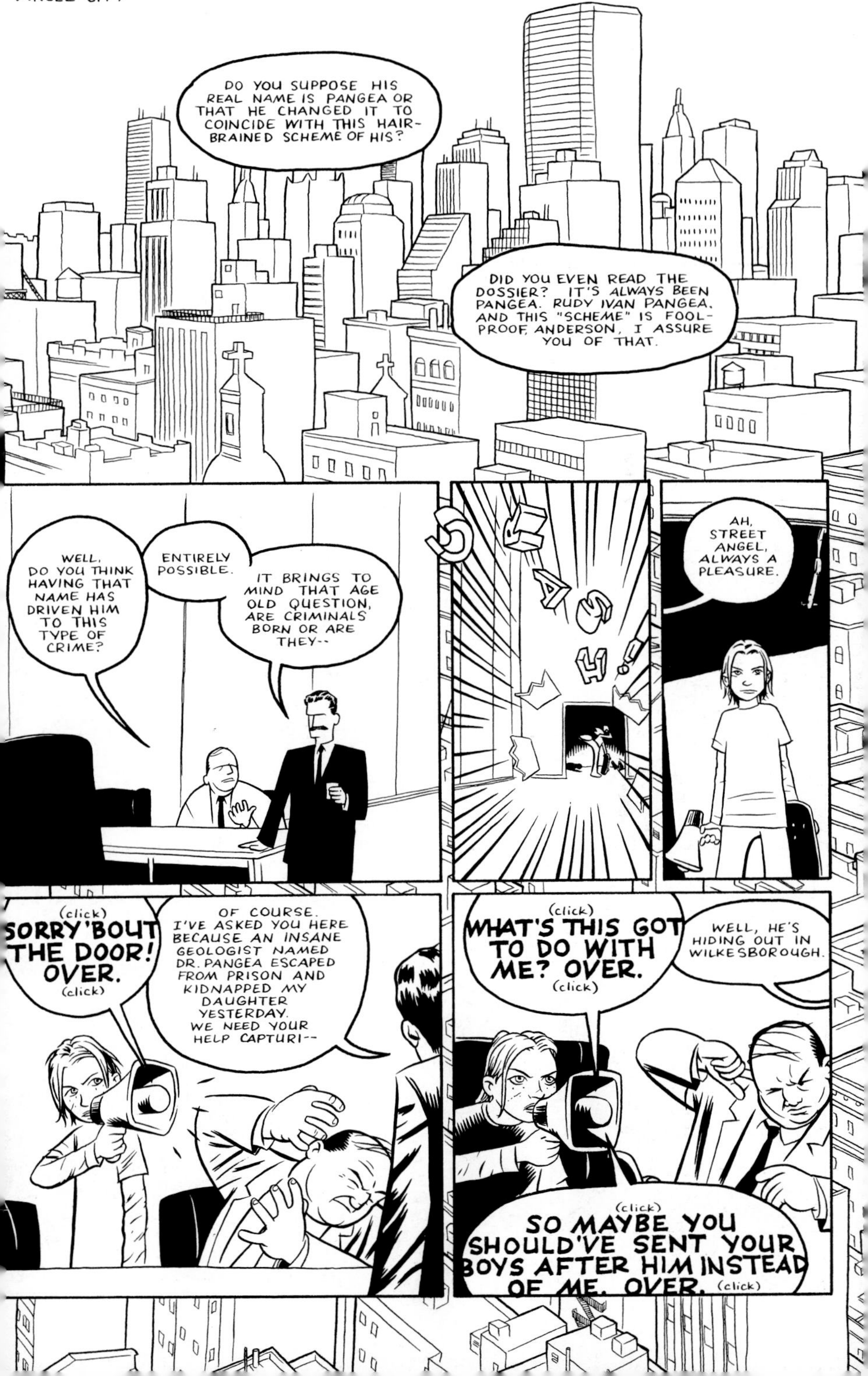
DO YOU SUPPOSE HIS REAL NAME IS PANGEA OR THAT HE CHANGED IT TO COINCIDE WITH THIS HAIR-BRAINED SCHEME OF HIS?
DID YOU EVEN READ THE DOSSIER? IT'S ALWAYS BEEN PANGEA. RUDY IVAN PANGEA. AND THIS "SCHEME" IS FOOL-PROOF, ANDERSON, I ASSURE YOU OF THAT.
WELL, DO YOU THINK HAVING THAT NAME HAS DRIVEN HIM TO THIS TYPE OF CRIME?
ENTIRELY POSSIBLE.
IT BRINGS TO MIND THAT AGE OLD QUESTION, ARE CRIMINALS BORN OR ARE THEY--
AH, STREET ANGEL, ALWAYS A PLEASURE.
(click) SORRY 'BOUT THE DOOR! OVER. (click)
OF COURSE. I'VE ASKED YOU HERE BECAUSE AN INSANE GEOLOGIST NAMED DR. PANGEA ESCAPED FROM PRISON AND KIDNAPPED MY DAUGHTER YESTERDAY. WE NEED YOUR HELP CAPTURI--
(click) WHAT'S THIS GOT TO DO WITH ME? OVER. (click)
WELL, HE'S HIDING OUT IN WILKESBOROUGH.
(click) SO MAYBE YOU SHOULD'VE SENT YOUR BOYS AFTER HIM INSTEAD OF ME. OVER. (click)

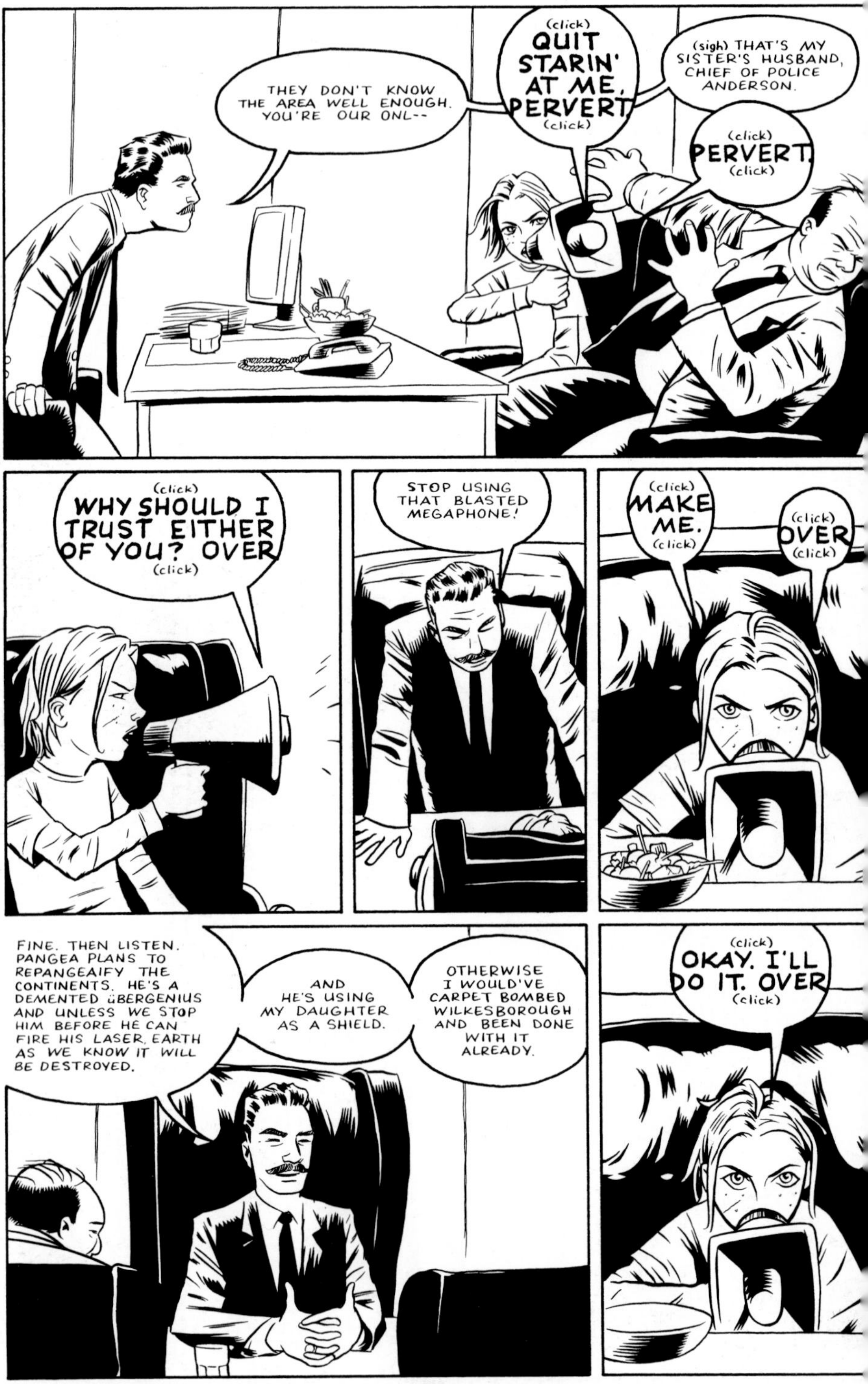
THEY DON'T KNOW THE AREA WELL ENOUGH. YOU'RE OUR ONL--
(click) QUIT STARIN' AT ME, PERVERT (click)
(sigh) THAT'S MY SISTER'S HUSBAND, CHIEF OF POLICE ANDERSON.
(click) PERVERT. (click)
(click) WHY SHOULD I TRUST EITHER OF YOU? OVER (click)
STOP USING THAT BLASTED MEGAPHONE!
(click) MAKE ME. (click)
(click) OVER (click)
FINE. THEN LISTEN. PANGEA PLANS TO REPANGEAIFY THE CONTINENTS. HE'S A DEMENTED üBERGENIUS AND UNLESS WE STOP HIM BEFORE HE CAN FIRE HIS LASER, EARTH AS WE KNOW IT WILL BE DESTROYED.
AND HE'S USING MY DAUGHTER AS A SHIELD.
OTHERWISE I WOULD'VE CARPET BOMBED WILKESBOROUGH AND BEEN DONE WITH IT ALREADY.
(click) OKAY. I'LL DO IT. OVER (click)

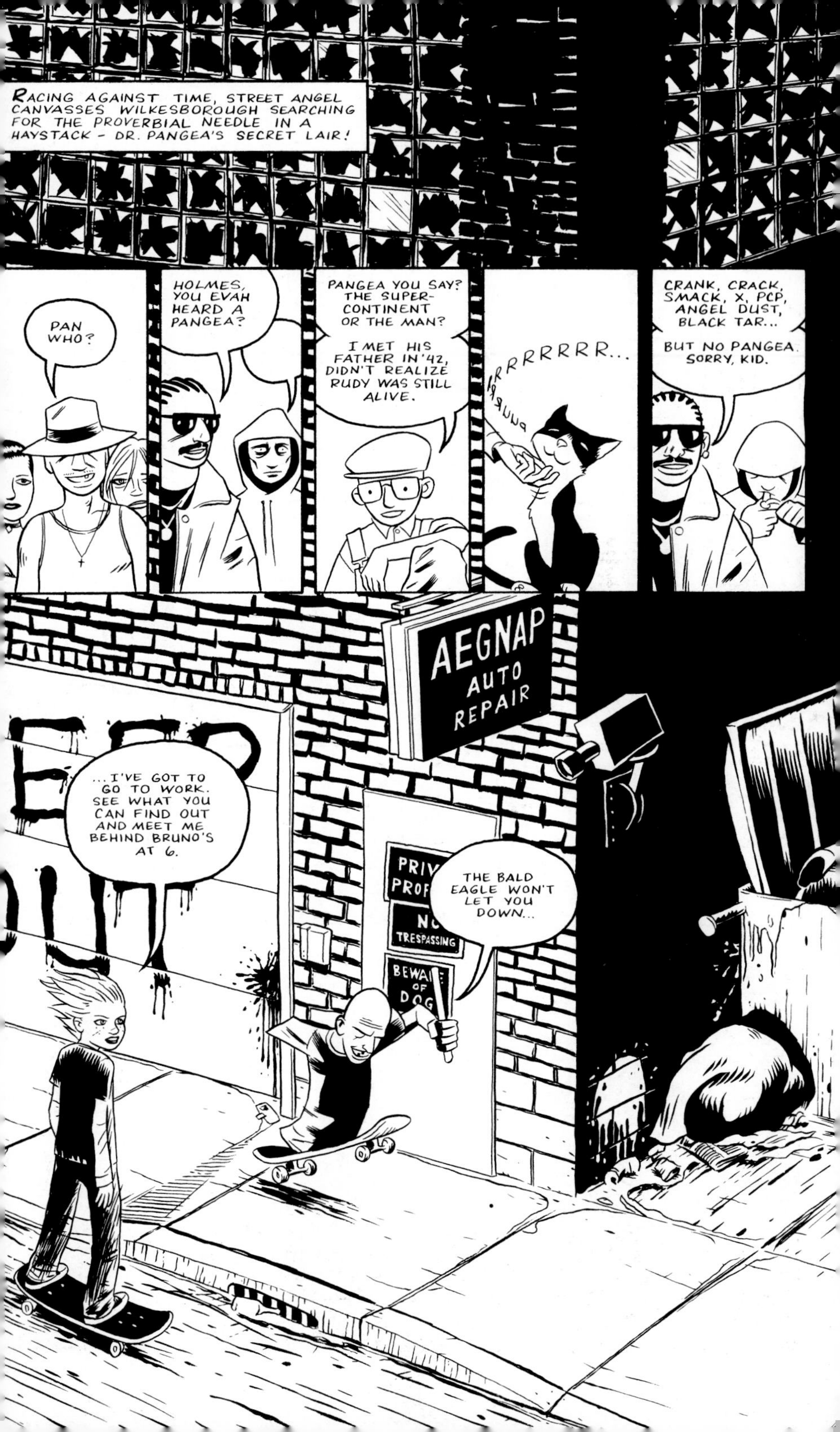
RACING AGAINST TIME, STREET ANGEL CANVASSES WILKESBOROUGH SEARCHING FOR THE PROVERBIAL NEEDLE IN A HAYSTACK - DR. PANGEA'S SECRET LAIR!
PAN WHO?
HOLMES, YOU EVAH HEARD A PANGEA?
PANGEA YOU SAY? THE SUPER-CONTINENT OR THE MAN?
I MET HIS FATHER IN '42, DIDN'T REALIZE RUDY WAS STILL ALIVE.
RRRRRRRRR...
CRANK, CRACK, SMACK, X, PCP, ANGEL DUST, BLACK TAR...
BUT NO PANGEA. SORRY, KID.
AEGNAP AUTO REPAIR
...I'VE GOT TO GO TO WORK. SEE WHAT YOU CAN FIND OUT AND MEET ME BEHIND BRUNO'S AT 6.
THE BALD EAGLE WON'T LET YOU DOWN...
NO TRESPASSING

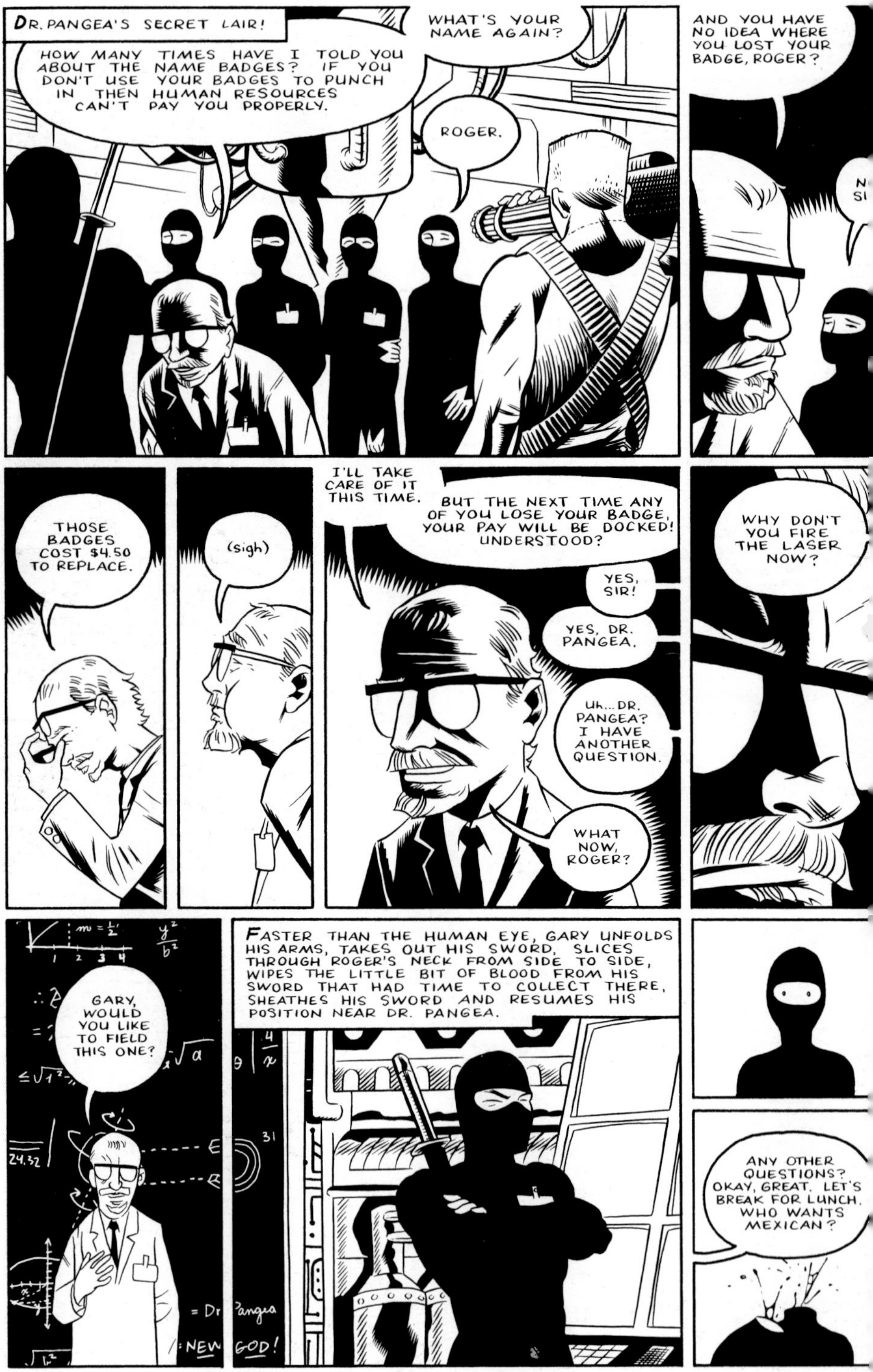
DR. PANGEA'S SECRET LAIR!
HOW MANY TIMES HAVE I TOLD YOU ABOUT THE NAME BADGES? IF YOU DON'T USE YOUR BADGES TO PUNCH IN THEN HUMAN RESOURCES CAN'T PAY YOU PROPERLY.
WHAT'S YOUR NAME AGAIN?
ROGER.
AND YOU HAVE NO IDEA WHERE YOU LOST YOUR BADGE, ROGER?
THOSE BADGES COST $4.50 TO REPLACE.
(sigh)
I'LL TAKE CARE OF IT THIS TIME.
BUT THE NEXT TIME ANY OF YOU LOSE YOUR BADGE, YOUR PAY WILL BE DOCKED! UNDERSTOOD?
YES, SIR!
YES, DR. PANGEA.
Uh... DR. PANGEA? I HAVE ANOTHER QUESTION.
WHAT NOW, ROGER?
WHY DON'T YOU FIRE THE LASER NOW?
GARY, WOULD YOU LIKE TO FIELD THIS ONE?
= Dr Pangea
= NEW GOD!
FASTER THAN THE HUMAN EYE, GARY UNFOLDS HIS ARMS, TAKES OUT HIS SWORD, SLICES THROUGH ROGER'S NECK FROM SIDE TO SIDE, WIPES THE LITTLE BIT OF BLOOD FROM HIS SWORD THAT HAD TIME TO COLLECT THERE, SHEATHES HIS SWORD AND RESUMES HIS POSITION NEAR DR. PANGEA.
ANY OTHER QUESTIONS? OKAY, GREAT. LET'S BREAK FOR LUNCH. WHO WANTS MEXICAN?

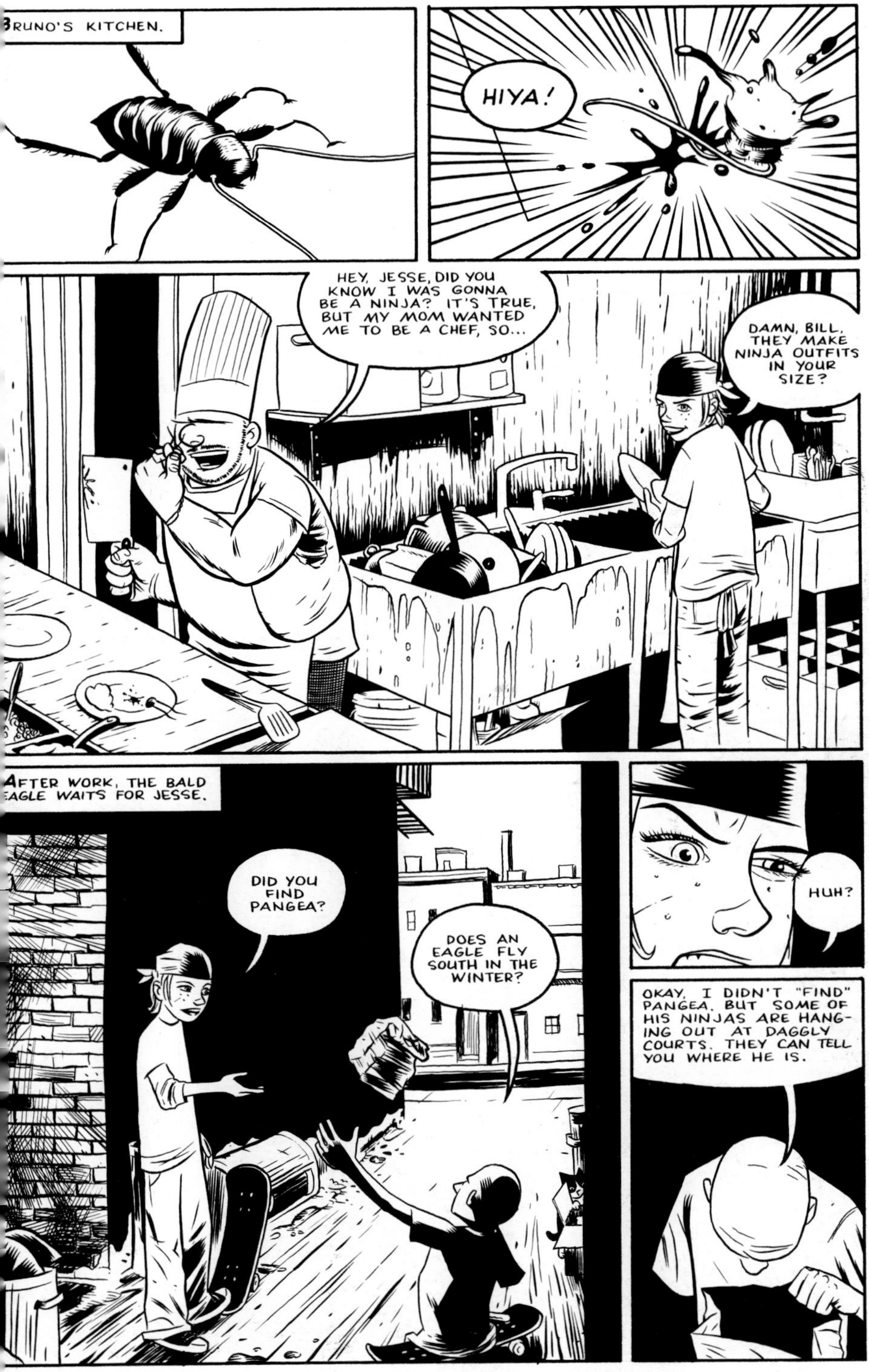
BRUNO'S KITCHEN.
HIYA!
HEY, JESSE, DID YOU KNOW I WAS GONNA BE A NINJA? IT'S TRUE, BUT MY MOM WANTED ME TO BE A CHEF, SO...
DAMN, BILL, THEY MAKE NINJA OUTFITS IN YOUR SIZE?
AFTER WORK, THE BALD EAGLE WAITS FOR JESSE.
DID YOU FIND PANGEA?
DOES AN EAGLE FLY SOUTH IN THE WINTER?
HUH?
OKAY, I DIDN'T "FIND" PANGEA. BUT SOME OF HIS NINJAS ARE HANGING OUT AT DAGGLY COURTS. THEY CAN TELL YOU WHERE HE IS.

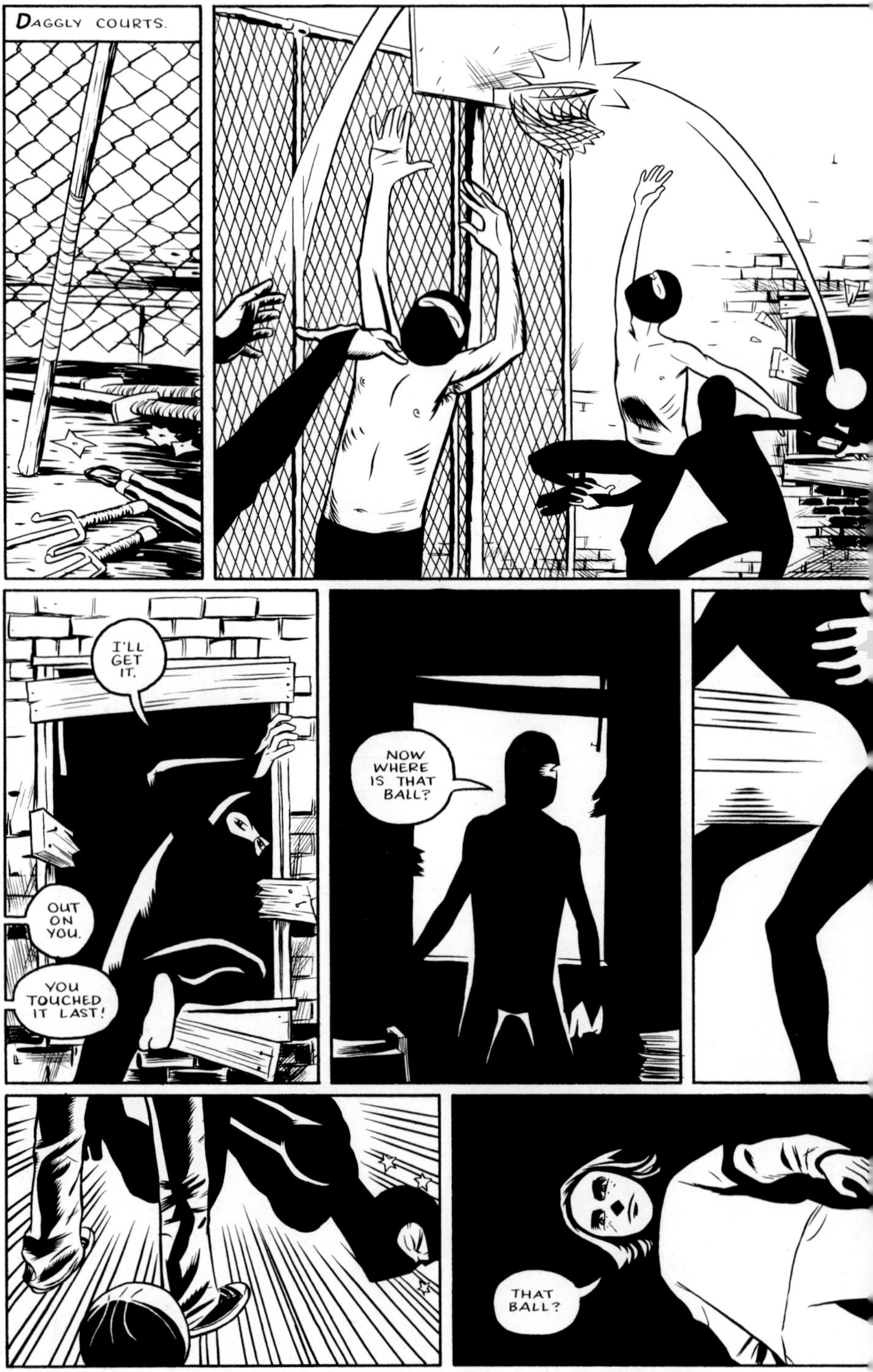
DAGGLY COURTS.
I'LL GET IT.
OUT ON YOU.
YOU TOUCHED IT LAST!
NOW WHERE IS THAT BALL?
THAT BALL?

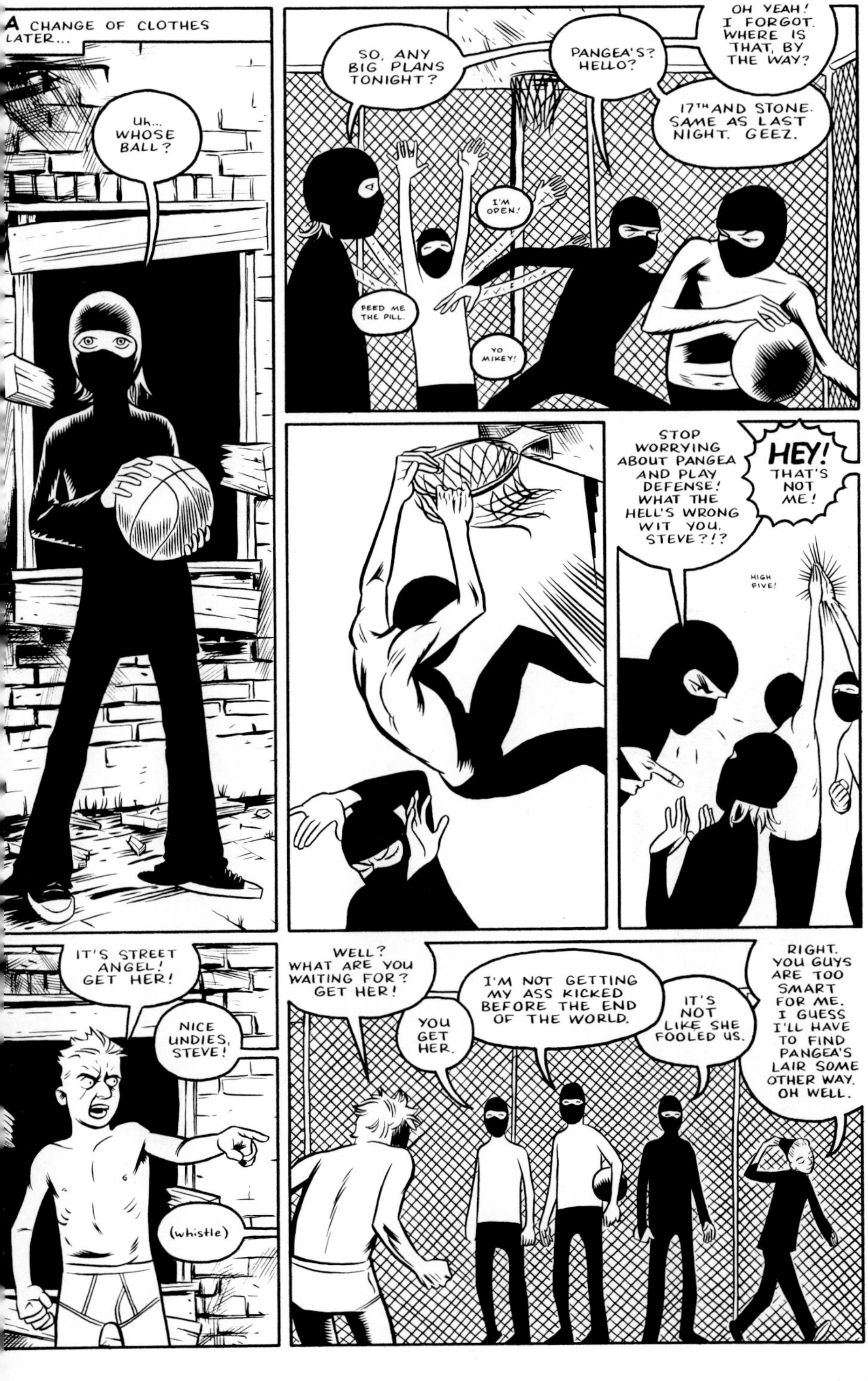
A CHANGE OF CLOTHES LATER...
Uh... WHOSE BALL?
SO, ANY BIG PLANS TONIGHT?
PANGEA'S? HELLO?
OH YEAH! I FORGOT. WHERE IS THAT, BY THE WAY?
17TH AND STONE. SAME AS LAST NIGHT. GEEZ.
I'M OPEN!
FEED ME THE PILL.
YO MIKEY!
STOP WORRYING ABOUT PANGEA AND PLAY DEFENSE! WHAT THE HELL'S WRONG WIT YOU, STEVE?!?
HEY! THAT'S NOT ME!
HIGH FIVE!
IT'S STREET ANGEL! GET HER!
NICE UNDIES, STEVE!
(whistle)
WELL? WHAT ARE YOU WAITING FOR? GET HER!
YOU GET HER.
I'M NOT GETTING MY ASS KICKED BEFORE THE END OF THE WORLD.
IT'S NOT LIKE SHE FOOLED US.
RIGHT. YOU GUYS ARE TOO SMART FOR ME. I GUESS I'LL HAVE TO FIND PANGEA'S LAIR SOME OTHER WAY. OH WELL.

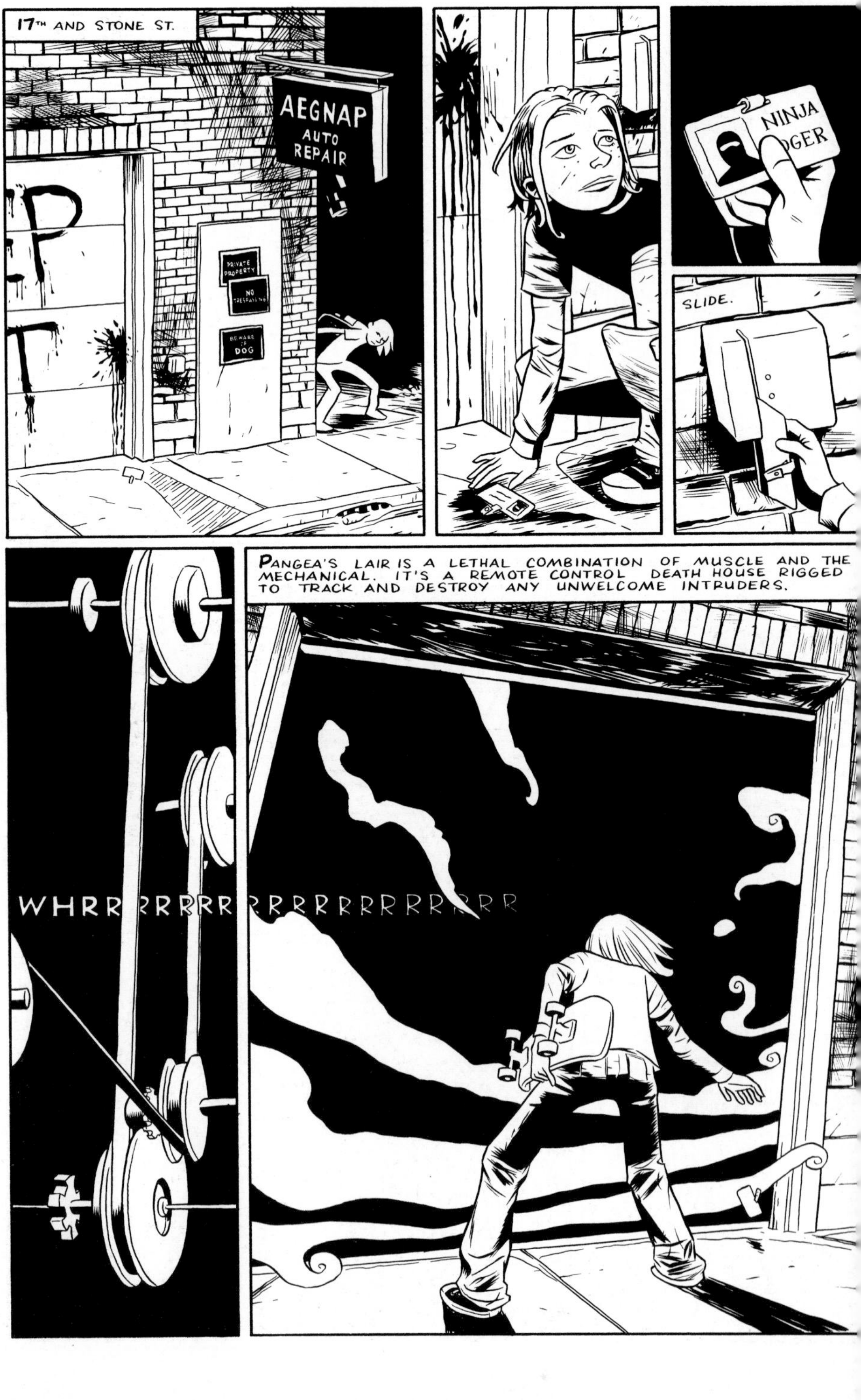
17TH AND STONE ST.
AEGNAP AUTO REPAIR
PRIVATE PROPERTY
NO TRESPASSING
BEWARE OF DOG
NINJA
OGER
SLIDE.
PANGEA'S LAIR IS A LETHAL COMBINATION OF MUSCLE AND THE MECHANICAL. IT'S A REMOTE CONTROL DEATH HOUSE RIGGED TO TRACK AND DESTROY ANY UNWELCOME INTRUDERS.
WHRRRRRRRRRRRRRRRRRRRR

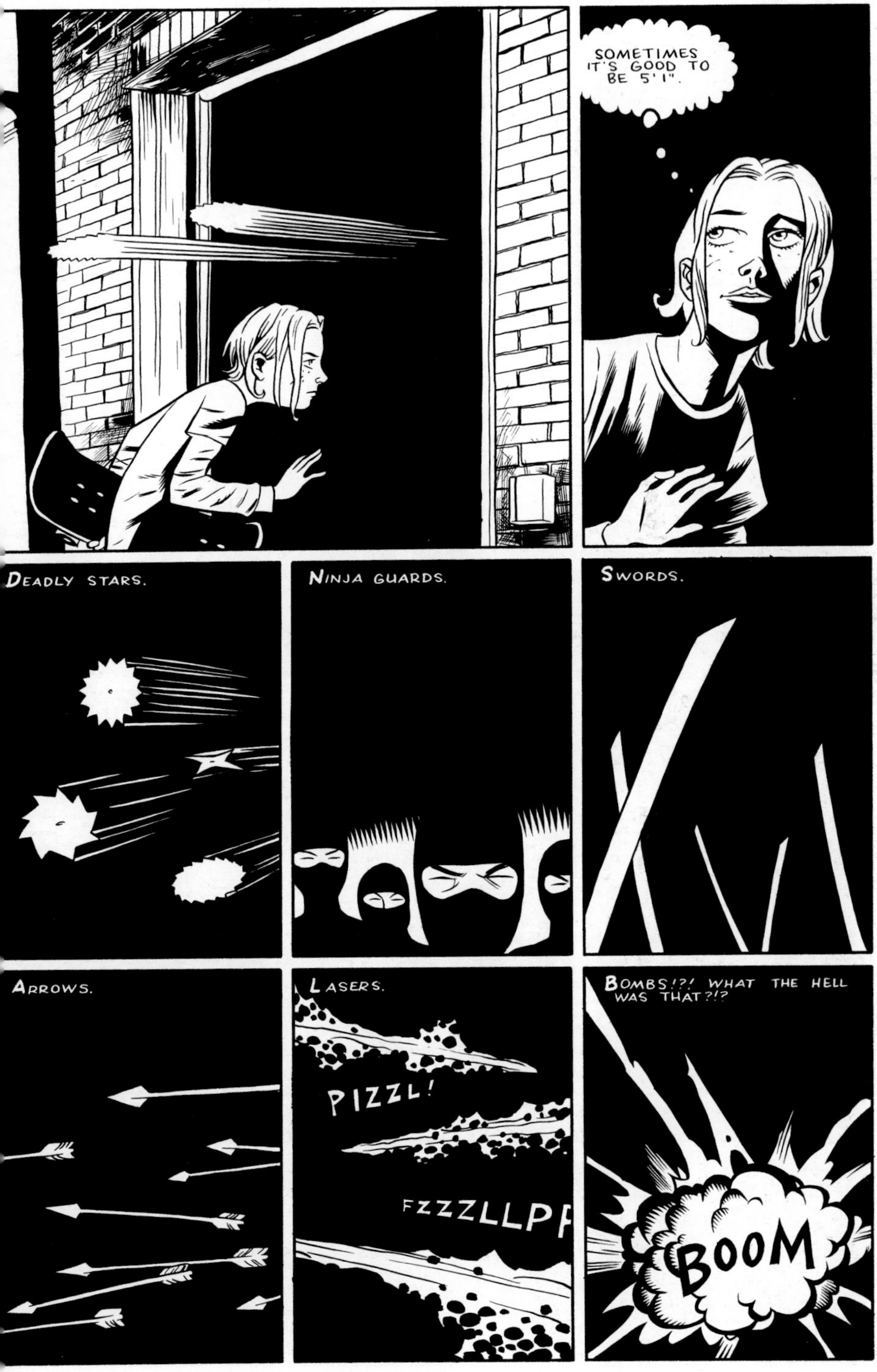
SOMETIMES IT'S GOOD TO BE 5'1".
DEADLY STARS.
NINJA GUARDS.
SWORDS.
ARROWS.
LASERS.
PIZZL!
FZZZLLPP
BOMBS!?! WHAT THE HELL WAS THAT?!?
BOOM

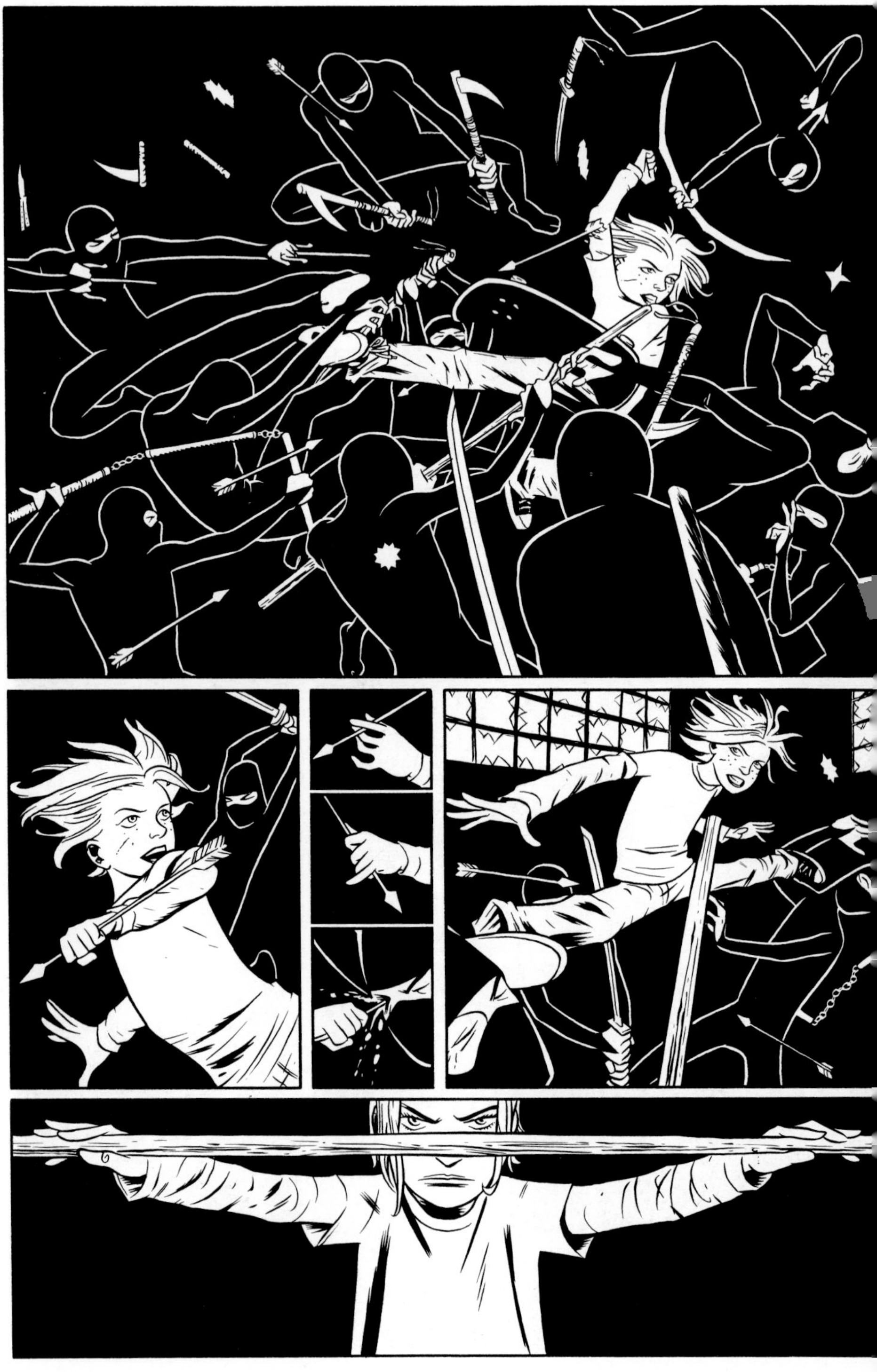

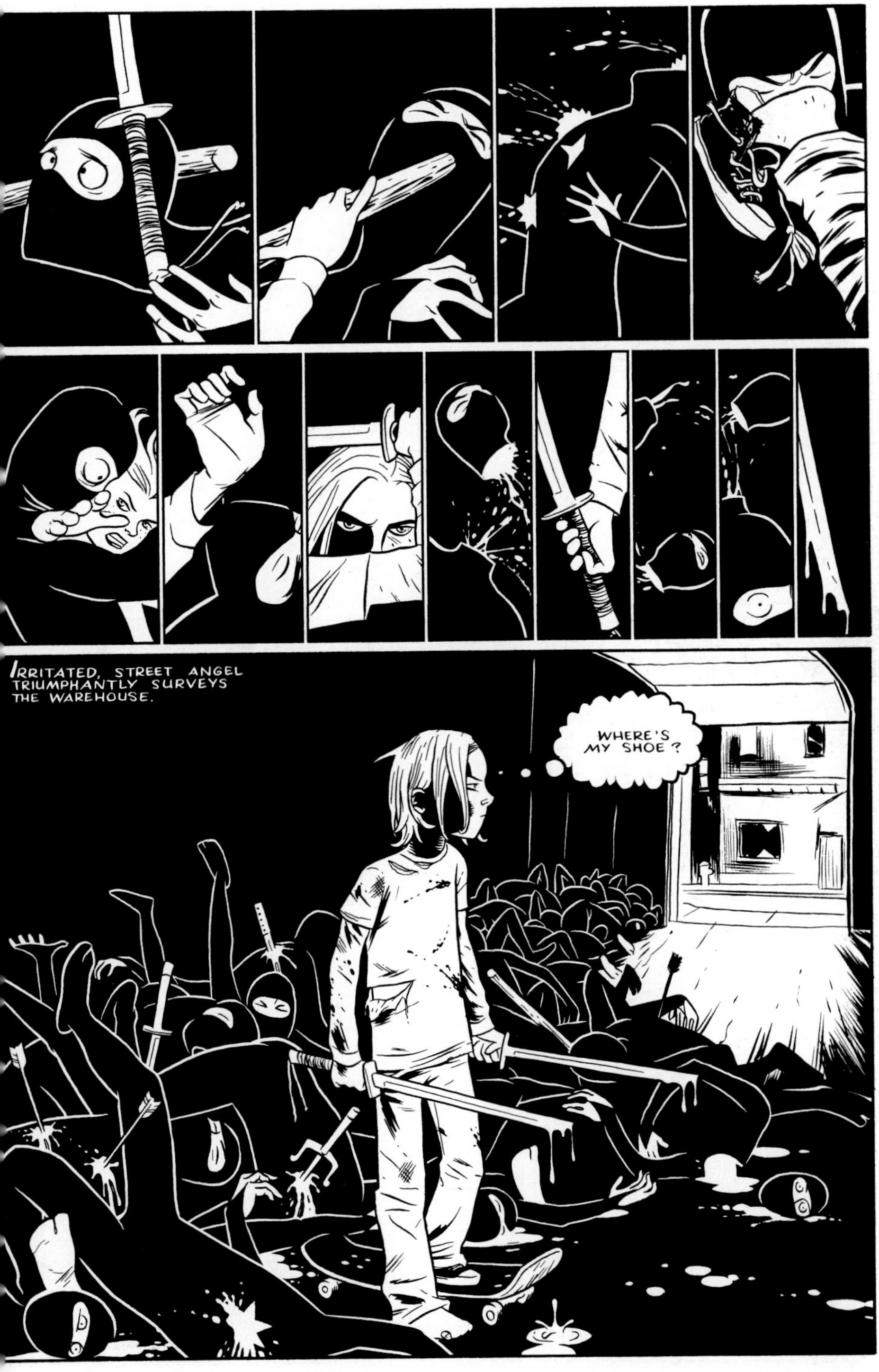
IRRITATED, STREET ANGEL TRIUMPHANTLY SURVEYS THE WAREHOUSE.
WHERE'S MY SHOE?

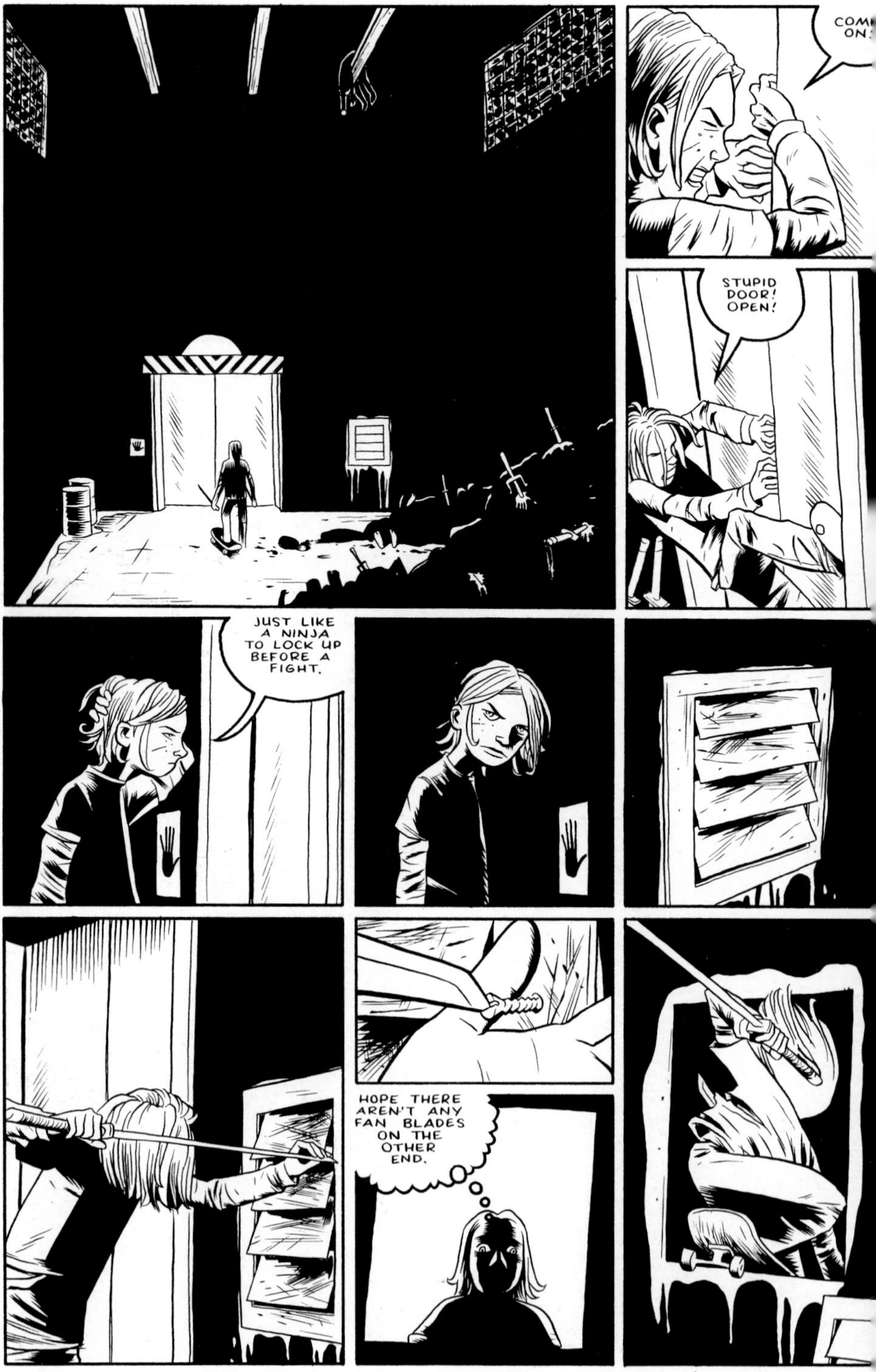
STUPID DOOR! OPEN!
JUST LIKE A NINJA TO LOCK UP BEFORE A FIGHT.
HOPE THERE AREN'T ANY FAN BLADES ON THE OTHER END.

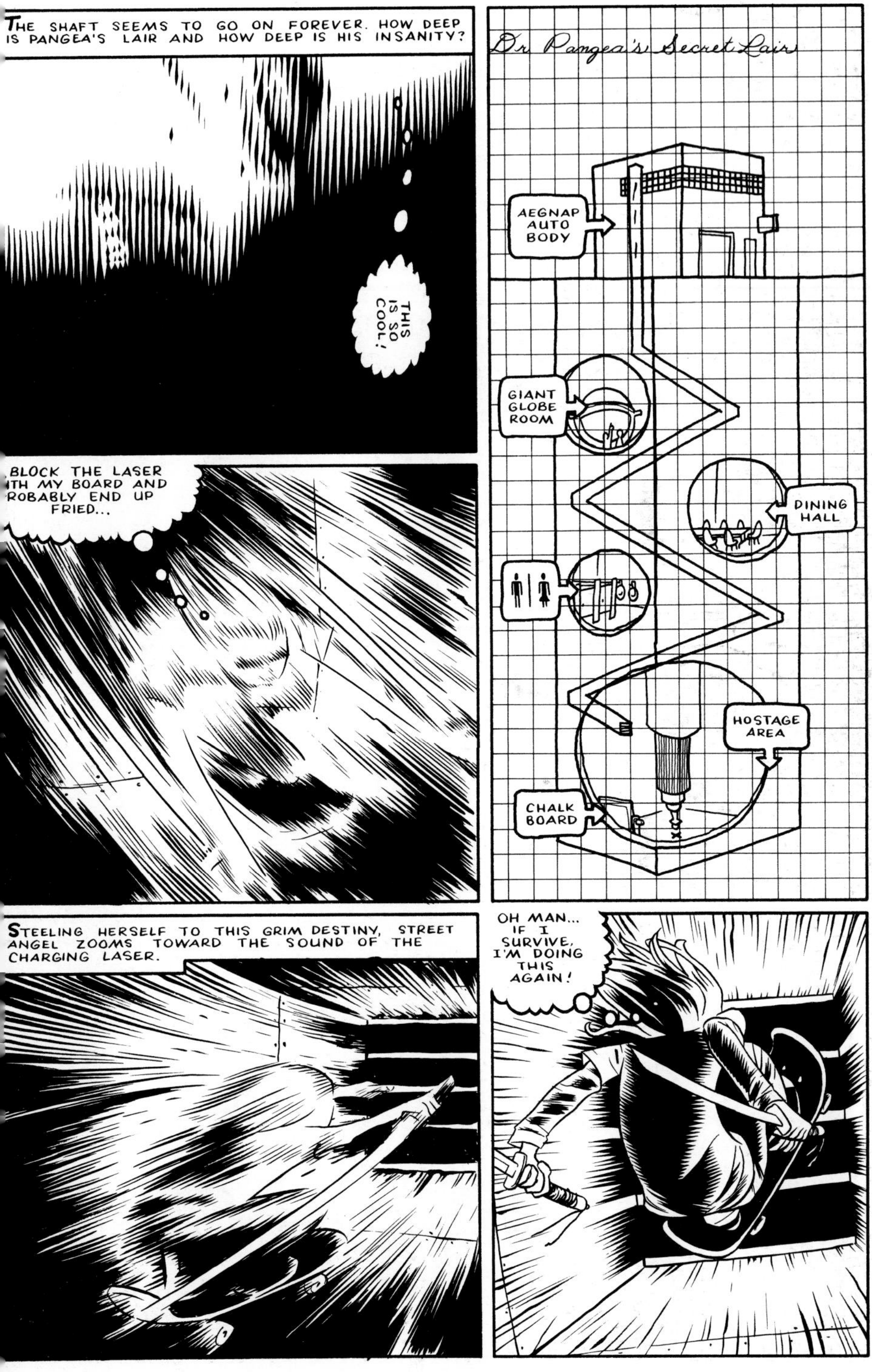

THE SHAFT SEEMS TO GO ON FOREVER. HOW DEEP IS PANGEA'S LAIR AND HOW DEEP IS HIS INSANITY?
THIS IS SO COOL!
BLOCK THE LASER
ITH MY BOARD AND
ROBABLY END UP
FRIED...
Dr Pangea's Secret Lair
AEGNAP AUTO BODY
GIANT GLOBE ROOM
DINING HALL
HOSTAGE AREA
CHALK BOARD
STEELING HERSELF TO THIS GRIM DESTINY, STREET ANGEL ZOOMS TOWARD THE SOUND OF THE CHARGING LASER.
OH MAN... IF I SURVIVE, I'M DOING THIS AGAIN!

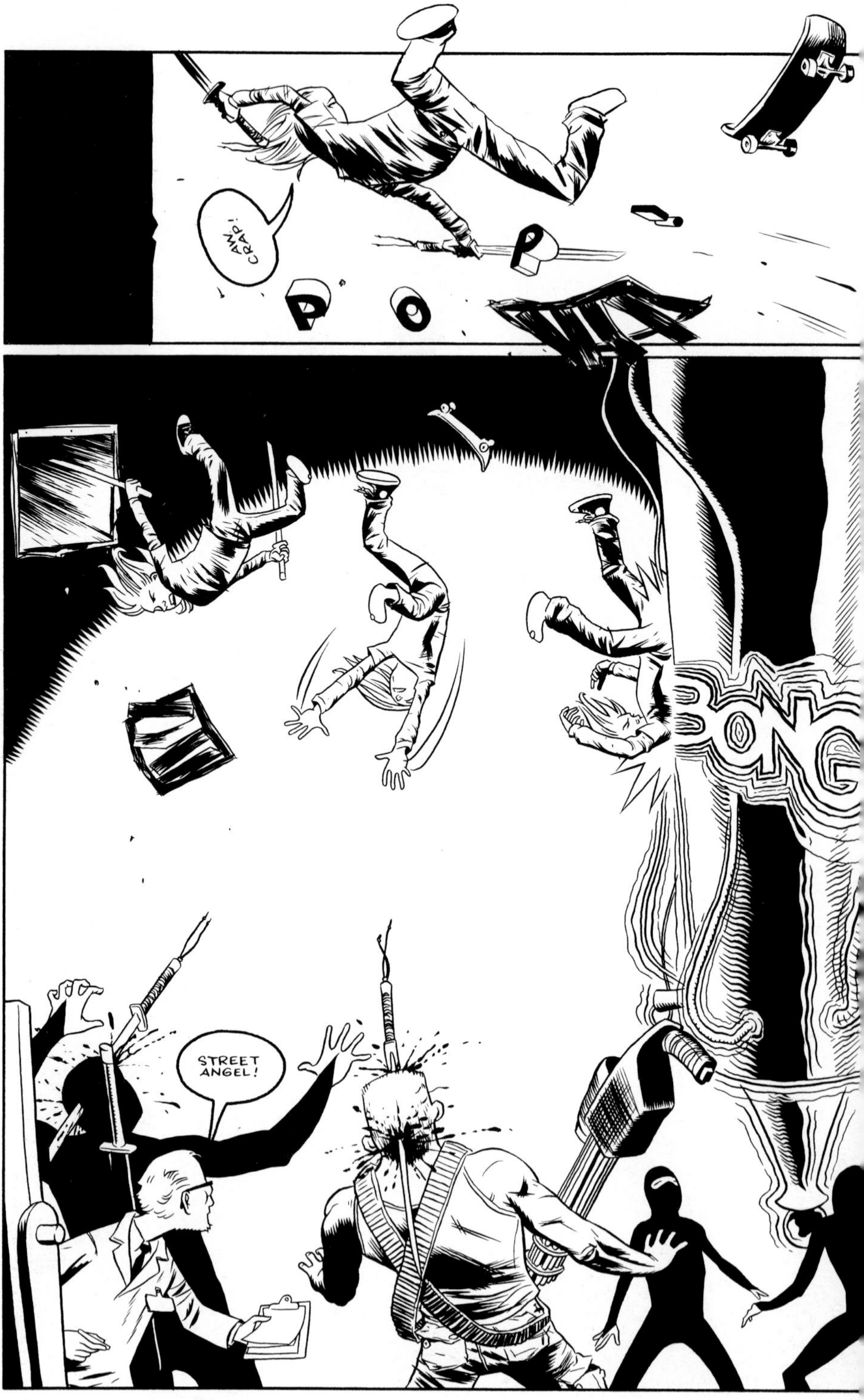
AW, CRAP!
POP
BONG
STREET ANGEL!

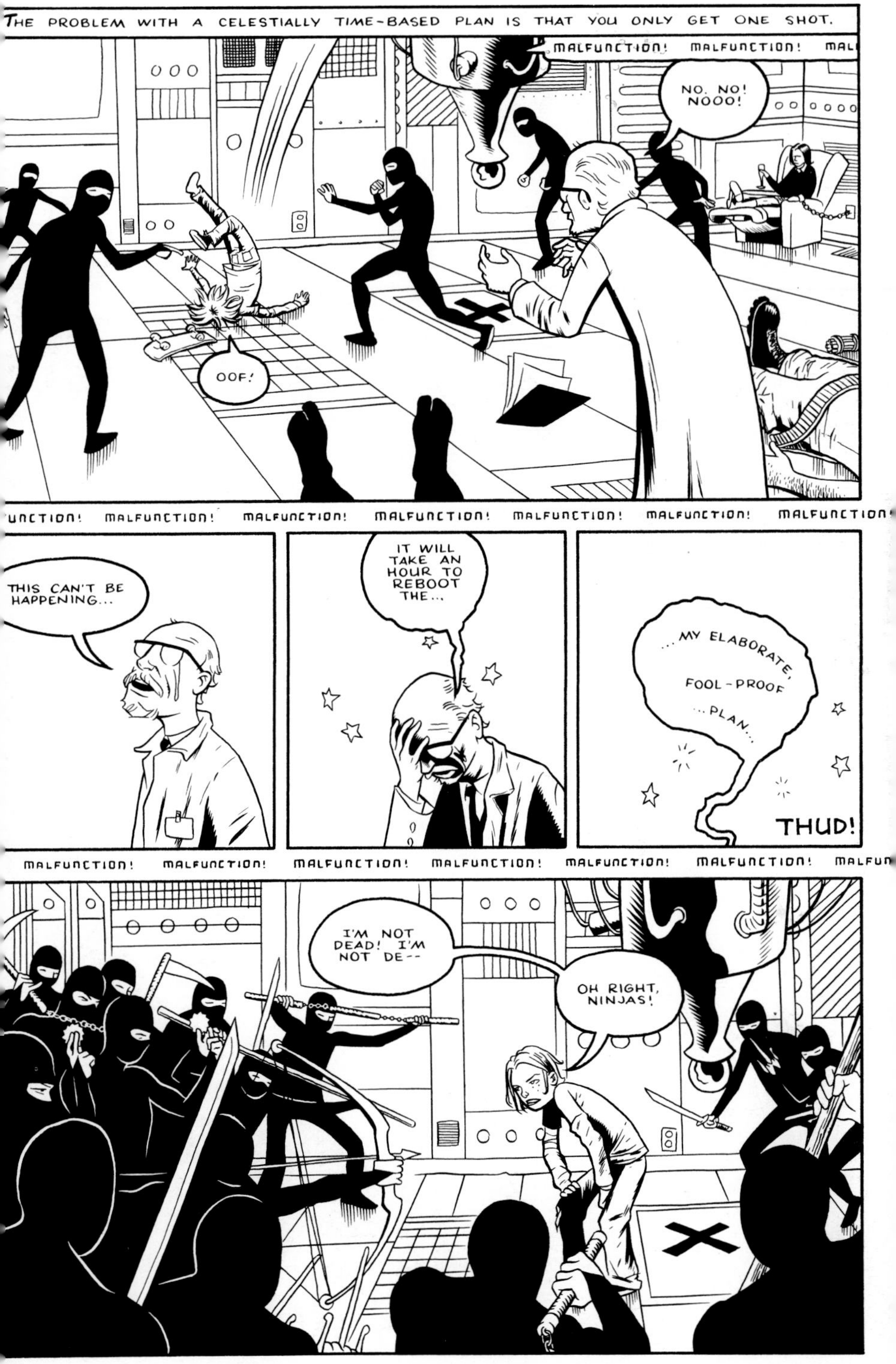
THE PROBLEM WITH A CELESTIALLY TIME-BASED PLAN IS THAT YOU ONLY GET ONE SHOT.
MALFUNCTION! MALFUNCTION!
NO. NO! NOOO!
OOF!
MALFUNCTION! MALFUNCTION! MALFUNCTION! MALFUNCTION! MALFUNCTION! MALFUNCTION!
THIS CAN'T BE HAPPENING...
IT WILL TAKE AN HOUR TO REBOOT THE...
...MY ELABORATE, FOOL-PROOF ...PLAN...
THUD!
MALFUNCTION! MALFUNCTION! MALFUNCTION! MALFUNCTION! MALFUNCTION! MALFUNCTION!
I'M NOT DEAD! I'M NOT DE--
OH RIGHT, NINJAS!

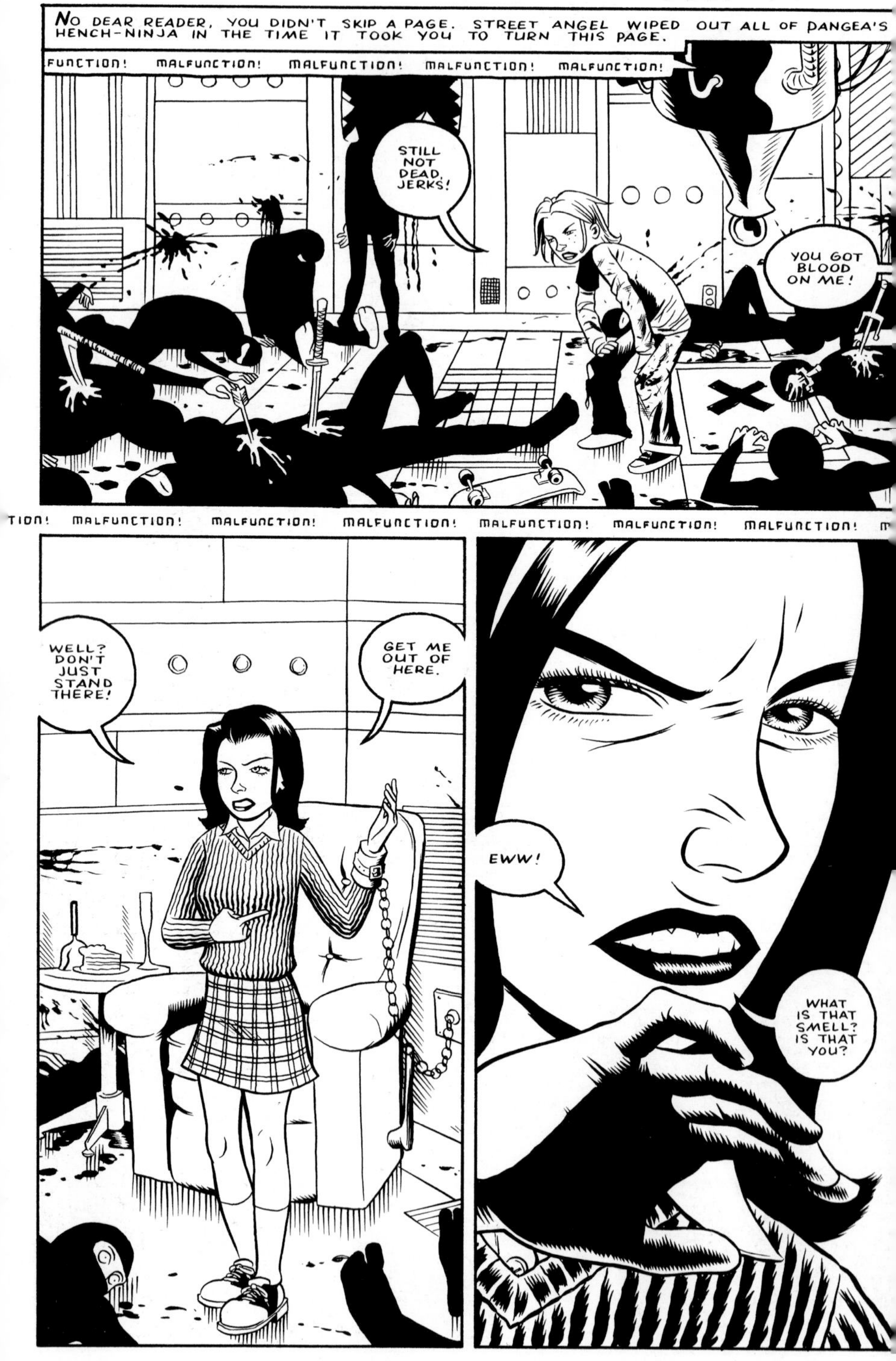

NO DEAR READER, YOU DIDN'T SKIP A PAGE. STREET ANGEL WIPED OUT ALL OF PANGEA'S HENCH-NINJA IN THE TIME IT TOOK YOU TO TURN THIS PAGE.
FUNCTION! MALFUNCTION! MALFUNCTION! MALFUNCTION! MALFUNCTION!
STILL NOT DEAD, JERKS!
YOU GOT BLOOD ON ME!
TION! MALFUNCTION! MALFUNCTION! MALFUNCTION! MALFUNCTION! MALFUNCTION! MALFUNCTION!
WELL? DON'T JUST STAND THERE!
GET ME OUT OF HERE.
EWW!
WHAT IS THAT SMELL? IS THAT YOU?

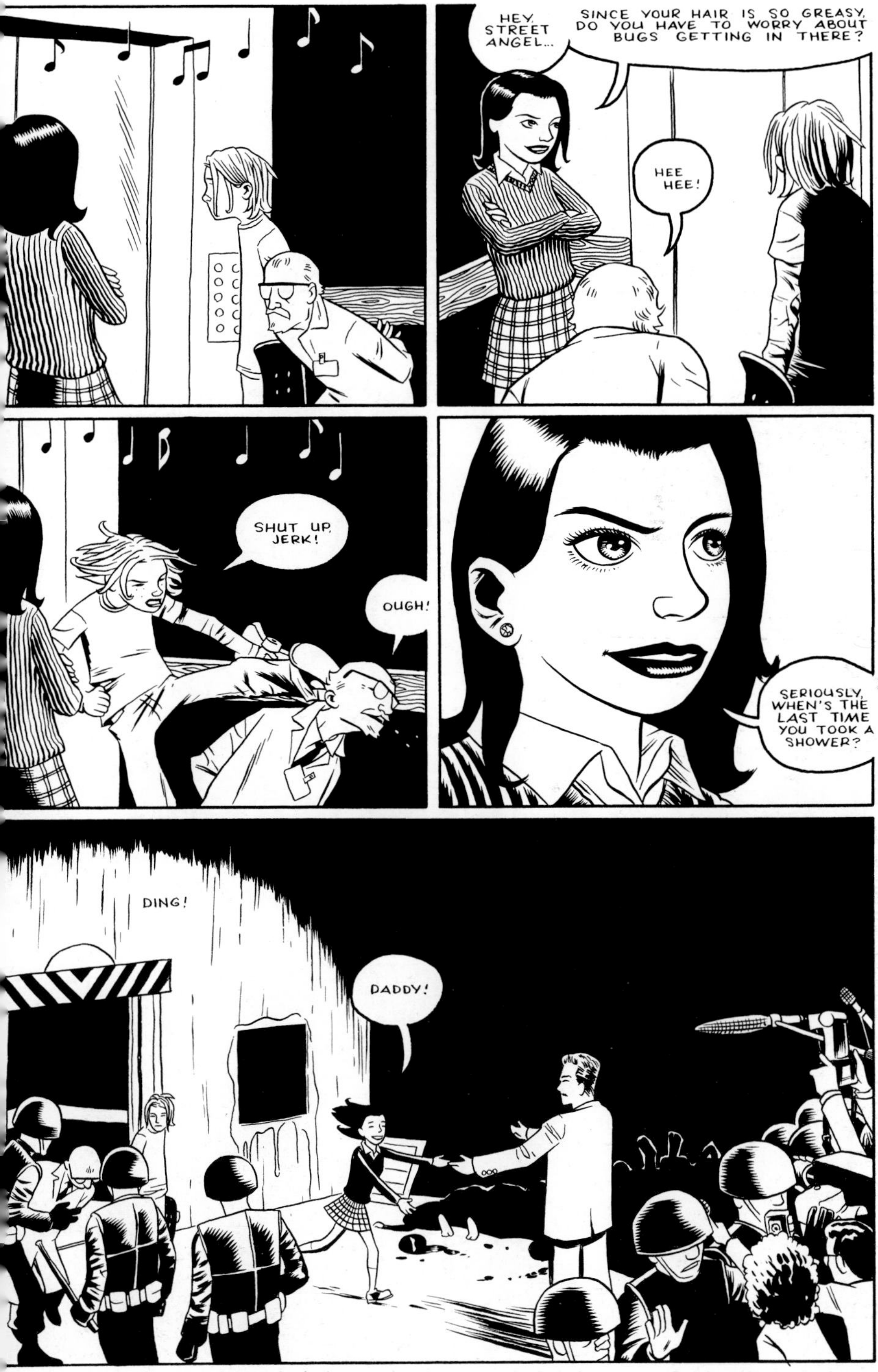
HEY, STREET ANGEL...
SINCE YOUR HAIR IS SO GREASY, DO YOU HAVE TO WORRY ABOUT BUGS GETTING IN THERE?
HEE HEE!
SHUT UP, JERK!
OUGH!
SERIOUSLY, WHEN'S THE LAST TIME YOU TOOK A SHOWER?
DING!
DADDY!

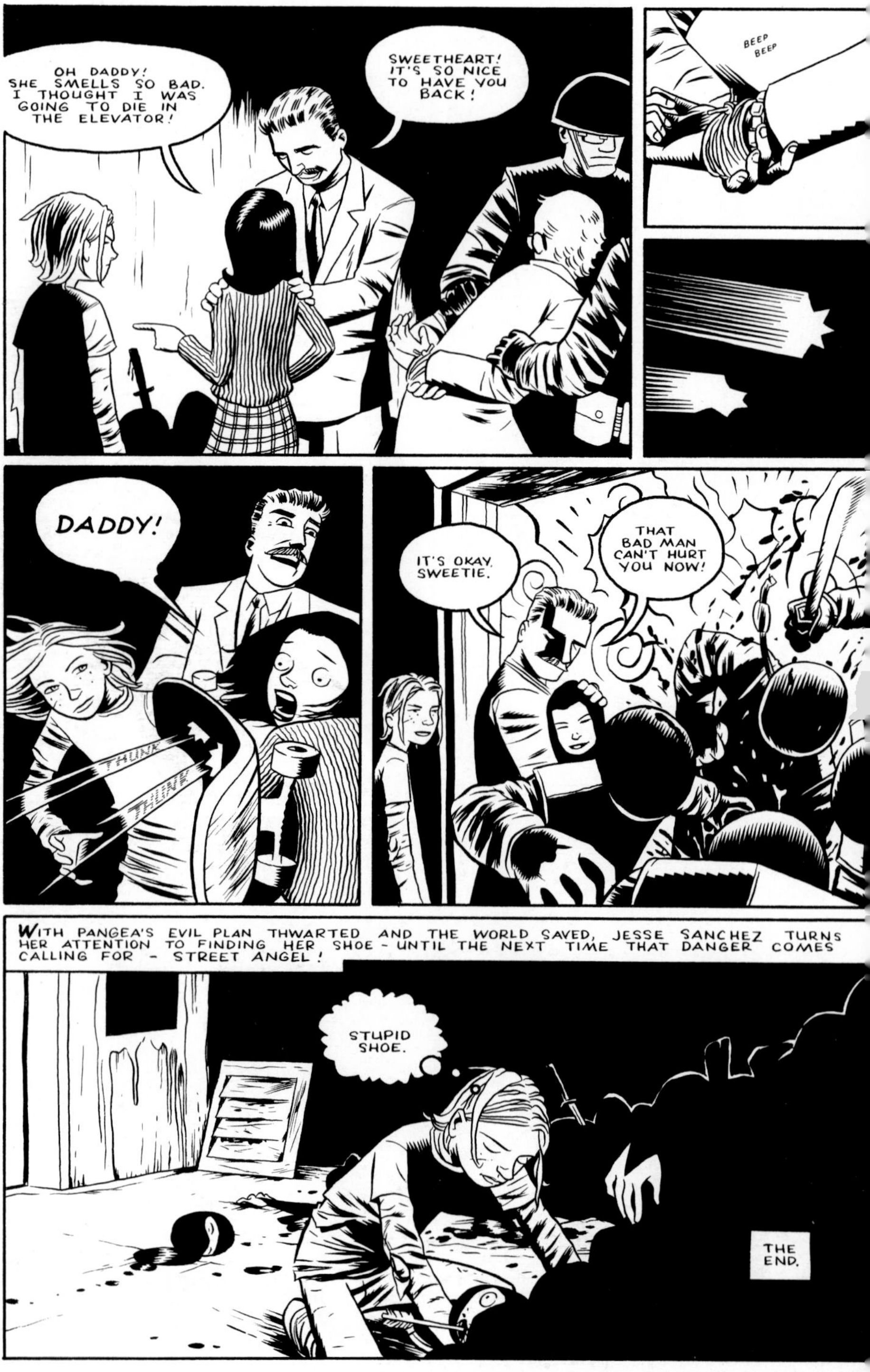
OH DADDY! SHE SMELLS SO BAD. I THOUGHT I WAS GOING TO DIE IN THE ELEVATOR!
SWEETHEART! IT'S SO NICE TO HAVE YOU BACK!
BEEP BEEP
DADDY!
THUNK
THUNK
IT'S OKAY, SWEETIE.
THAT BAD MAN CAN'T HURT YOU NOW!
WITH PANGEA'S EVIL PLAN THWARTED AND THE WORLD SAVED, JESSE SANCHEZ TURNS HER ATTENTION TO FINDING HER SHOE - UNTIL THE NEXT TIME THAT DANGER COMES CALLING FOR - STREET ANGEL!
STUPID SHOE.
THE END.

Street Angel

Name: Jesse Sanchez
Height: 5'1
Weight: 87 lbs
Eyes: Green
Hair: Red

History: Little is known about this tiny avenger: some believe she is allowed to meddle in the mayor's affairs because she is one of his illegitimate children; the homeless brotherhood contend an infant, rescued from a dumpster and, with great sacrifice, nursed back to health, now lives as protector of the community; old ninja mothers speak of a graceful ninjina, falling in love with a Skate Lord. Betrayed by her clan and besieged by ninjas at the Skate Lord mansion, all were killed except an infant, now bent on revenge; local clergy maintain that nuns found the young girl, with no memory, atop a mound of corpses, clutching a katana, her hair permanently stained red from the blood...

Her earliest memories are of the people closest to her dying.

Powers: All-world skateboardist; Can't-be-beat martial artist; Phat dumpster diving skills; Olympic-level gymnast; Optimist

First Appearance: Street Angel #1

Abilities Matrix	0	1	2	3	4	5	6	7
Agility/Speed	■	■	■	■				
Smarts	■							
Energy Protection	■							
Fight Skills	■	■	■	■	■	■	■	
Skate Skills	■	■	■	■	■	■	■	■
Basketball Skills	■							
Strength	■							

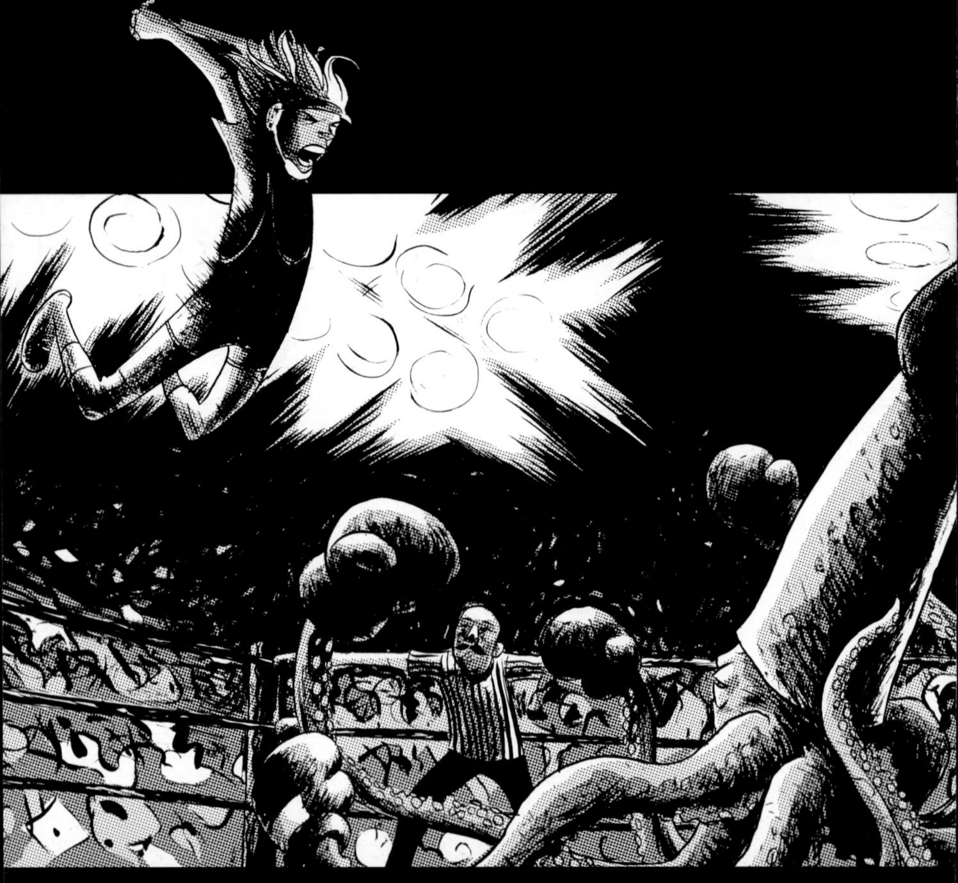

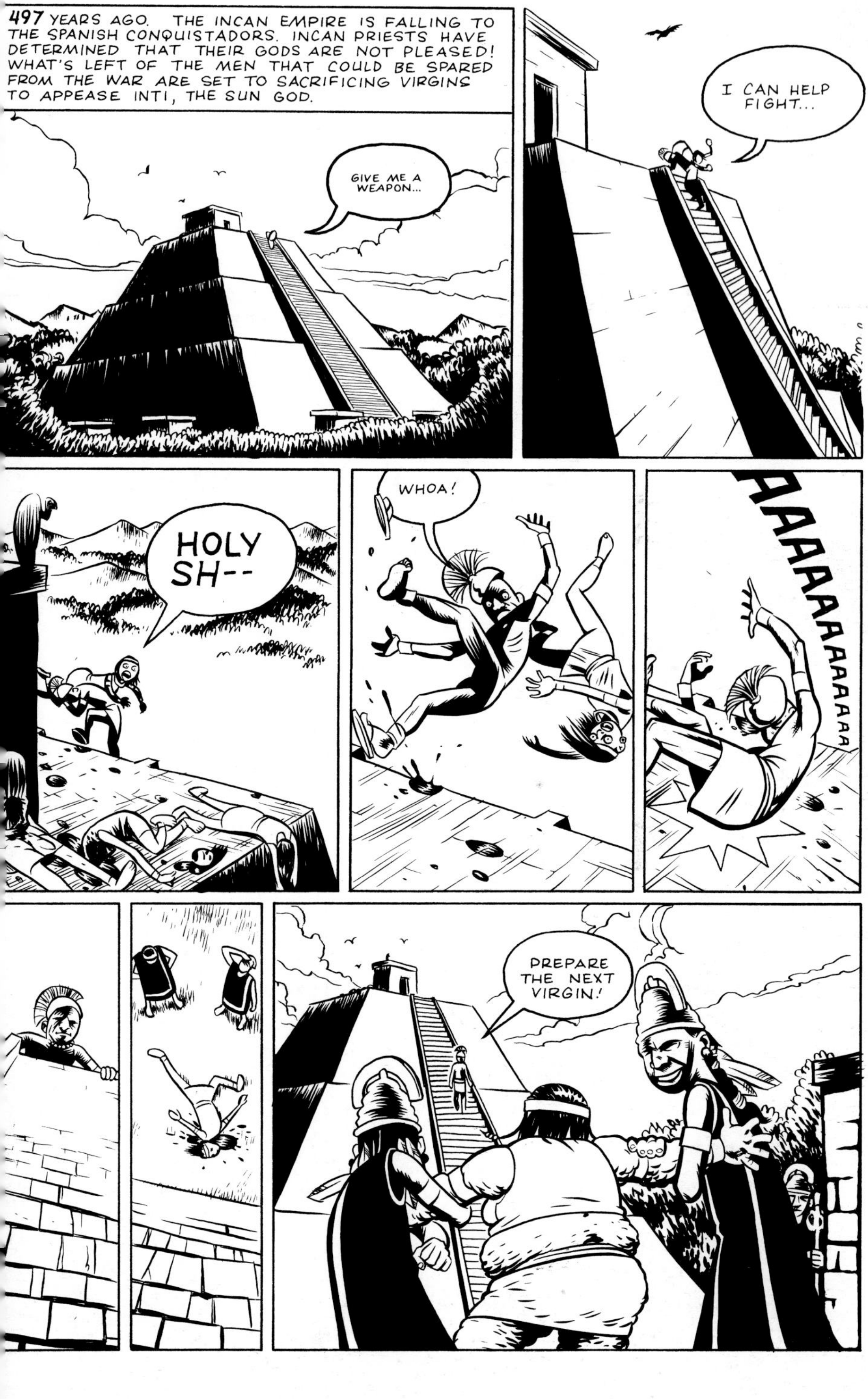
497 YEARS AGO. THE INCAN EMPIRE IS FALLING TO THE SPANISH CONQUISTADORS. INCAN PRIESTS HAVE DETERMINED THAT THEIR GODS ARE NOT PLEASED! WHAT'S LEFT OF THE MEN THAT COULD BE SPARED FROM THE WAR ARE SET TO SACRIFICING VIRGINS TO APPEASE INTI, THE SUN GOD.
GIVE ME A WEAPON...
I CAN HELP FIGHT...
HOLY SH--
WHOA!
AAAAAAAAAAAAAAA
PREPARE THE NEXT VIRGIN!

INCAdinkaDOOM

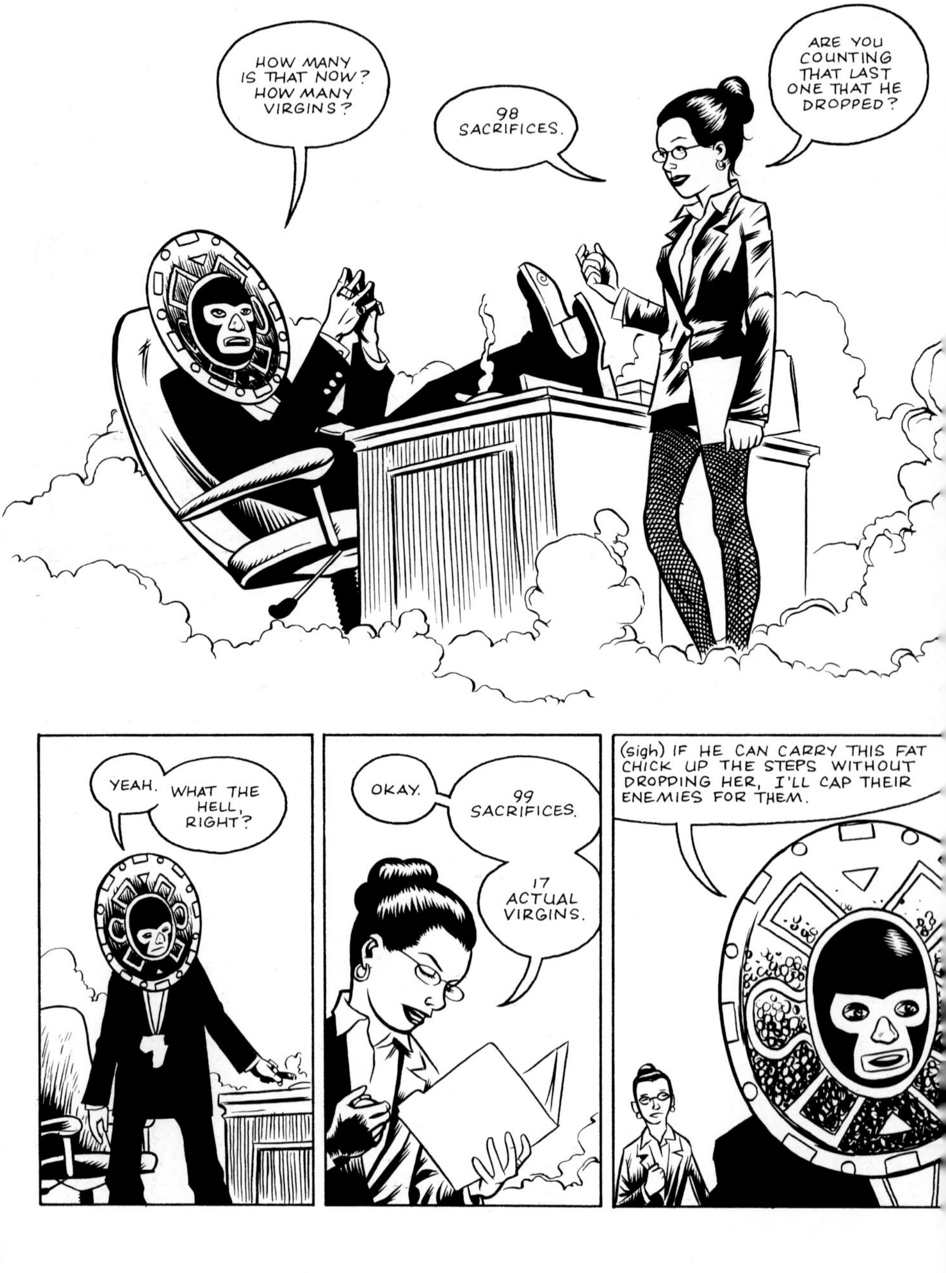
HOW MANY IS THAT NOW? HOW MANY VIRGINS?
98 SACRIFICES.
ARE YOU COUNTING THAT LAST ONE THAT HE DROPPED?
YEAH.
WHAT THE HELL, RIGHT?
OKAY.
99 SACRIFICES.
17 ACTUAL VIRGINS.
(sigh) IF HE CAN CARRY THIS FAT CHICK UP THE STEPS WITHOUT DROPPING HER, I'LL CAP THEIR ENEMIES FOR THEM.

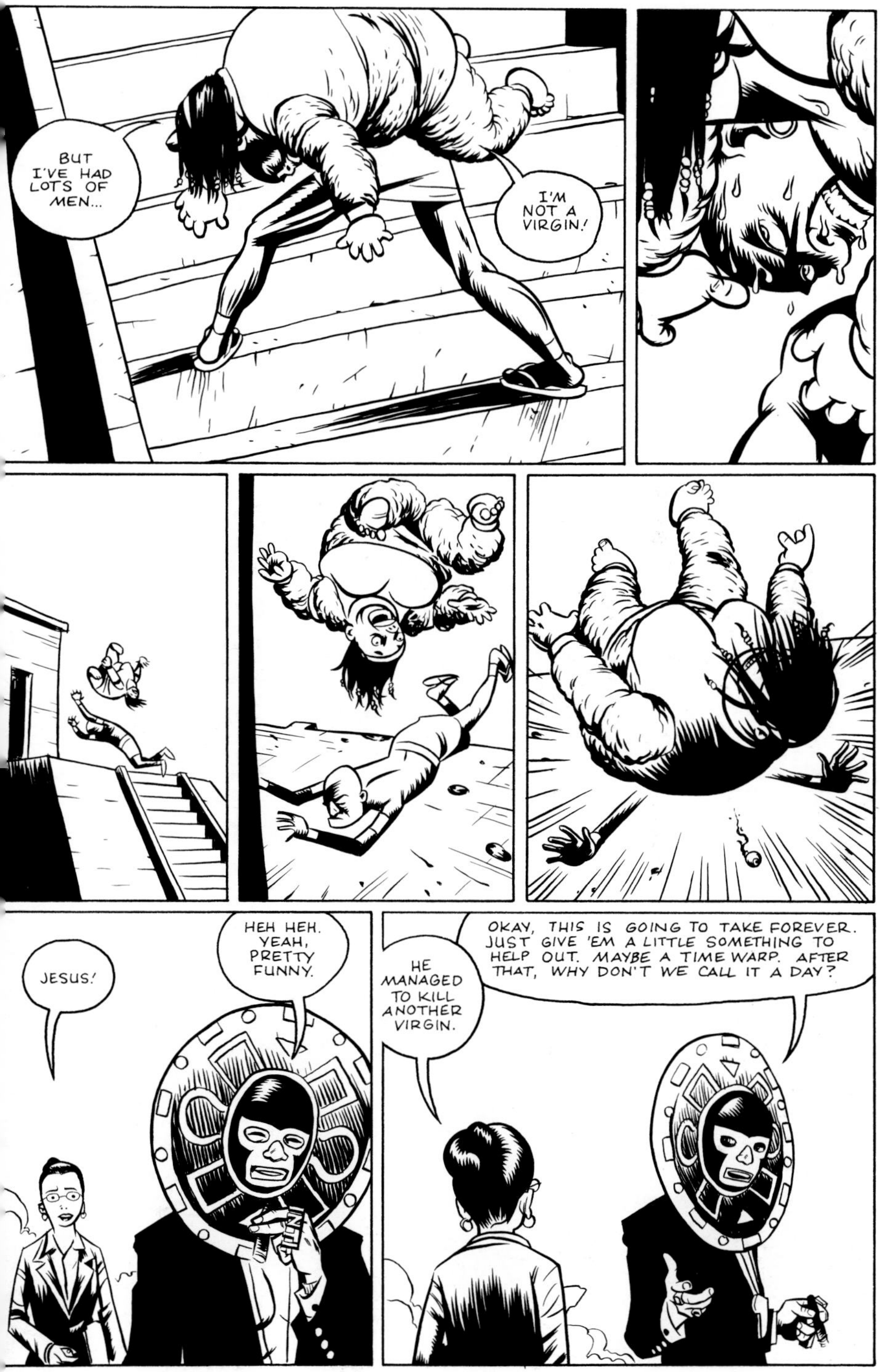
BUT I'VE HAD LOTS OF MEN...
I'M NOT A VIRGIN!
JESUS!
HEH HEH. YEAH, PRETTY FUNNY.
HE MANAGED TO KILL ANOTHER VIRGIN.
OKAY, THIS IS GOING TO TAKE FOREVER. JUST GIVE 'EM A LITTLE SOMETHING TO HELP OUT. MAYBE A TIME WARP. AFTER THAT, WHY DON'T WE CALL IT A DAY?

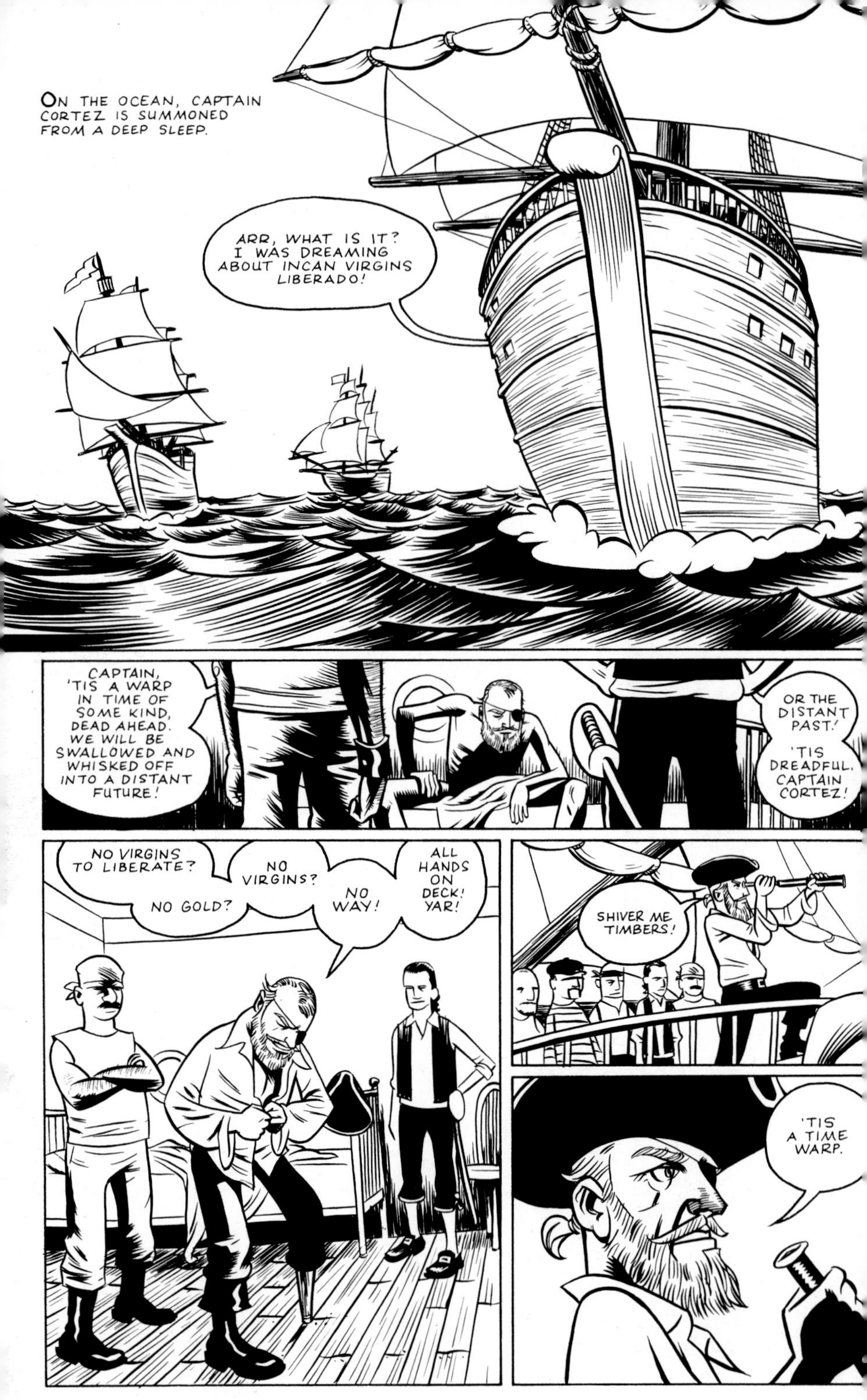
ON THE OCEAN, CAPTAIN CORTEZ IS SUMMONED FROM A DEEP SLEEP.
ARR, WHAT IS IT? I WAS DREAMING ABOUT INCAN VIRGINS LIBERADO!
CAPTAIN, 'TIS A WARP IN TIME OF SOME KIND, DEAD AHEAD. WE WILL BE SWALLOWED AND WHISKED OFF INTO A DISTANT FUTURE!
OR THE DISTANT PAST!
'TIS DREADFUL, CAPTAIN CORTEZ!
NO VIRGINS TO LIBERATE?
NO GOLD?
NO VIRGINS?
NO WAY!
ALL HANDS ON DECK! YAR!
SHIVER ME TIMBERS!
'TIS A TIME WARP.

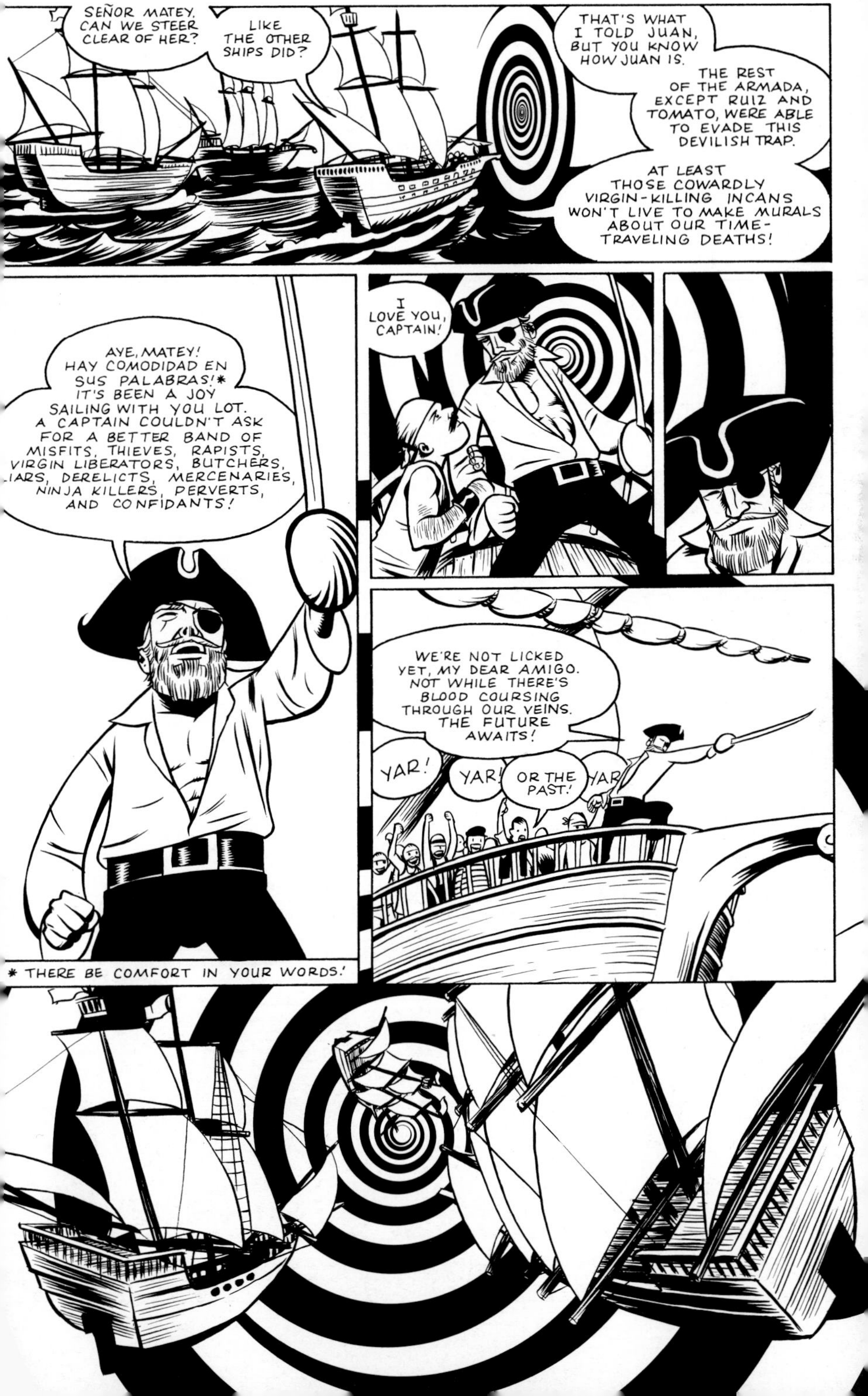
SEÑOR MATEY, CAN WE STEER CLEAR OF HER?
LIKE THE OTHER SHIPS DID?
THAT'S WHAT I TOLD JUAN, BUT YOU KNOW HOW JUAN IS.
THE REST OF THE ARMADA, EXCEPT RUIZ AND TOMATO, WERE ABLE TO EVADE THIS DEVILISH TRAP.
AT LEAST THOSE COWARDLY VIRGIN-KILLING INCANS WON'T LIVE TO MAKE MURALS ABOUT OUR TIME-TRAVELING DEATHS!
AYE, MATEY! HAY COMODIDAD EN SUS PALABRAS!* IT'S BEEN A JOY SAILING WITH YOU LOT. A CAPTAIN COULDN'T ASK FOR A BETTER BAND OF MISFITS, THIEVES, RAPISTS, VIRGIN LIBERATORS, BUTCHERS, LIARS, DERELICTS, MERCENARIES, NINJA KILLERS, PERVERTS, AND CONFIDANTS!
* THERE BE COMFORT IN YOUR WORDS!
I LOVE YOU, CAPTAIN!
WE'RE NOT LICKED YET, MY DEAR AMIGO. NOT WHILE THERE'S BLOOD COURSING THROUGH OUR VEINS. THE FUTURE AWAITS!
YAR!
YAR!
OR THE PAST!
YAR

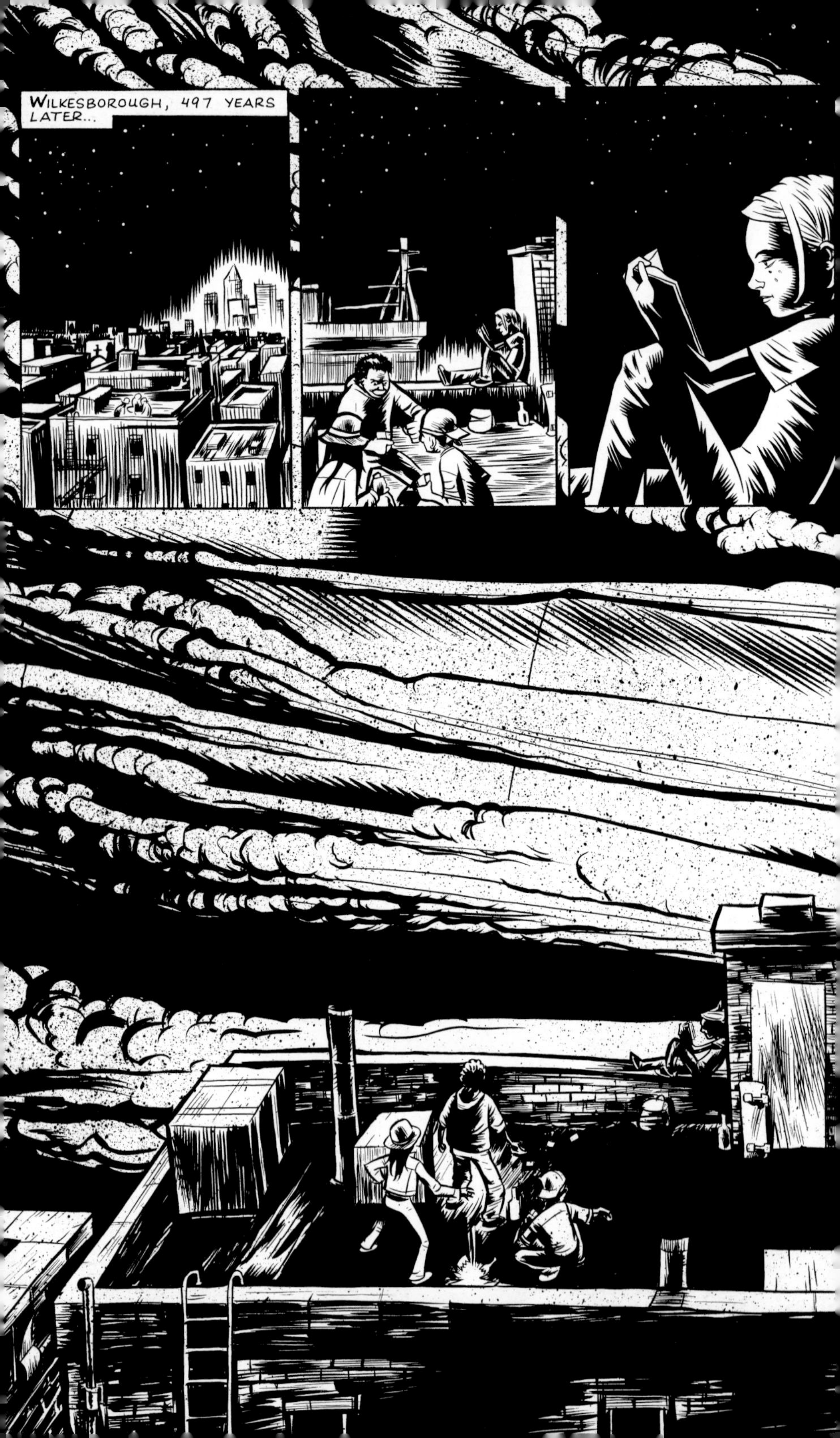
WILKESBOROUGH, 497 YEARS LATER...

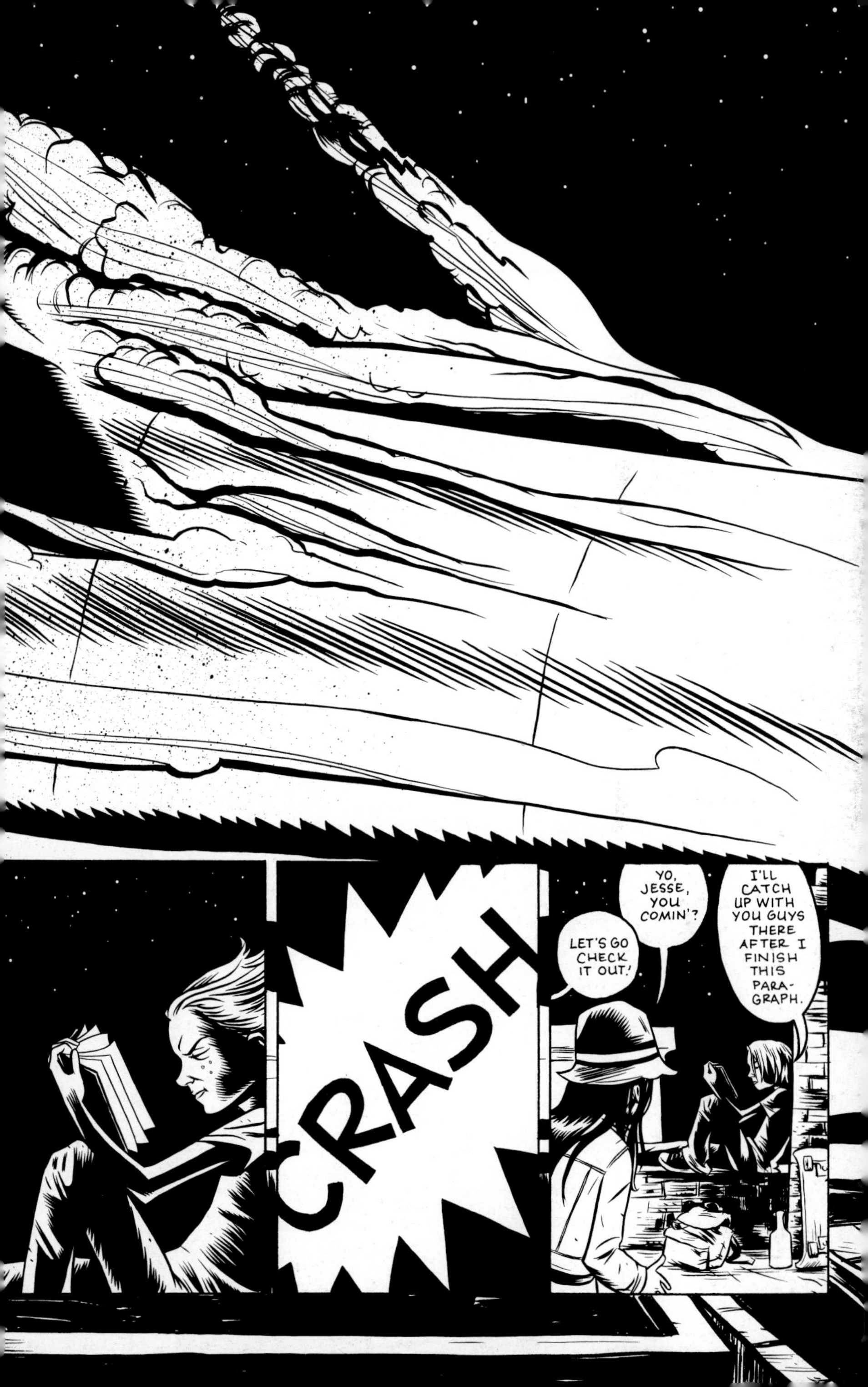
CRASH
LET'S GO CHECK IT OUT!
YO, JESSE, YOU COMIN'?
I'LL CATCH UP WITH YOU GUYS THERE AFTER I FINISH THIS PARA-GRAPH.

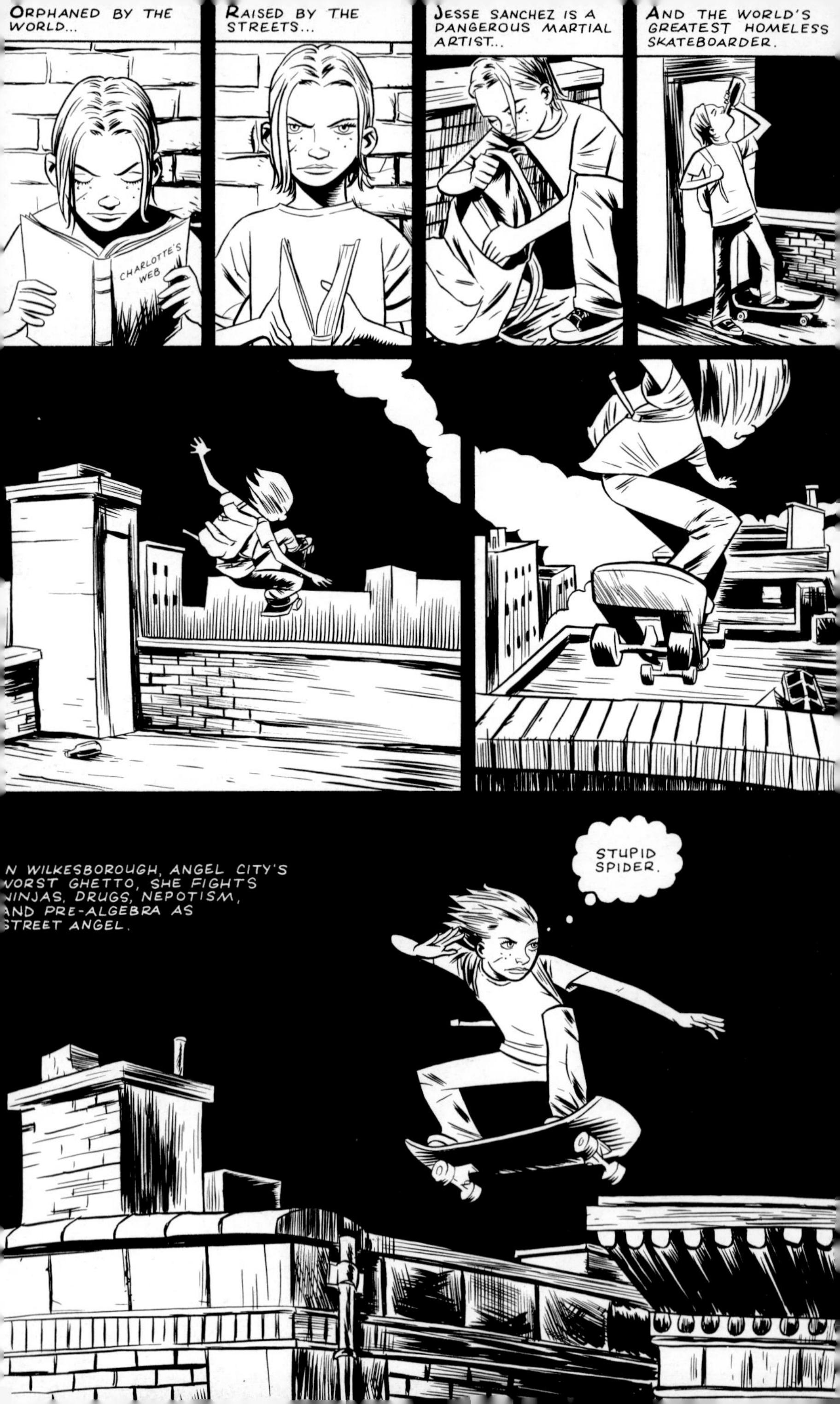
ORPHANED BY THE WORLD...
RAISED BY THE STREETS...
JESSE SANCHEZ IS A DANGEROUS MARTIAL ARTIST...
AND THE WORLD'S GREATEST HOMELESS SKATEBOARDER.
CHARLOTTE'S WEB
N WILKESBOROUGH, ANGEL CITY'S VORST GHETTO, SHE FIGHTS NINJAS, DRUGS, NEPOTISM, AND PRE-ALGEBRA AS STREET ANGEL.
STUPID SPIDER.

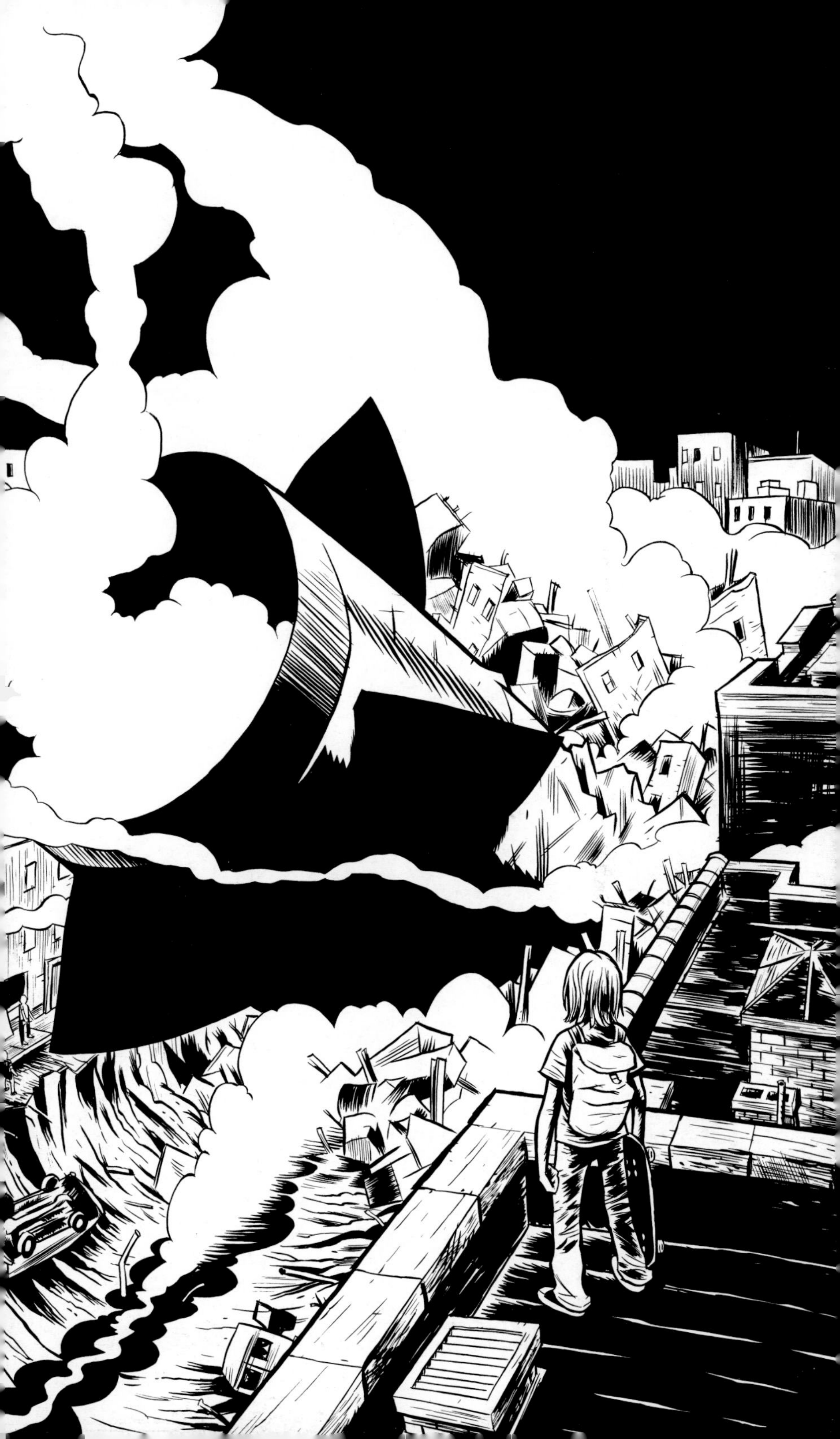

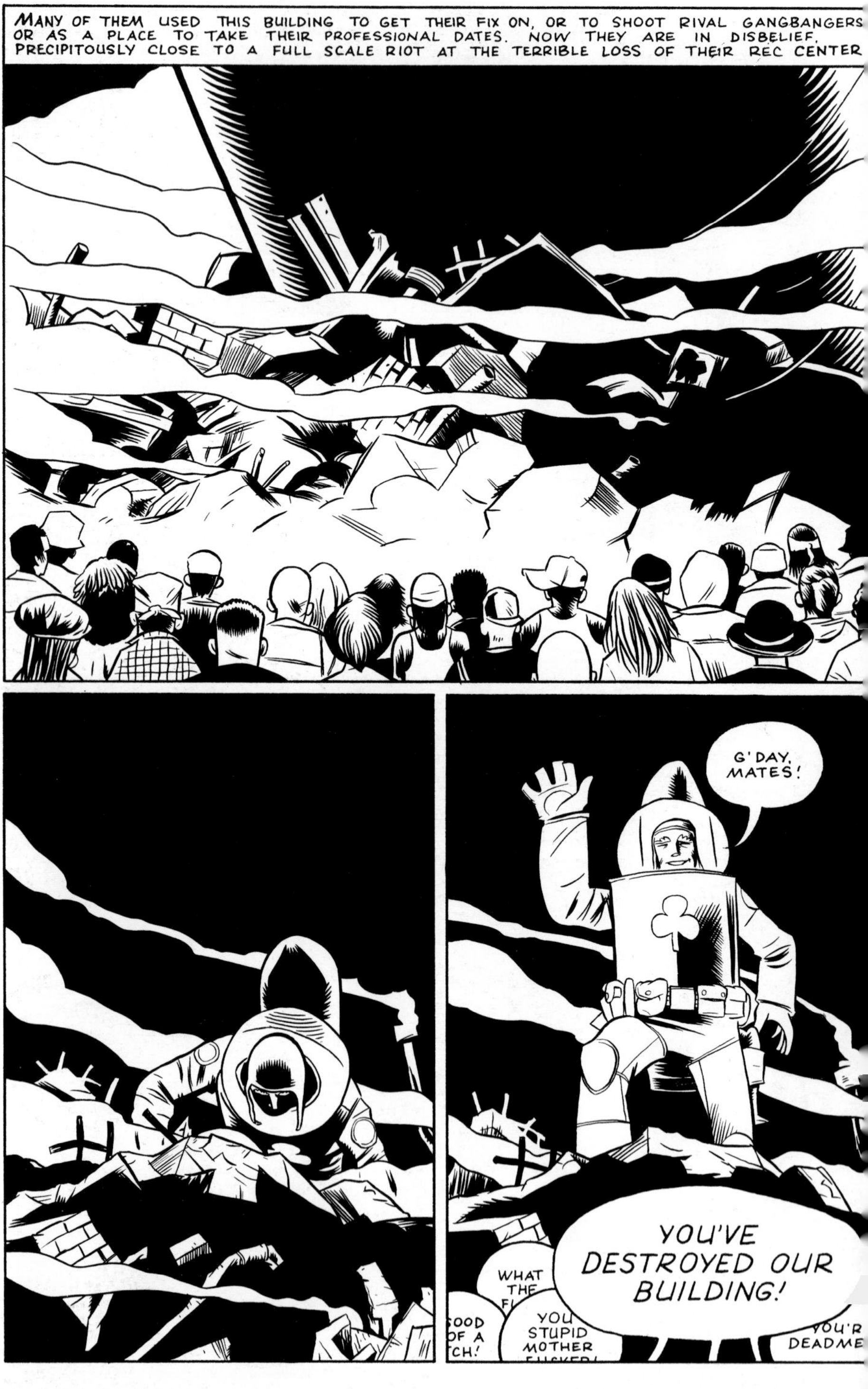
MANY OF THEM USED THIS BUILDING TO GET THEIR FIX ON, OR TO SHOOT RIVAL GANGBANGERS OR AS A PLACE TO TAKE THEIR PROFESSIONAL DATES. NOW THEY ARE IN DISBELIEF, PRECIPITOUSLY CLOSE TO A FULL SCALE RIOT AT THE TERRIBLE LOSS OF THEIR REC CENTER
G'DAY, MATES!
YOU'VE DESTROYED OUR BUILDING!
WHAT THE
YOU STUPID MOTHER

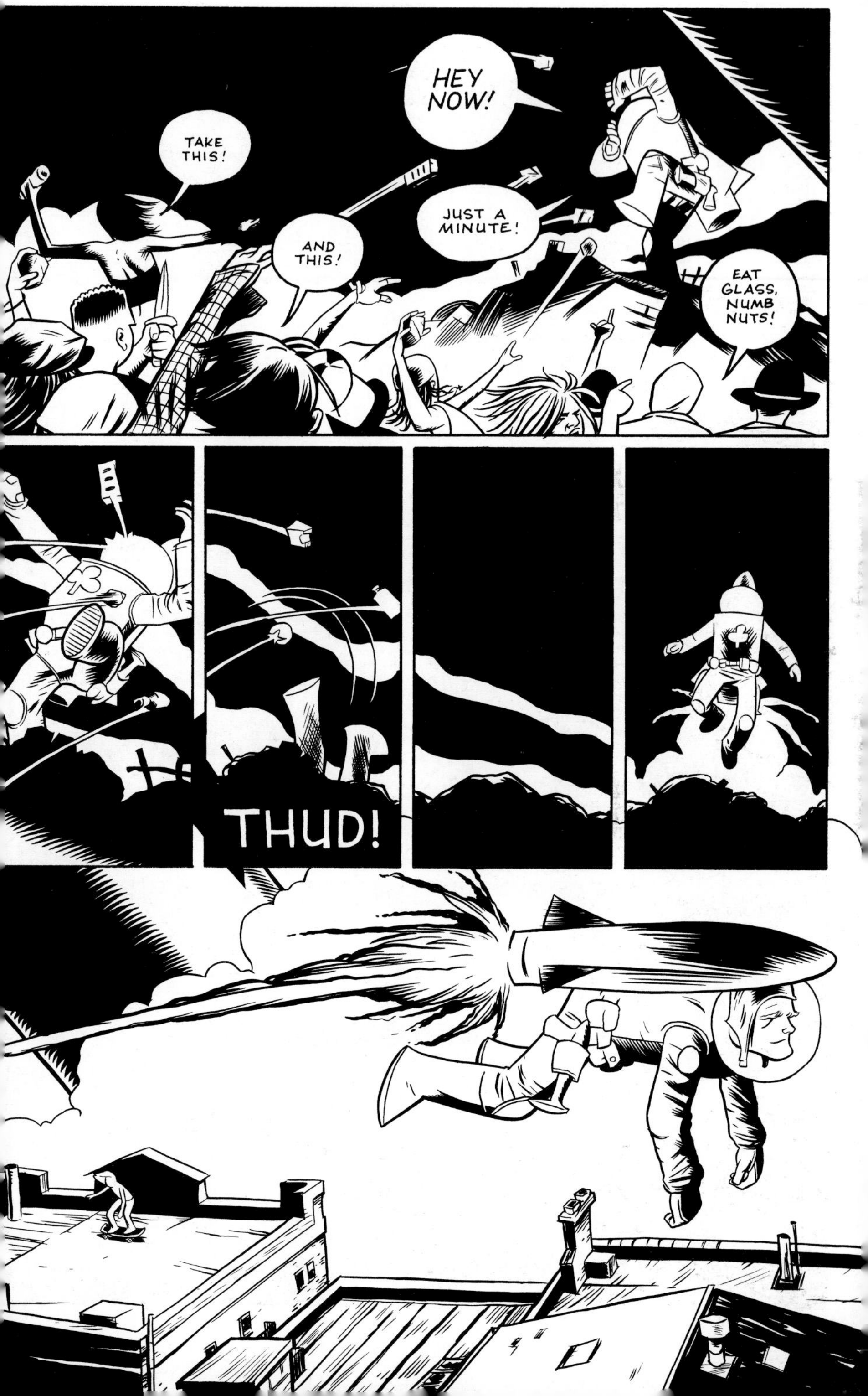
TAKE THIS!
AND THIS!
HEY NOW!
JUST A MINUTE!
EAT GLASS, NUMB NUTS!
THUD!

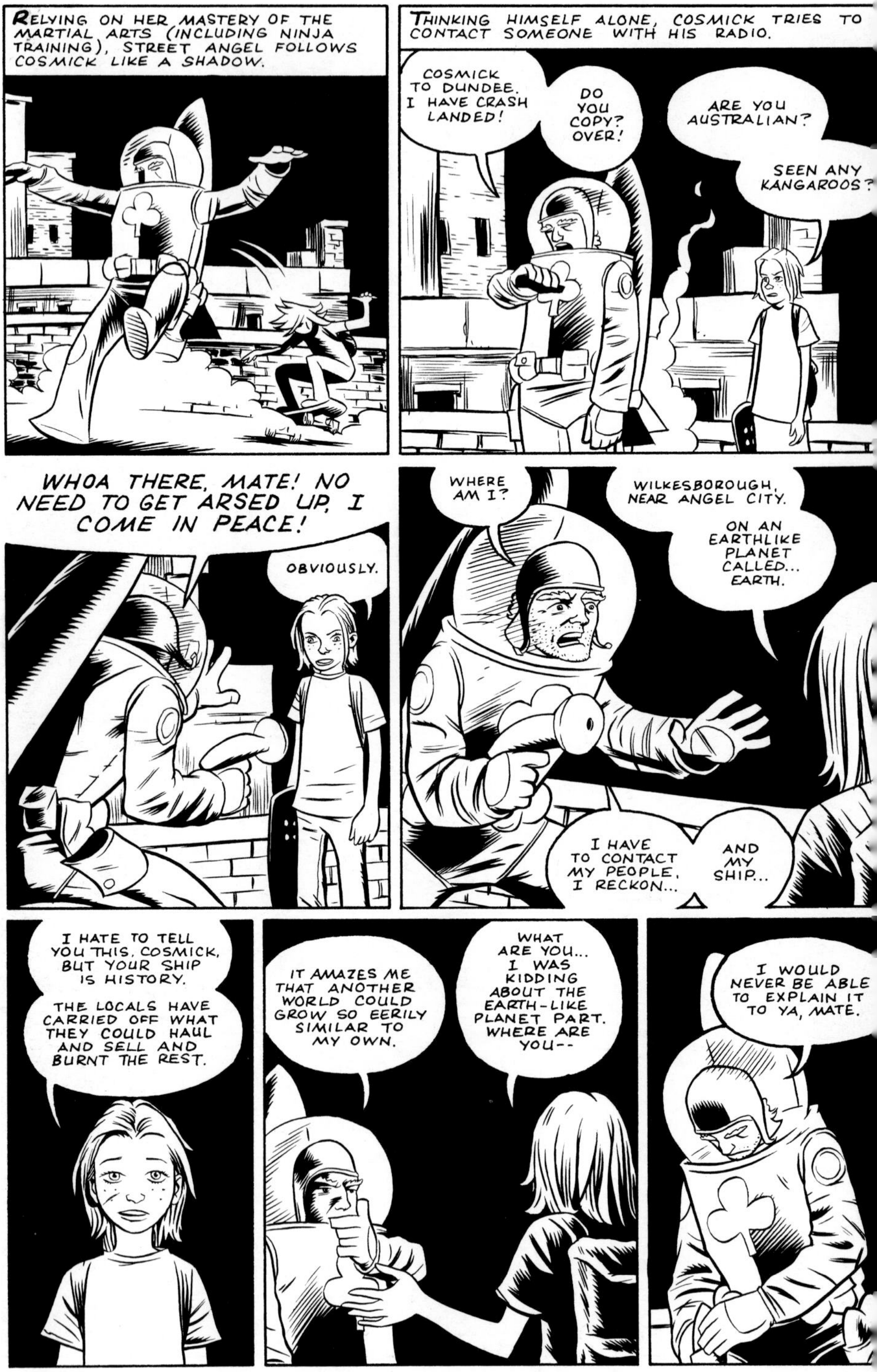
RELYING ON HER MASTERY OF THE MARTIAL ARTS (INCLUDING NINJA TRAINING), STREET ANGEL FOLLOWS COSMICK LIKE A SHADOW.
THINKING HIMSELF ALONE, COSMICK TRIES TO CONTACT SOMEONE WITH HIS RADIO.
COSMICK TO DUNDEE. I HAVE CRASH LANDED!
DO YOU COPY? OVER!
ARE YOU AUSTRALIAN?
SEEN ANY KANGAROOS?
WHOA THERE, MATE! NO NEED TO GET ARSED UP, I COME IN PEACE!
OBVIOUSLY.
WHERE AM I?
WILKESBOROUGH, NEAR ANGEL CITY.
ON AN EARTHLIKE PLANET CALLED... EARTH.
I HAVE TO CONTACT MY PEOPLE, I RECKON...
AND MY SHIP...
I HATE TO TELL YOU THIS, COSMICK, BUT YOUR SHIP IS HISTORY.
THE LOCALS HAVE CARRIED OFF WHAT THEY COULD HAUL AND SELL AND BURNT THE REST.
IT AMAZES ME THAT ANOTHER WORLD COULD GROW SO EERILY SIMILAR TO MY OWN.
WHAT ARE YOU... I WAS KIDDING ABOUT THE EARTH-LIKE PLANET PART. WHERE ARE YOU--
I WOULD NEVER BE ABLE TO EXPLAIN IT TO YA, MATE.

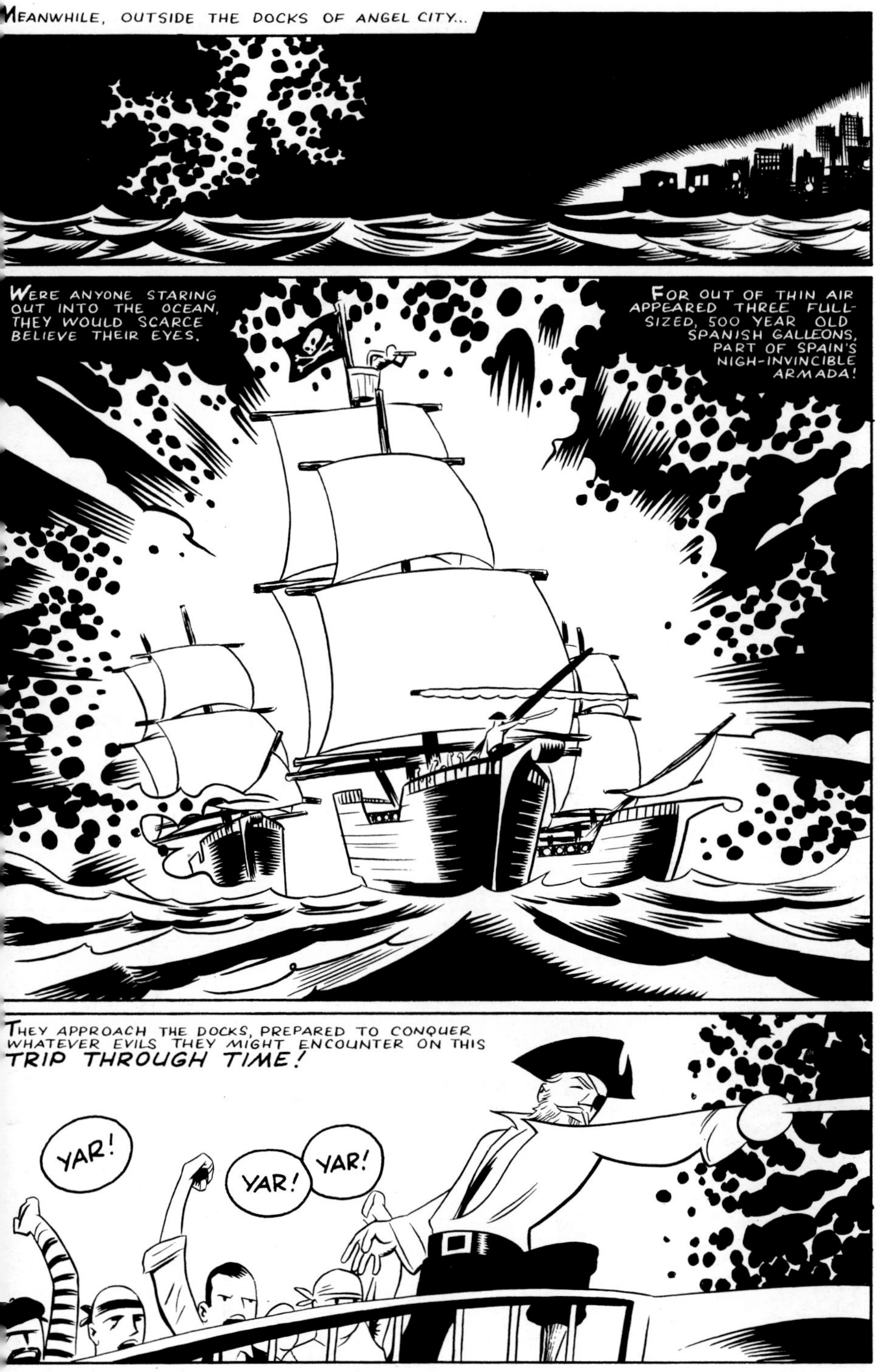
MEANWHILE, OUTSIDE THE DOCKS OF ANGEL CITY...
WERE ANYONE STARING OUT INTO THE OCEAN, THEY WOULD SCARCE BELIEVE THEIR EYES.
FOR OUT OF THIN AIR APPEARED THREE FULL-SIZED, 500 YEAR OLD SPANISH GALLEONS, PART OF SPAIN'S NIGH-INVINCIBLE ARMADA!
THEY APPROACH THE DOCKS, PREPARED TO CONQUER WHATEVER EVILS THEY MIGHT ENCOUNTER ON THIS TRIP THROUGH TIME!
YAR!
YAR!
YAR!

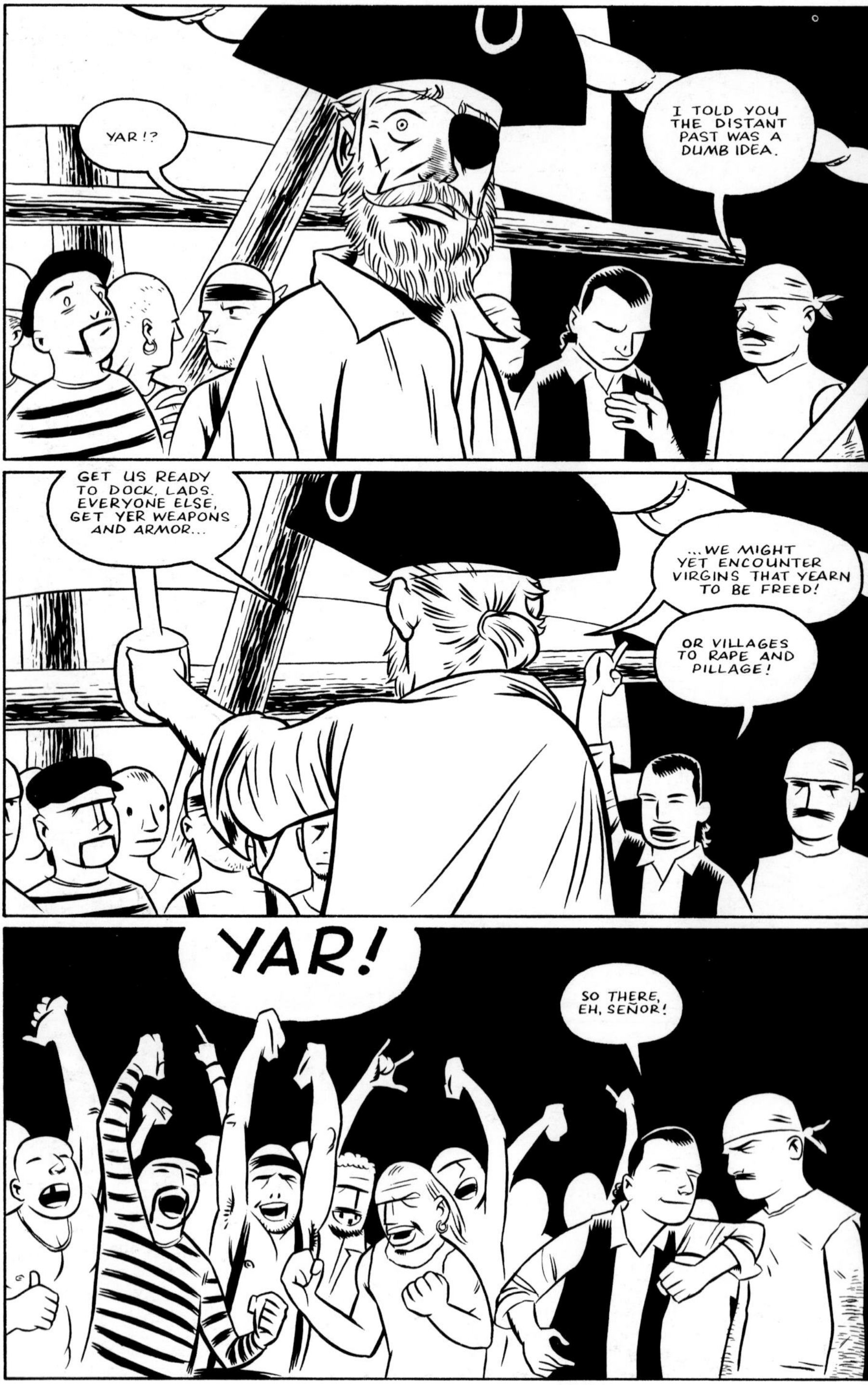
YAR!?
I TOLD YOU THE DISTANT PAST WAS A DUMB IDEA.
GET US READY TO DOCK, LADS. EVERYONE ELSE, GET YER WEAPONS AND ARMOR...
...WE MIGHT YET ENCOUNTER VIRGINS THAT YEARN TO BE FREED!
OR VILLAGES TO RAPE AND PILLAGE!
YAR!
SO THERE, EH, SEÑOR!

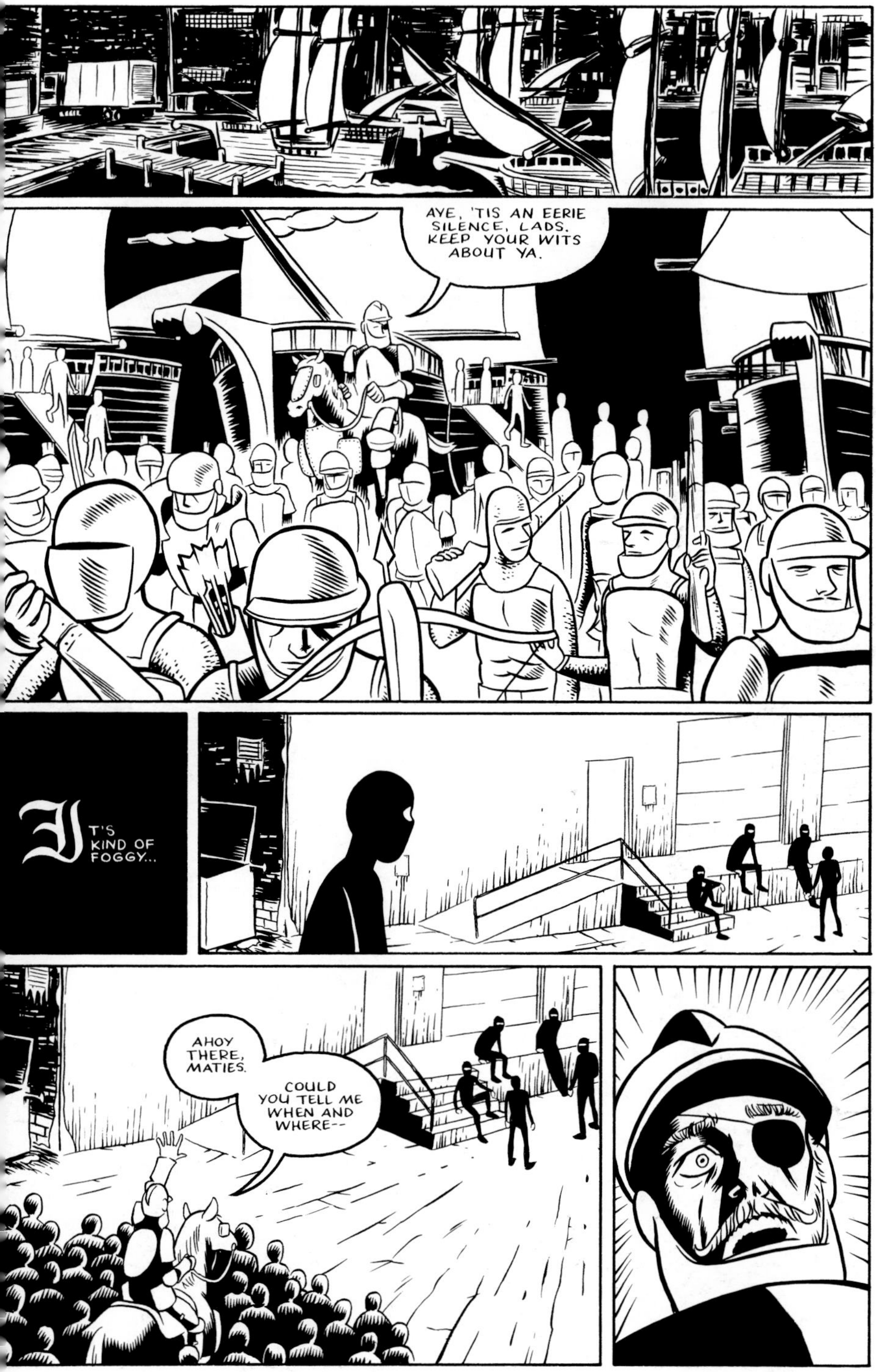
AYE, 'TIS AN EERIE SILENCE, LADS. KEEP YOUR WITS ABOUT YA.
IT'S KIND OF FOGGY...
AHOY THERE, MATIES.
COULD YOU TELL ME WHEN AND WHERE--

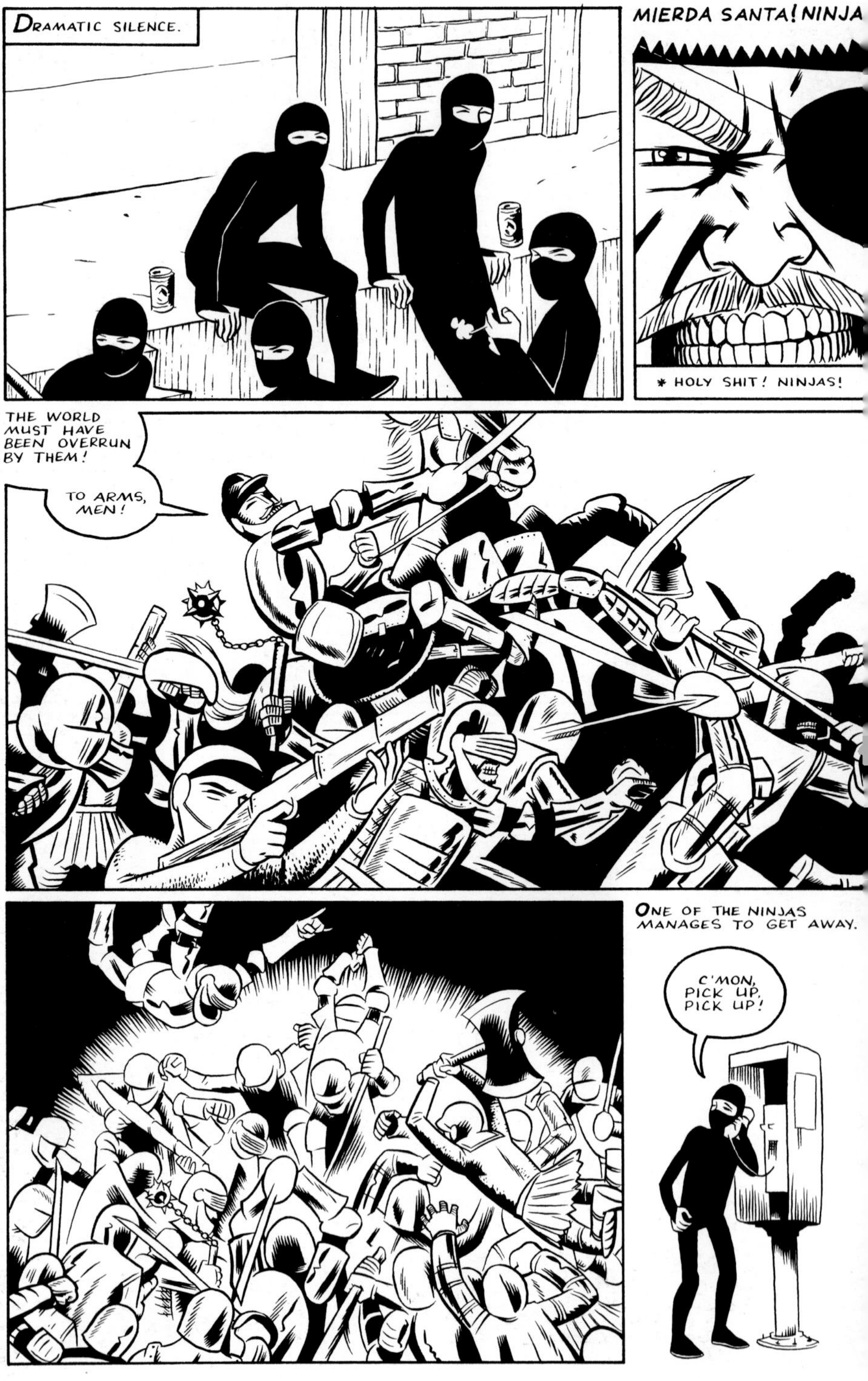
Dramatic silence.
MIERDA SANTA! NINJA
* HOLY SHIT! NINJAS!
THE WORLD MUST HAVE BEEN OVERRUN BY THEM!
TO ARMS, MEN!
One of the ninjas manages to get away.
C'MON, PICK UP, PICK UP!

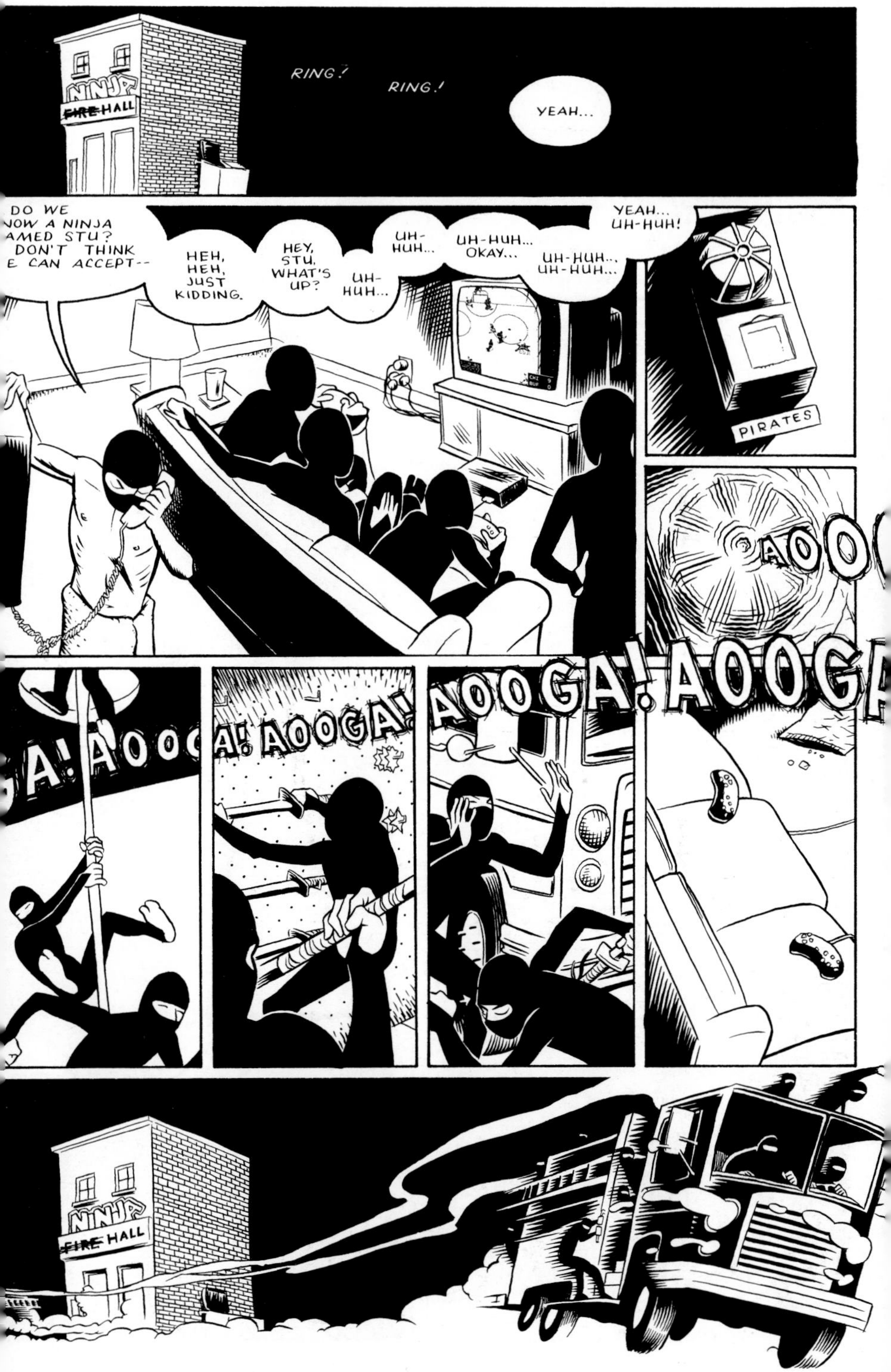
NINJA
FIRE HALL
RING!
RING!
YEAH...
DO WE
NOW A NINJA
AMED STU?
DON'T THINK
E CAN ACCEPT--
HEH,
HEH,
JUST
KIDDING.
HEY,
STU,
WHAT'S
UP?
UH-
HUH...
UH-
HUH...
UH-HUH...
OKAY...
UH-HUH...
UH-HUH...
YEAH...
UH-HUH!
PIRATES
AOO
GA! AOOGA! AOOGA! AOOGA! AOOGA! AOOG
NINJA
FIRE HALL

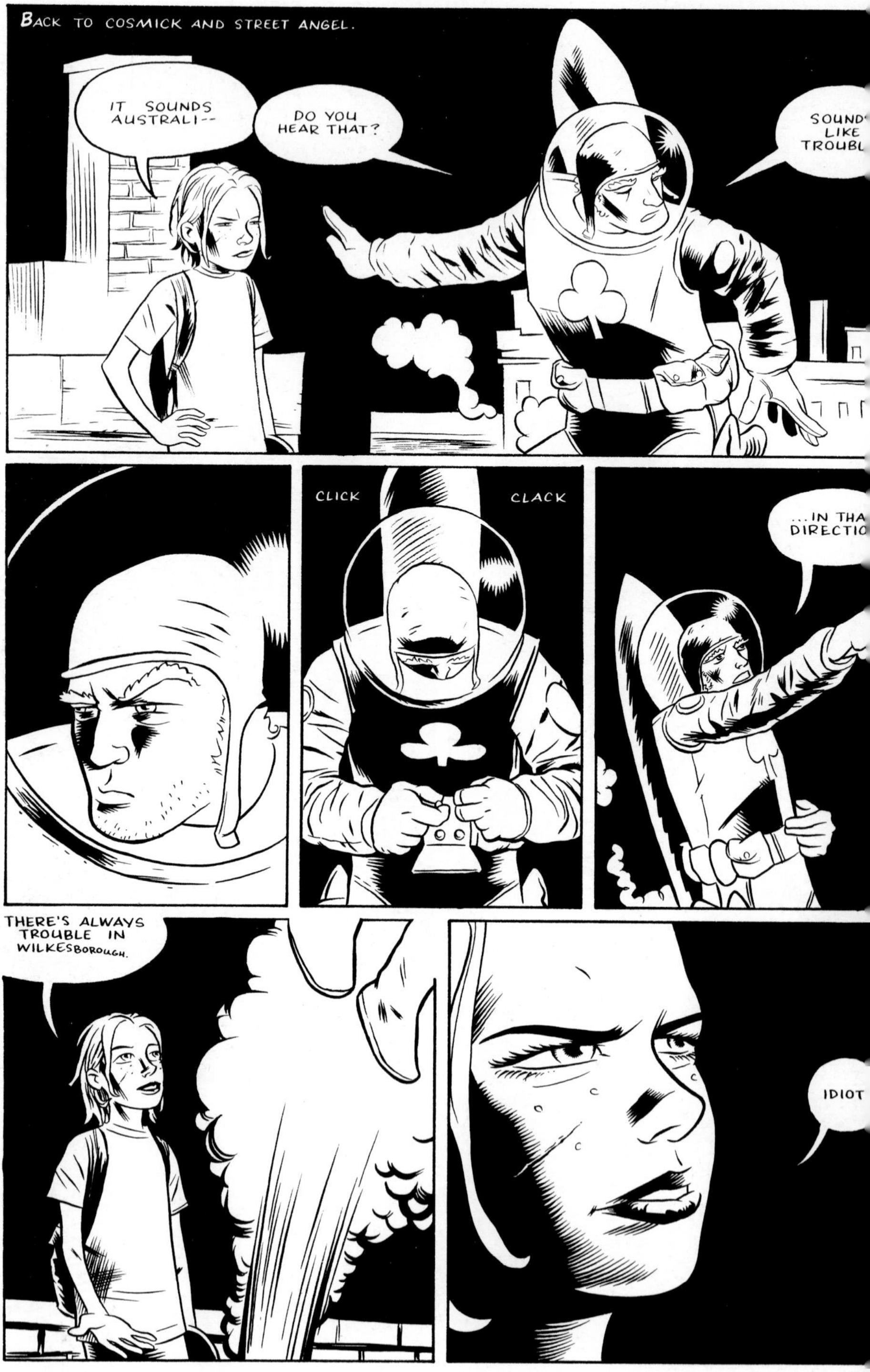
BACK TO COSMICK AND STREET ANGEL.
IT SOUNDS AUSTRALI--
DO YOU HEAR THAT?
SOUND' LIKE TROUBL
CLICK
CLACK
...IN THA DIRECTIO
THERE'S ALWAYS TROUBLE IN WILKESBOROUGH.
IDIOT

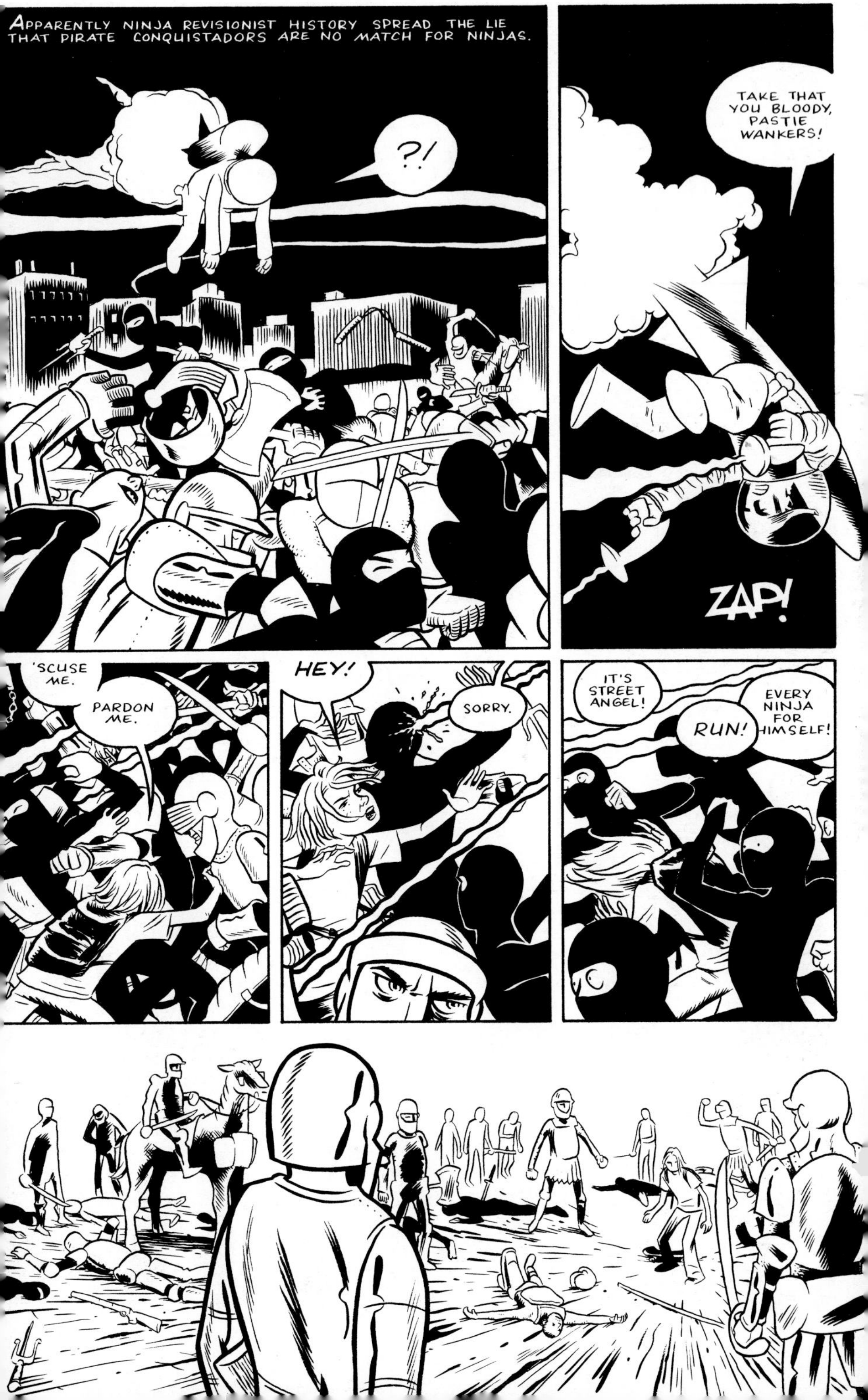
APPARENTLY NINJA REVISIONIST HISTORY SPREAD THE LIE THAT PIRATE CONQUISTADORS ARE NO MATCH FOR NINJAS.
?!
TAKE THAT YOU BLOODY, PASTIE WANKERS!
ZAP!
'SCUSE ME.
PARDON ME.
HEY!
SORRY.
IT'S STREET ANGEL!
EVERY NINJA FOR HIMSELF!
RUN!

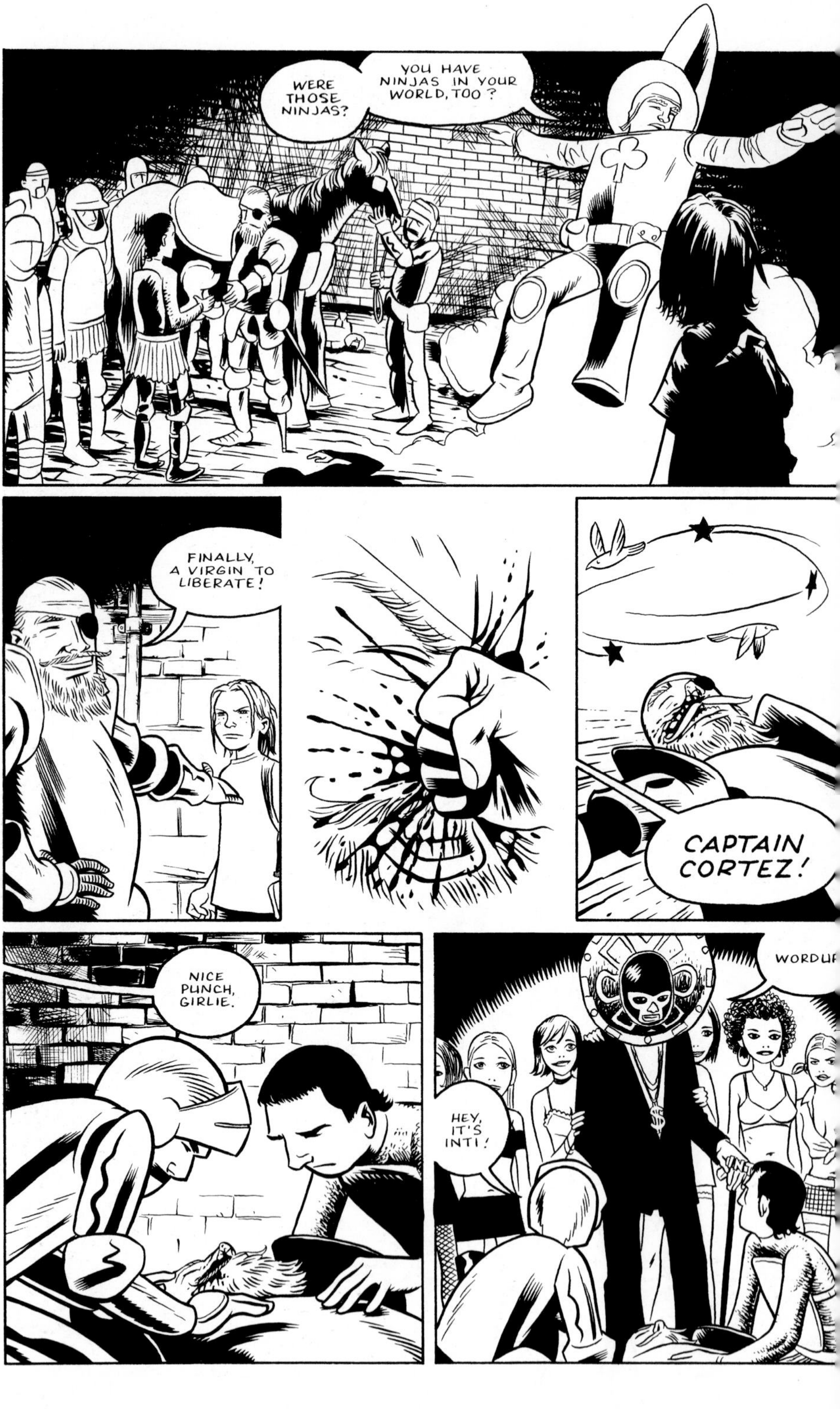
WERE THOSE NINJAS?
YOU HAVE NINJAS IN YOUR WORLD, TOO?
FINALLY, A VIRGIN TO LIBERATE!
CAPTAIN CORTEZ!
NICE PUNCH, GIRLIE.
HEY, IT'S INTI!

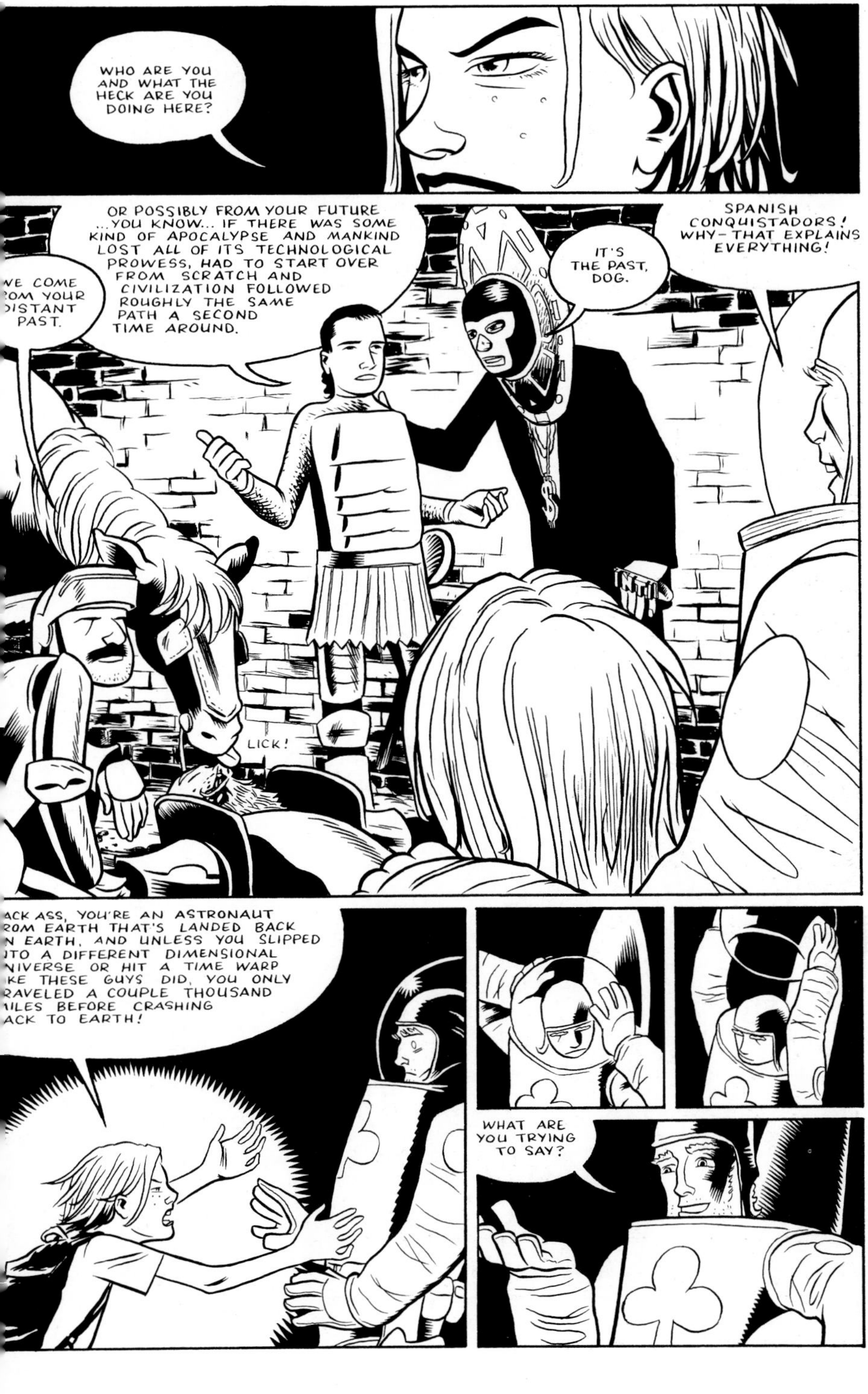
WHO ARE YOU AND WHAT THE HECK ARE YOU DOING HERE?
WE COME FROM YOUR DISTANT PAST.
OR POSSIBLY FROM YOUR FUTURE ...YOU KNOW... IF THERE WAS SOME KIND OF APOCALYPSE AND MANKIND LOST ALL OF ITS TECHNOLOGICAL PROWESS, HAD TO START OVER FROM SCRATCH AND CIVILIZATION FOLLOWED ROUGHLY THE SAME PATH A SECOND TIME AROUND.
IT'S THE PAST, DOG.
SPANISH CONQUISTADORS! WHY-THAT EXPLAINS EVERYTHING!
LICK!
ACK ASS, YOU'RE AN ASTRONAUT ROM EARTH THAT'S LANDED BACK N EARTH, AND UNLESS YOU SLIPPED NTO A DIFFERENT DIMENSIONAL NIVERSE OR HIT A TIME WARP IKE THESE GUYS DID, YOU ONLY RAVELED A COUPLE THOUSAND MILES BEFORE CRASHING ACK TO EARTH!
WHAT ARE YOU TRYING TO SAY?

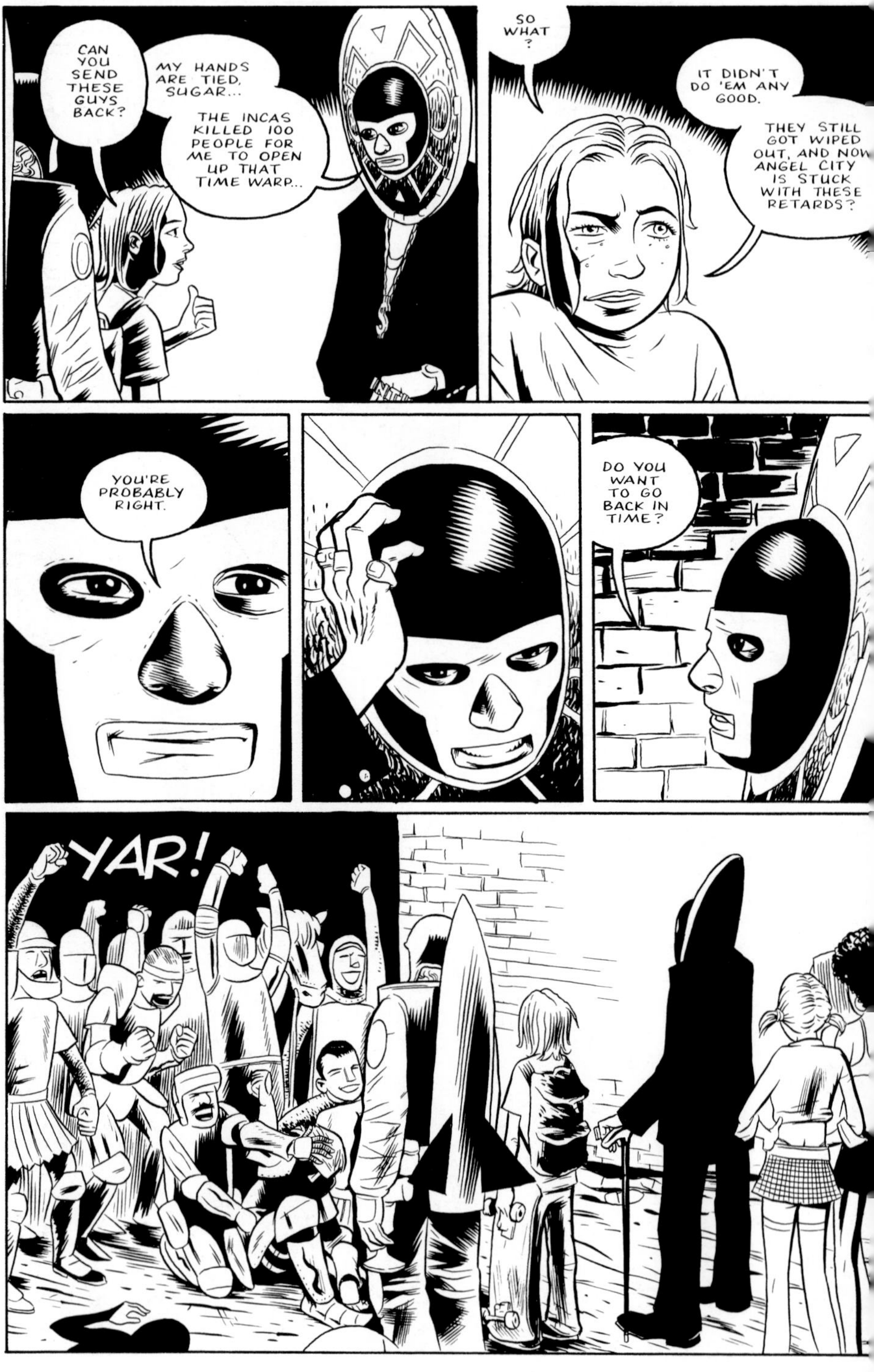
CAN YOU SEND THESE GUYS BACK?
MY HANDS ARE TIED, SUGAR...
THE INCAS KILLED 100 PEOPLE FOR ME TO OPEN UP THAT TIME WARP...
SO WHAT?
IT DIDN'T DO 'EM ANY GOOD.
THEY STILL GOT WIPED OUT, AND NOW ANGEL CITY IS STUCK WITH THESE RETARDS?
YOU'RE PROBABLY RIGHT.
DO YOU WANT TO GO BACK IN TIME?
YAR!

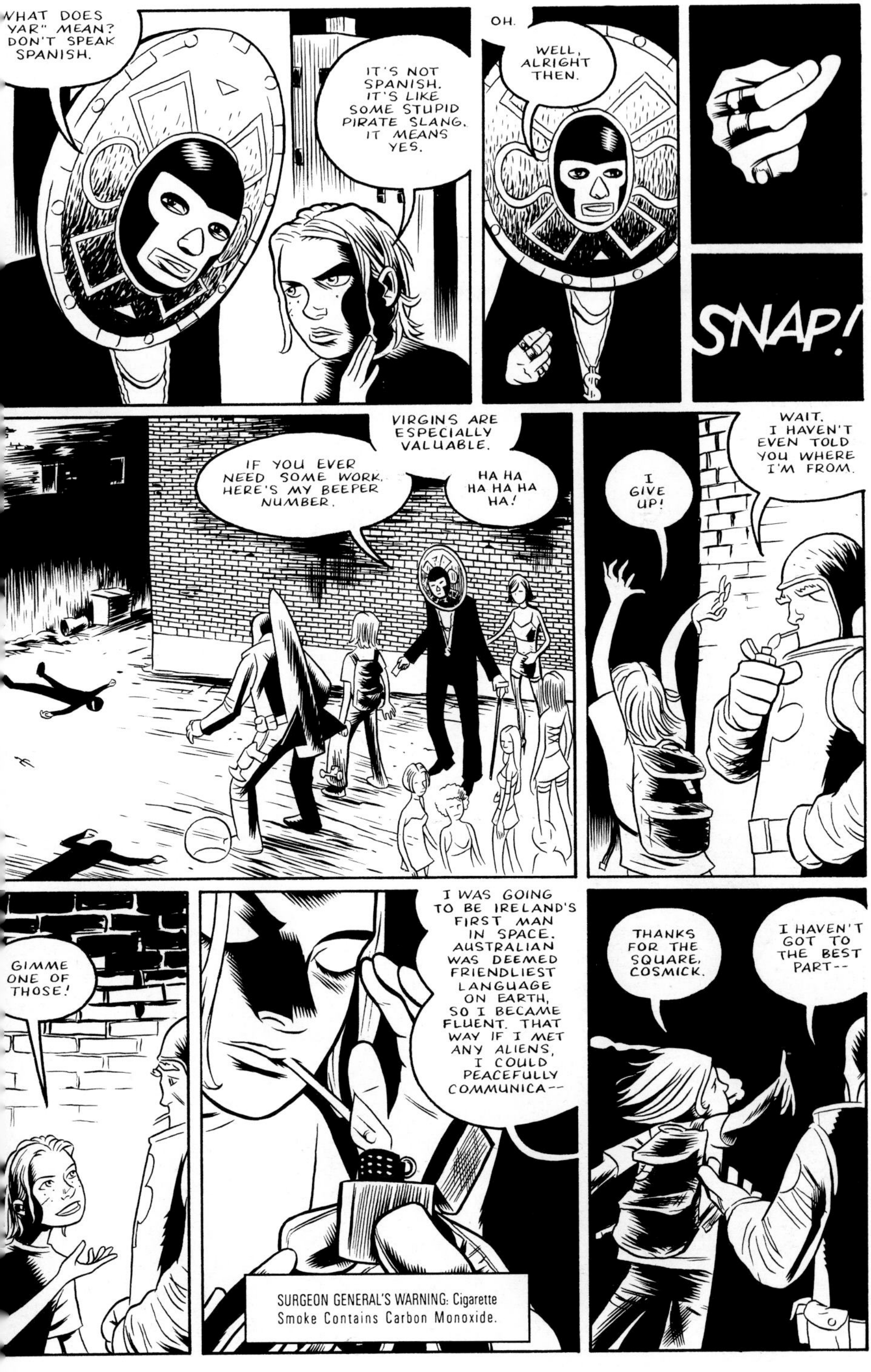
WHAT DOES "YAR" MEAN? I DON'T SPEAK SPANISH.
IT'S NOT SPANISH. IT'S LIKE SOME STUPID PIRATE SLANG. IT MEANS YES.
OH.
WELL, ALRIGHT THEN.
SNAP!
IF YOU EVER NEED SOME WORK, HERE'S MY BEEPER NUMBER.
VIRGINS ARE ESPECIALLY VALUABLE.
HA HA HA HA HA HA!
I GIVE UP!
WAIT. I HAVEN'T EVEN TOLD YOU WHERE I'M FROM.
GIMME ONE OF THOSE!
I WAS GOING TO BE IRELAND'S FIRST MAN IN SPACE. AUSTRALIAN WAS DEEMED FRIENDLIEST LANGUAGE ON EARTH, SO I BECAME FLUENT. THAT WAY IF I MET ANY ALIENS, I COULD PEACEFULLY COMMUNICA--
SURGEON GENERAL'S WARNING: Cigarette Smoke Contains Carbon Monoxide.
THANKS FOR THE SQUARE, COSMICK.
I HAVEN'T GOT TO THE BEST PART--

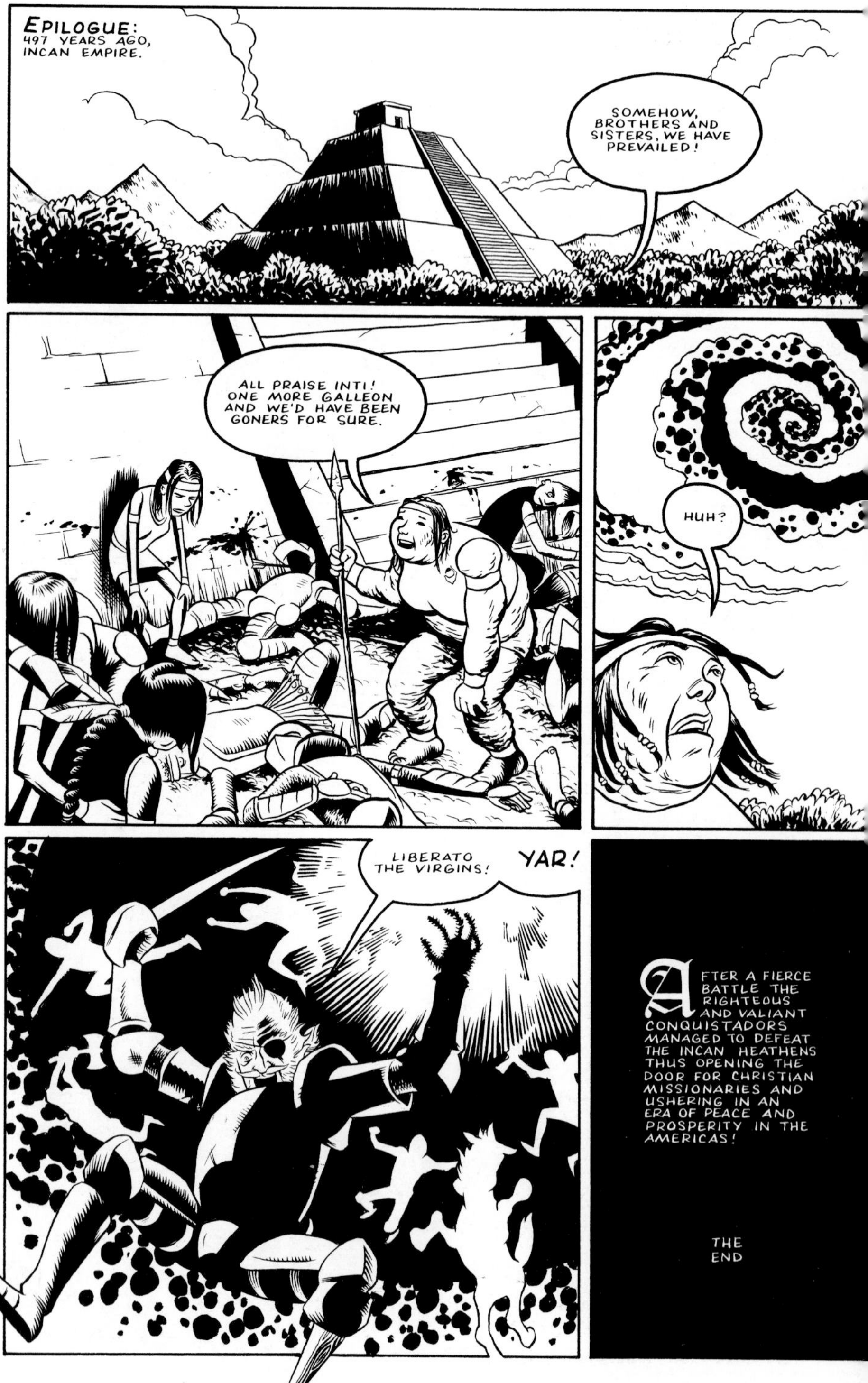
EPILOGUE:
497 YEARS AGO, INCAN EMPIRE.
SOMEHOW, BROTHERS AND SISTERS, WE HAVE PREVAILED!
ALL PRAISE INTI! ONE MORE GALLEON AND WE'D HAVE BEEN GONERS FOR SURE.
HUH?
LIBERATO THE VIRGINS!
YAR!
AFTER A FIERCE BATTLE THE RIGHTEOUS AND VALIANT CONQUISTADORS MANAGED TO DEFEAT THE INCAN HEATHENS THUS OPENING THE DOOR FOR CHRISTIAN MISSIONARIES AND USHERING IN AN ERA OF PEACE AND PROSPERITY IN THE AMERICAS!
THE END

CosMick

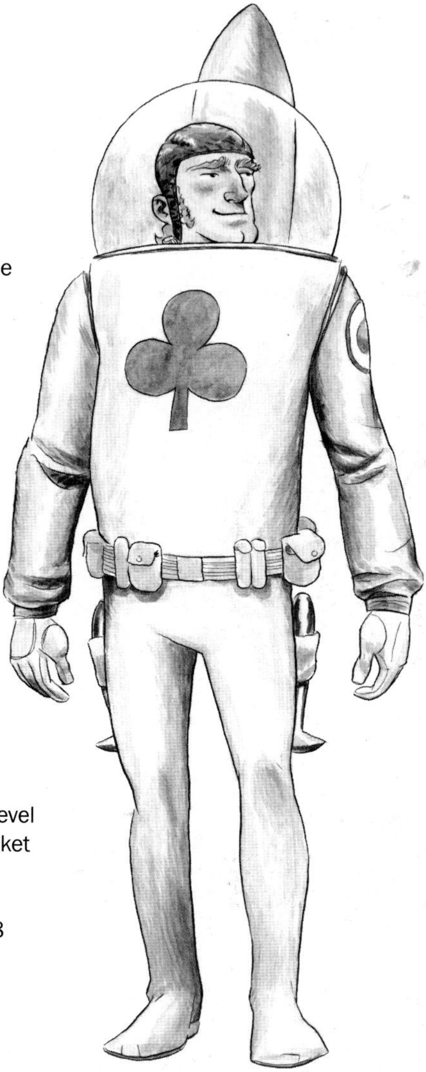

Name: Mickey O'Brannigan
Height: 6'2"
Weight: 215 lbs
Eyes: Emerald
Hair: Red

History: Because of his uncanny resemblance to a captured lieutenant of the IRDS (Irish Republican Death Squads), the Irish government implored IASCAR's (Irish Association for Stock Car Auto Racing) top driver, CosMick, to infiltrate the terrorist group and bring it down from the inside. Before CosMick could complete his mission, his doppleganger escaped. Confronted by his terrorist twin, and with the terrorist compound burning all around them, CosMick engaged in a battle to the death. It was not until his twin lay dying that CosMick learned the terrorist's true identity. Inconsolable about killing his long lost twin brother, CosMick joined the IASA (Irish Aeronautics and Space Administration) to try to forget.

Powers: Pilot; Excellent marksman; Olympic-level boxer; One of the few living masters of the rocket pack (Olympic level)

First Appearance: Amazing Irish Funnies #28

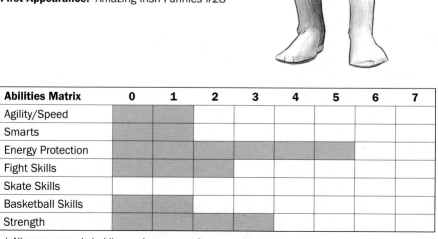

Abilities Matrix	0	1	2	3	4	5	6	7
Agility/Speed	▓	▓						
Smarts	▓	▓						
Energy Protection	▓	▓	▓	▓	▓	▓		
Fight Skills	▓	▓						
Skate Skills								
Basketball Skills	▓	▓						
Strength	▓	▓	▓	▓				

* All scores recorded while wearing space suit.

Going Street to Hell!

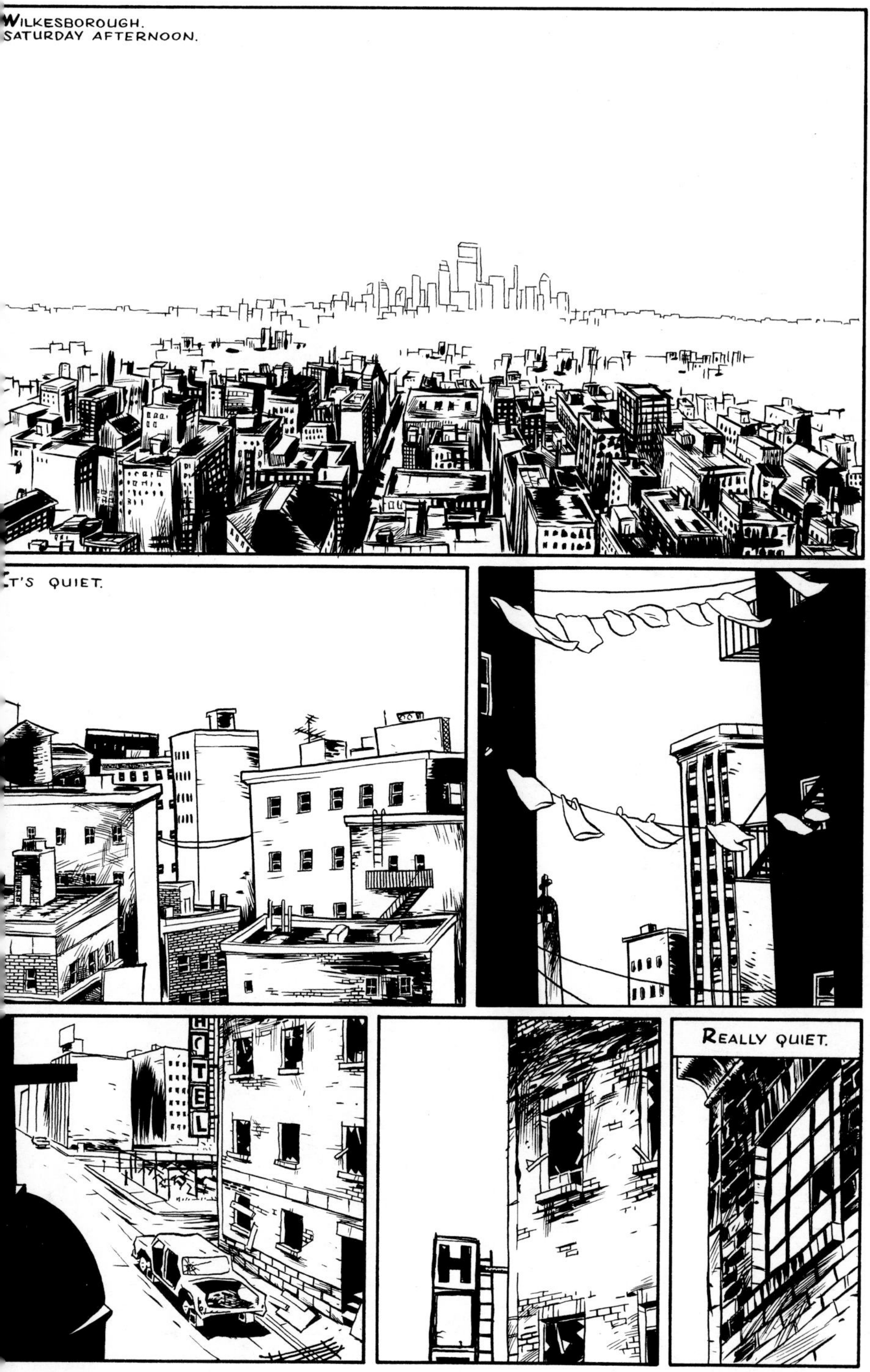
WILKESBOROUGH.
SATURDAY AFTERNOON.
IT'S QUIET.
HOTEL
REALLY QUIET.

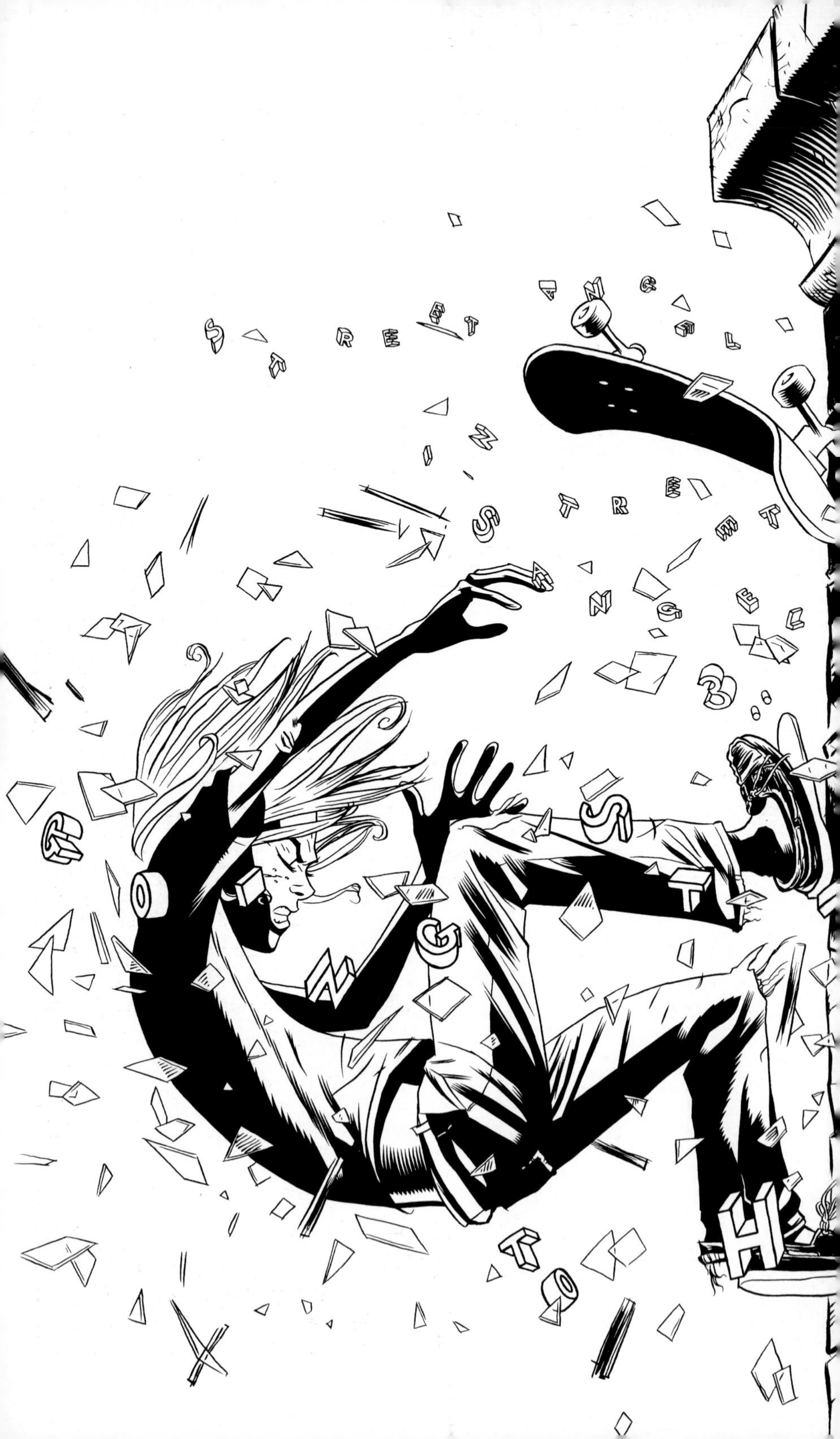

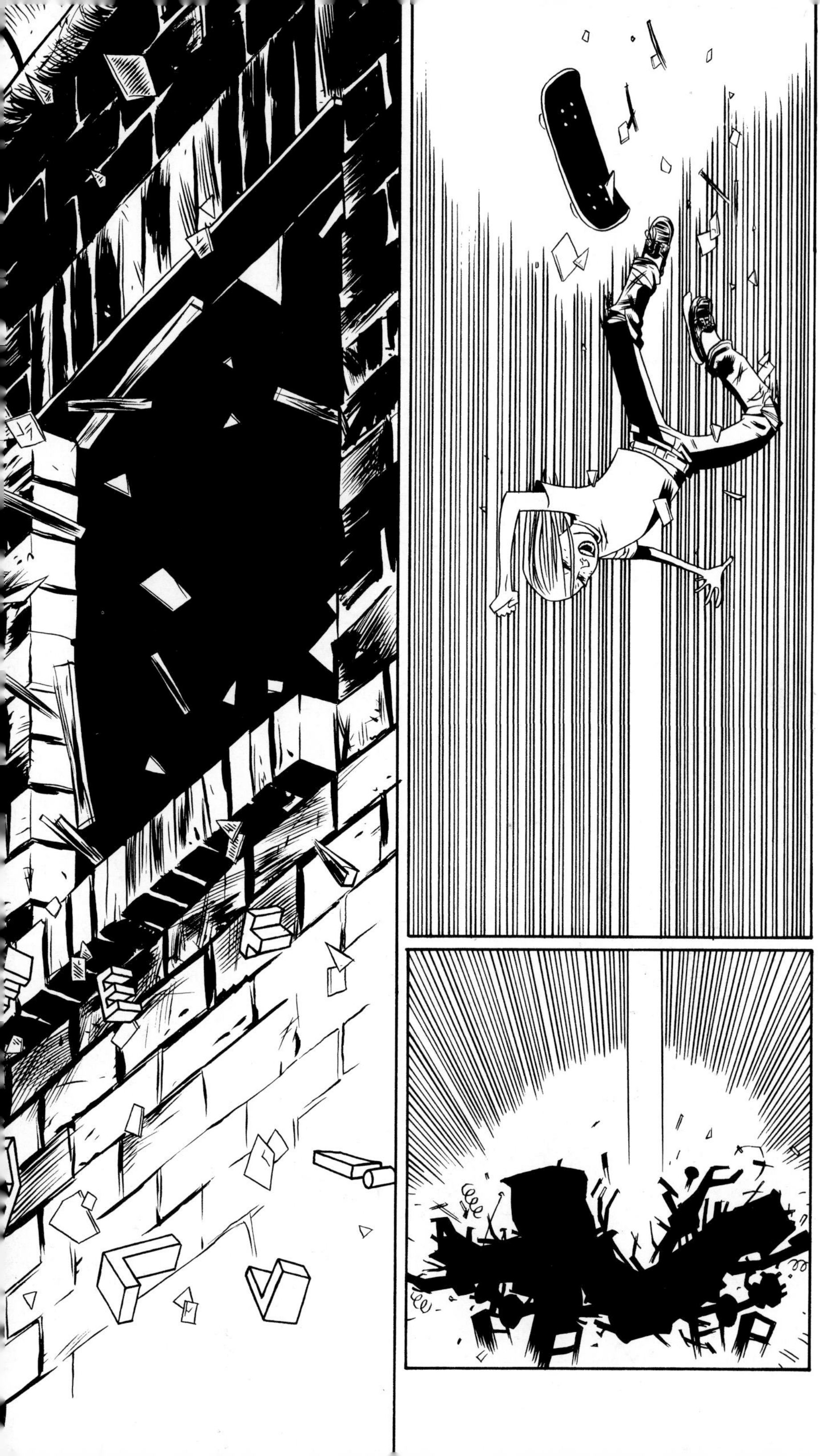

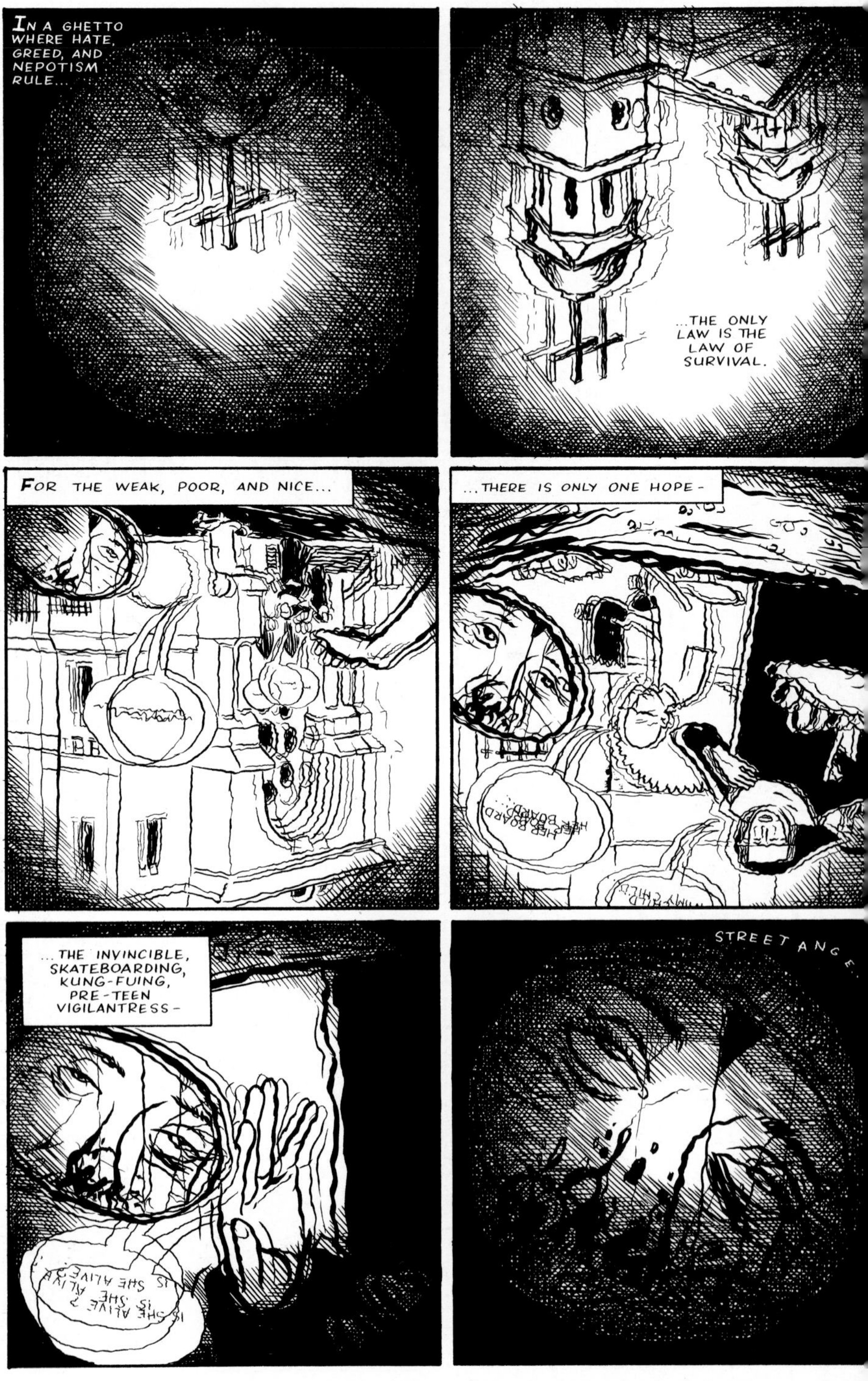
IN A GHETTO WHERE HATE, GREED, AND NEPOTISM RULE...
...THE ONLY LAW IS THE LAW OF SURVIVAL.
FOR THE WEAK, POOR, AND NICE...
...THERE IS ONLY ONE HOPE-
HER BOARD HER BOARD...
...THE INVINCIBLE, SKATEBOARDING, KUNG-FUING, PRE-TEEN VIGILANTRESS-
IS SHE ALIVE? IS SHE ALIVE? IS SHE ALIVE?
STREET ANG

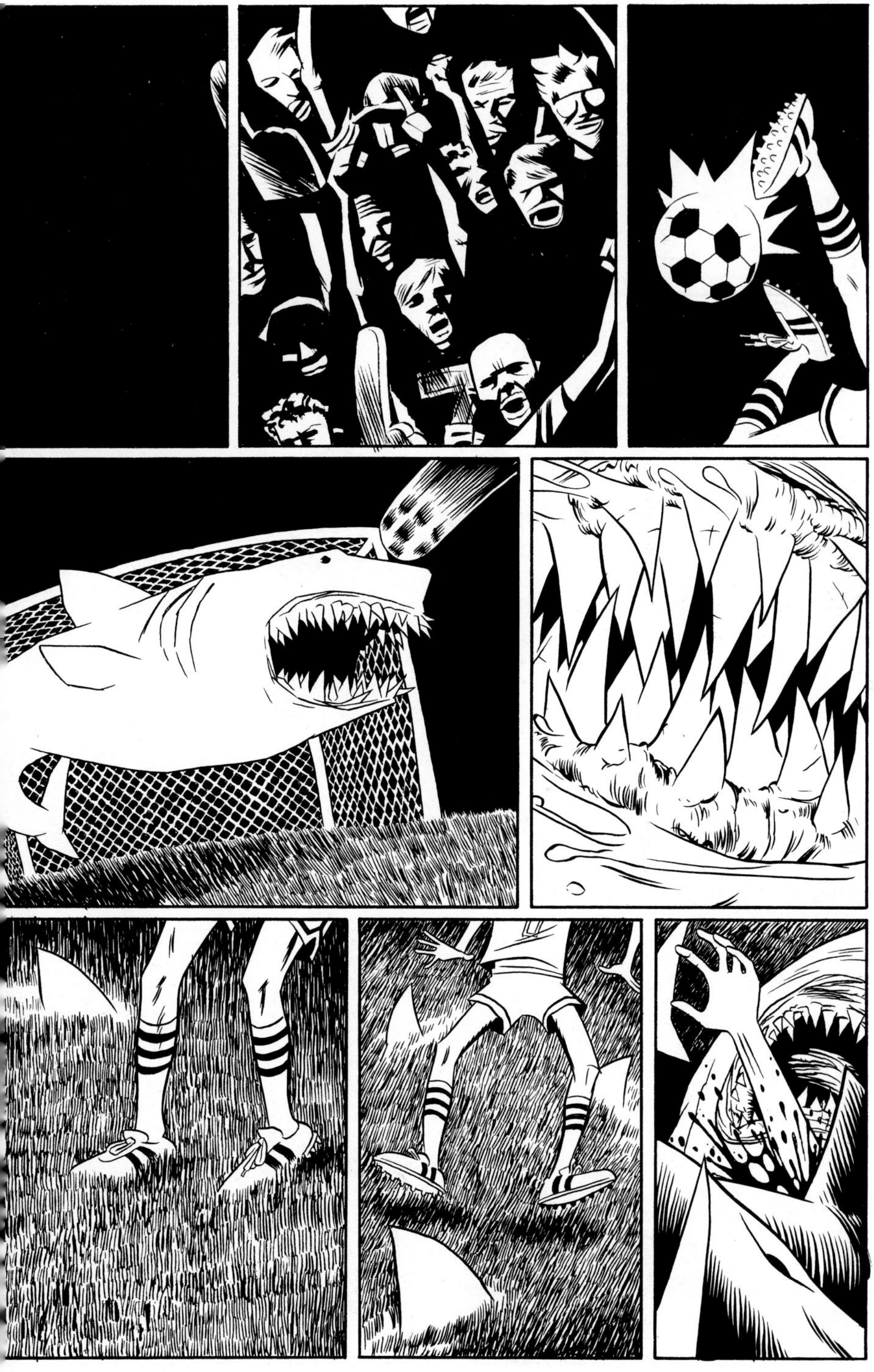

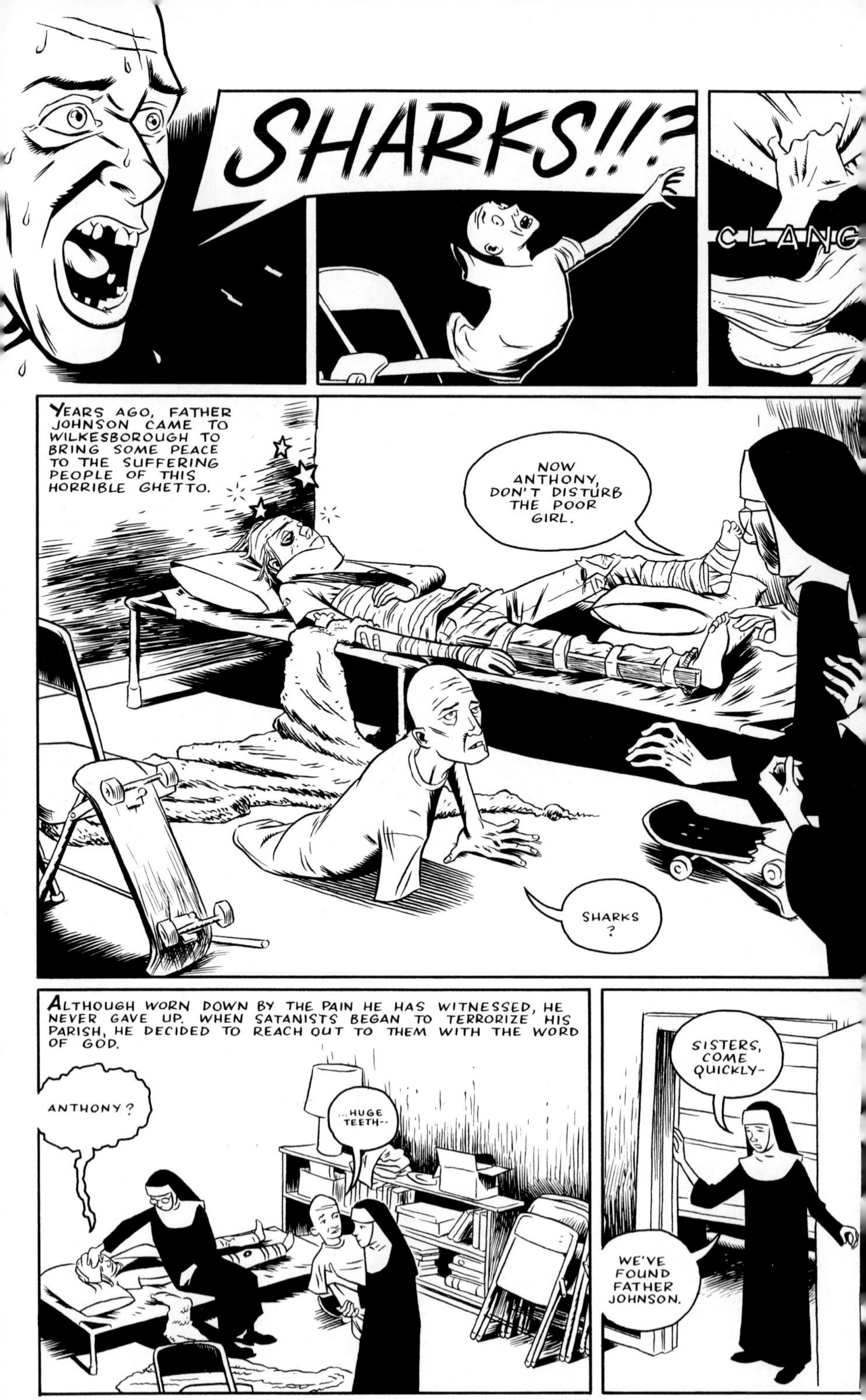
SHARKS!!?
CLANG
YEARS AGO, FATHER JOHNSON CAME TO WILKESBOROUGH TO BRING SOME PEACE TO THE SUFFERING PEOPLE OF THIS HORRIBLE GHETTO.
NOW ANTHONY, DON'T DISTURB THE POOR GIRL.
SHARKS ?
ALTHOUGH WORN DOWN BY THE PAIN HE HAS WITNESSED, HE NEVER GAVE UP. WHEN SATANISTS BEGAN TO TERRORIZE HIS PARISH, HE DECIDED TO REACH OUT TO THEM WITH THE WORD OF GOD.
ANTHONY?
...HUGE TEETH--
SISTERS, COME QUICKLY-
WE'VE FOUND FATHER JOHNSON.

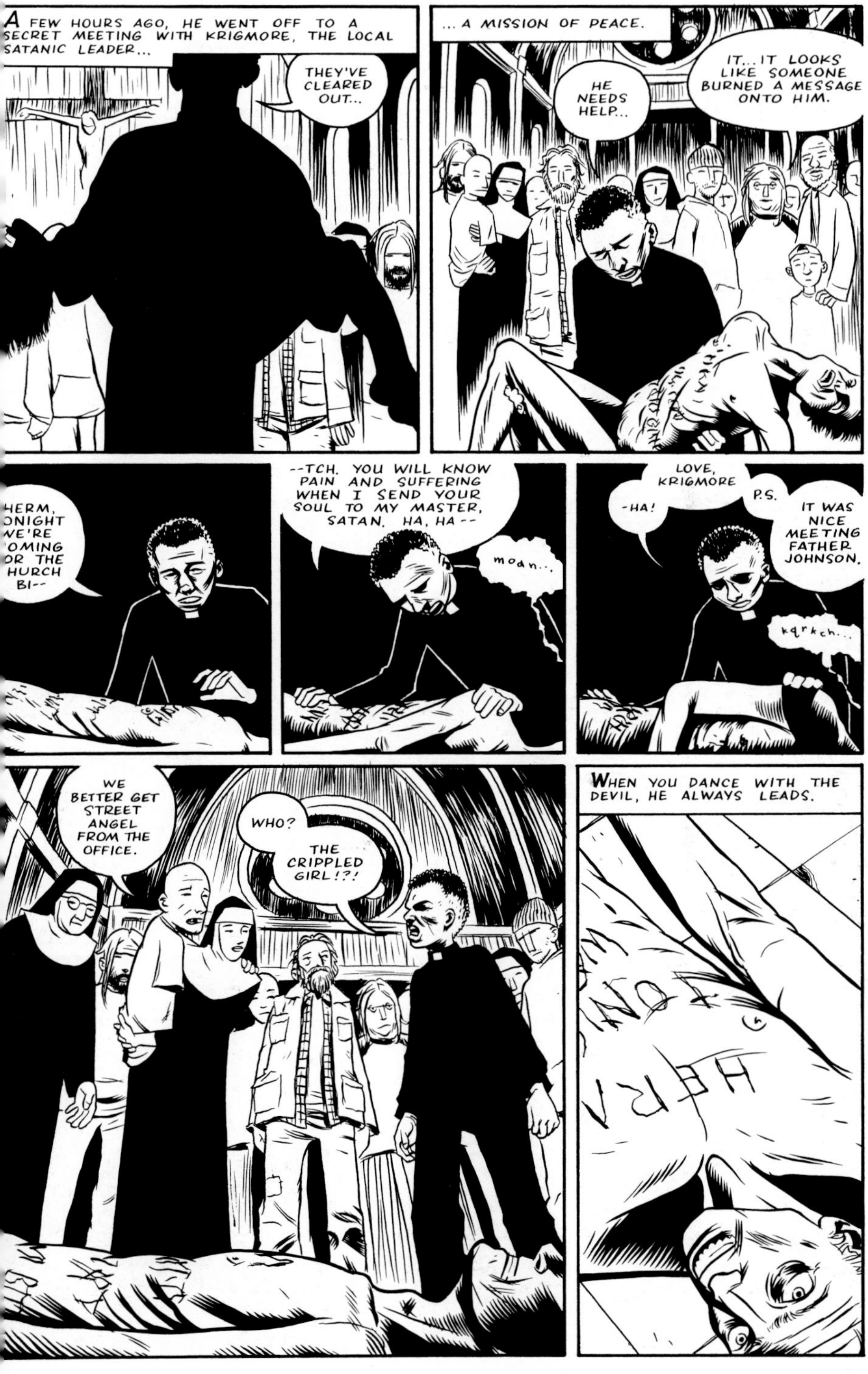
A FEW HOURS AGO, HE WENT OFF TO A SECRET MEETING WITH KRIGMORE, THE LOCAL SATANIC LEADER...
THEY'VE CLEARED OUT...
... A MISSION OF PEACE.
HE NEEDS HELP...
IT... IT LOOKS LIKE SOMEONE BURNED A MESSAGE ONTO HIM.
HERM, ONIGHT WE'RE OMING OR THE HURCH BI--
--TCH. YOU WILL KNOW PAIN AND SUFFERING WHEN I SEND YOUR SOUL TO MY MASTER, SATAN. HA, HA--
moan...
LOVE, KRIGMORE
-HA!
P.S.
IT WAS NICE MEETING FATHER JOHNSON.
kqrkch...
WE BETTER GET STREET ANGEL FROM THE OFFICE.
WHO?
THE CRIPPLED GIRL!?!
WHEN YOU DANCE WITH THE DEVIL, HE ALWAYS LEADS.
HERM

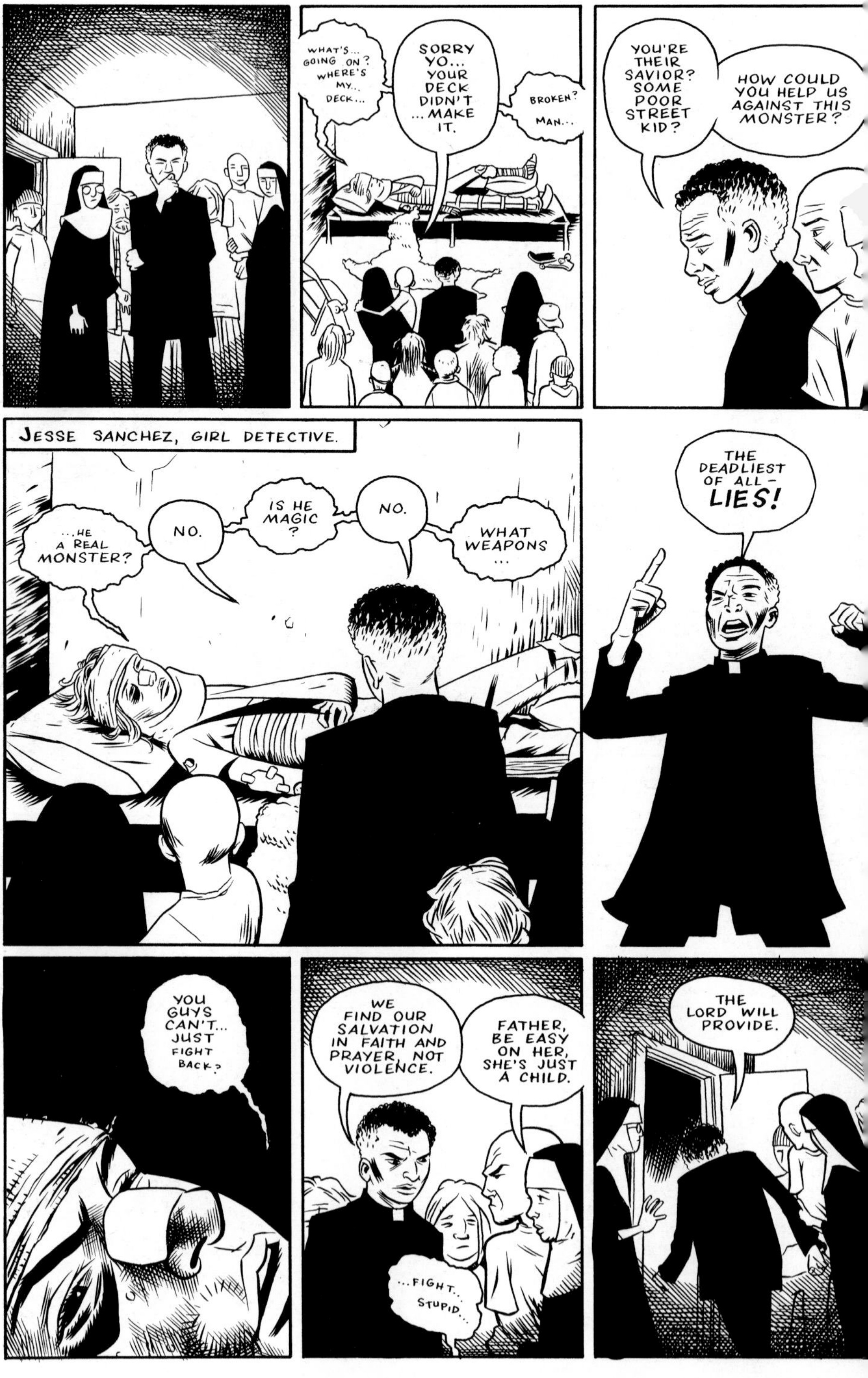
WHAT'S... GOING ON? WHERE'S MY... DECK...
SORRY YO... YOUR DECK DIDN'T ...MAKE IT.
BROKEN? MAN...
YOU'RE THEIR SAVIOR? SOME POOR STREET KID?
HOW COULD YOU HELP US AGAINST THIS MONSTER?
JESSE SANCHEZ, GIRL DETECTIVE.
...HE A REAL MONSTER?
NO.
IS HE MAGIC?
NO.
WHAT WEAPONS...
THE DEADLIEST OF ALL- LIES!
YOU GUYS CAN'T... JUST FIGHT BACK?
WE FIND OUR SALVATION IN FAITH AND PRAYER, NOT VIOLENCE.
FATHER, BE EASY ON HER, SHE'S JUST A CHILD.
...FIGHT... STUPID...
THE LORD WILL PROVIDE.

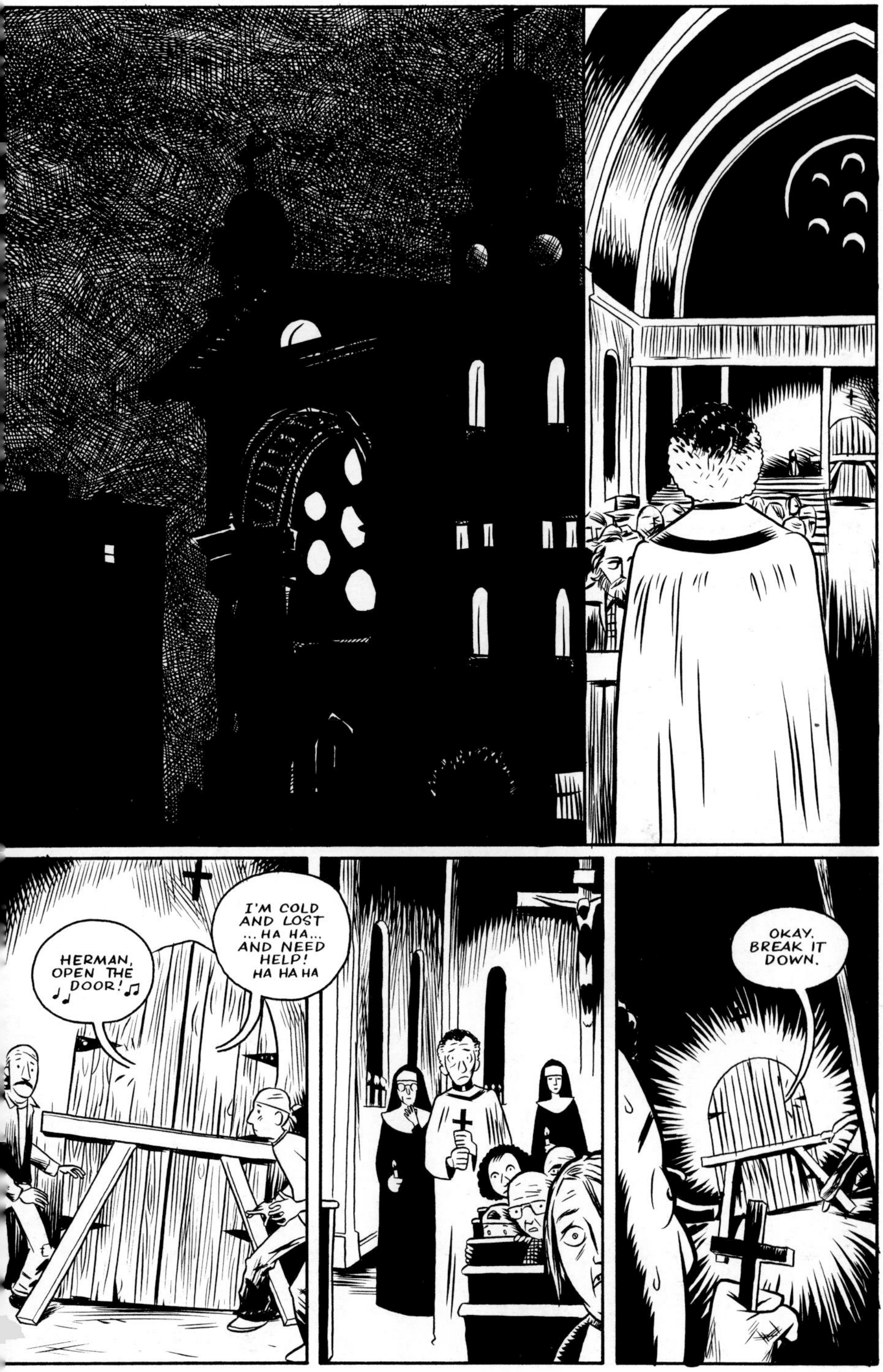
HERMAN, OPEN THE DOOR! ♪♪ ♫
I'M COLD AND LOST ...HA HA... AND NEED HELP! HA HA HA
OKAY. BREAK IT DOWN.

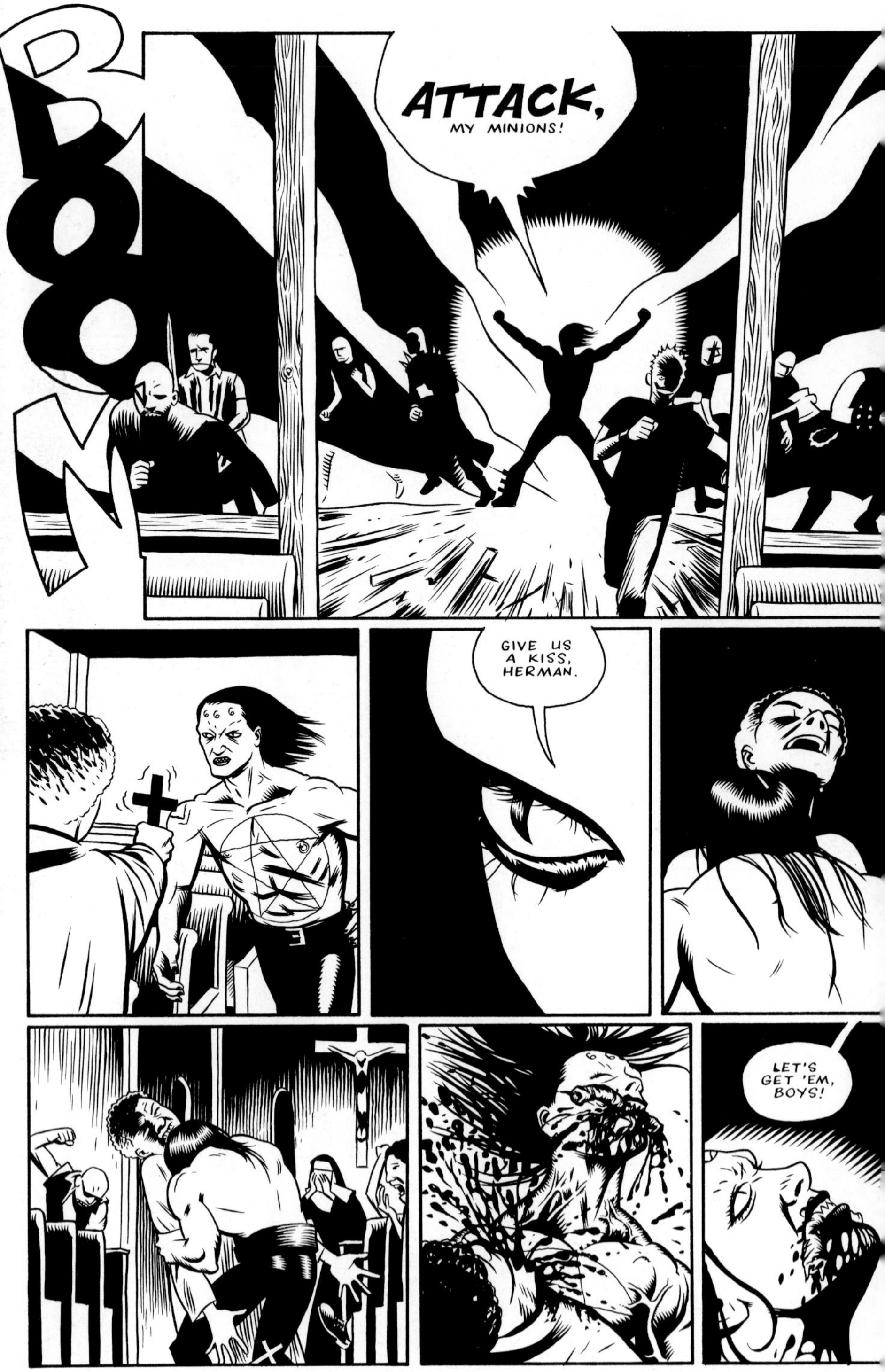
BOOM
ATTACK, MY MINIONS!
GIVE US A KISS, HERMAN.
LET'S GET 'EM, BOYS!

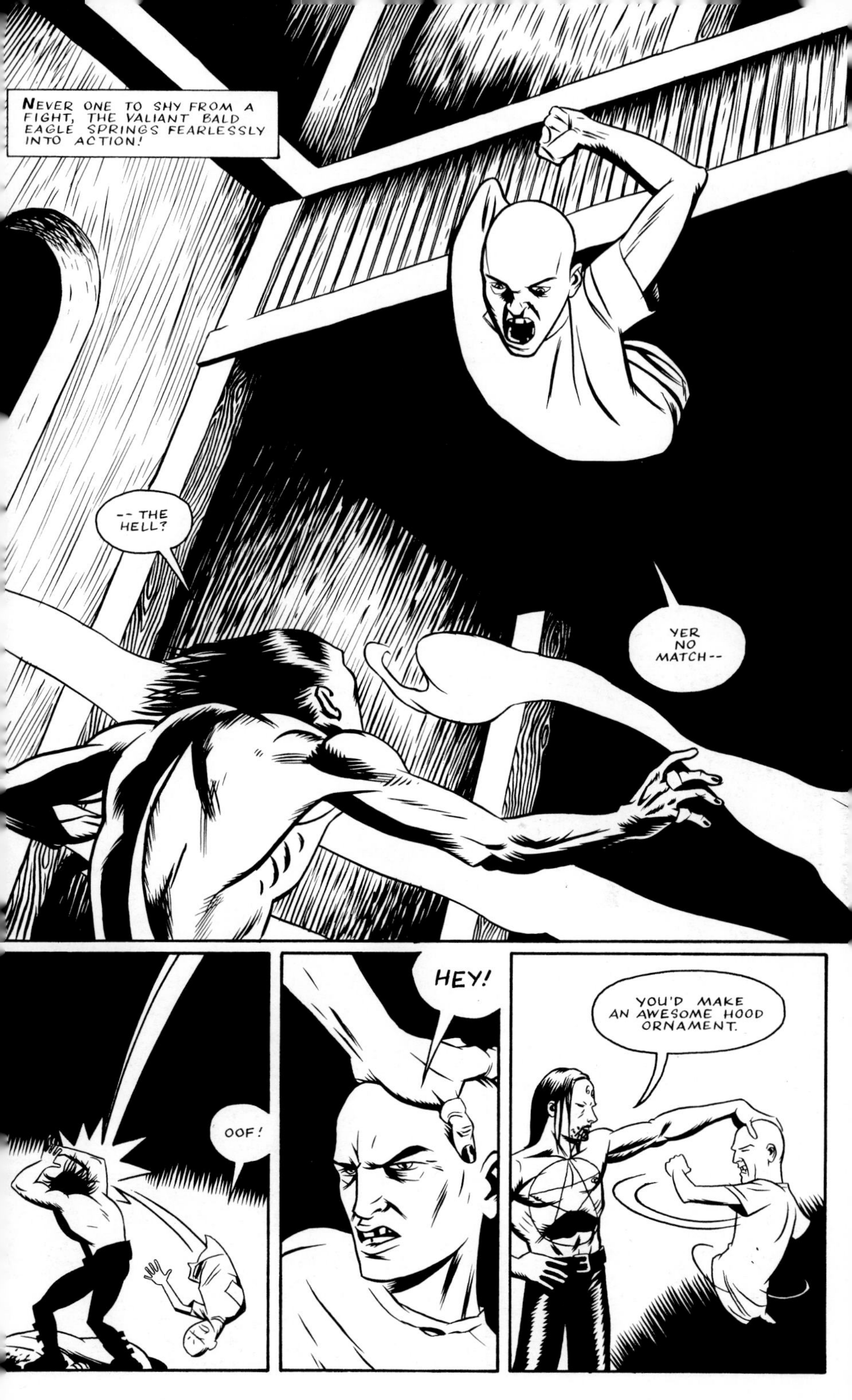
NEVER ONE TO SHY FROM A FIGHT, THE VALIANT BALD EAGLE SPRINGS FEARLESSLY INTO ACTION!
-- THE HELL?
YER NO MATCH --
OOF!
HEY!
YOU'D MAKE AN AWESOME HOOD ORNAMENT.

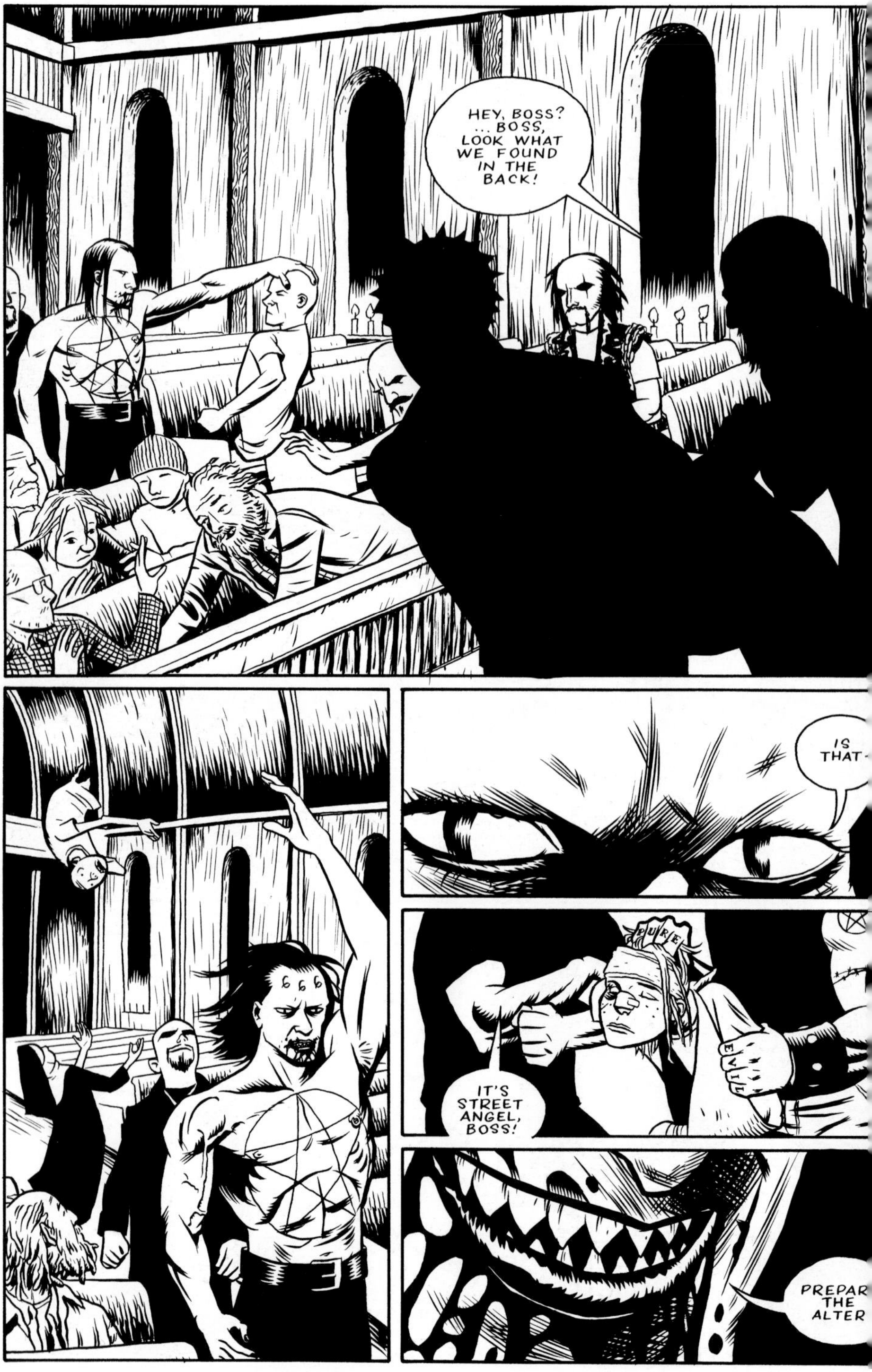
HEY, BOSS? ... BOSS, LOOK WHAT WE FOUND IN THE BACK!
IS THAT-
PURE
EVIL
IT'S STREET ANGEL, BOSS!
PREPAR THE ALTER

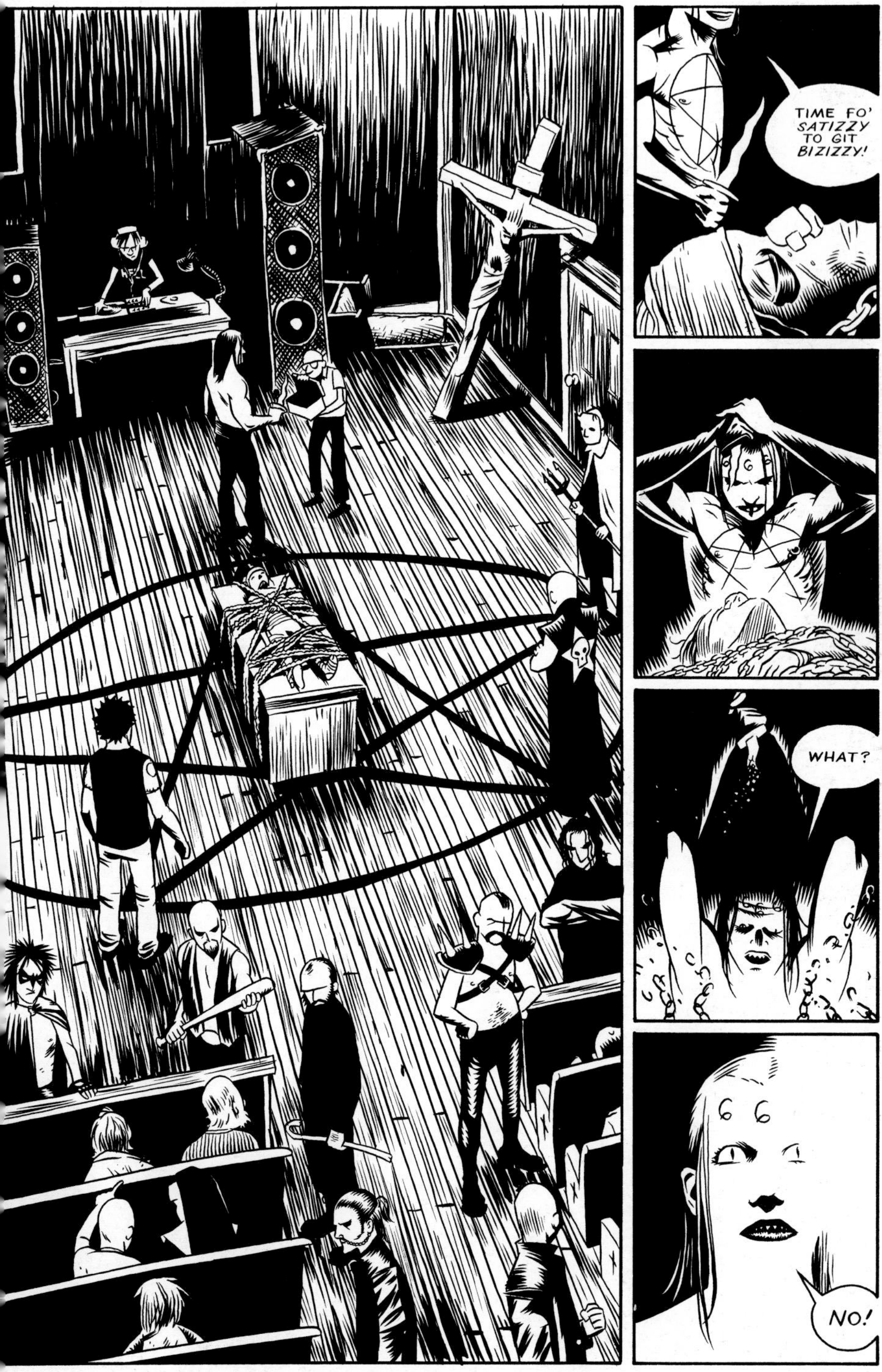
TIME FO' SATIZZY TO GIT BIZIZZY!
WHAT?
NO!

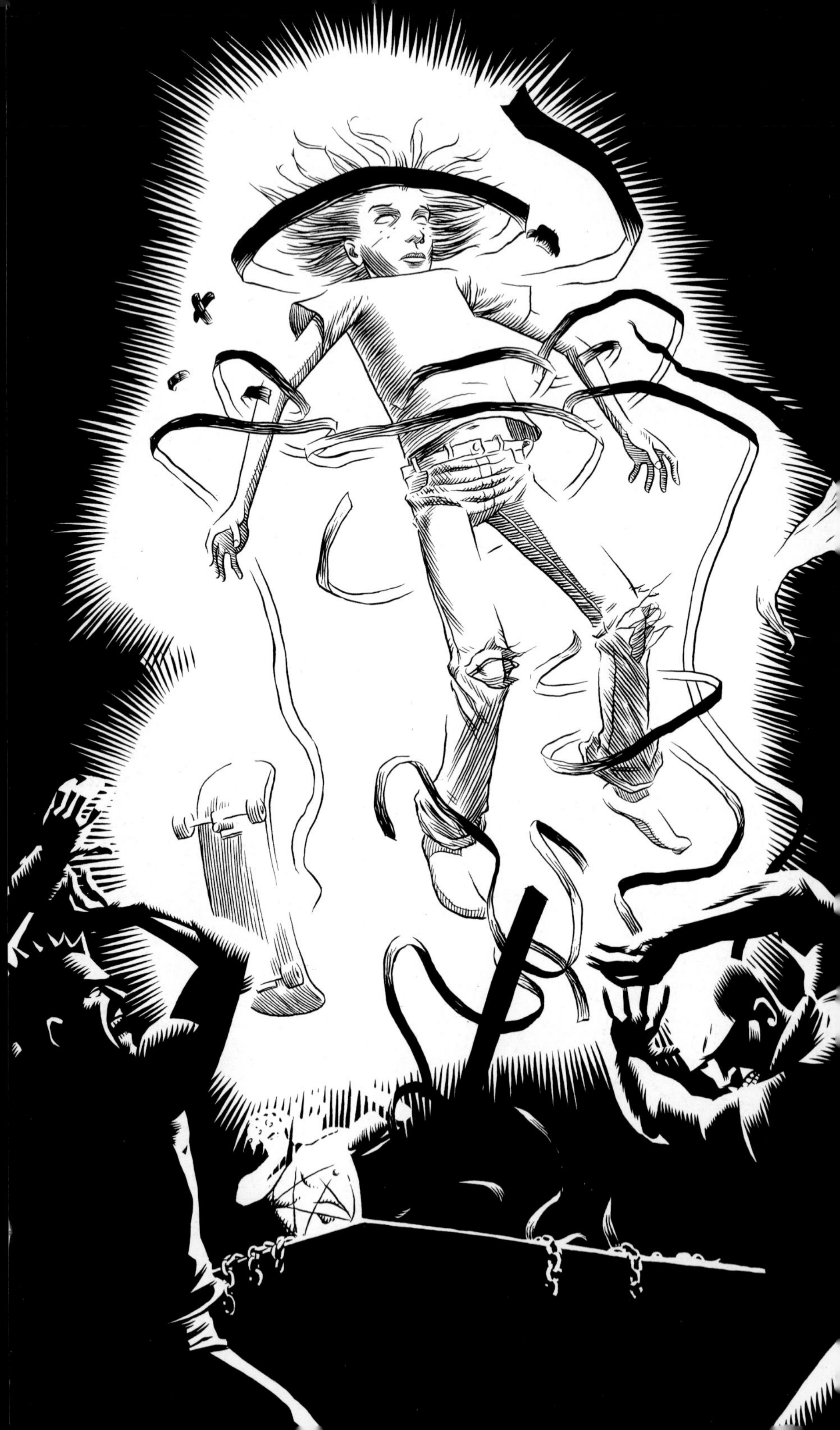

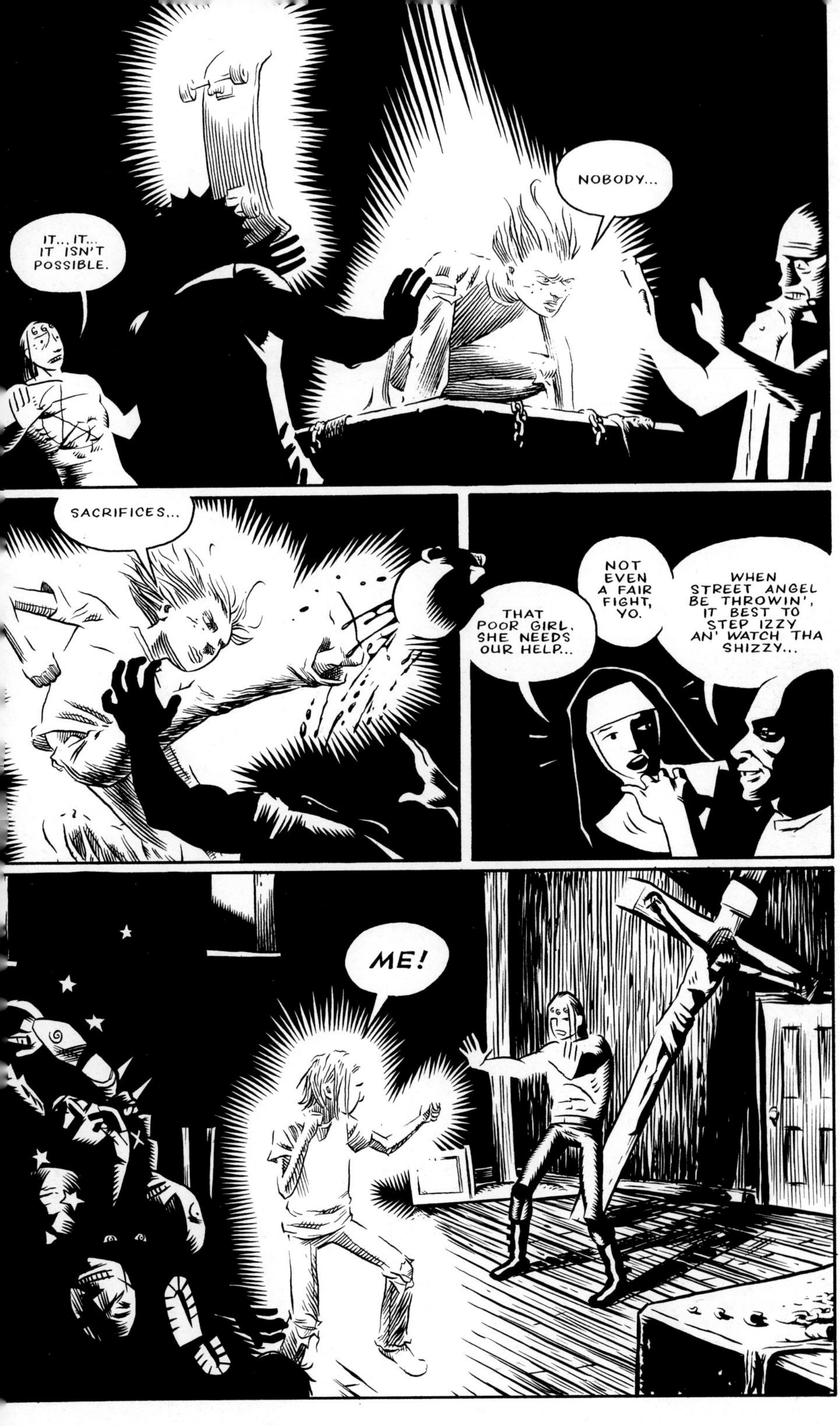

NOBODY...
IT... IT... IT ISN'T POSSIBLE.
SACRIFICES...
THAT POOR GIRL, SHE NEEDS OUR HELP...
NOT EVEN A FAIR FIGHT, YO.
WHEN STREET ANGEL BE THROWIN', IT BEST TO STEP IZZY AN' WATCH THA SHIZZY...
ME!

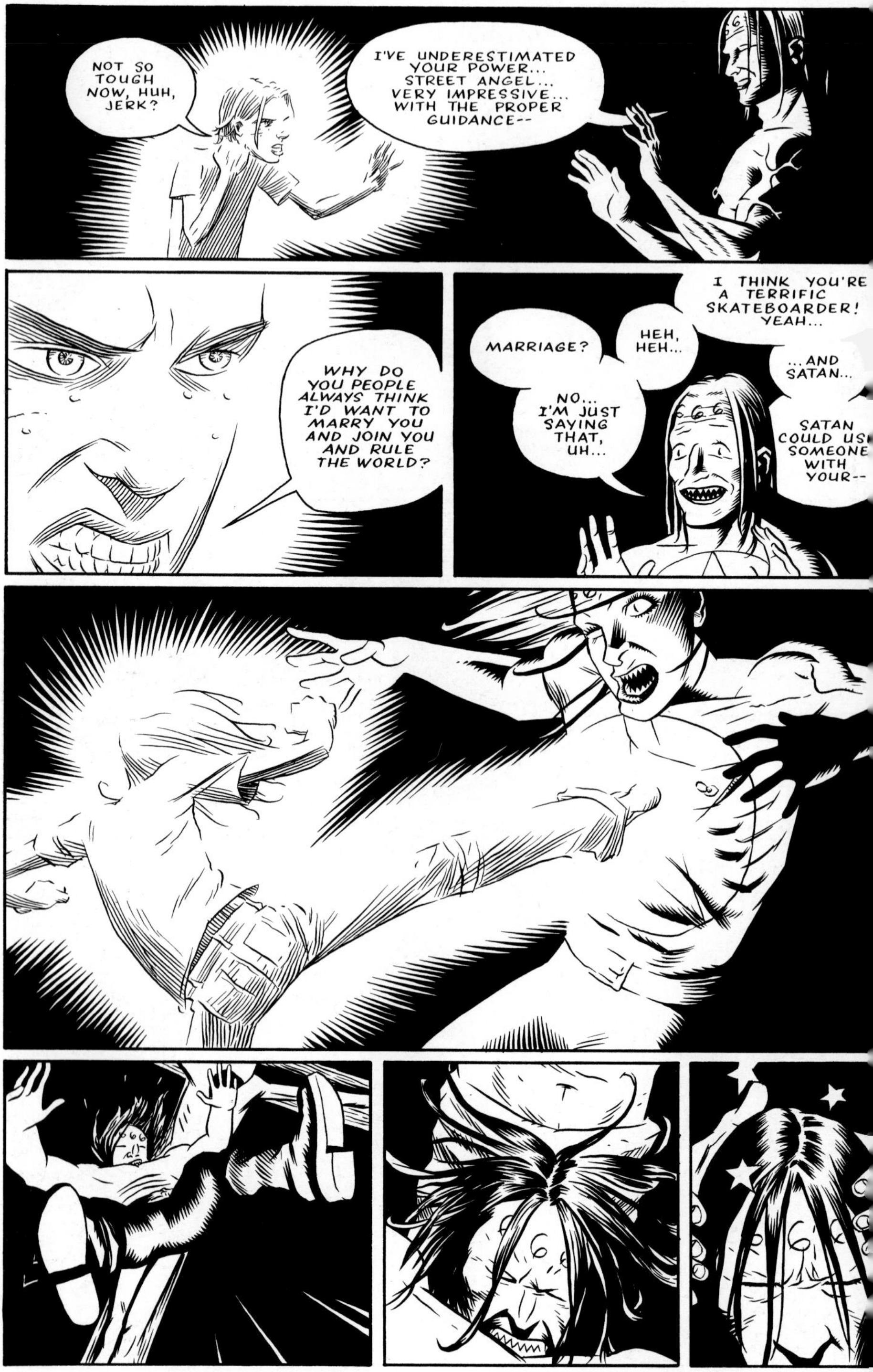
NOT SO TOUGH NOW, HUH, JERK?
I'VE UNDERESTIMATED YOUR POWER... STREET ANGEL... VERY IMPRESSIVE... WITH THE PROPER GUIDANCE--
WHY DO YOU PEOPLE ALWAYS THINK I'D WANT TO MARRY YOU AND JOIN YOU AND RULE THE WORLD?
MARRIAGE?
HEH, HEH...
I THINK YOU'RE A TERRIFIC SKATEBOARDER! YEAH...
NO... I'M JUST SAYING THAT, UH...
...AND SATAN...
SATAN COULD US SOMEONE WITH YOUR--

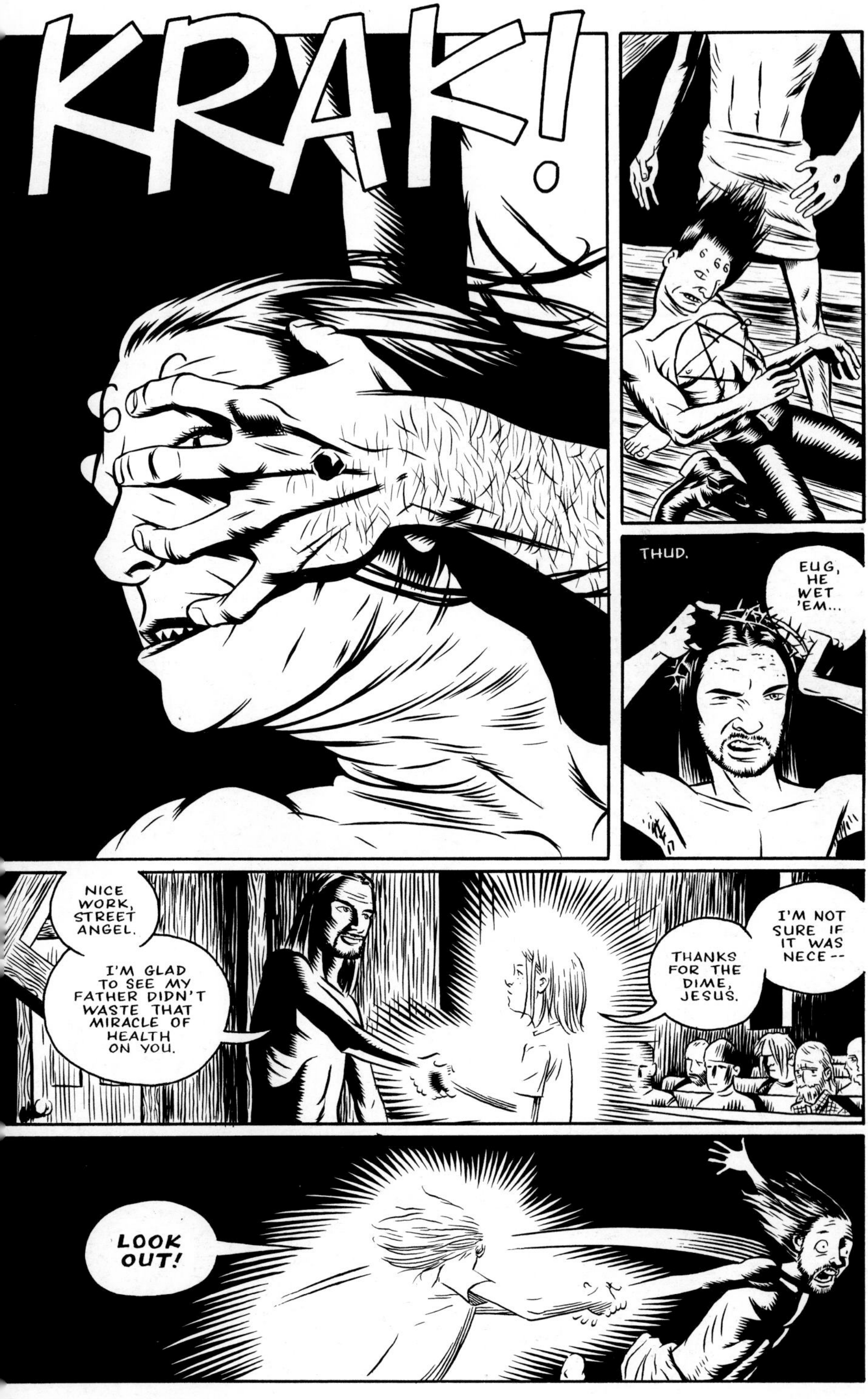
KRAK!
THUD.
EUG, HE WET 'EM...
NICE WORK, STREET ANGEL.
I'M GLAD TO SEE MY FATHER DIDN'T WASTE THAT MIRACLE OF HEALTH ON YOU.
THANKS FOR THE DIME, JESUS.
I'M NOT SURE IF IT WAS NECE--
LOOK OUT!

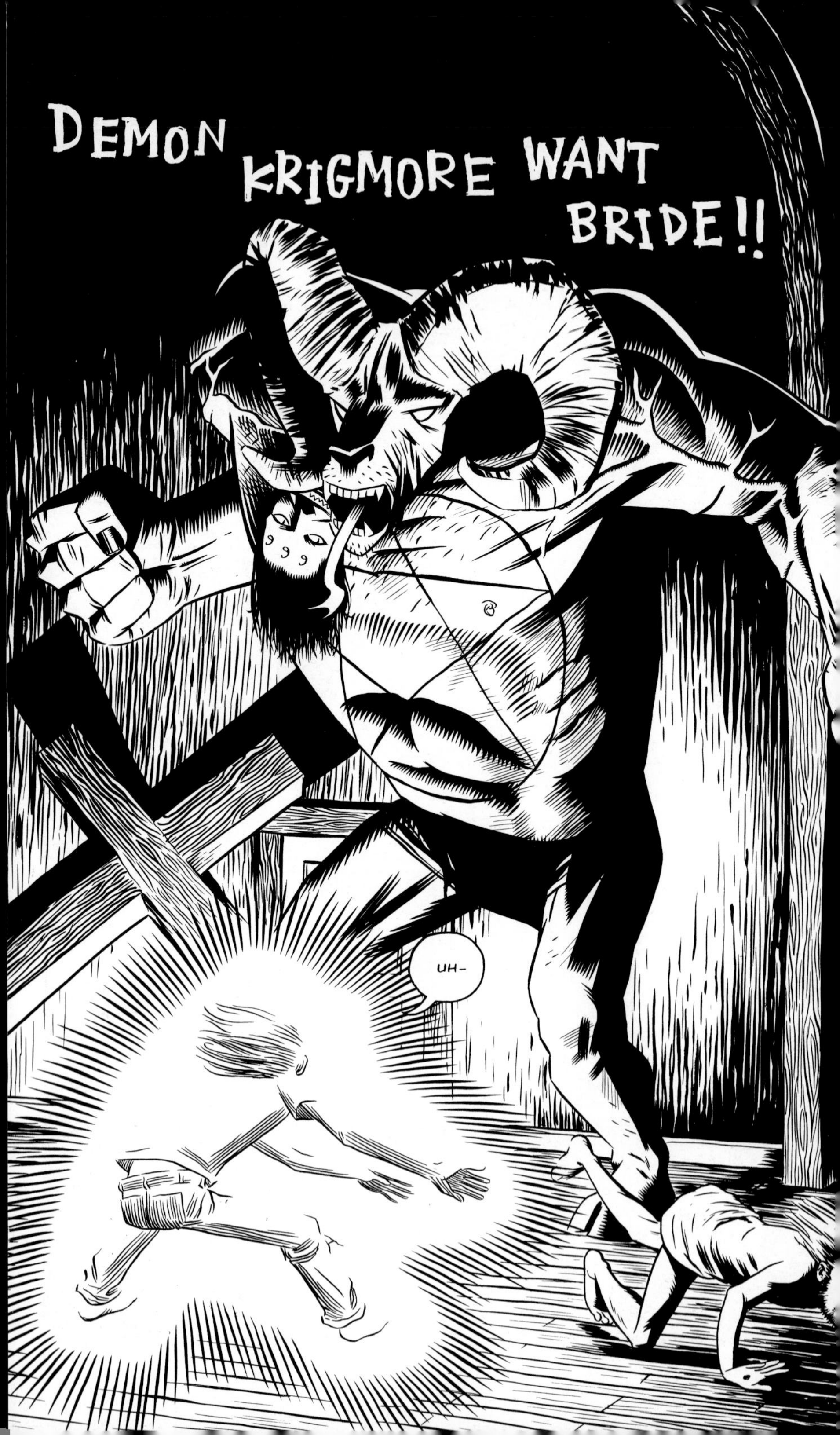
DEMON KRIGMORE WANT BRIDE!!
UH-

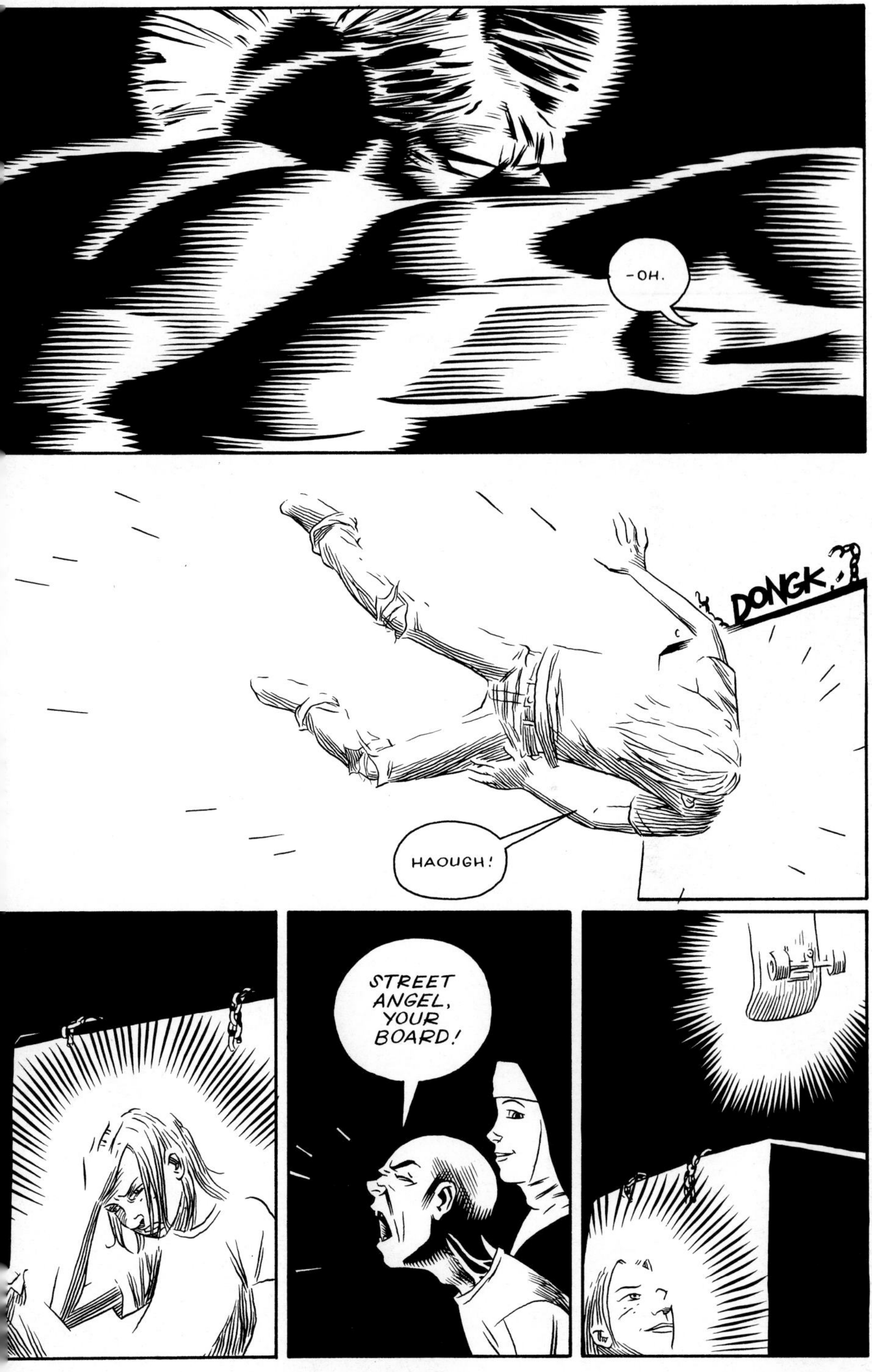
-OH.
DONGK
HAOUGH!
STREET ANGEL, YOUR BOARD!

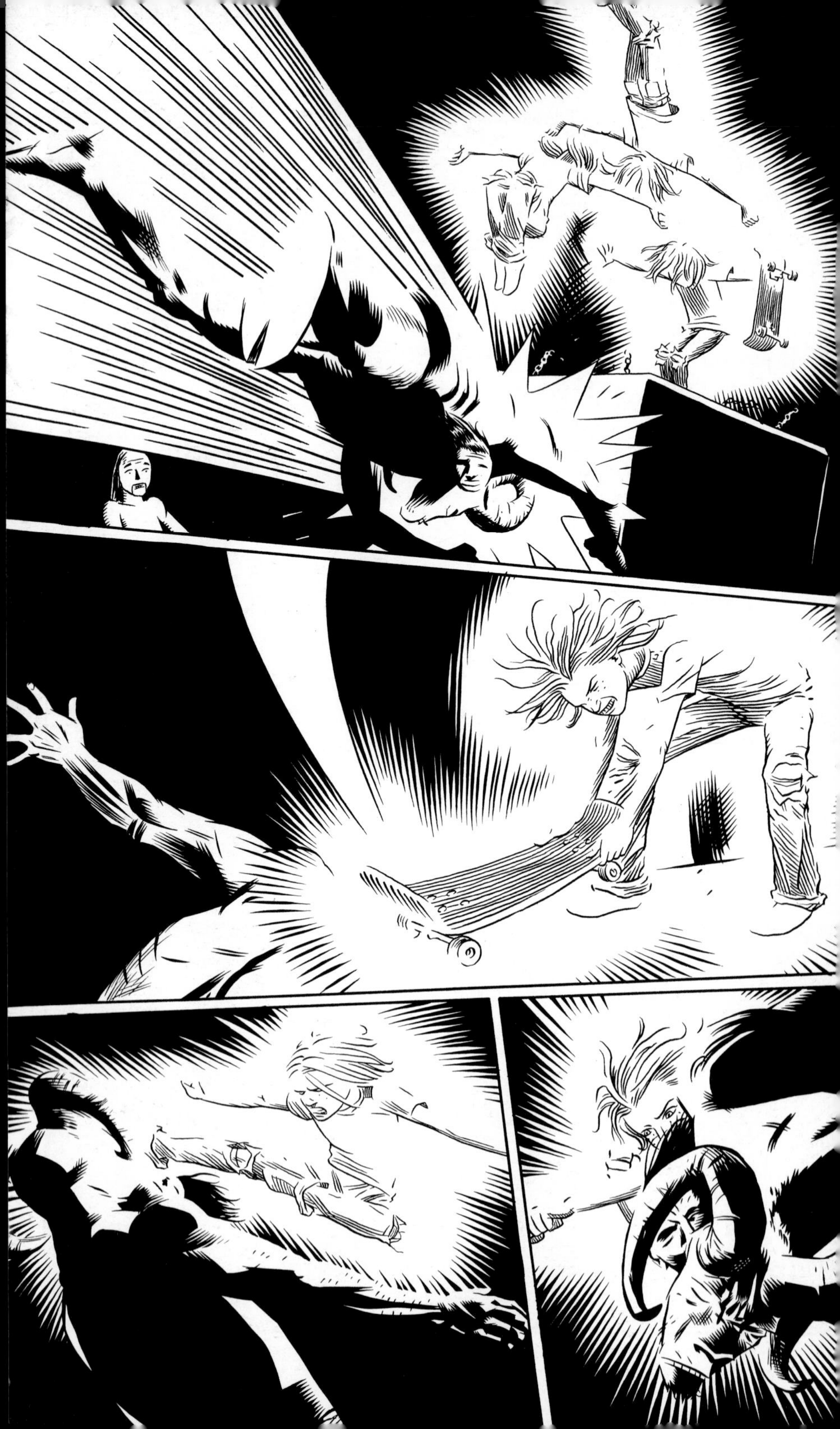

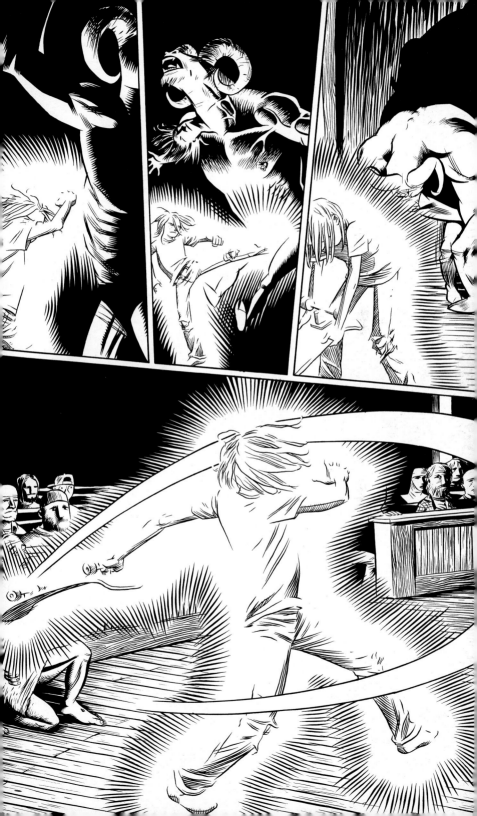

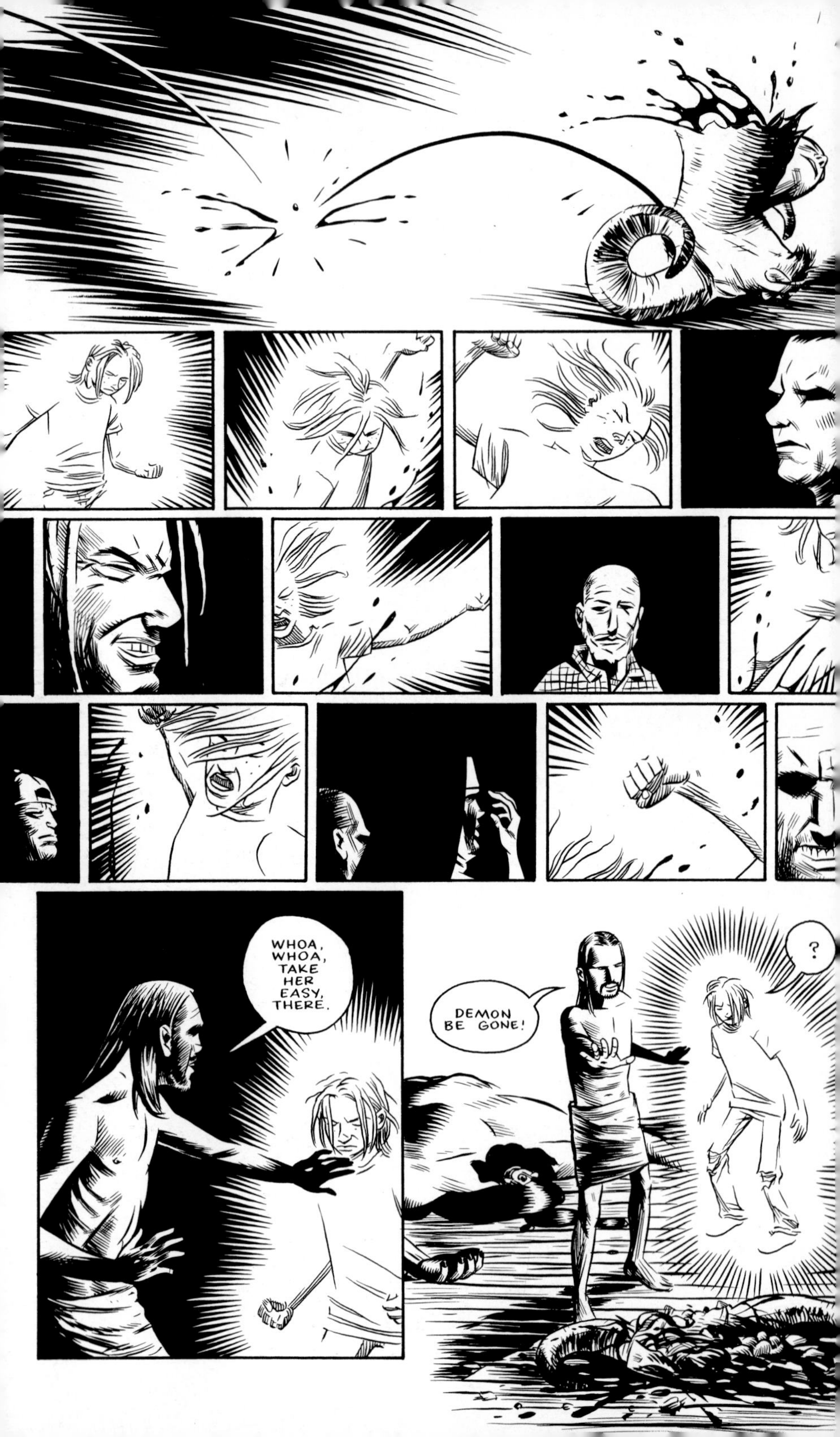
WHOA, WHOA, TAKE HER EASY, THERE.
DEMON BE GONE!
?

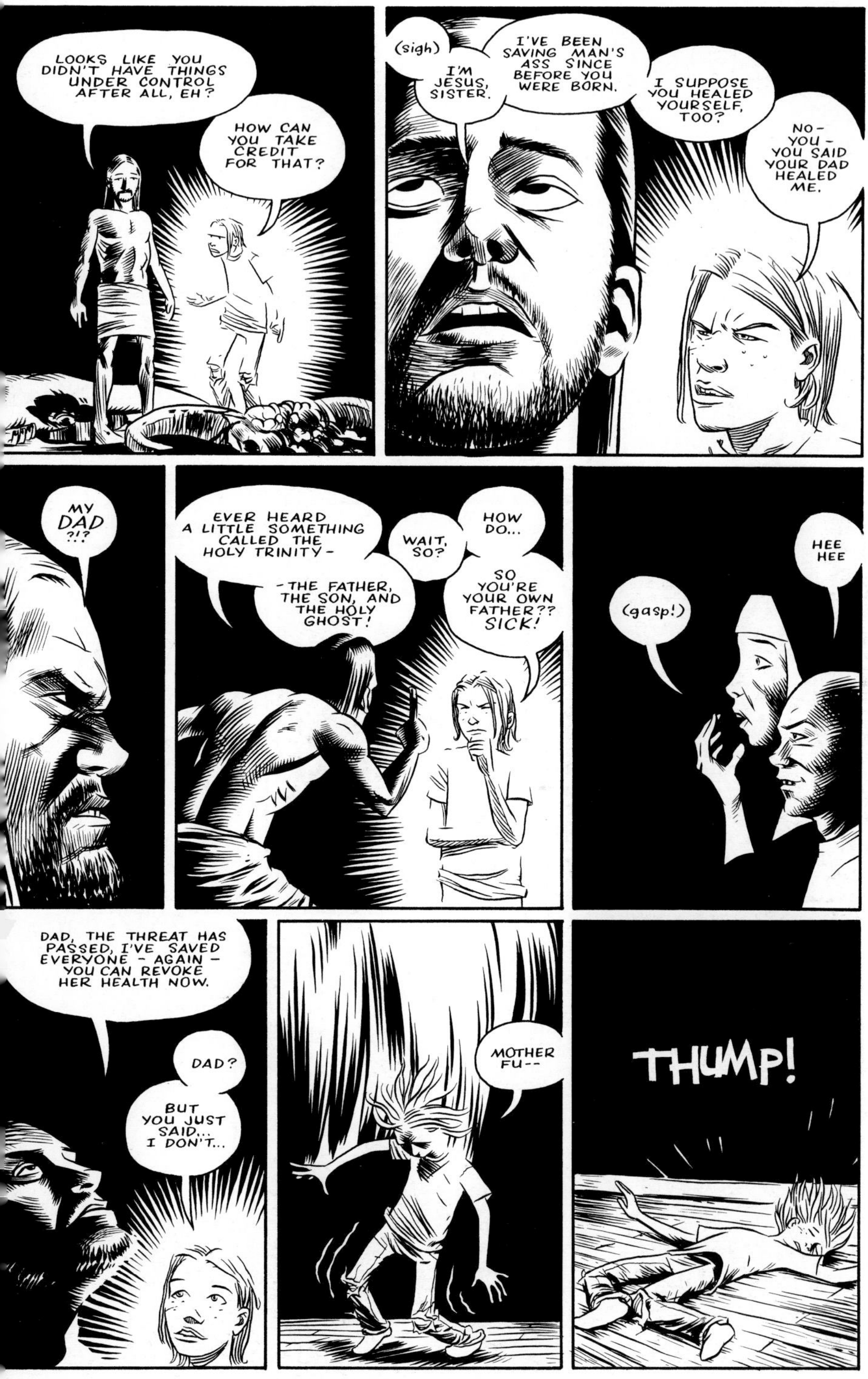
LOOKS LIKE YOU DIDN'T HAVE THINGS UNDER CONTROL AFTER ALL, EH?
HOW CAN YOU TAKE CREDIT FOR THAT?
(sigh)
I'M JESUS, SISTER.
I'VE BEEN SAVING MAN'S ASS SINCE BEFORE YOU WERE BORN.
I SUPPOSE YOU HEALED YOURSELF, TOO?
NO- YOU- YOU SAID YOUR DAD HEALED ME.
MY DAD ?!?
EVER HEARD A LITTLE SOMETHING CALLED THE HOLY TRINITY-
-THE FATHER, THE SON, AND THE HOLY GHOST!
WAIT, SO?
HOW DO...
SO YOU'RE YOUR OWN FATHER?? SICK!
(gasp!)
HEE HEE
DAD, THE THREAT HAS PASSED, I'VE SAVED EVERYONE - AGAIN - YOU CAN REVOKE HER HEALTH NOW.
DAD?
BUT YOU JUST SAID... I DON'T...
MOTHER FU--
THUMP!

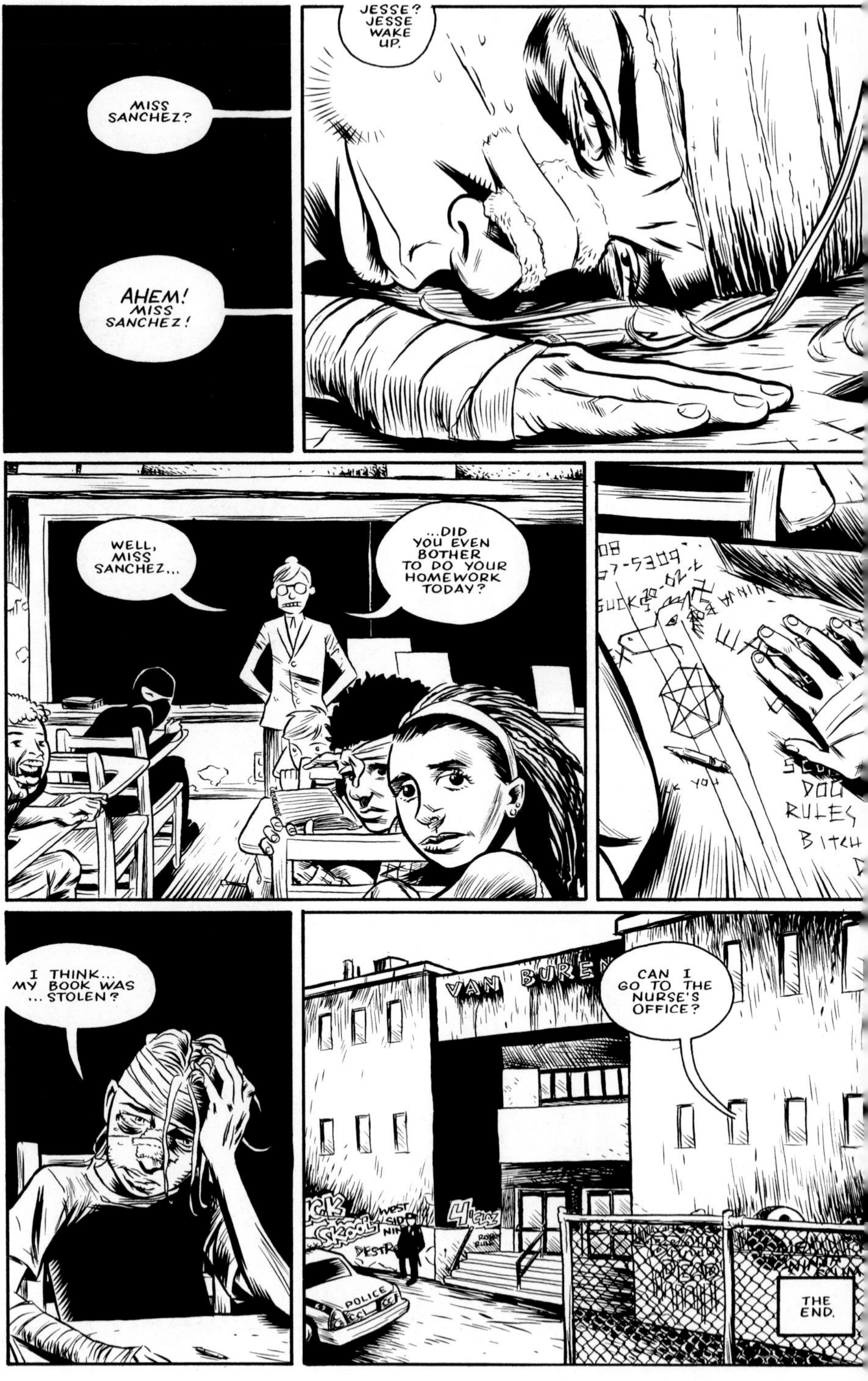
JESSE? JESSE WAKE UP.
MISS SANCHEZ?
AHEM! MISS SANCHEZ!
WELL, MISS SANCHEZ...
...DID YOU EVEN BOTHER TO DO YOUR HOMEWORK TODAY?
RULES
I THINK... MY BOOK WAS ... STOLEN?
VAN BUREN
CAN I GO TO THE NURSE'S OFFICE?
POLICE
THE END.

Wereshark

Name: N/A
Shark Length: 15' 6"
Were Height: 7'3"
Shark Weight: 3950 lbs
Were Weight: 560 lbs
Eyes: Black
Shark Hair: N/A
Were Hair: Reddish-brown

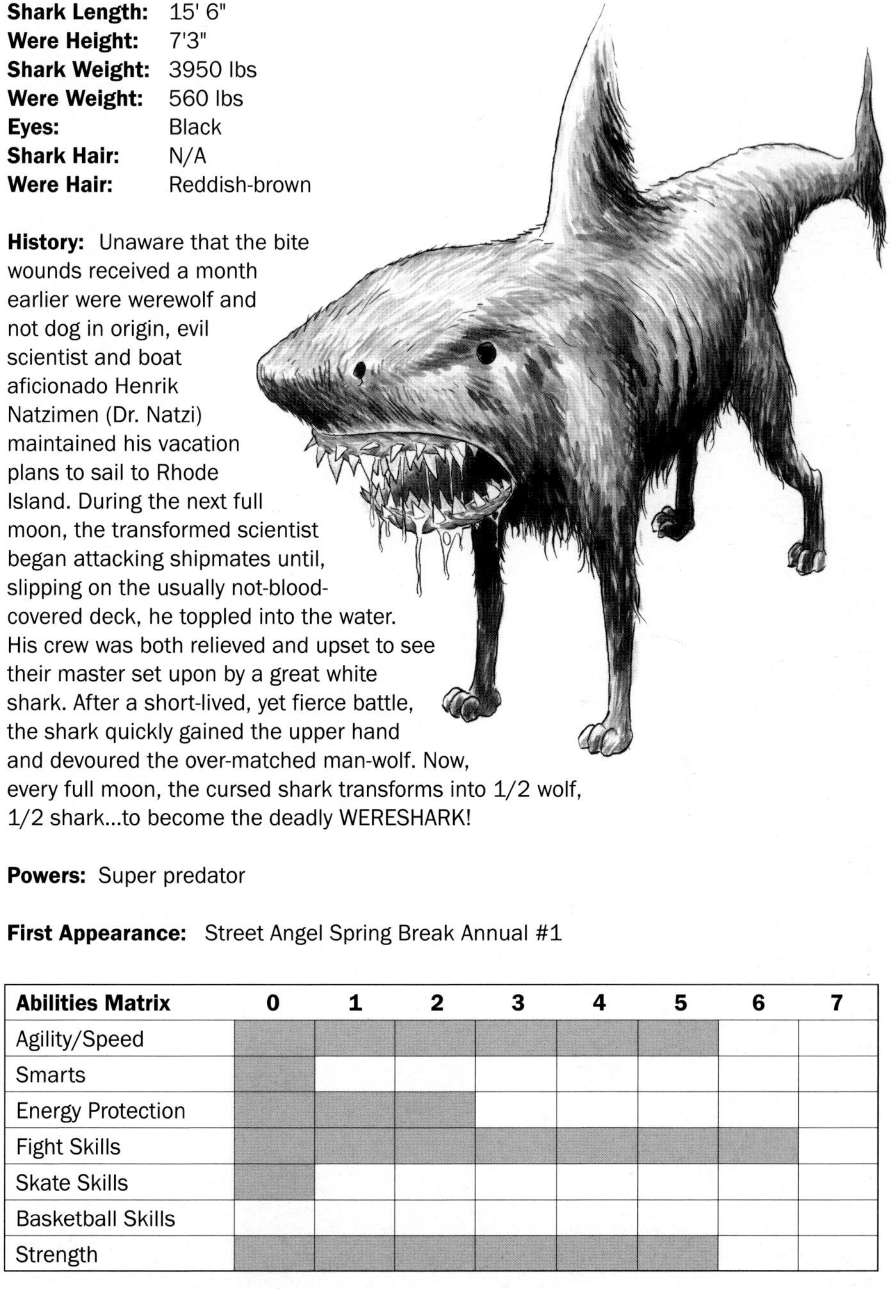

History: Unaware that the bite wounds received a month earlier were werewolf and not dog in origin, evil scientist and boat aficionado Henrik Natzimen (Dr. Natzi) maintained his vacation plans to sail to Rhode Island. During the next full moon, the transformed scientist began attacking shipmates until, slipping on the usually not-blood-covered deck, he toppled into the water. His crew was both relieved and upset to see their master set upon by a great white shark. After a short-lived, yet fierce battle, the shark quickly gained the upper hand and devoured the over-matched man-wolf. Now, every full moon, the cursed shark transforms into 1/2 wolf, 1/2 shark...to become the deadly WERESHARK!

Powers: Super predator

First Appearance: Street Angel Spring Break Annual #1

Abilities Matrix	**0**	**1**	**2**	**3**	**4**	**5**	**6**	**7**
Agility/Speed								
Smarts								
Energy Protection								
Fight Skills								
Skate Skills								
Basketball Skills								
Strength								

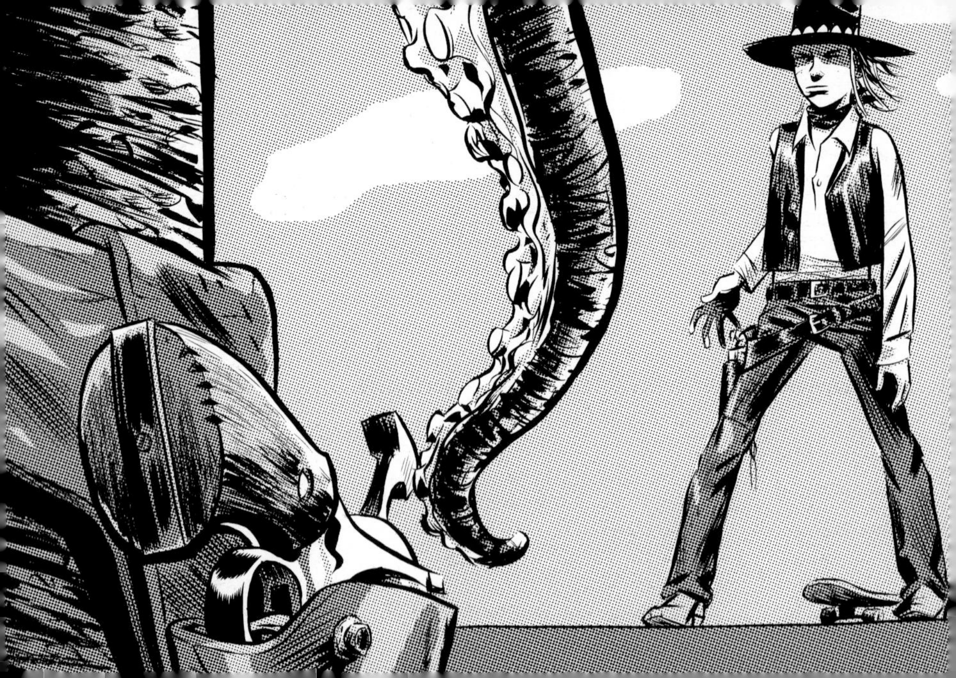

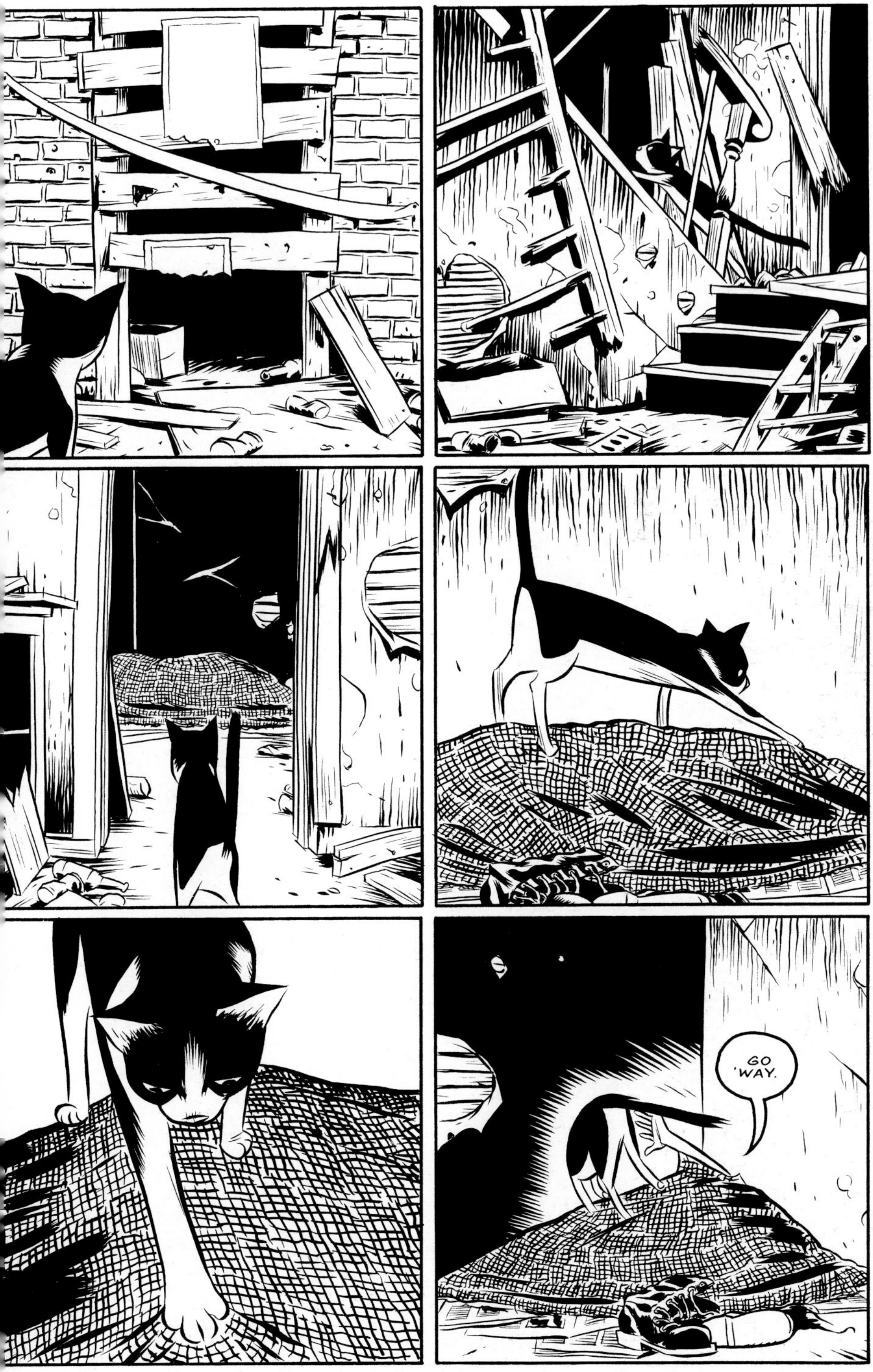
GO 'WAY.

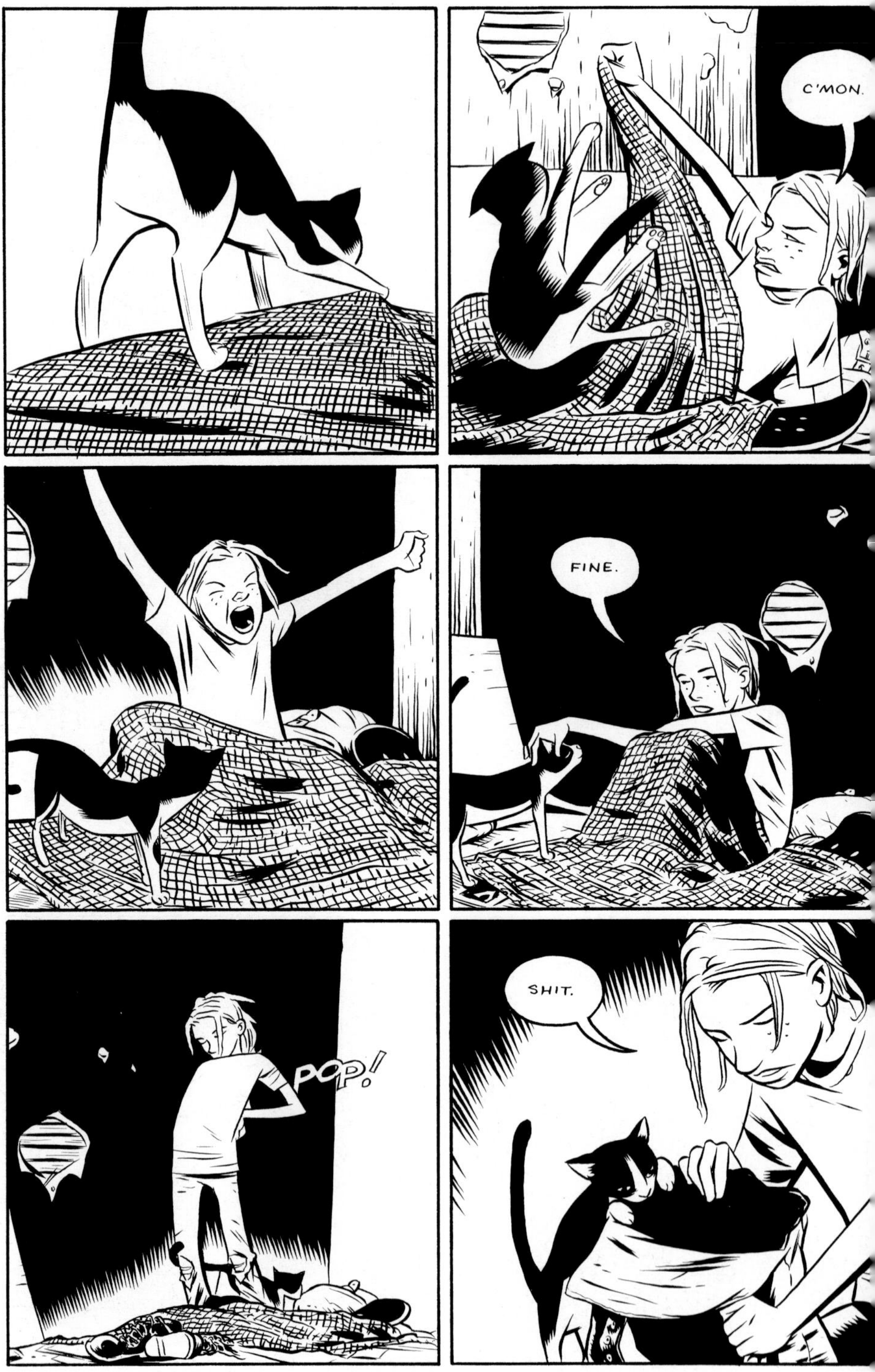
C'MON.
FINE.
POP!
SHIT.

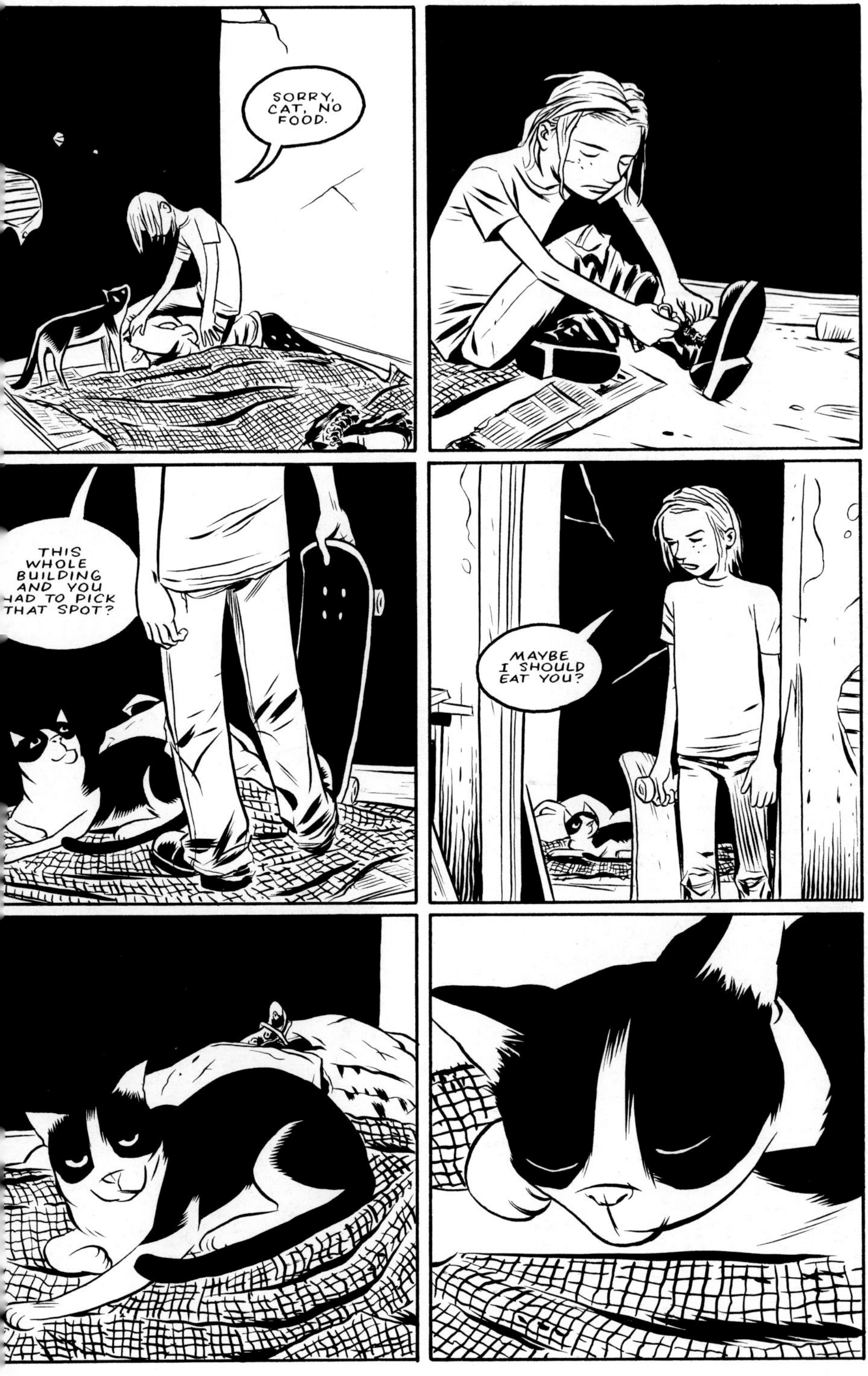
SORRY, CAT, NO FOOD.
THIS WHOLE BUILDING AND YOU HAD TO PICK THAT SPOT?
MAYBE I SHOULD EAT YOU?

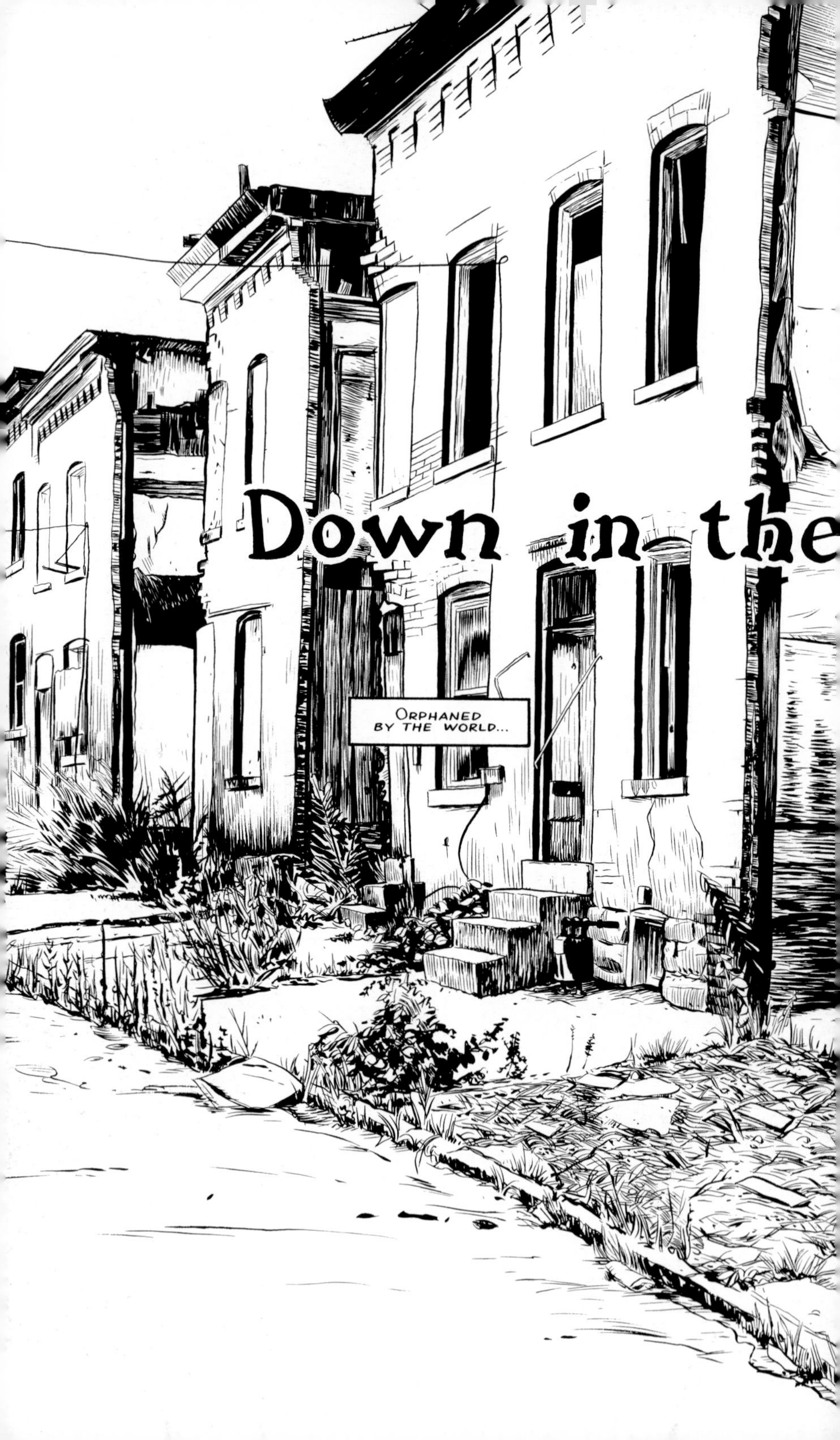
Down in the
ORPHANED BY THE WORLD...

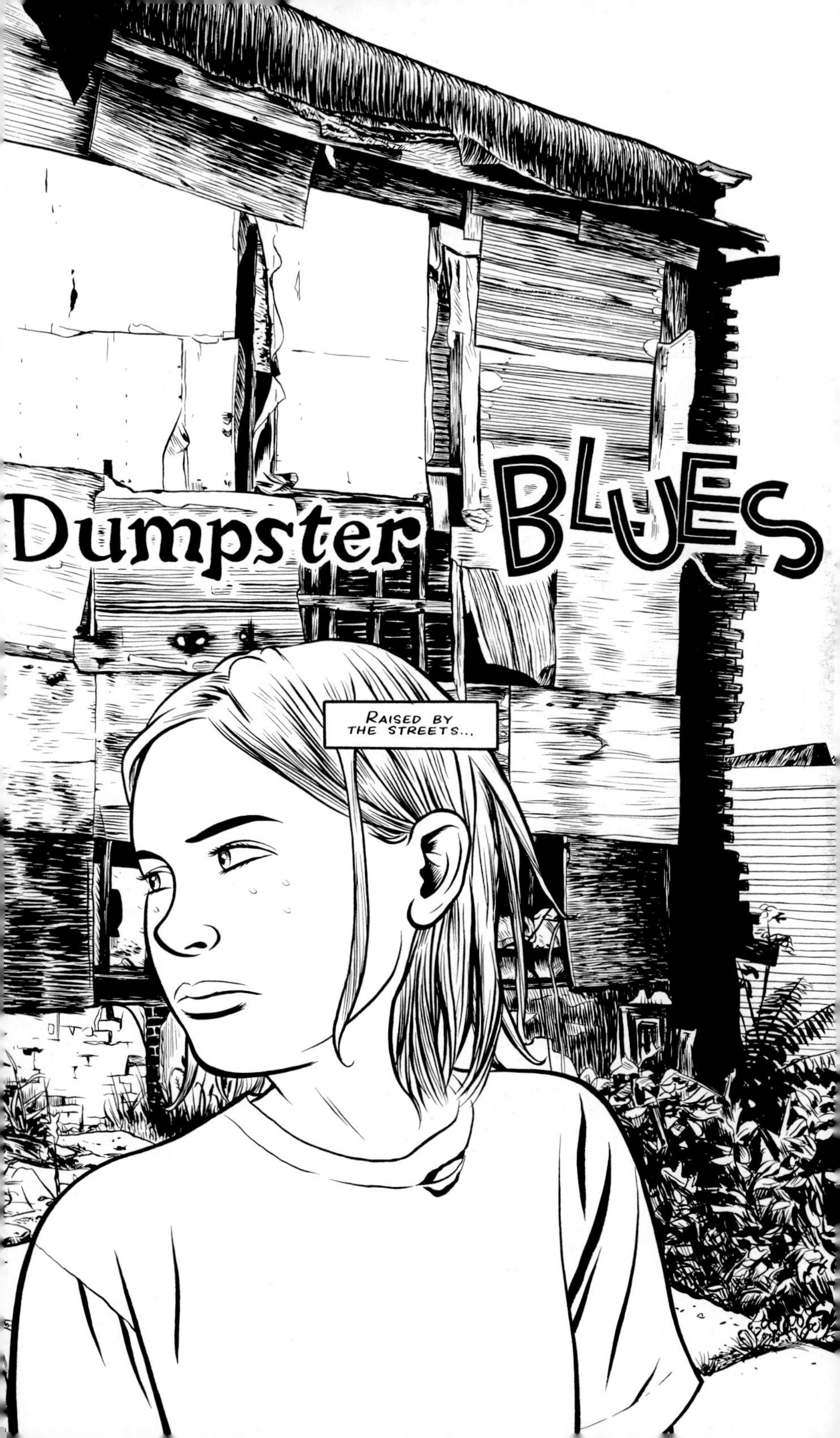
Dumpster BLUES
RAISED BY THE STREETS...

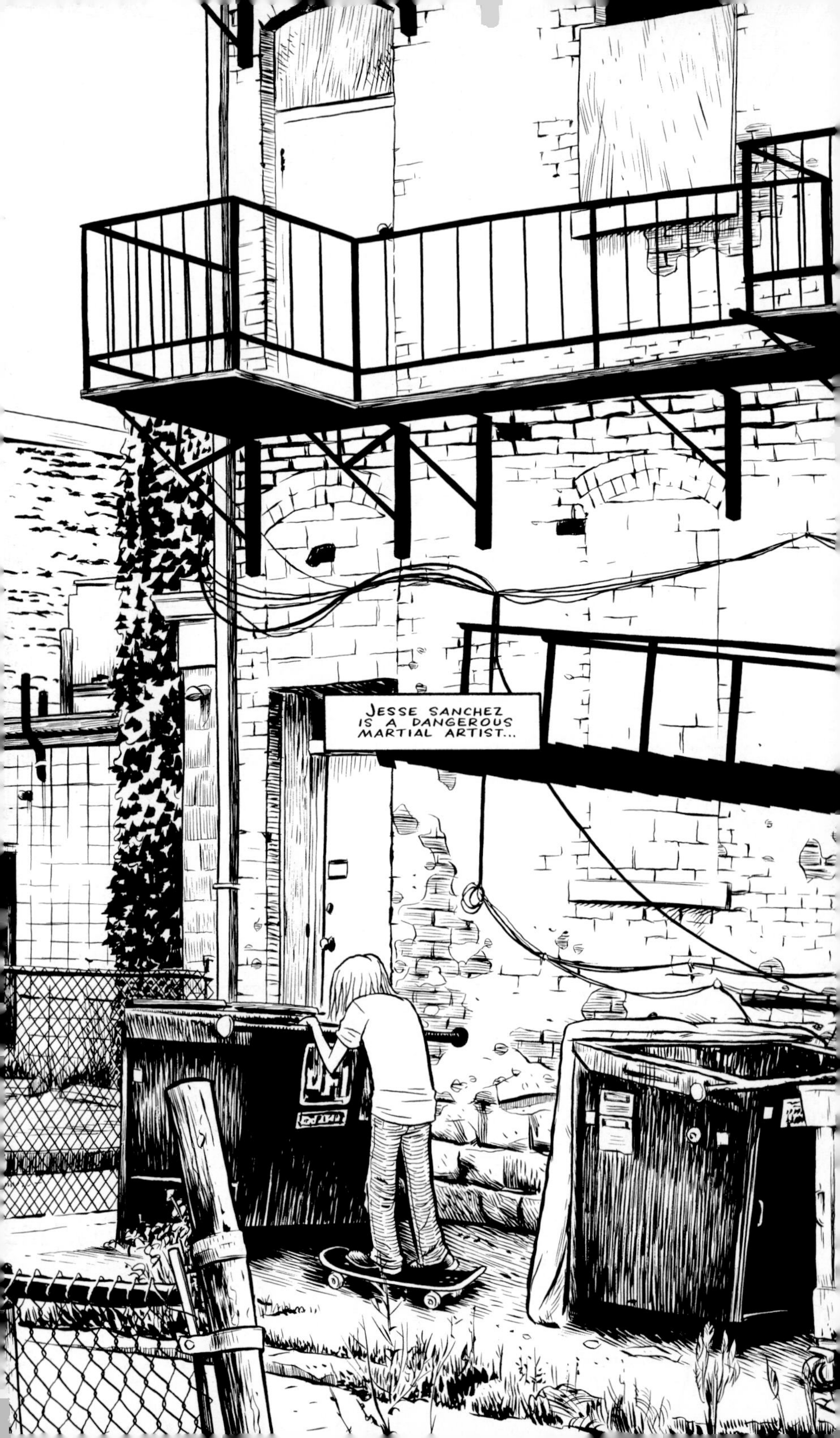
JESSE SANCHEZ IS A DANGEROUS MARTIAL ARTIST...

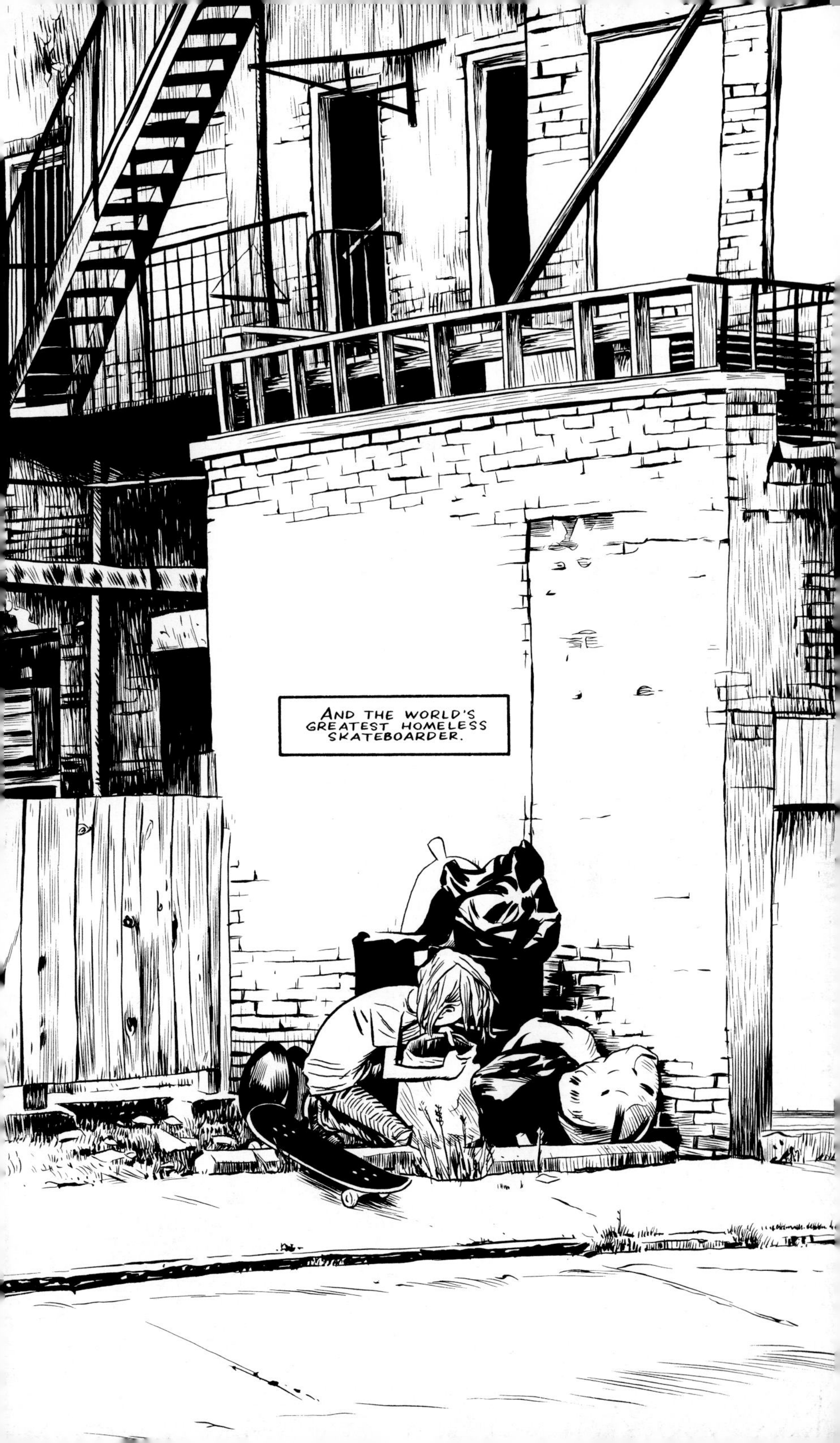
AND THE WORLD'S GREATEST HOMELESS SKATEBOARDER.

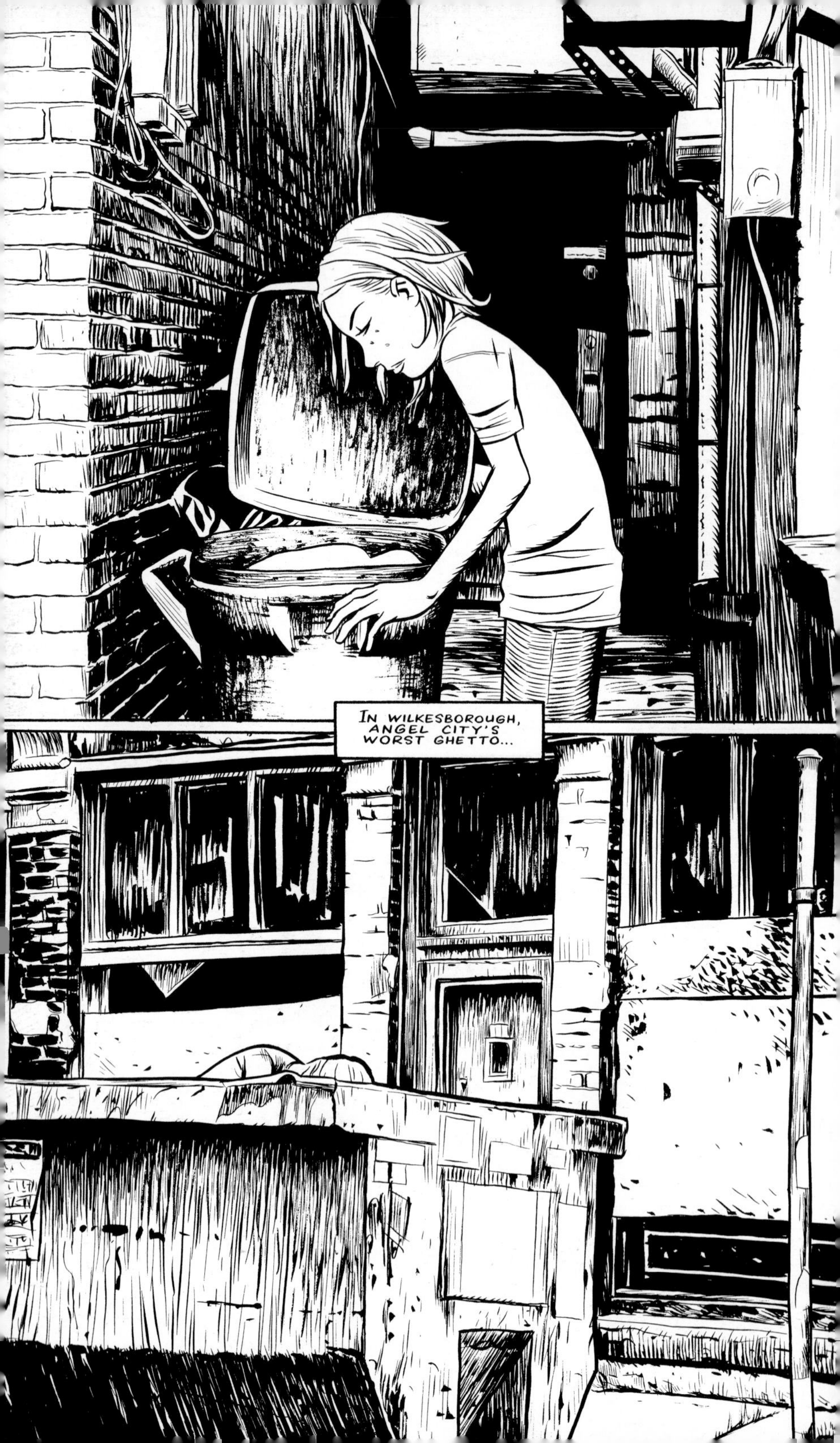
IN WILKESBOROUGH, ANGEL CITY'S WORST GHETTO...

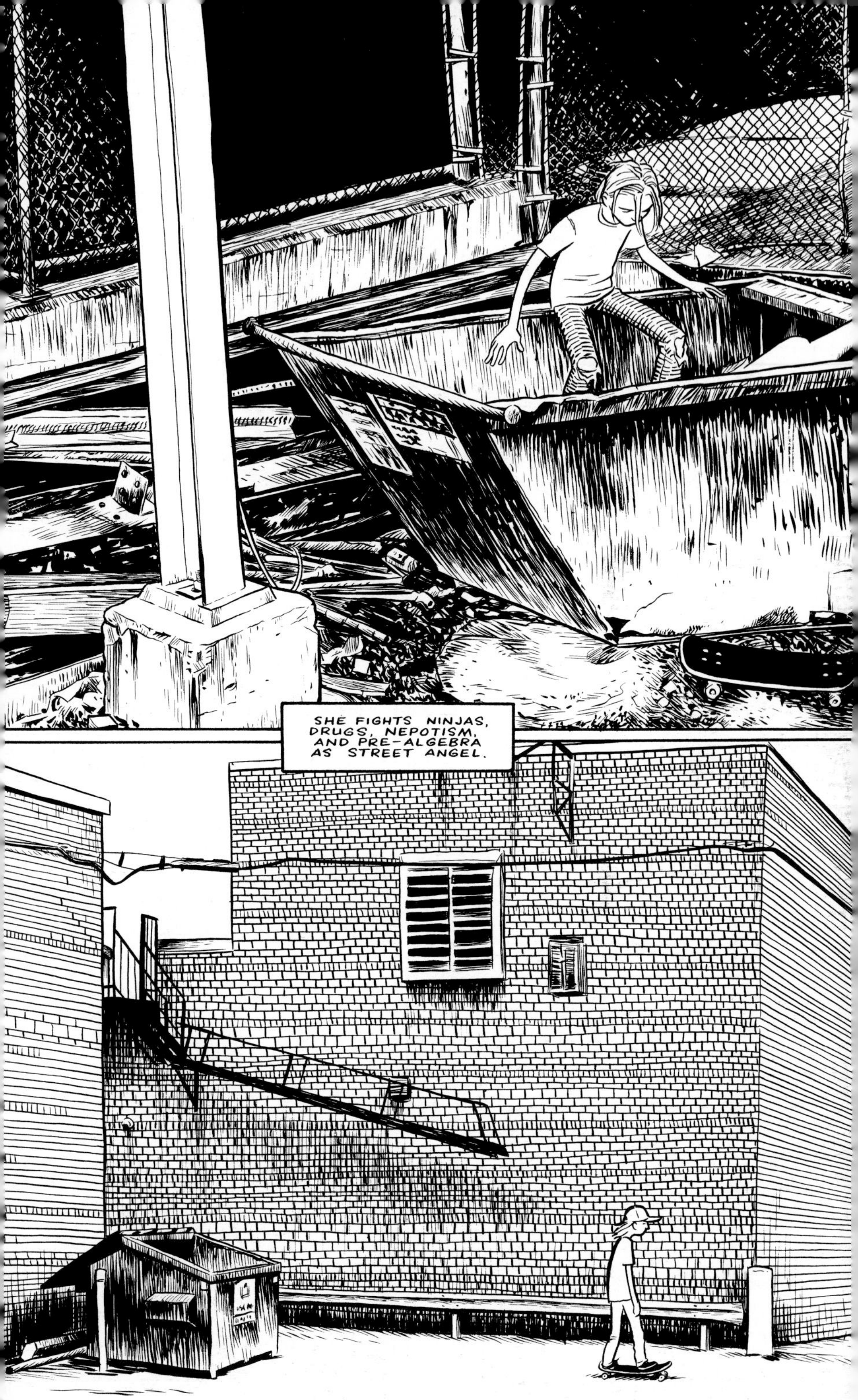
SHE FIGHTS NINJAS, DRUGS, NEPOTISM, AND PRE-ALGEBRA AS STREET ANGEL.

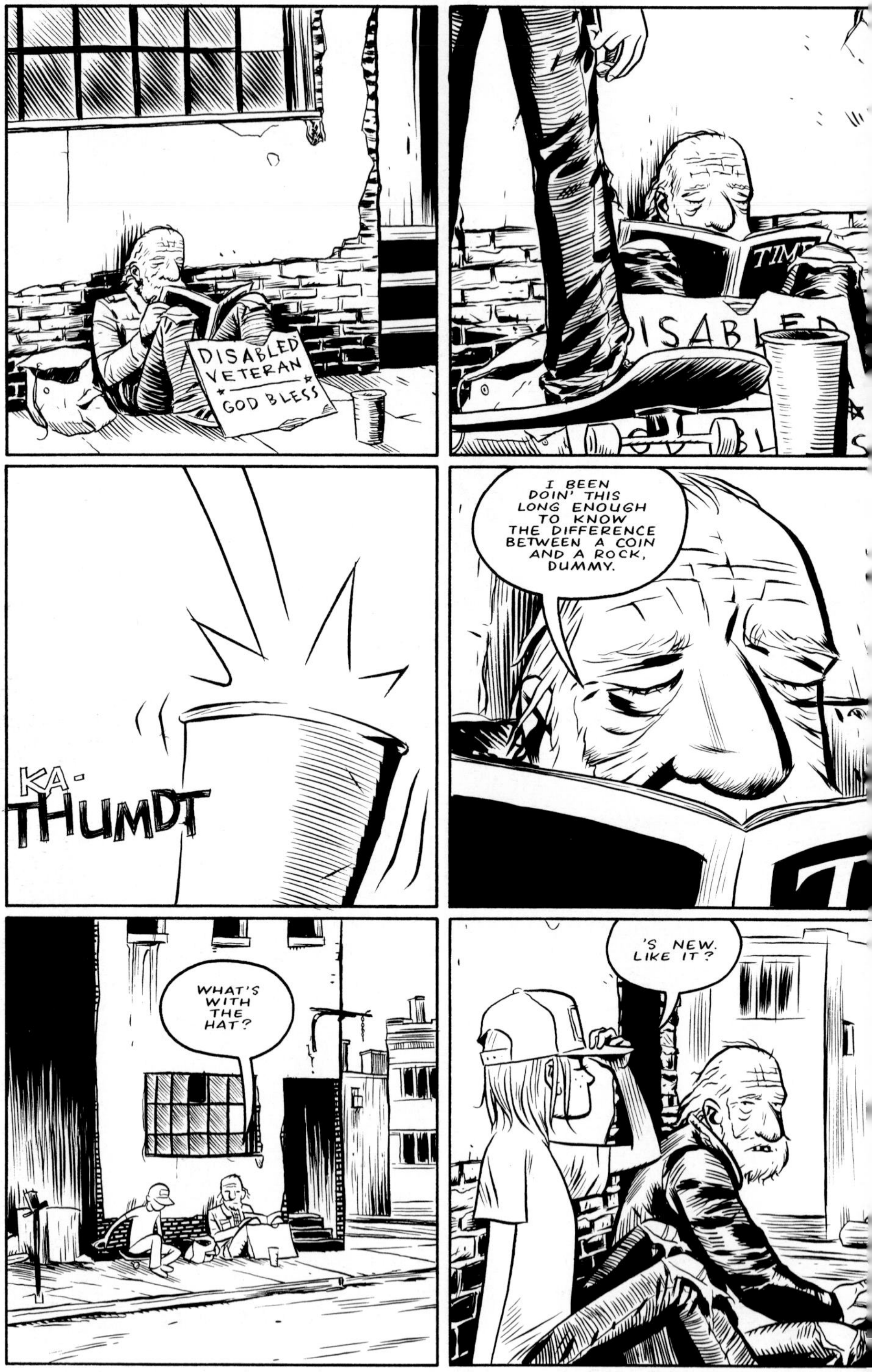
DISABLED VETERAN
GOD BLESS
TIME
DISABLED
KA-THUMDT
I BEEN DOIN' THIS LONG ENOUGH TO KNOW THE DIFFERENCE BETWEEN A COIN AND A ROCK, DUMMY.
WHAT'S WITH THE HAT?
'S NEW. LIKE IT?

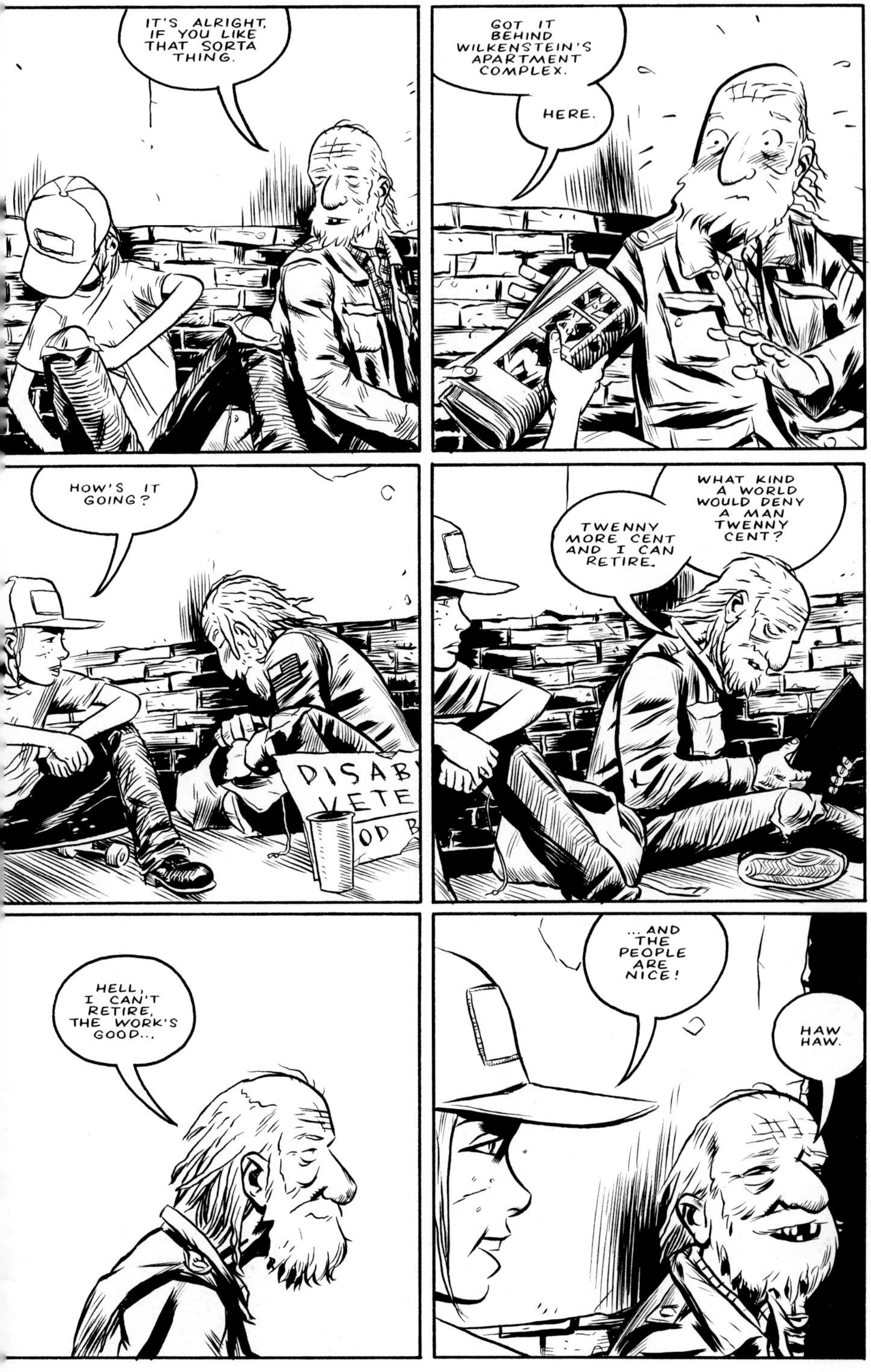

IT'S ALRIGHT, IF YOU LIKE THAT SORTA THING.
GOT IT BEHIND WILKENSTEIN'S APARTMENT COMPLEX.
HERE.
HOW'S IT GOING?
DISAB
VETE
OD B
TWENNY MORE CENT AND I CAN RETIRE.
WHAT KIND A WORLD WOULD DENY A MAN TWENNY CENT?
HELL, I CAN'T RETIRE, THE WORK'S GOOD...
...AND THE PEOPLE ARE NICE!
HAW HAW.

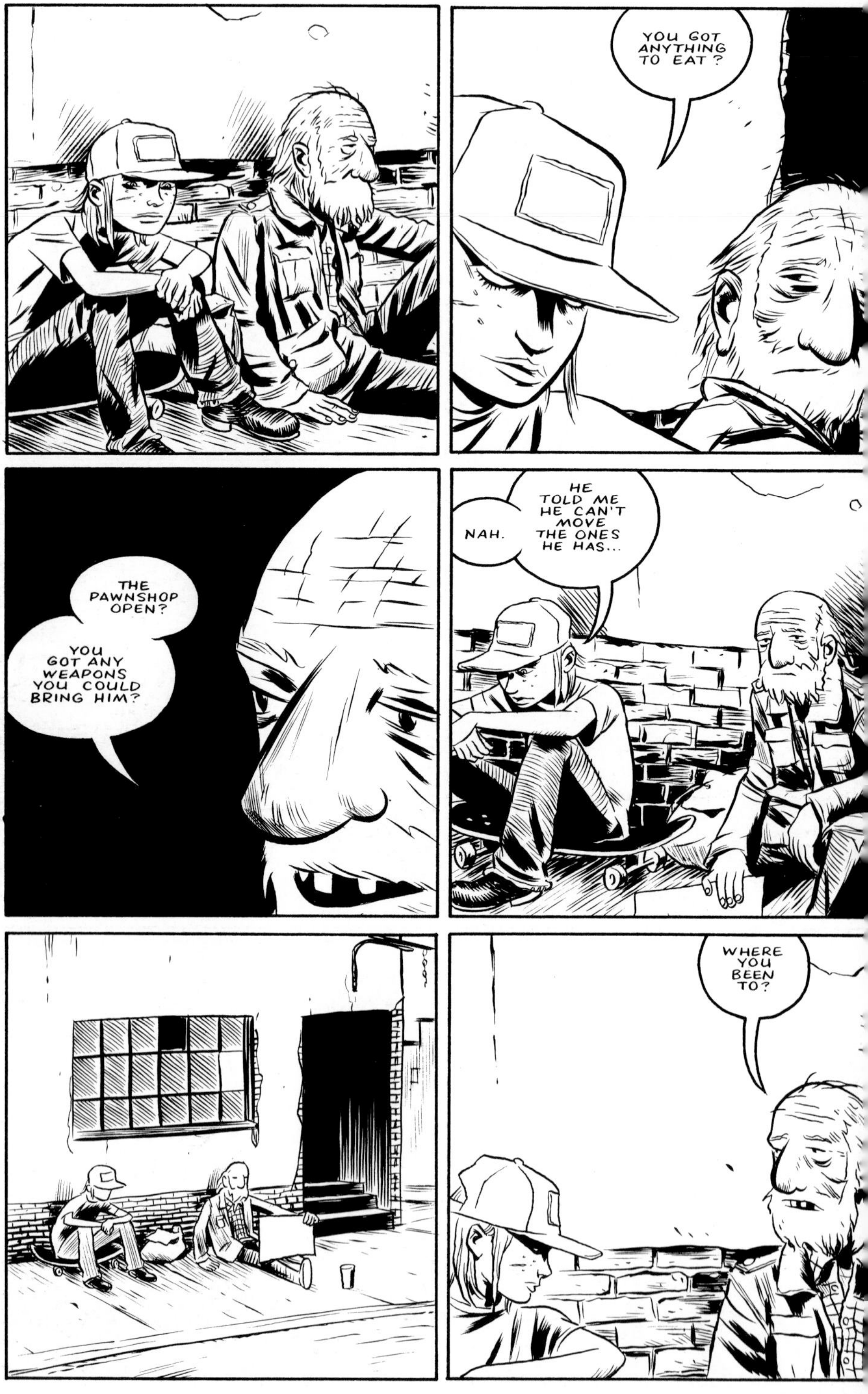
YOU GOT ANYTHING TO EAT?
THE PAWNSHOP OPEN?
YOU GOT ANY WEAPONS YOU COULD BRING HIM?
NAH.
HE TOLD ME HE CAN'T MOVE THE ONES HE HAS...
WHERE YOU BEEN TO?

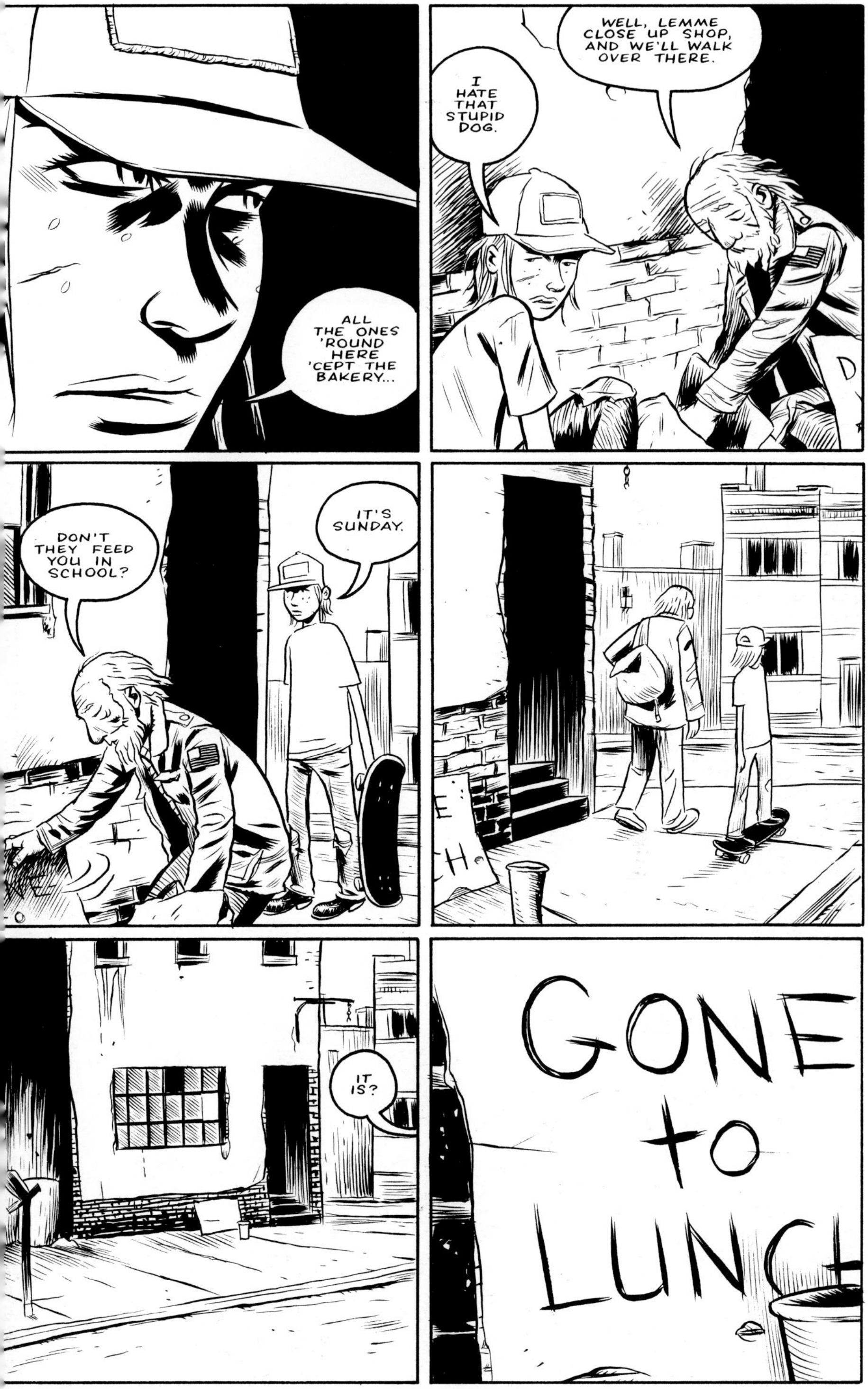
ALL THE ONES 'ROUND HERE 'CEPT THE BAKERY...
I HATE THAT STUPID DOG.
WELL, LEMME CLOSE UP SHOP, AND WE'LL WALK OVER THERE.
DON'T THEY FEED YOU IN SCHOOL?
IT'S SUNDAY.
IT IS?
GONE to LUNC

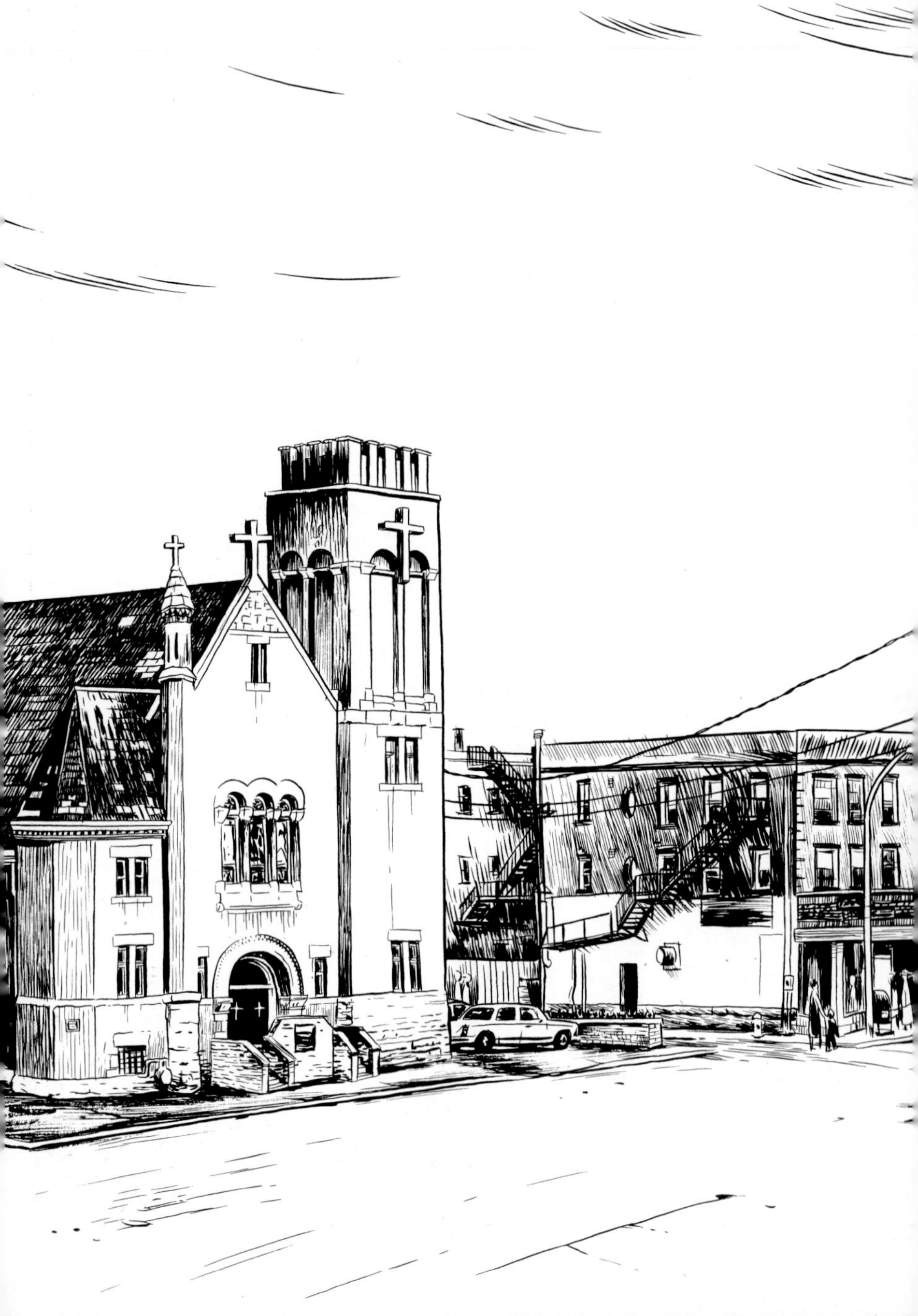

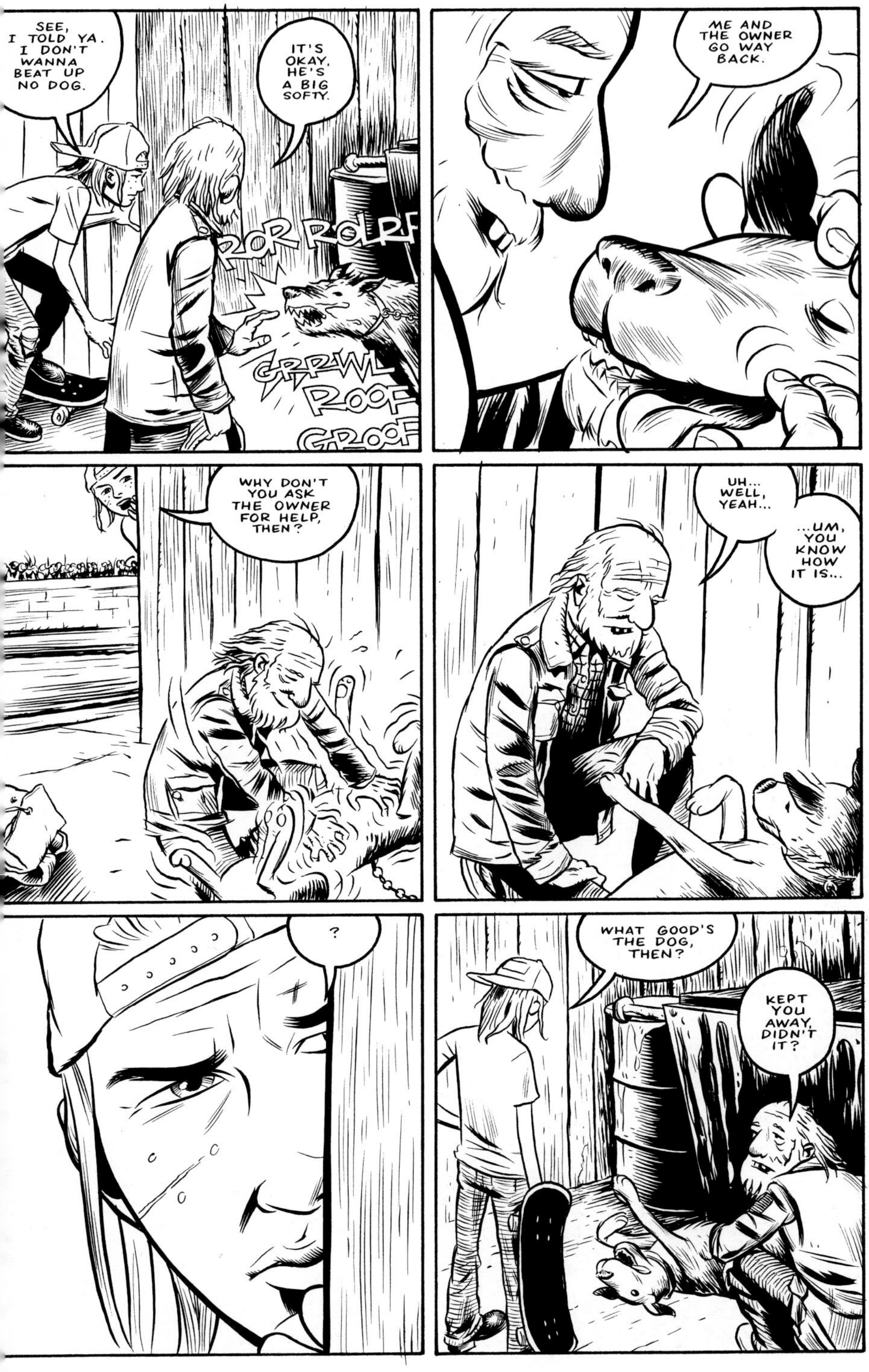
SEE, I TOLD YA. I DON'T WANNA BEAT UP NO DOG.
IT'S OKAY, HE'S A BIG SOFTY.
RORRORF
GRRWL
ROOF
GROOF
ME AND THE OWNER GO WAY BACK.
WHY DON'T YOU ASK THE OWNER FOR HELP, THEN?
UH... WELL, YEAH...
...UM, YOU KNOW HOW IT IS...
?
WHAT GOOD'S THE DOG, THEN?
KEPT YOU AWAY, DIDN'T IT?

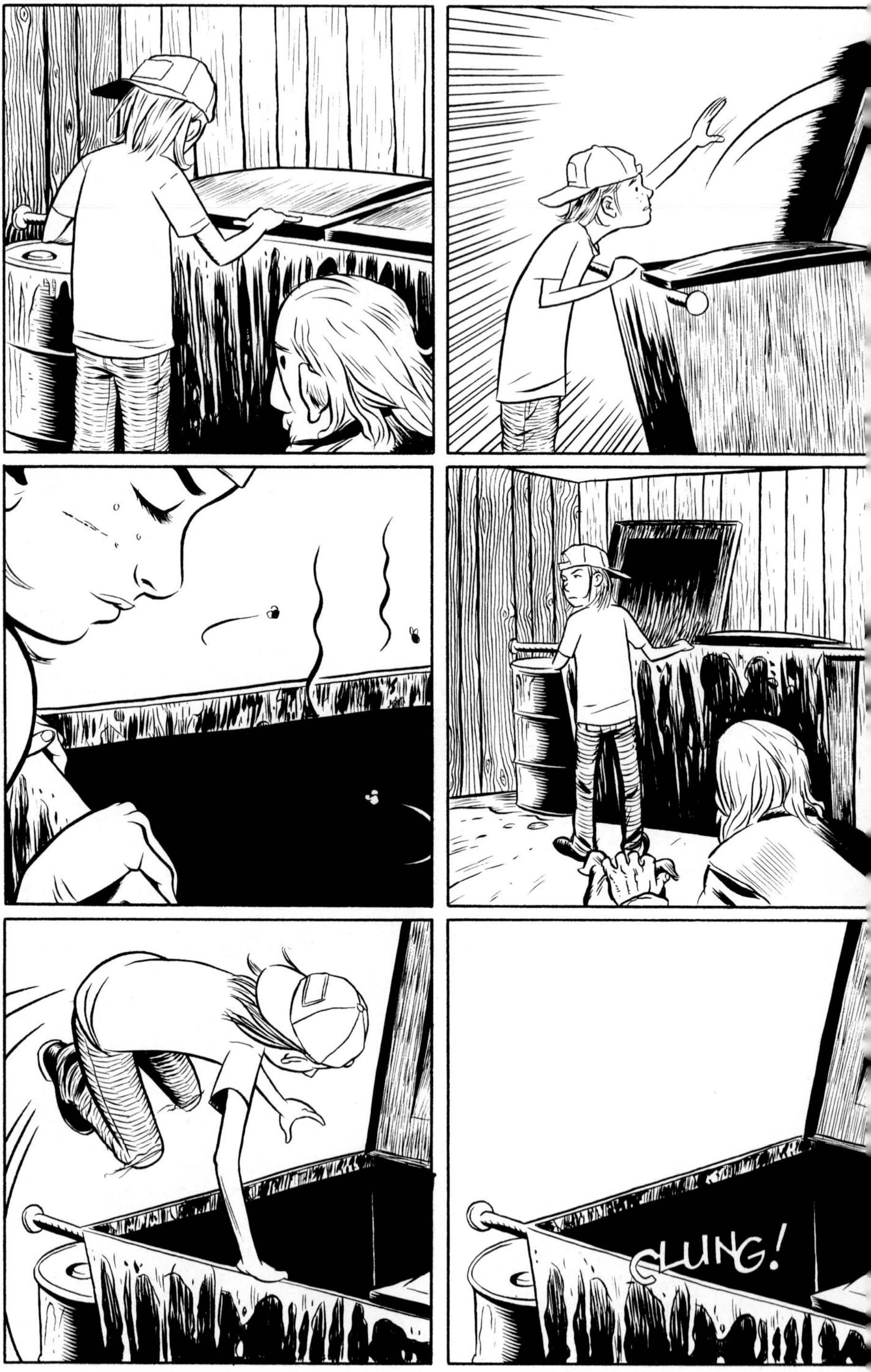
CLUNG!

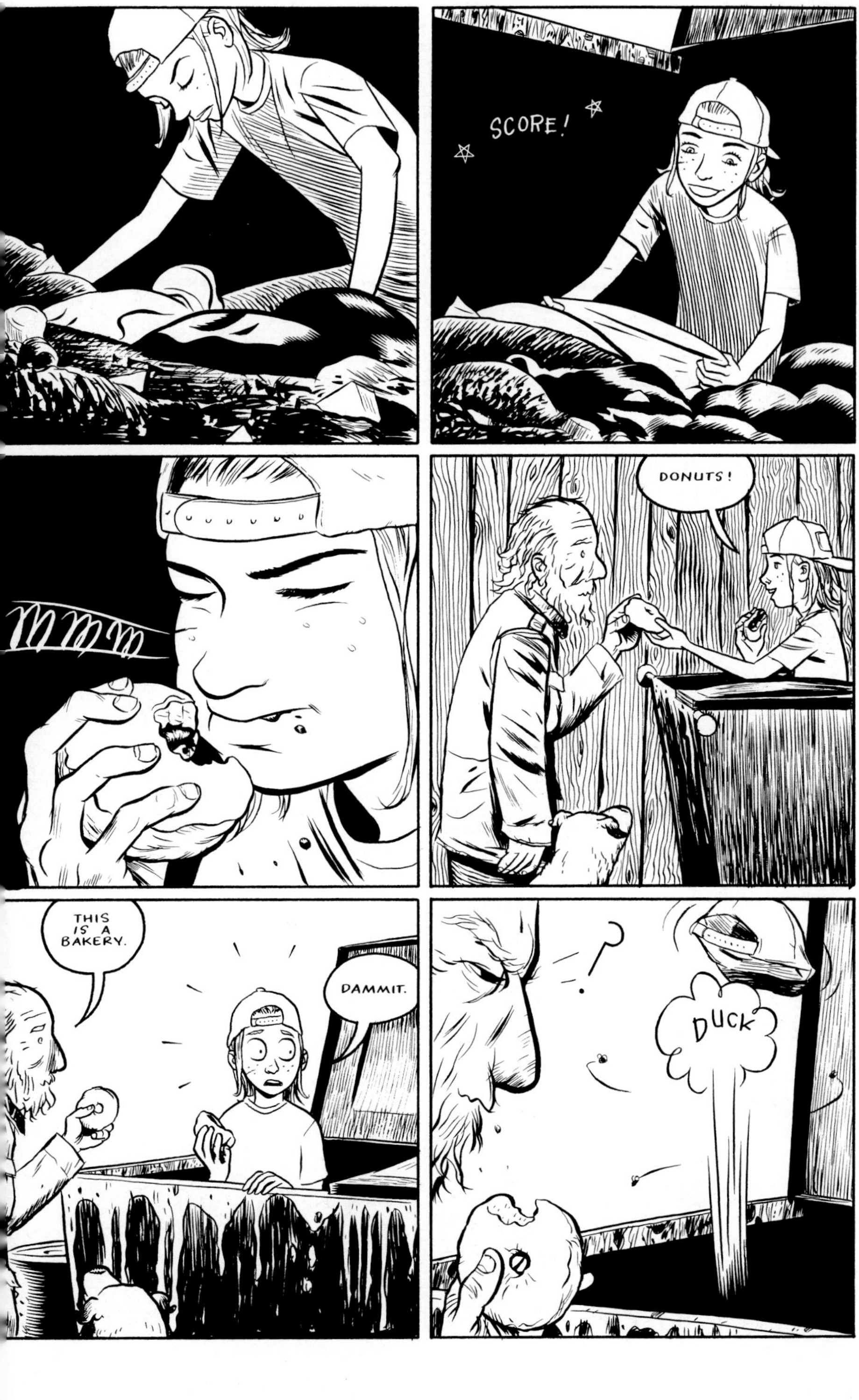
SCORE!
MMMM
DONUTS!
THIS IS A BAKERY.
DAMMIT.
DUCK

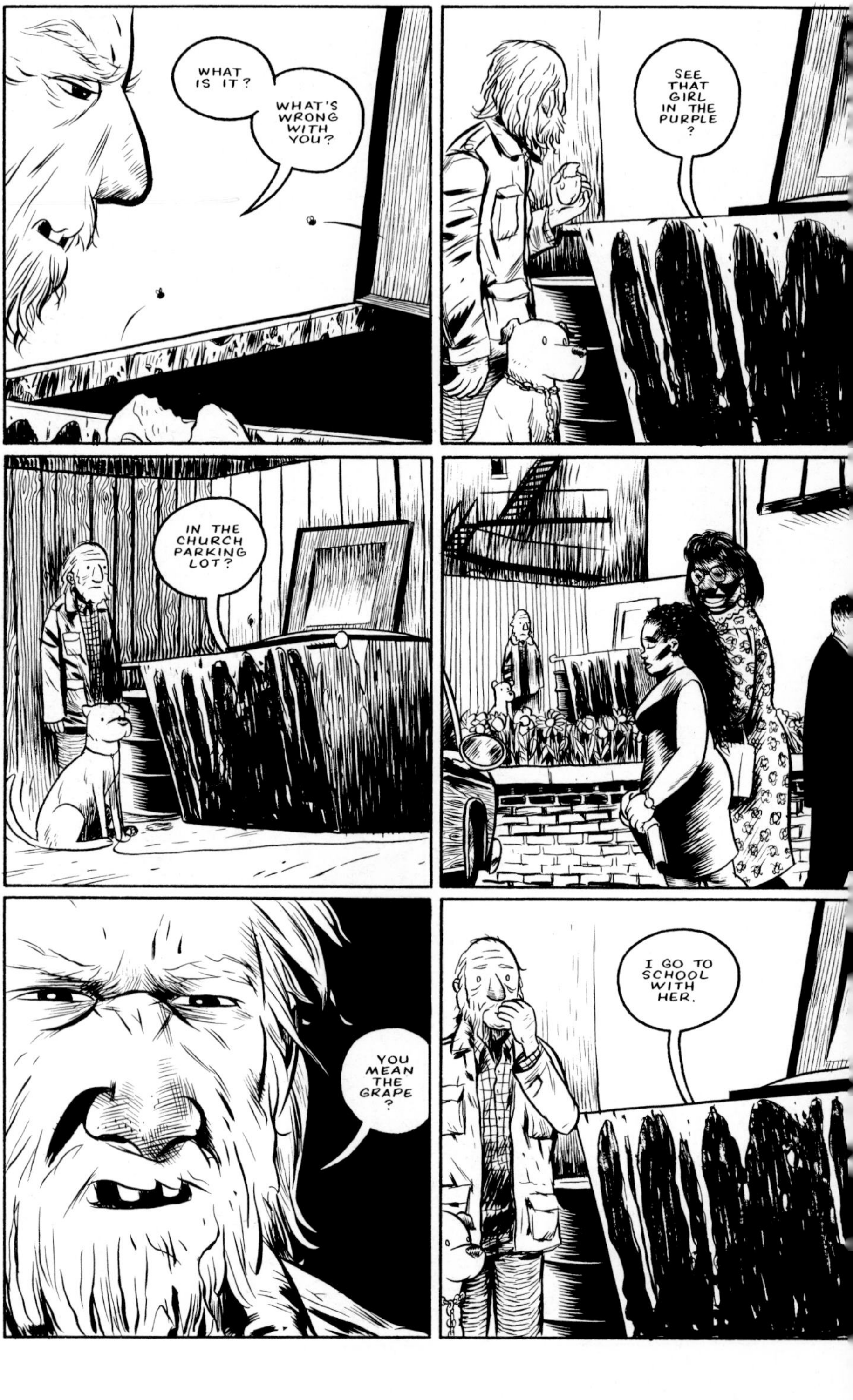
WHAT IS IT?
WHAT'S WRONG WITH YOU?
SEE THAT GIRL IN THE PURPLE?
IN THE CHURCH PARKING LOT?
YOU MEAN THE GRAPE?
I GO TO SCHOOL WITH HER.

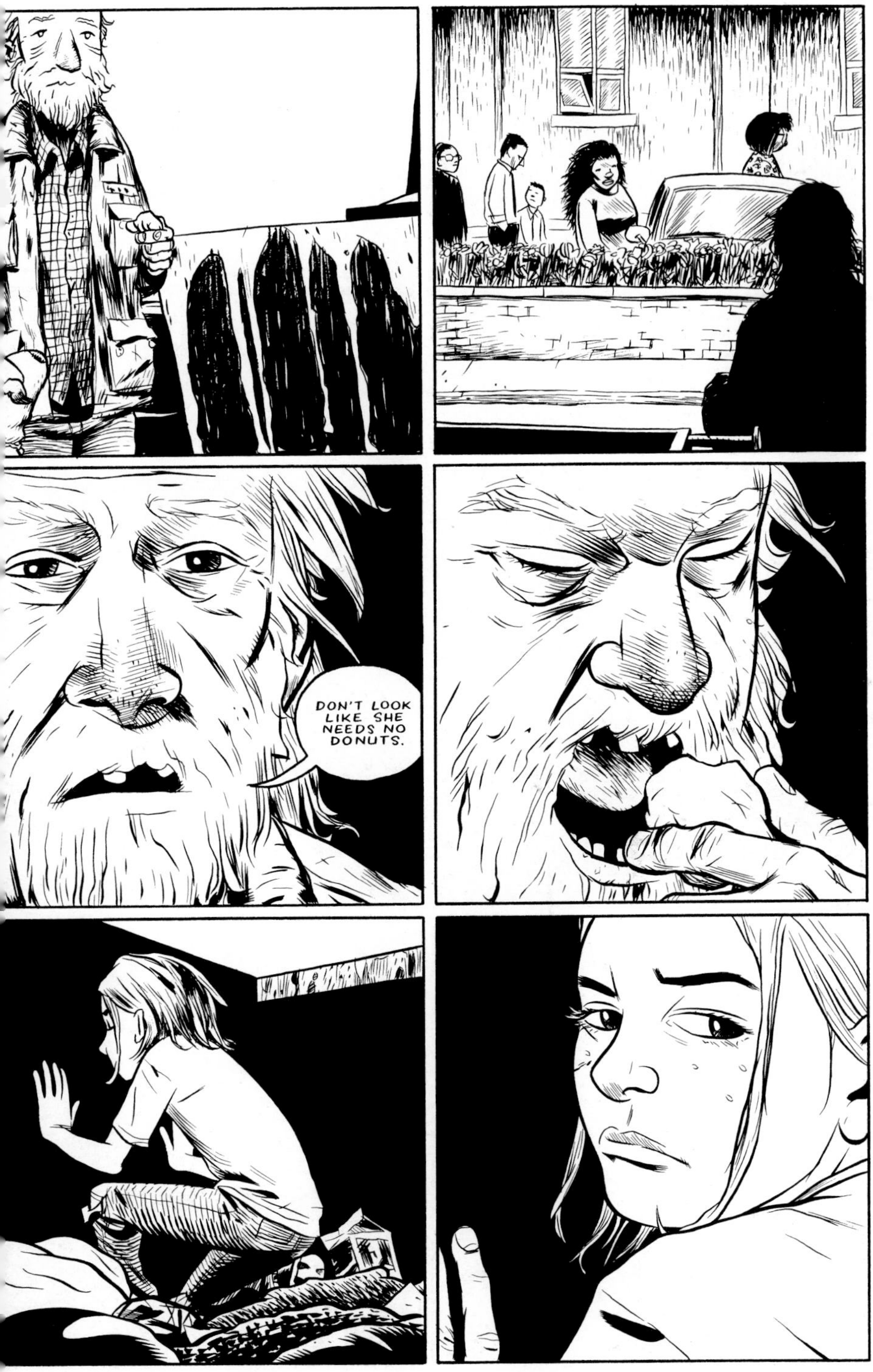
DON'T LOOK LIKE SHE NEEDS NO DONUTS.

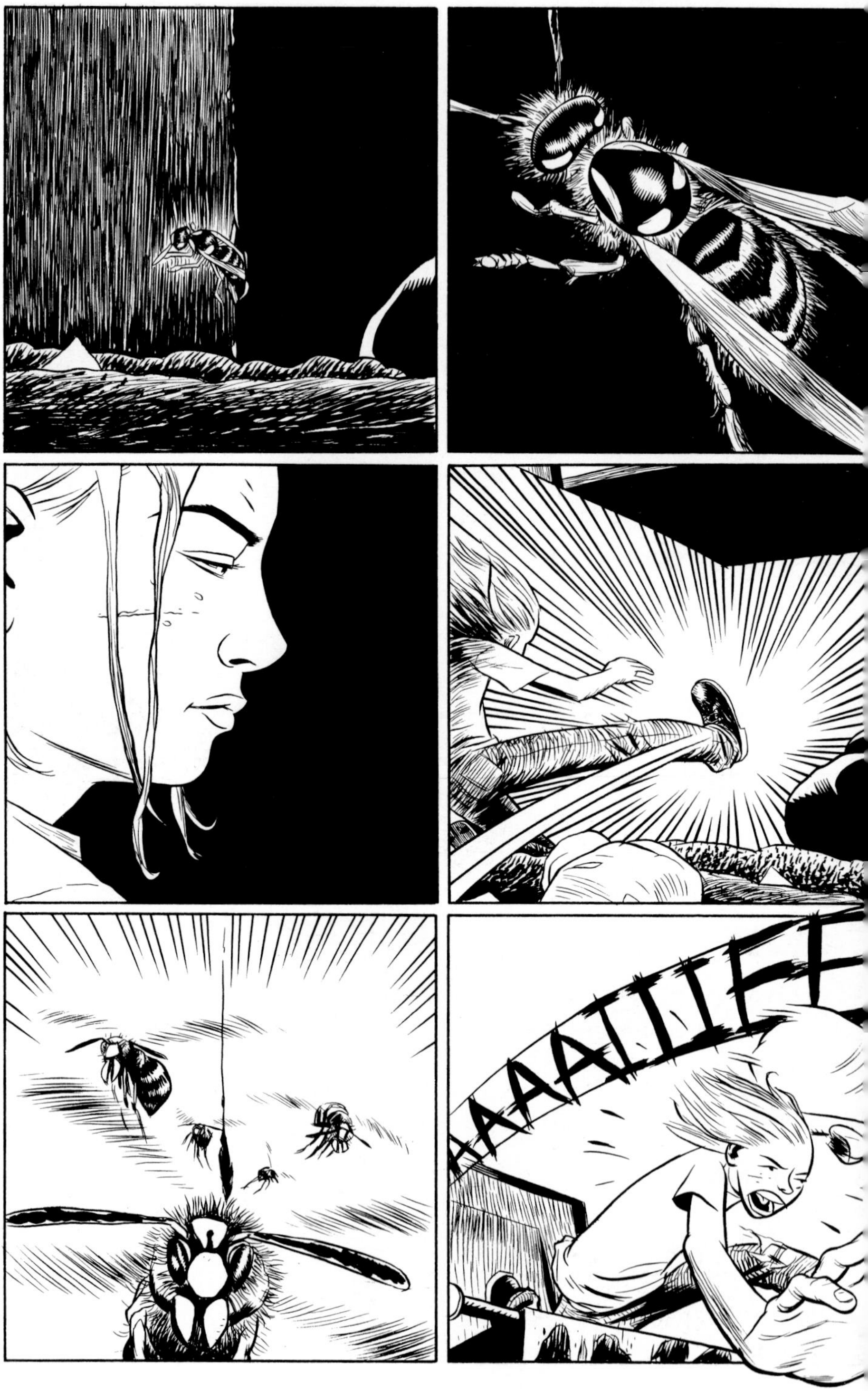
AAAAIIIIE

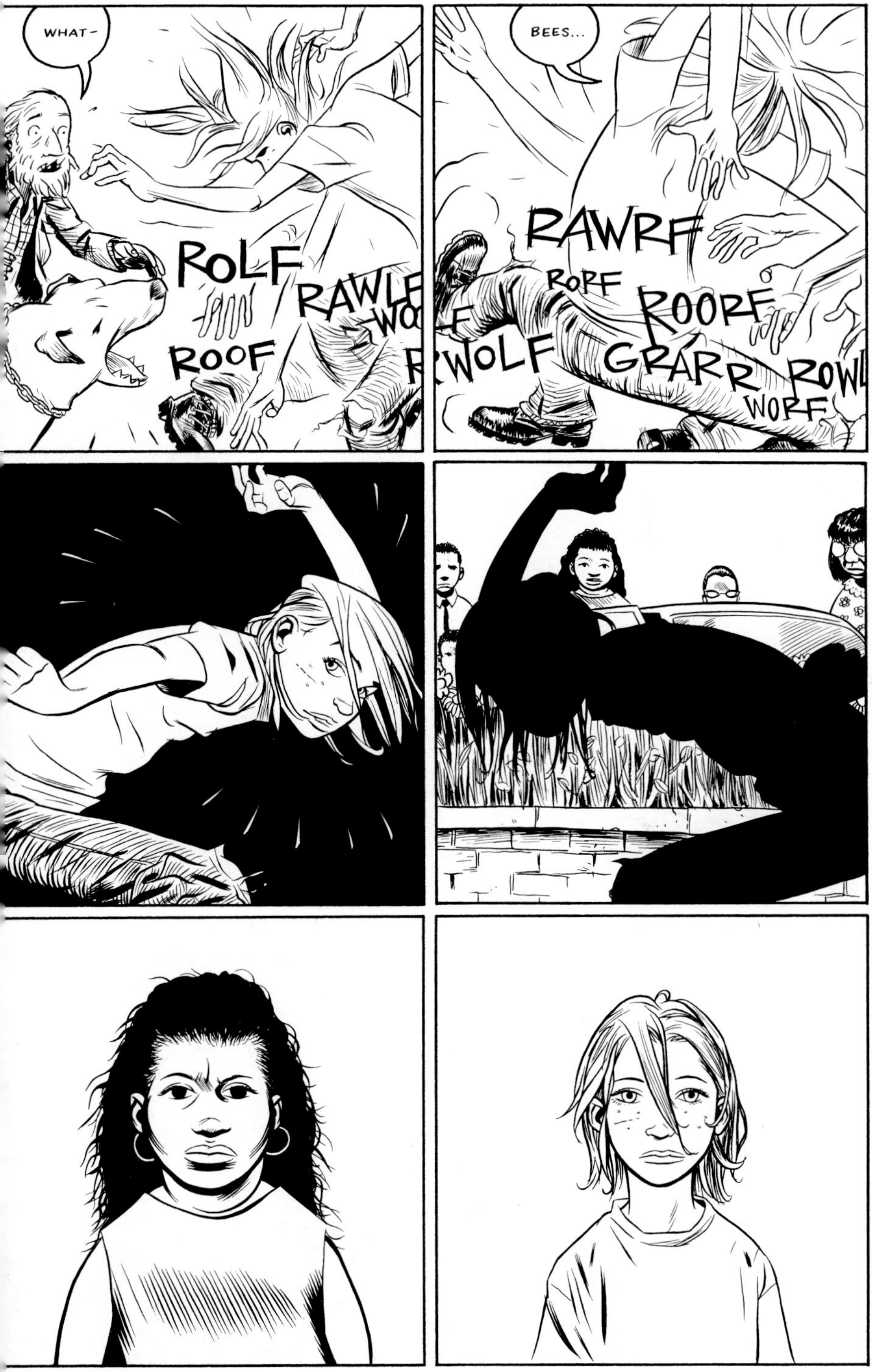
WHAT-
ROLF
RAWLF
ROOF
BEES...
RAWRF
ROPF
ROORF
RWOLF
GRARR
WORF

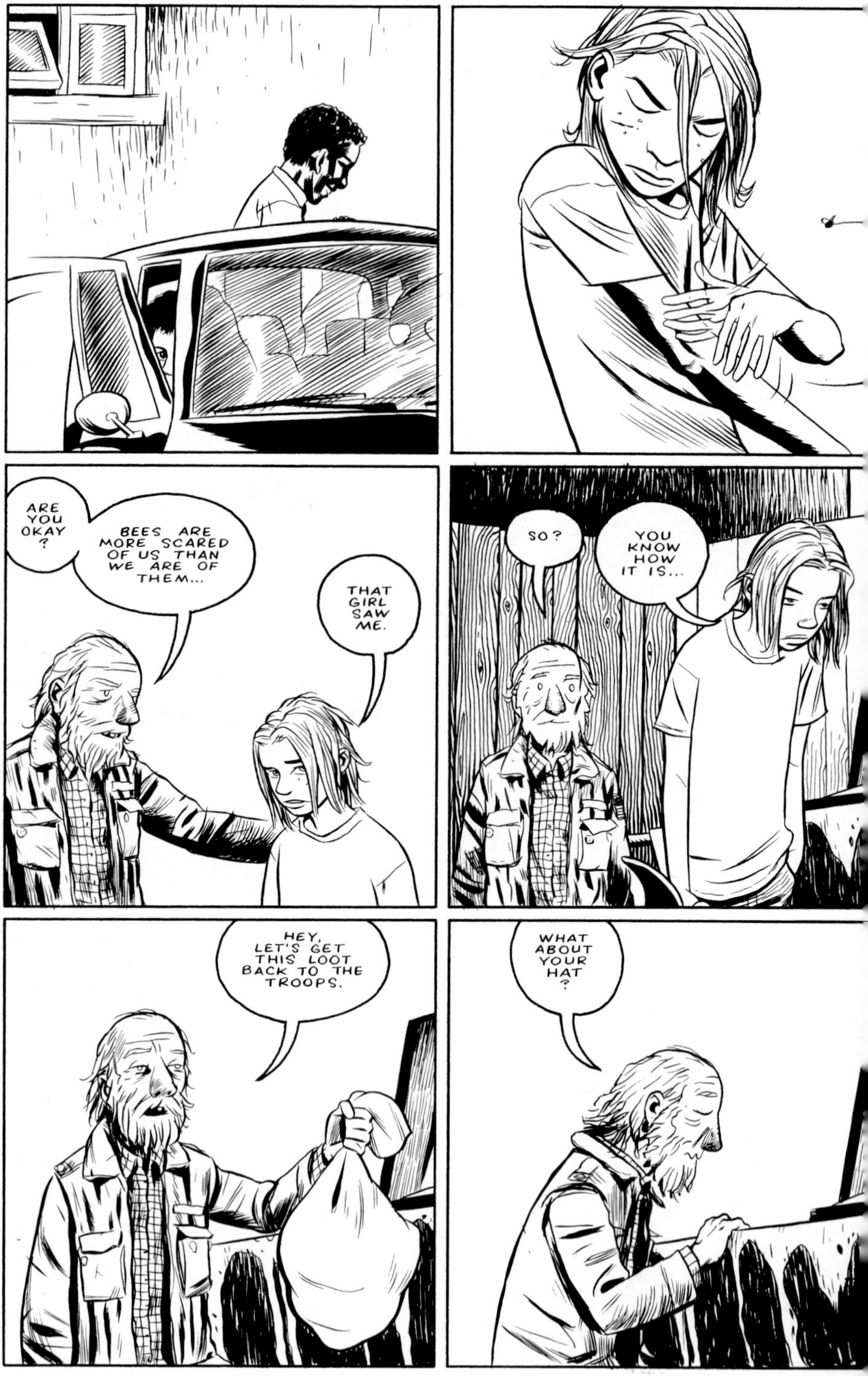
ARE YOU OKAY ?
BEES ARE MORE SCARED OF US THAN WE ARE OF THEM...
THAT GIRL SAW ME.
SO ?
YOU KNOW HOW IT IS...
HEY, LET'S GET THIS LOOT BACK TO THE TROOPS.
WHAT ABOUT YOUR HAT ?

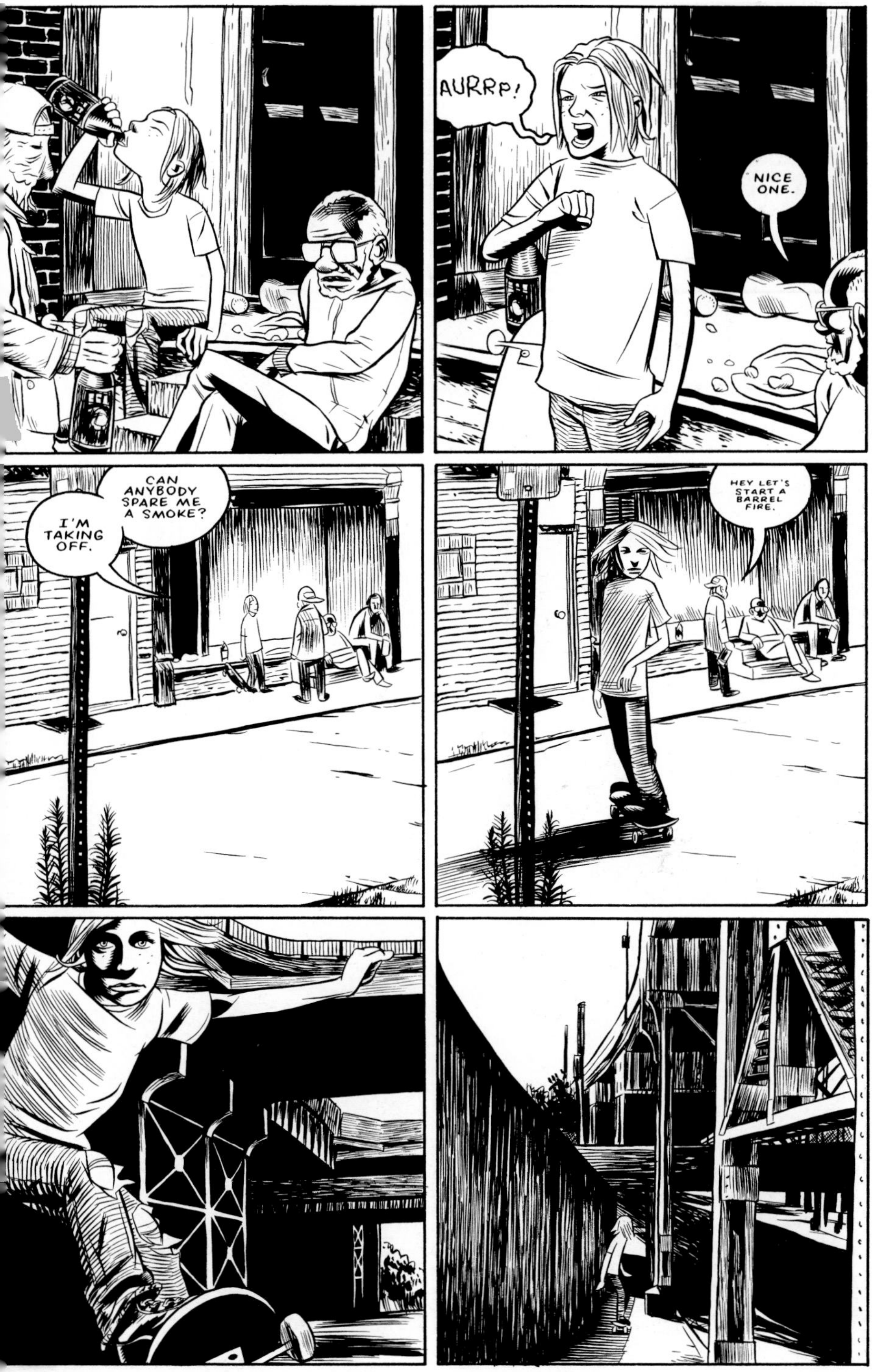
AURRP!
NICE ONE.
I'M TAKING OFF.
CAN ANYBODY SPARE ME A SMOKE?
HEY LET'S START A BARREL FIRE.

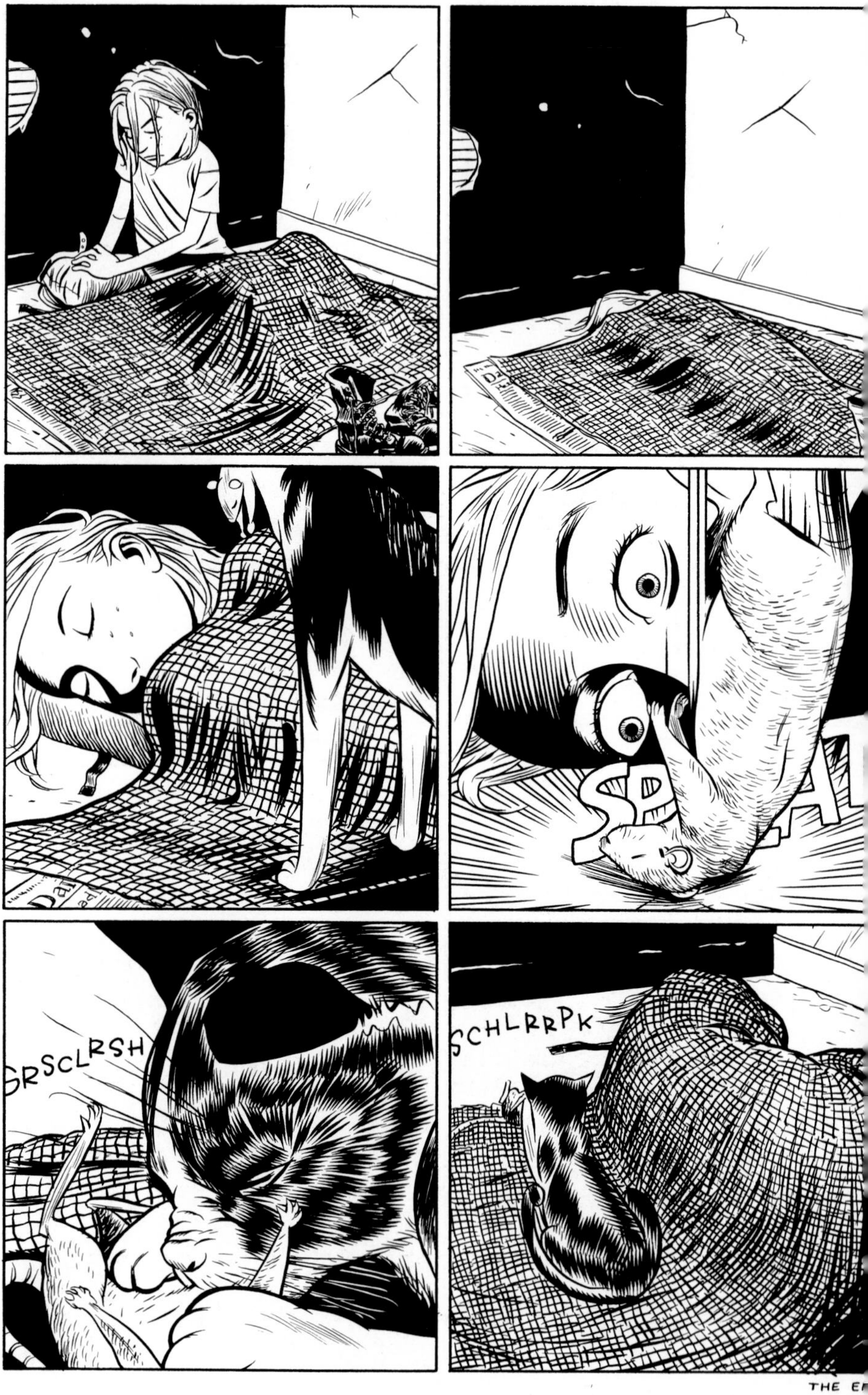
GRSCLRSH
SCHLRRPK

THE E

Dr. Pangea

Name: Rudy Ivan Pangea
Height: 5'7"
Weight: 132 lbs
Eyes: grayish-blue
Hair: white

History: Rudy's talent for the dark arts of Geology lay hidden until he was discovered by Oxford Associate Professor Walter Heffler, secret identity: the super-villain, "Earthquake." Heffler sensed the young man's potential and awakened the always bright, but never focused, Pangea. Pangea soon surpassed his mentor and a falling out ensued; the race was on to master geology! When Heffler was granted tenure, Pangea realized that he was beaten - and made a deal with Oxford's ninja fraternity. It was there, in ninja house, that Pangea jumped headfirst over the line into darkness.

Powers: Extremely intelligent; Gifted pianist; Master of the dark arts of Geology

First Appearance: Street Angel #1

Abilities Matrix	0	1	2	3	4	5	6	7
Agility/Speed								
Smarts								
Energy Protection								
Fight Skills								
Skate Skills								
Basketball Skills								
Strength								

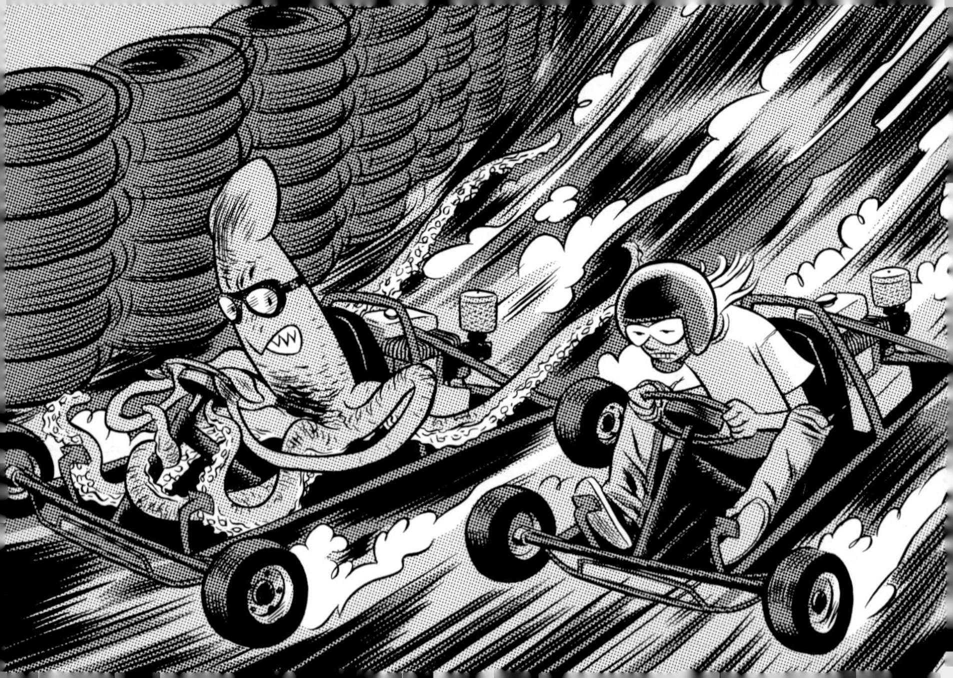

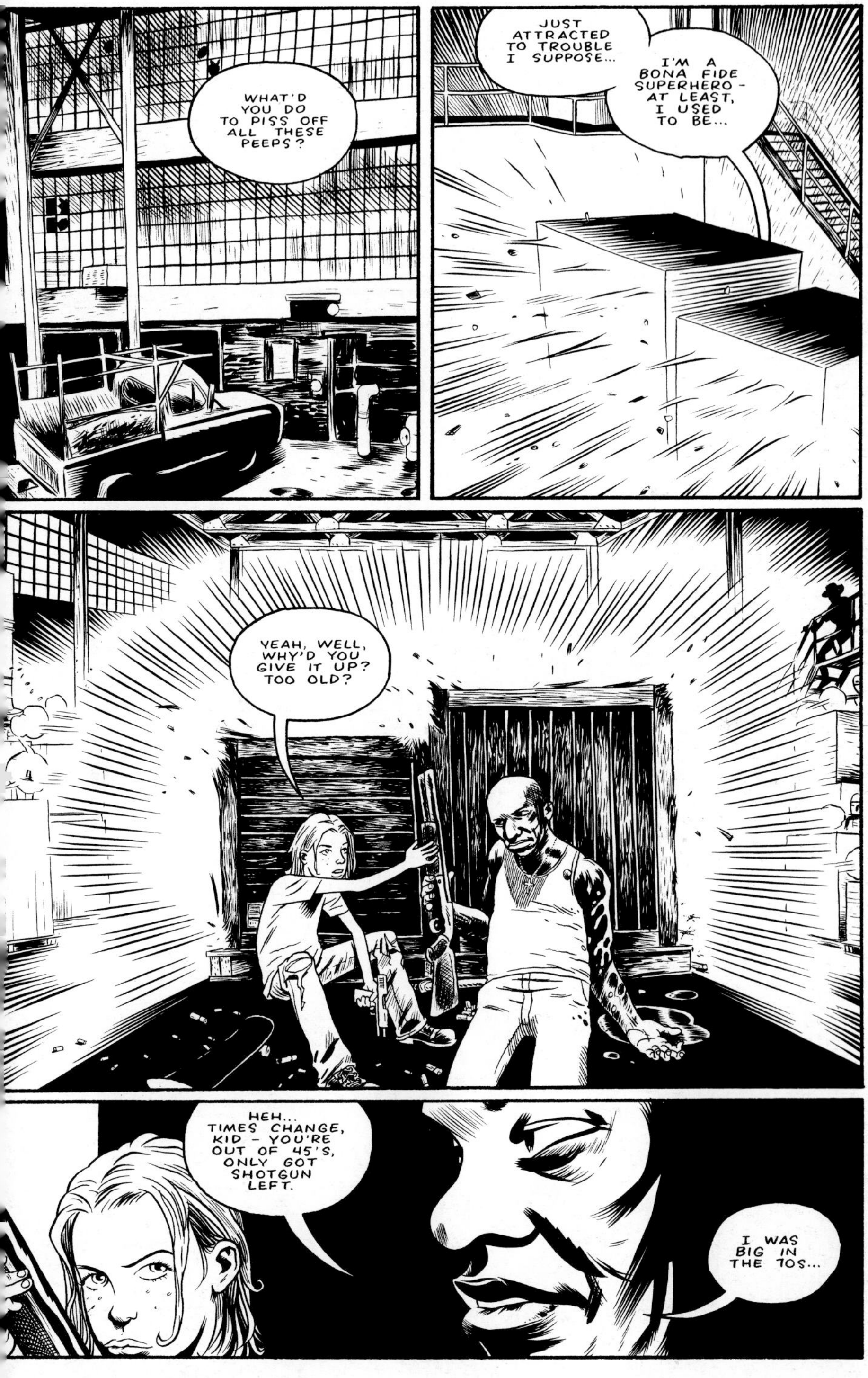
WHAT'D YOU DO TO PISS OFF ALL THESE PEEPS?
JUST ATTRACTED TO TROUBLE I SUPPOSE...
I'M A BONA FIDE SUPERHERO - AT LEAST, I USED TO BE...
YEAH, WELL, WHY'D YOU GIVE IT UP? TOO OLD?
HEH... TIMES CHANGE, KID - YOU'RE OUT OF 45'S, ONLY GOT SHOTGUN LEFT.
I WAS BIG IN THE 70S...

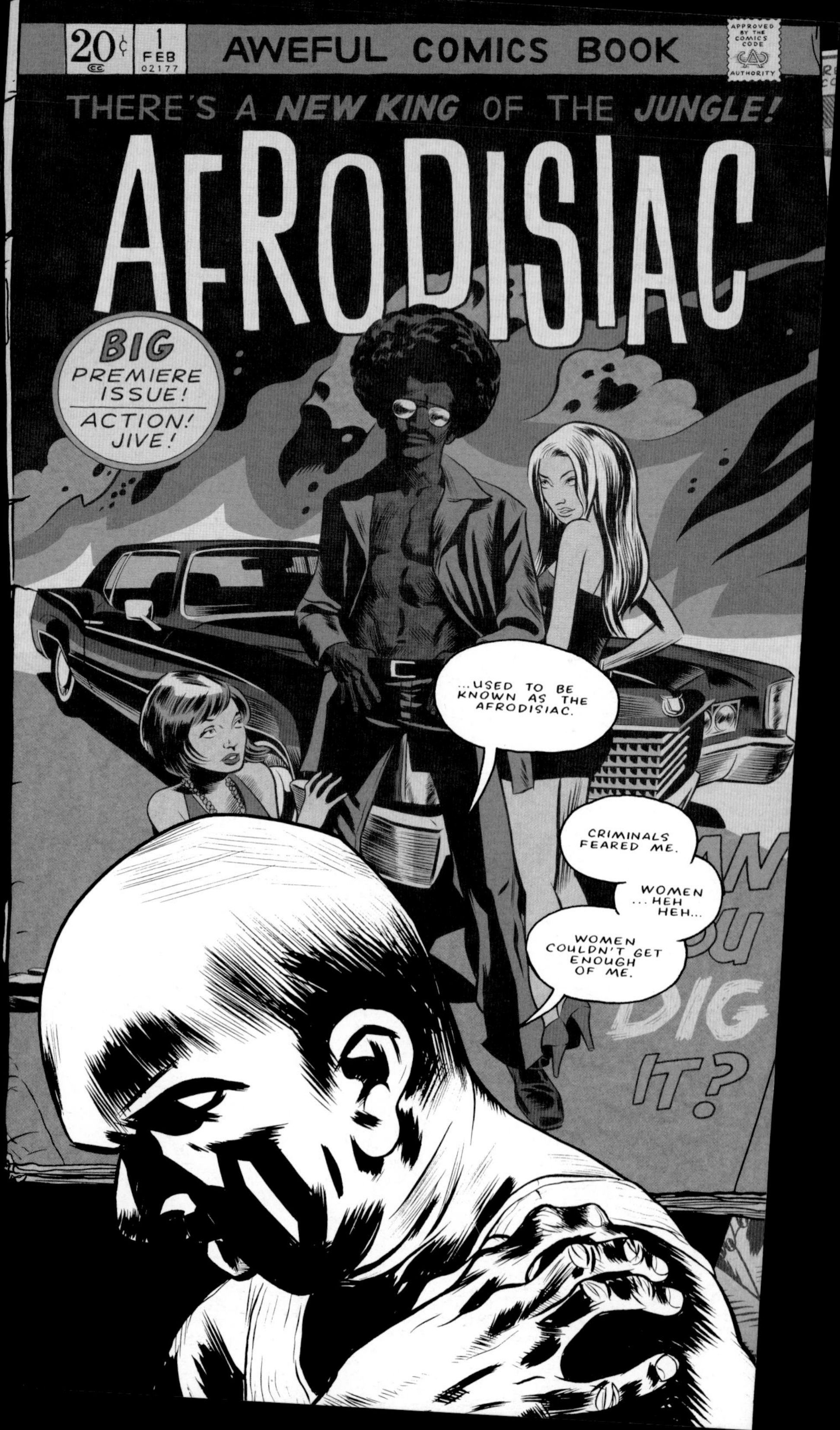
20¢
1 FEB 02177
AWEFUL COMICS BOOK
APPROVED BY THE COMICS CODE AUTHORITY
THERE'S A NEW KING OF THE JUNGLE!
AFRODISIAC
BIG PREMIERE ISSUE!
ACTION! JIVE!
...USED TO BE KNOWN AS THE AFRODISIAC.
CRIMINALS FEARED ME.
WOMEN ...HEH HEH...
WOMEN COULDN'T GET ENOUGH OF ME.
DIG IT?

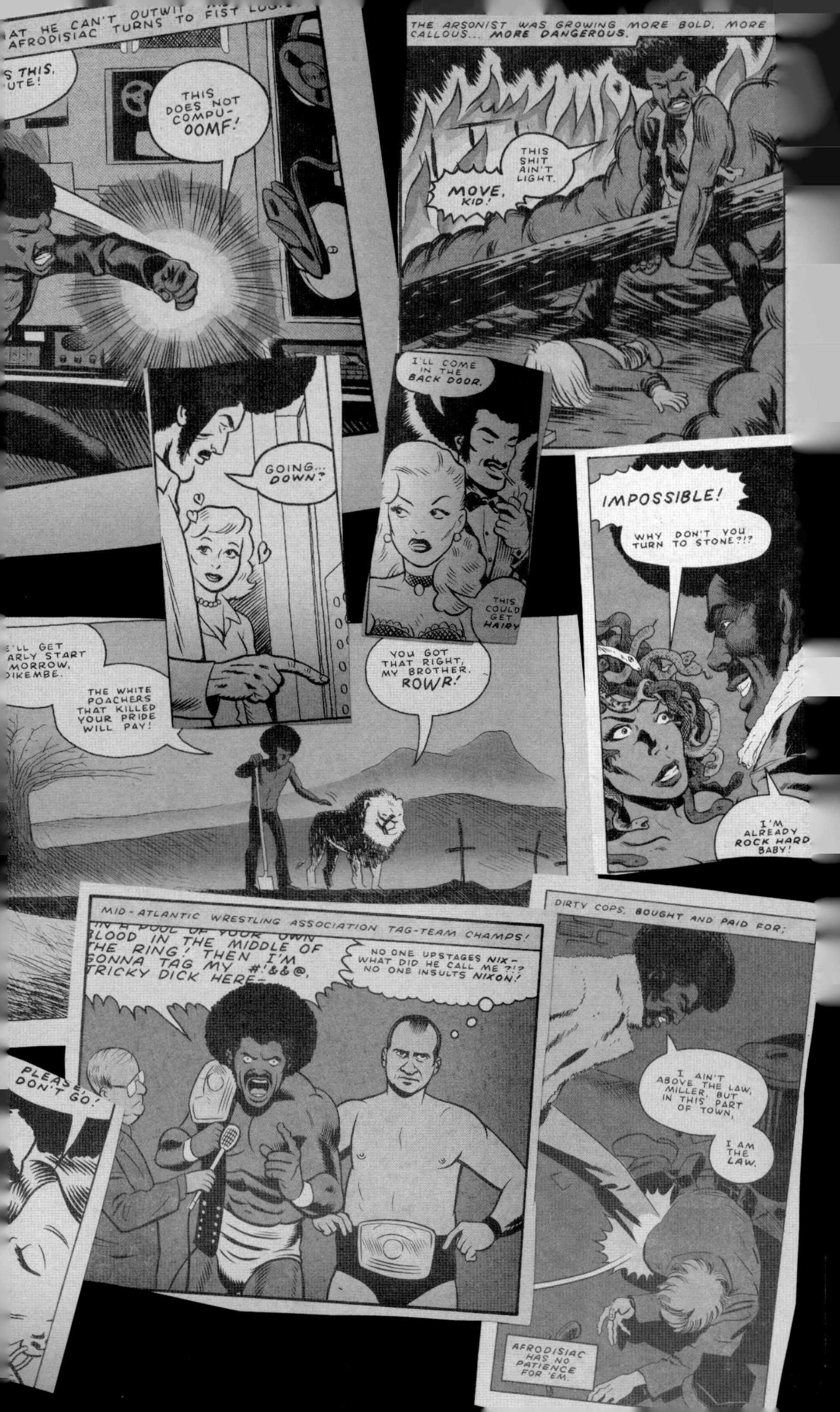

AT HE CAN'T OUTWIT
AFRODISIAC TURNS TO FIST
S THIS, UTE!
THIS DOES NOT COMPU- OOMF!
THE ARSONIST WAS GROWING MORE BOLD, MORE CALLOUS... MORE DANGEROUS.
THIS SHIT AIN'T LIGHT.
MOVE, KID!
GOING... DOWN?
I'LL COME IN THE BACK DOOR.
THIS COULD GET HAIRY
IMPOSSIBLE!
WHY DON'T YOU TURN TO STONE?!?
I'M ALREADY ROCK HARD, BABY!
E'LL GET ARLY START MORROW, DIKEMBE.
THE WHITE POACHERS THAT KILLED YOUR PRIDE WILL PAY!
YOU GOT THAT RIGHT, MY BROTHER. ROWR!
MID-ATLANTIC WRESTLING ASSOCIATION TAG-TEAM CHAMPS!
BLOOD IN THE MIDDLE OF THE RING! THEN I'M GONNA TAG MY #!&&@, TRICKY DICK HERE-
NO ONE UPSTAGES NIX- WHAT DID HE CALL ME?!? NO ONE INSULTS NIXON!
PLEASE, DON'T GO!
DIRTY COPS, BOUGHT AND PAID FOR;
I AIN'T ABOVE THE LAW, MILLER, BUT IN THIS PART OF TOWN,
I AM THE LAW.
AFRODISIAC HAS NO PATIENCE FOR 'EM.

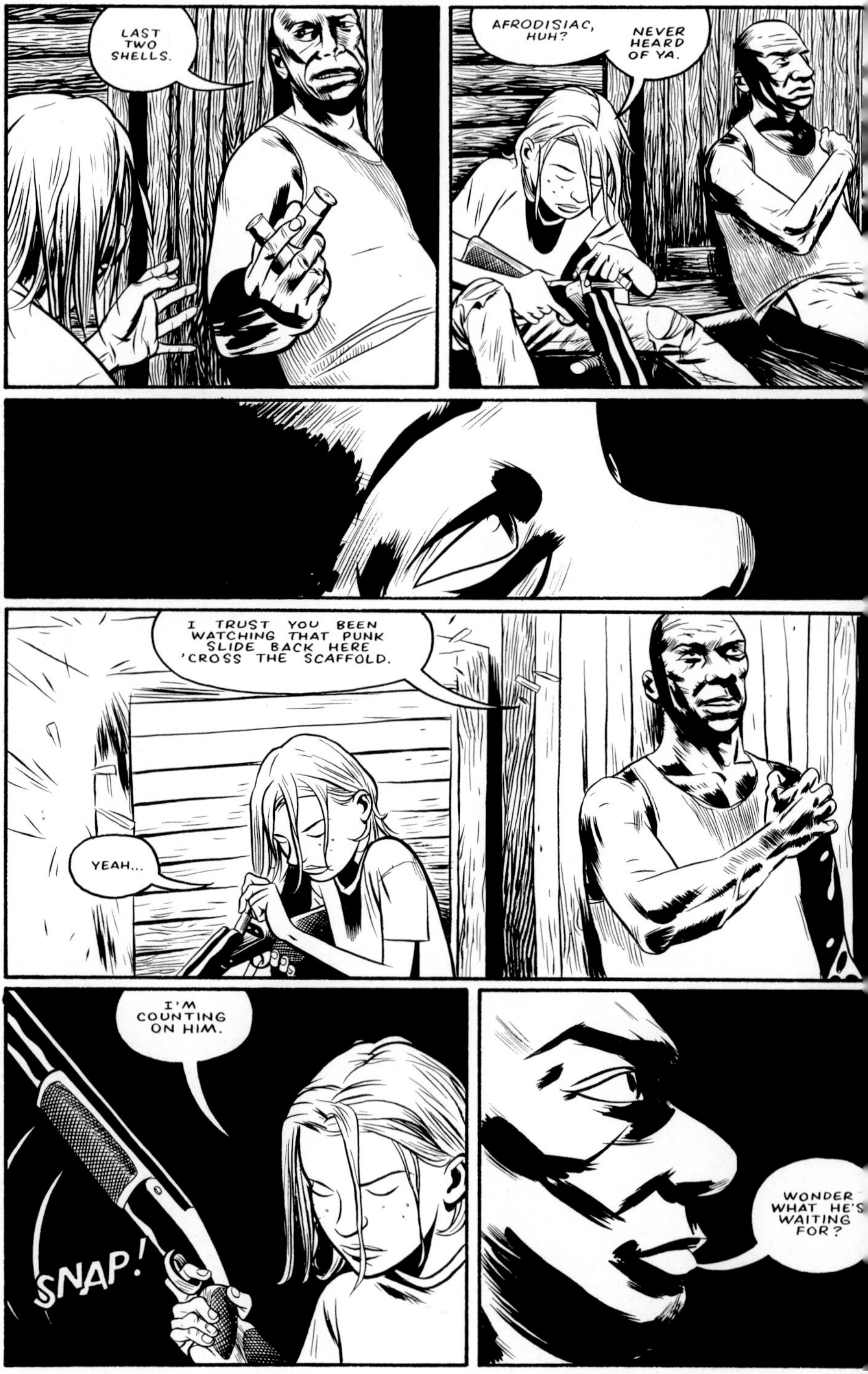
LAST TWO SHELLS.
AFRODISIAC, HUH?
NEVER HEARD OF YA.
I TRUST YOU BEEN WATCHING THAT PUNK SLIDE BACK HERE 'CROSS THE SCAFFOLD.
YEAH...
I'M COUNTING ON HIM.
SNAP!
WONDER WHAT HE'S WAITING FOR?

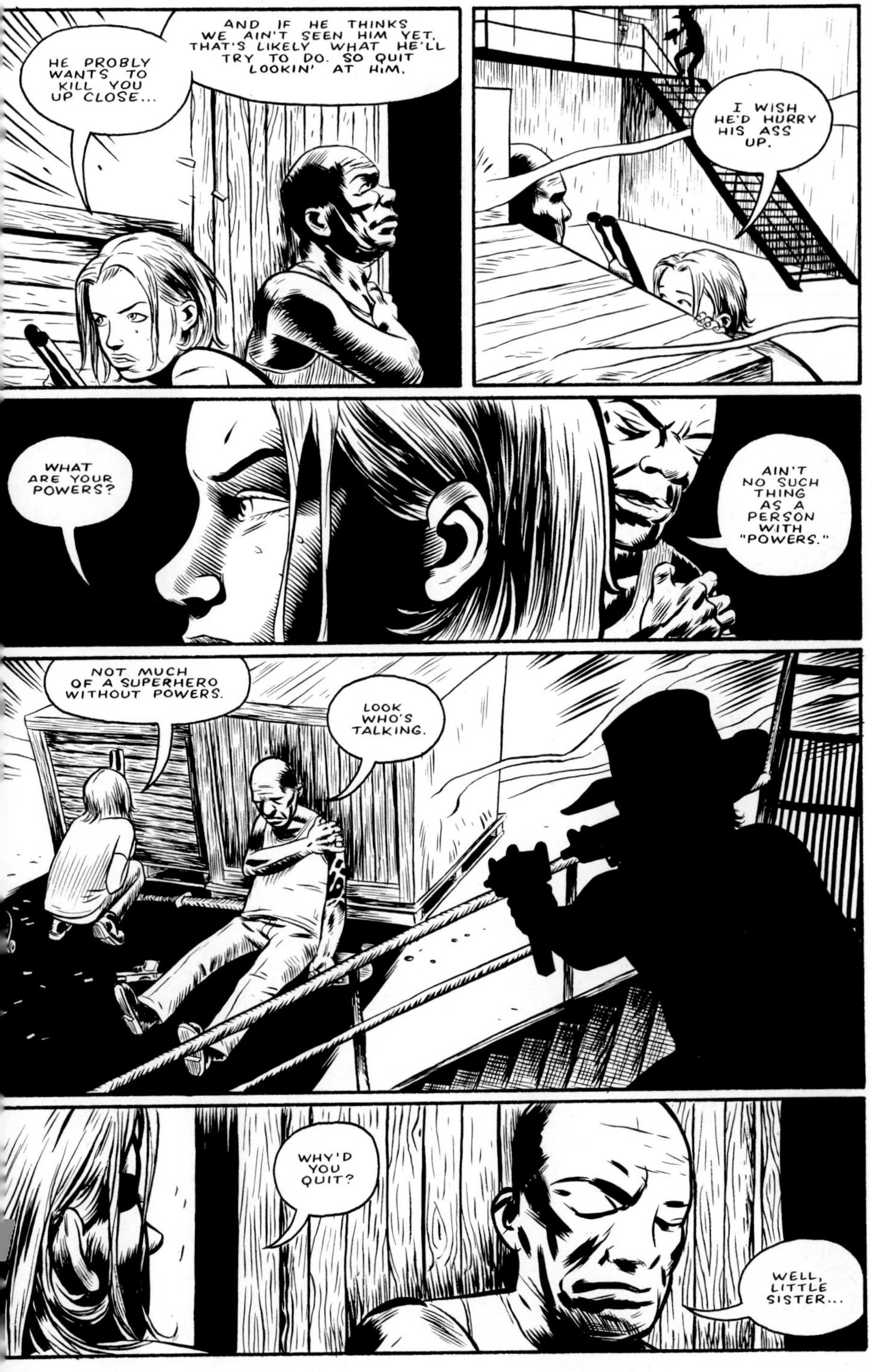
HE PROBLY WANTS TO KILL YOU UP CLOSE...
AND IF HE THINKS WE AIN'T SEEN HIM YET, THAT'S LIKELY WHAT HE'LL TRY TO DO. SO QUIT LOOKIN' AT HIM.
I WISH HE'D HURRY HIS ASS UP.
WHAT ARE YOUR POWERS?
AIN'T NO SUCH THING AS A PERSON WITH "POWERS."
NOT MUCH OF A SUPERHERO WITHOUT POWERS.
LOOK WHO'S TALKING.
WHY'D YOU QUIT?
WELL, LITTLE SISTER...

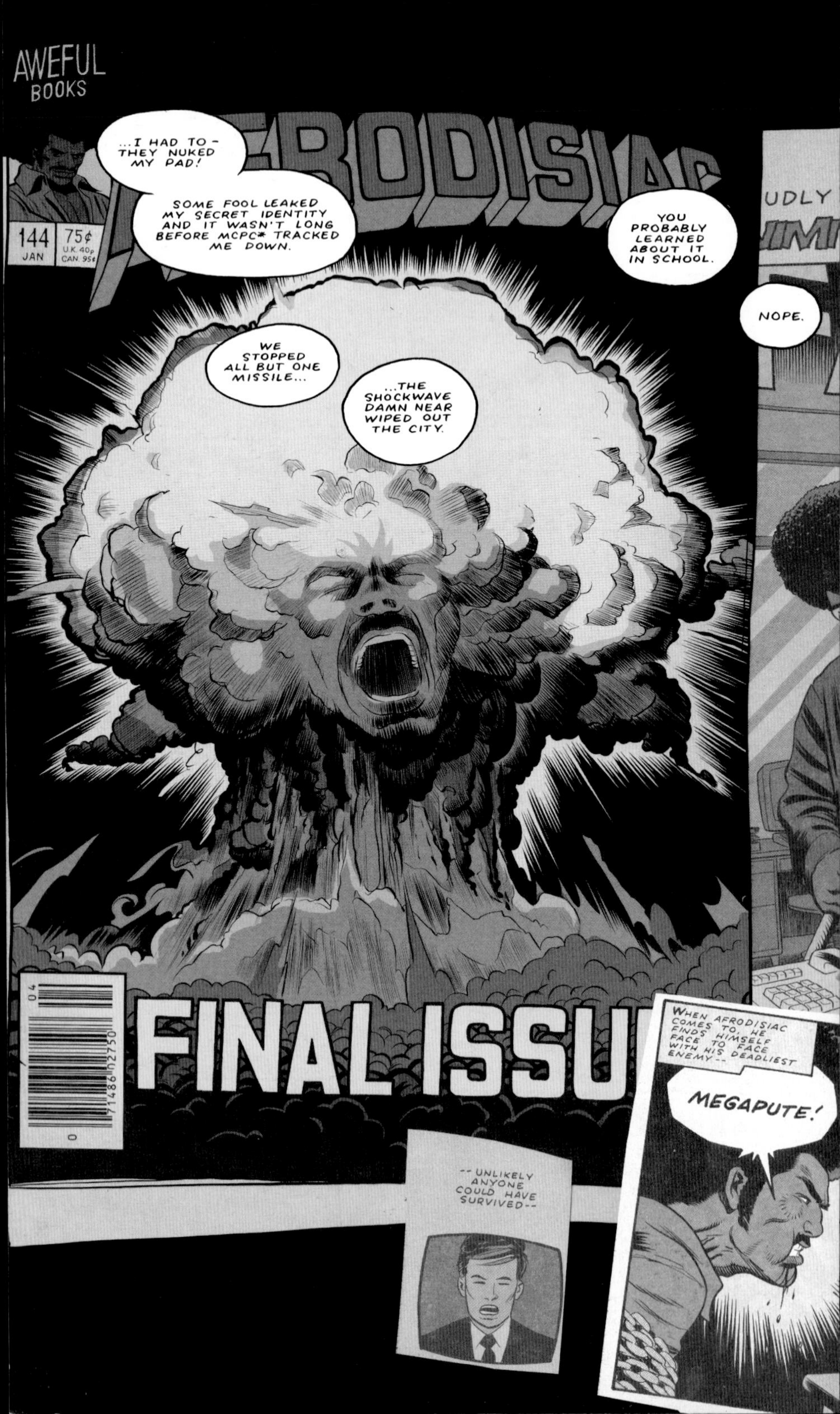
AWEFUL BOOKS
...I HAD TO - THEY NUKED MY PAD!
SOME FOOL LEAKED MY SECRET IDENTITY AND IT WASN'T LONG BEFORE MCPC* TRACKED ME DOWN.
144 JAN
75¢ U.K. 40p CAN. 95¢
YOU PROBABLY LEARNED ABOUT IT IN SCHOOL.
NOPE.
WE STOPPED ALL BUT ONE MISSILE...
...THE SHOCKWAVE DAMN NEAR WIPED OUT THE CITY.
FINAL ISSU
WHEN AFRODISIAC COMES TO, HE FINDS HIMSELF FACE TO FACE WITH HIS DEADLIEST ENEMY--
MEGAPUTE!
--UNLIKELY ANYONE COULD HAVE SURVIVED--

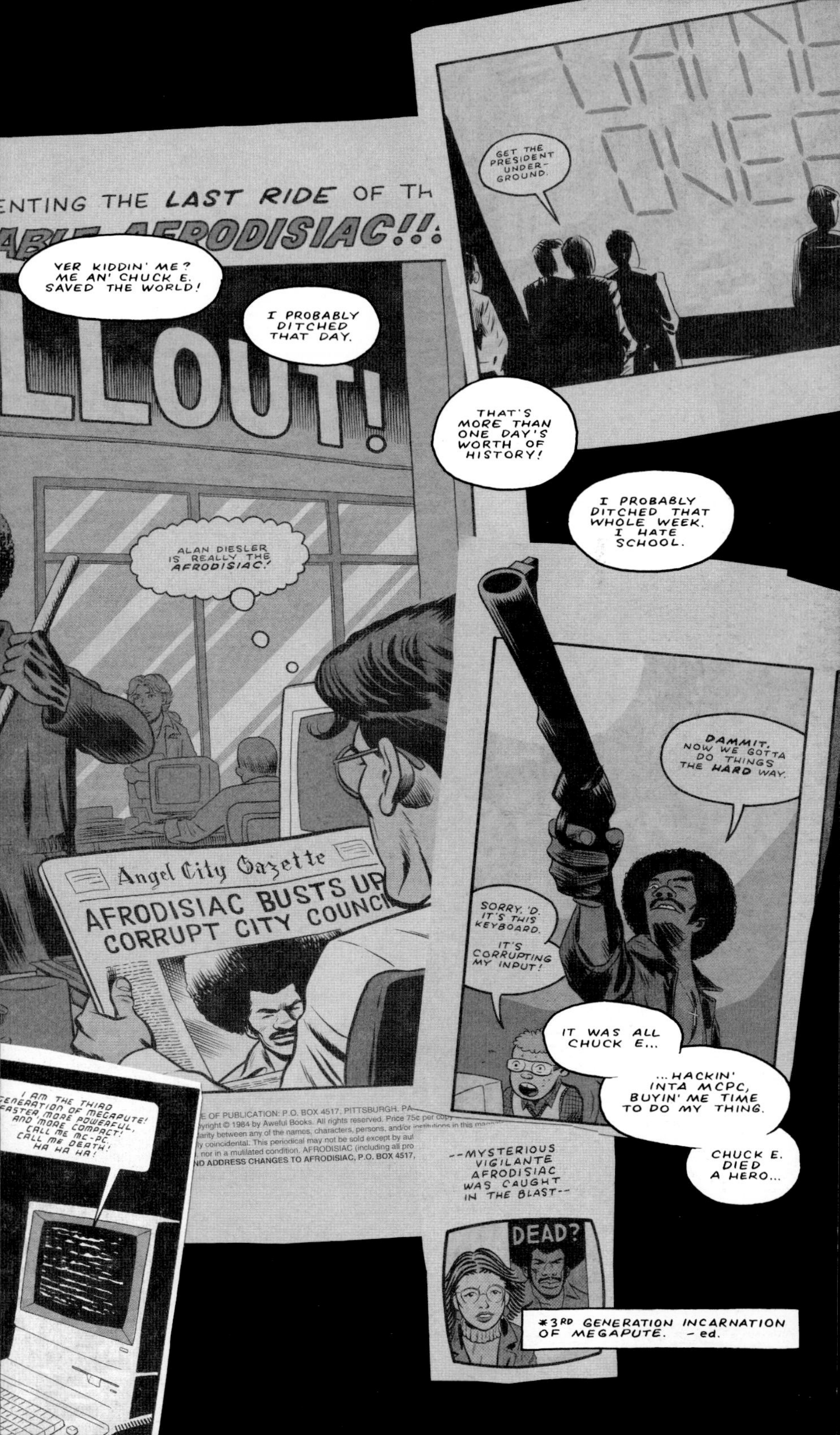
ENTING THE LAST RIDE OF TH
YER KIDDIN' ME? ME AN' CHUCK E. SAVED THE WORLD!
I PROBABLY DITCHED THAT DAY.
LLOUT!
ALAN DIESLER IS REALLY THE AFRODISIAC!
Angel City Gazette
AFRODISIAC BUSTS UP CORRUPT CITY COUNCI
GET THE PRESIDENT UNDER-GROUND.
THAT'S MORE THAN ONE DAY'S WORTH OF HISTORY!
I PROBABLY DITCHED THAT WHOLE WEEK. I HATE SCHOOL.
DAMMIT. NOW WE GOTTA DO THINGS THE HARD WAY.
SORRY, 'D. IT'S THIS KEYBOARD.
IT'S CORRUPTING MY INPUT!
IT WAS ALL CHUCK E...
...HACKIN' INTA MCPC, BUYIN' ME TIME TO DO MY THING.
I AM THE THIRD GENERATION OF MEGAPUTE! FASTER, MORE POWERFUL, AND MORE COMPACT! CALL ME MC-PC. CALL ME DEATH! HA HA HA!
E OF PUBLICATION: P.O. BOX 4517, PITTSBURGH, PA
pyright © 1984 by Aweful Books. All rights reserved. Price 75¢ per
larity between any of the names, characters, persons, and/or
ly coincidental. This periodical may not be sold except by aut
, nor in a mutilated condition. AFRODISIAC (including all pro
ND ADDRESS CHANGES TO AFRODISIAC, P.O. BOX 4517,
--MYSTERIOUS VIGILANTE AFRODISIAC WAS CAUGHT IN THE BLAST--
CHUCK E. DIED A HERO...
DEAD?
*3RD GENERATION INCARNATION OF MEGAPUTE. -ed.

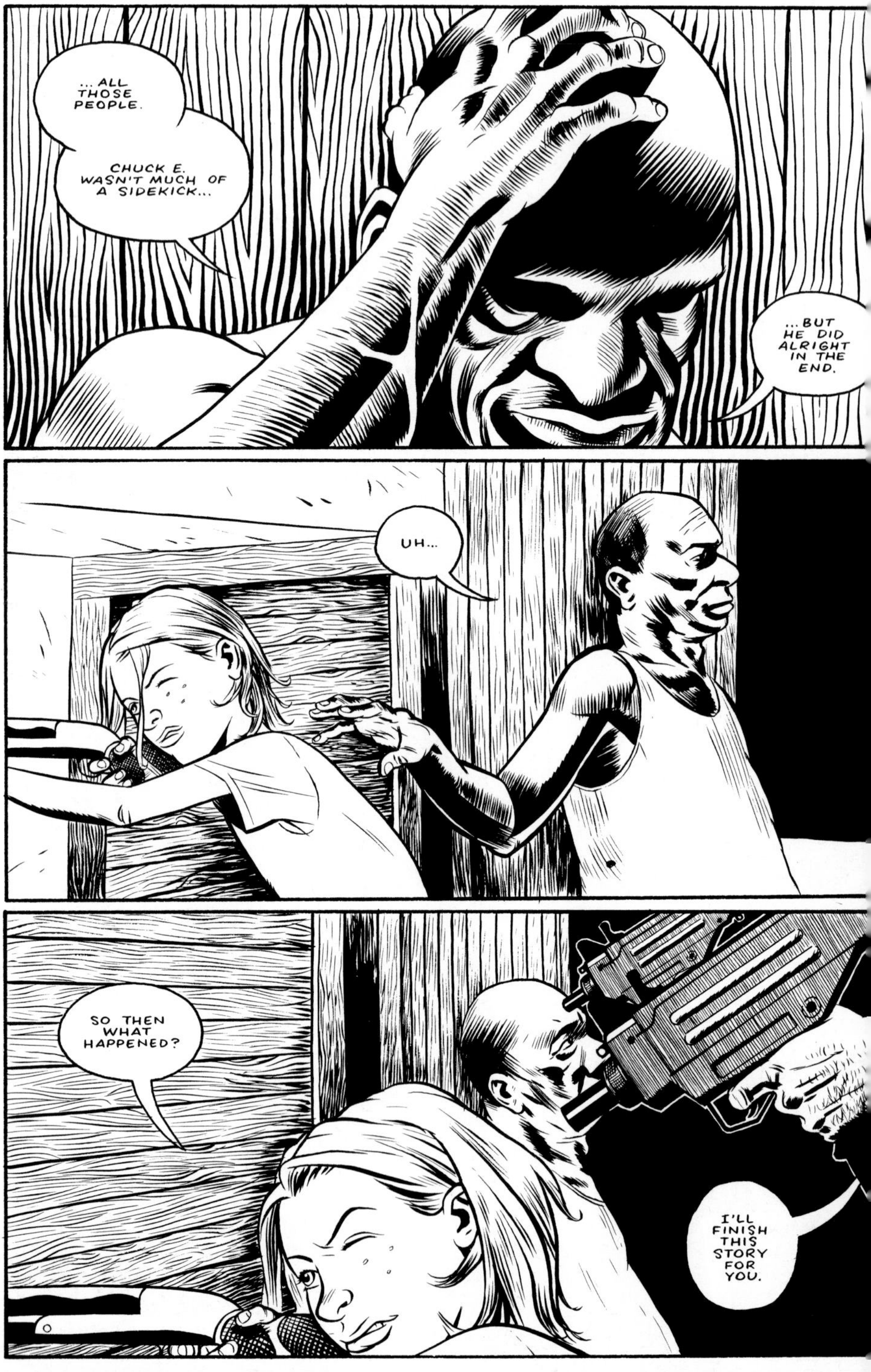
...ALL THOSE PEOPLE.
CHUCK E. WASN'T MUCH OF A SIDEKICK...
...BUT HE DID ALRIGHT IN THE END.
UH...
SO THEN WHAT HAPPENED?
I'LL FINISH THIS STORY FOR YOU.

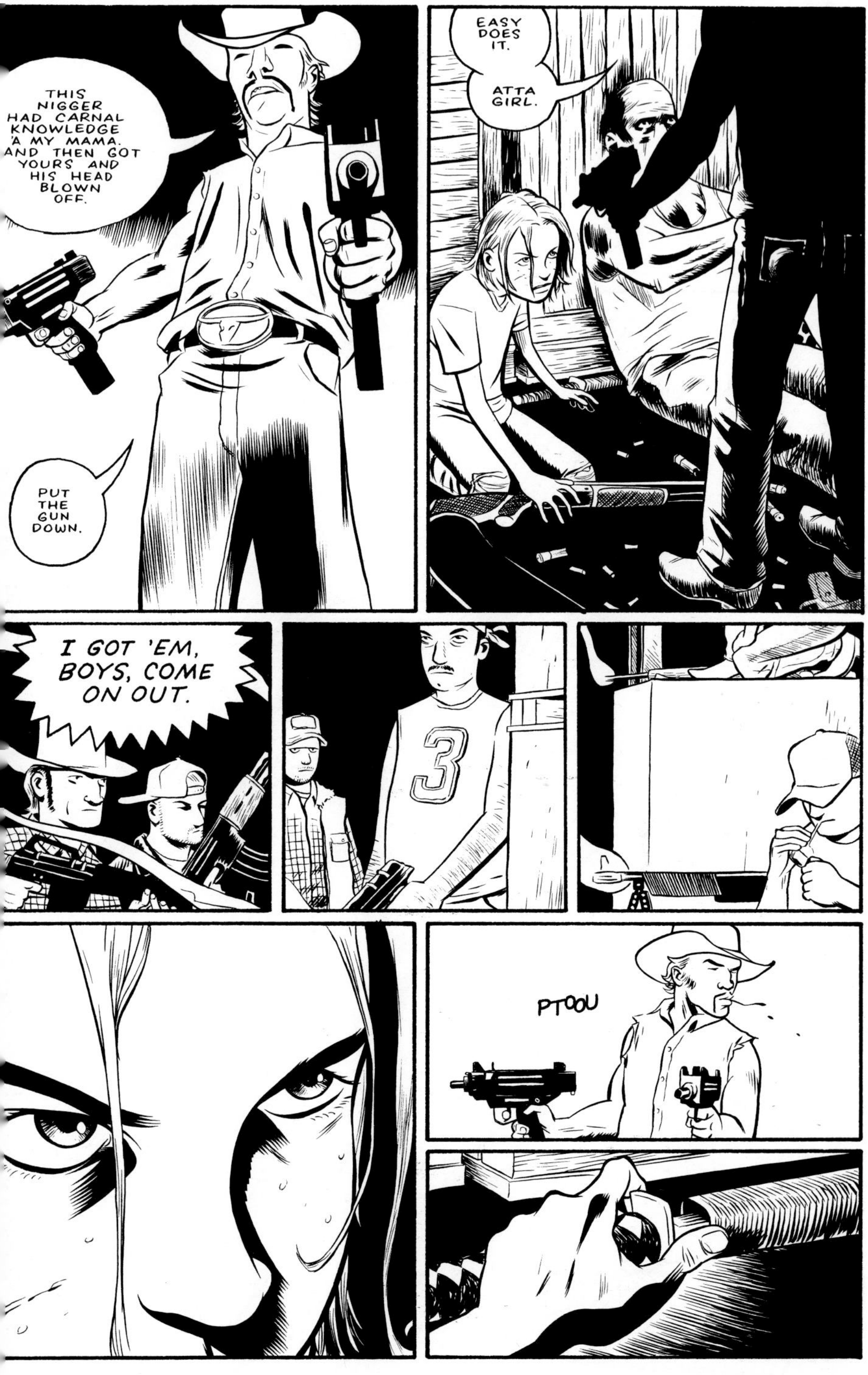
THIS NIGGER HAD CARNAL KNOWLEDGE 'A MY MAMA. AND THEN GOT YOURS AND HIS HEAD BLOWN OFF.
PUT THE GUN DOWN.
EASY DOES IT.
ATTA GIRL.
I GOT 'EM, BOYS, COME ON OUT.
3
PTOOU

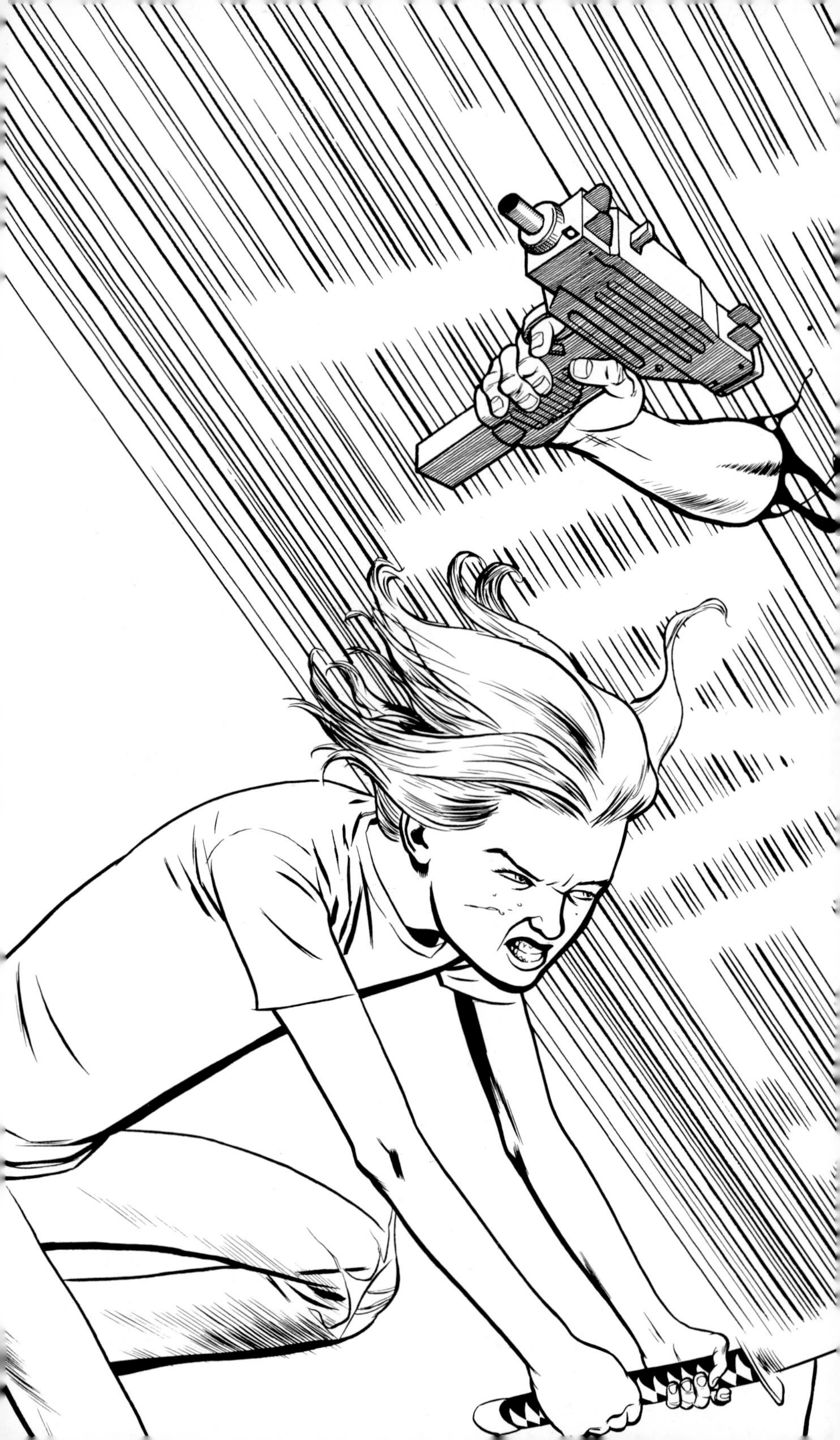

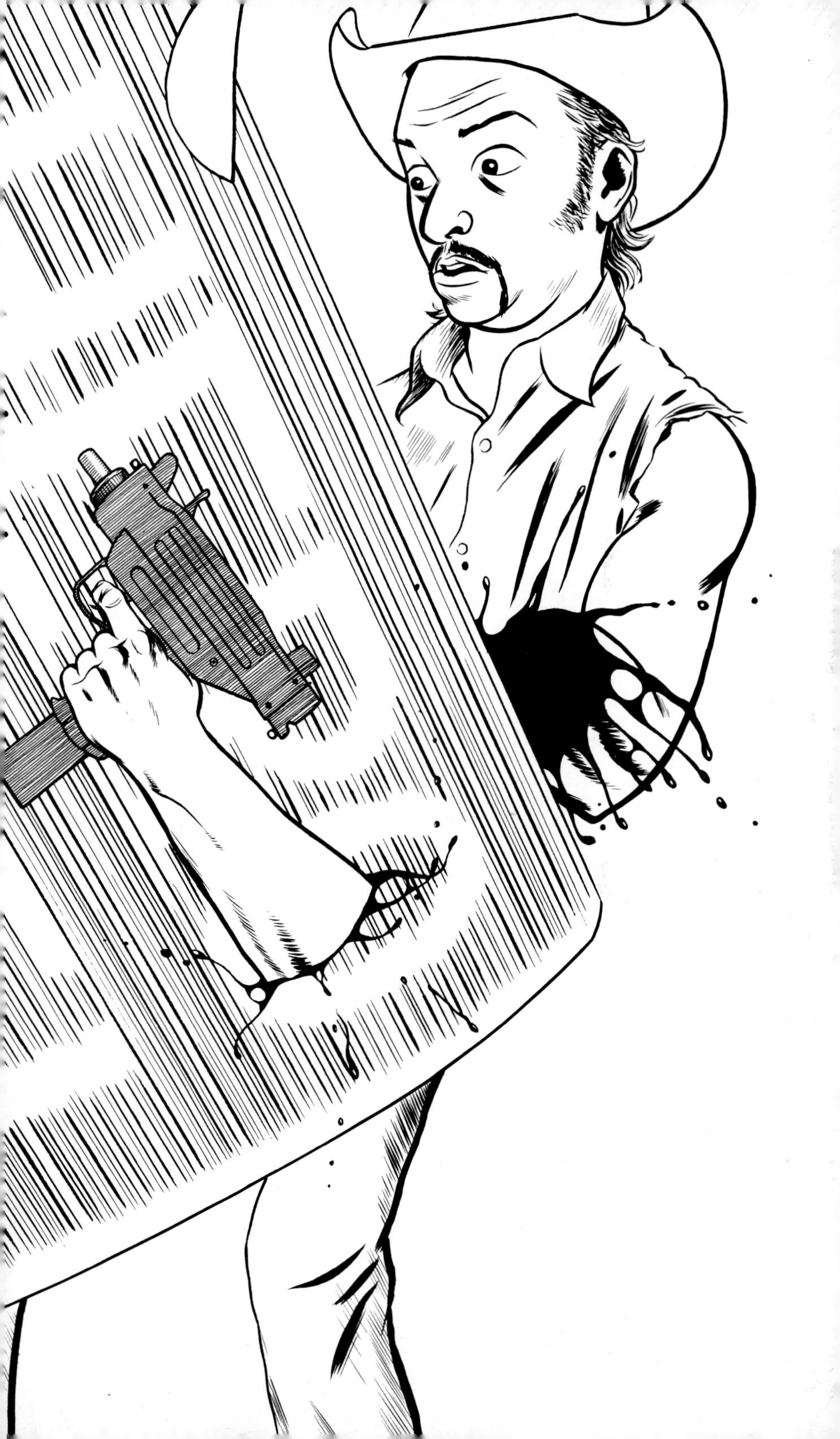

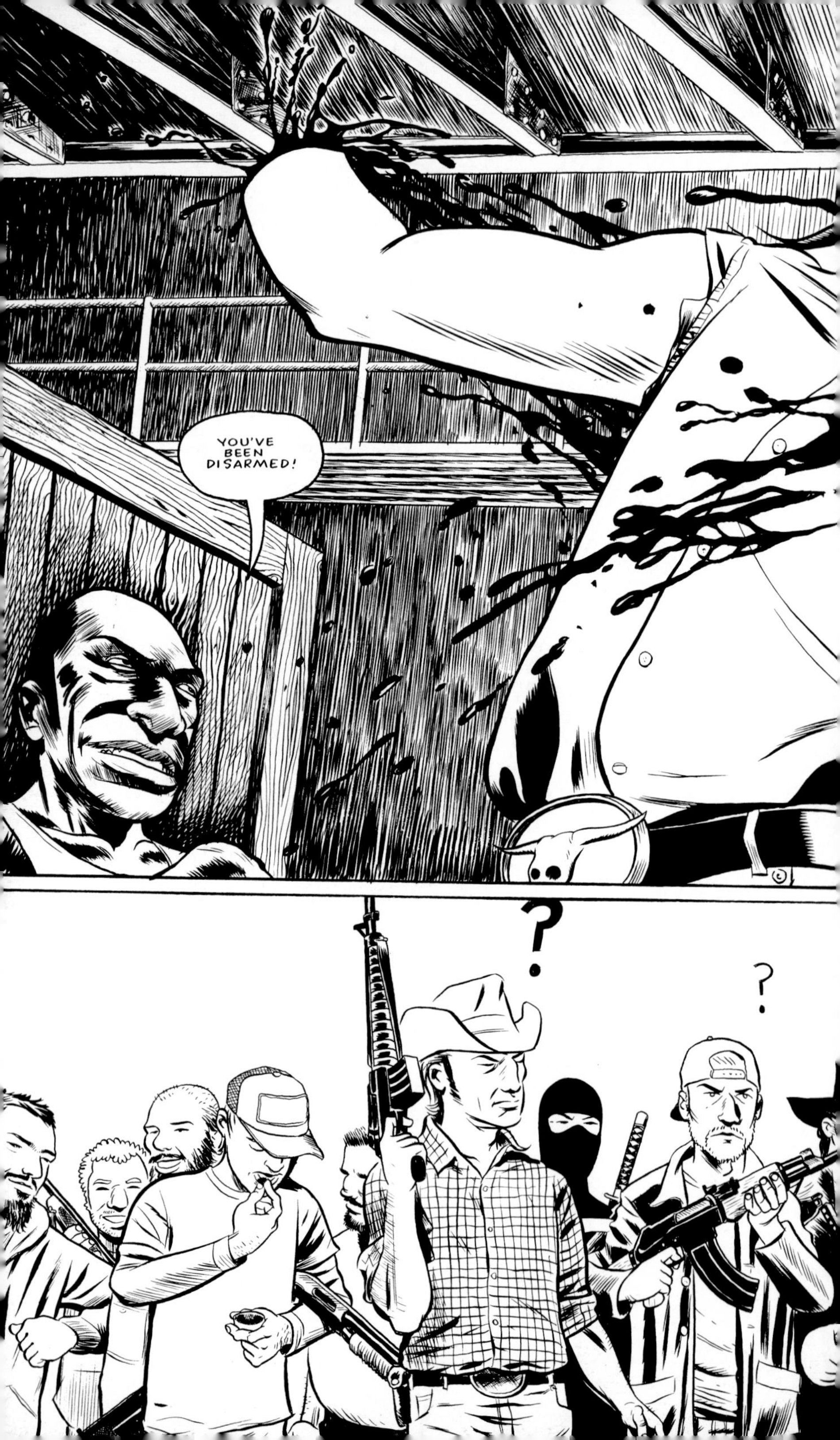
YOU'VE BEEN DISARMED!
?
?

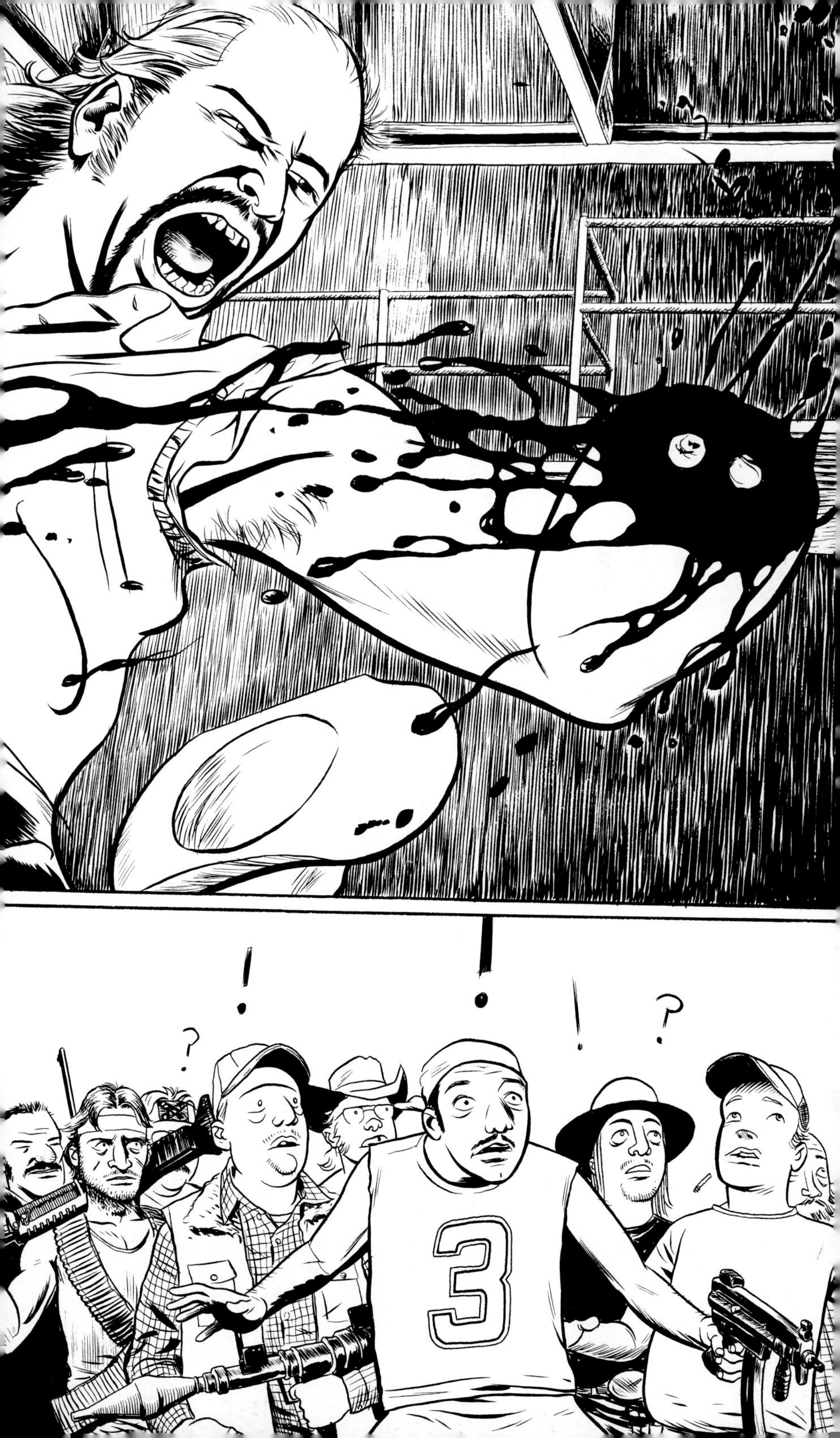
?
!
!
!
?

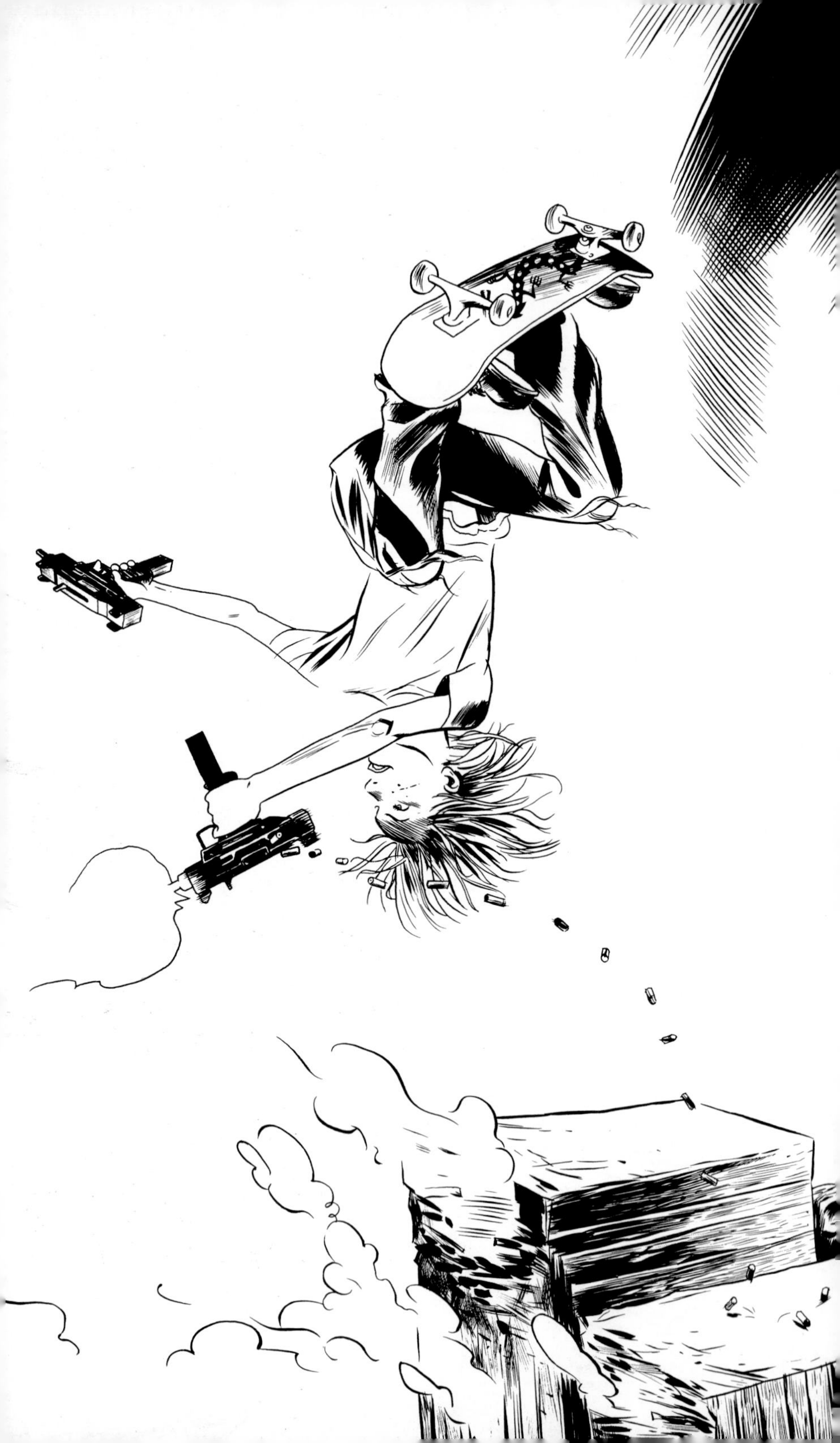

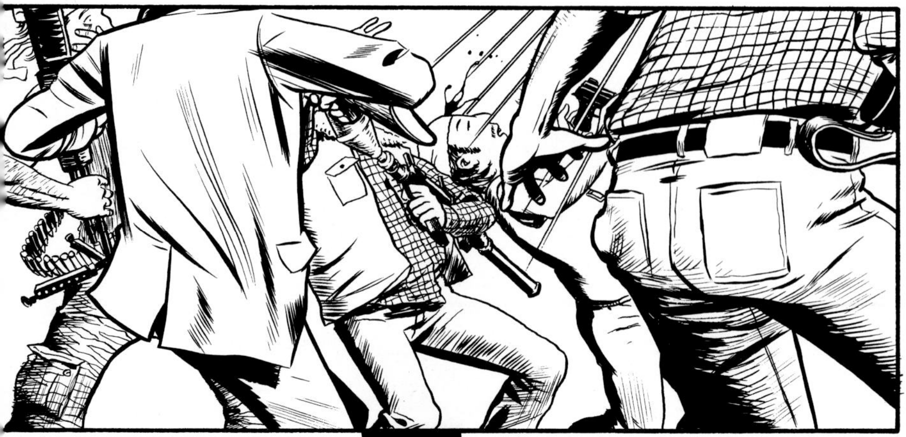
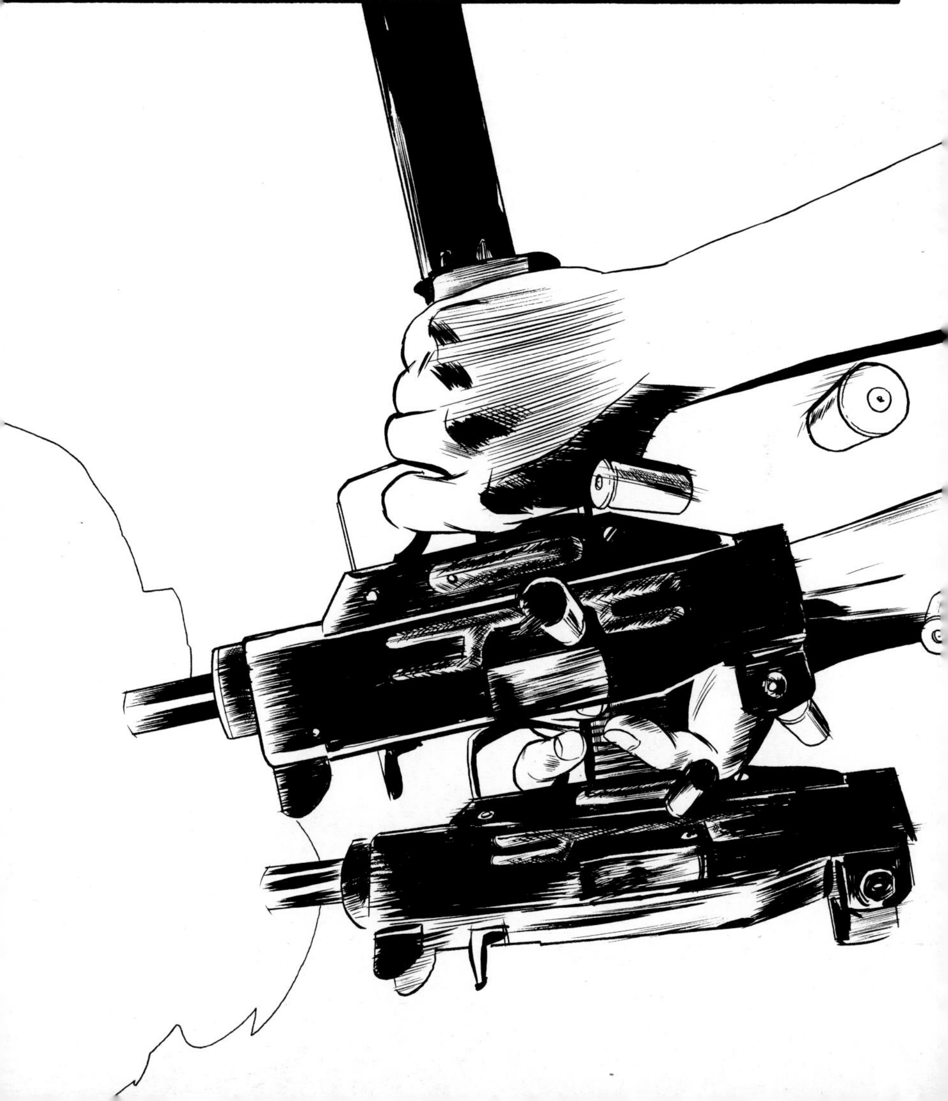

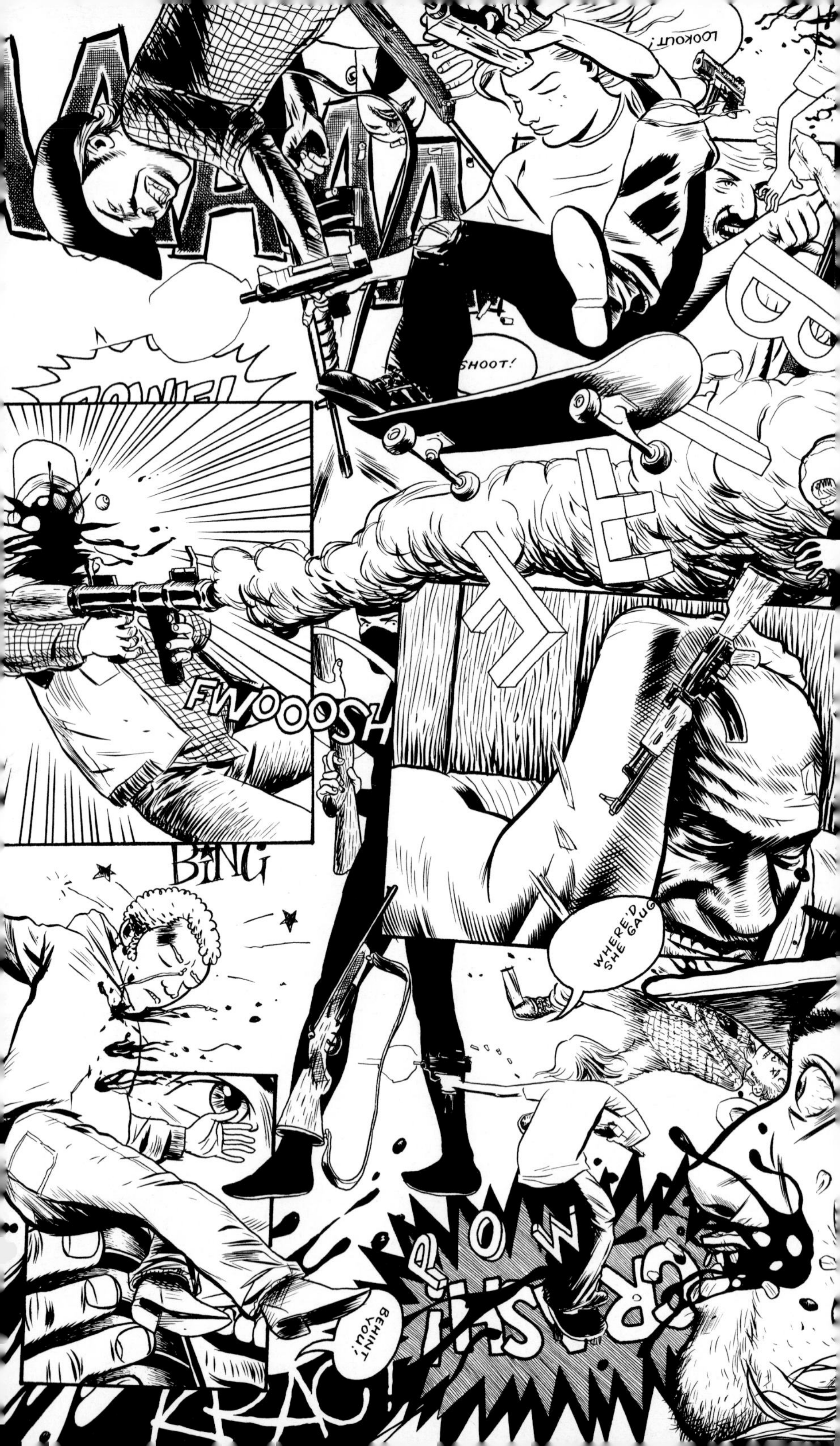
LOOKOUT!
SHOOT!
FWOOOSH
BING
BEHINT YOU!
KRAC!

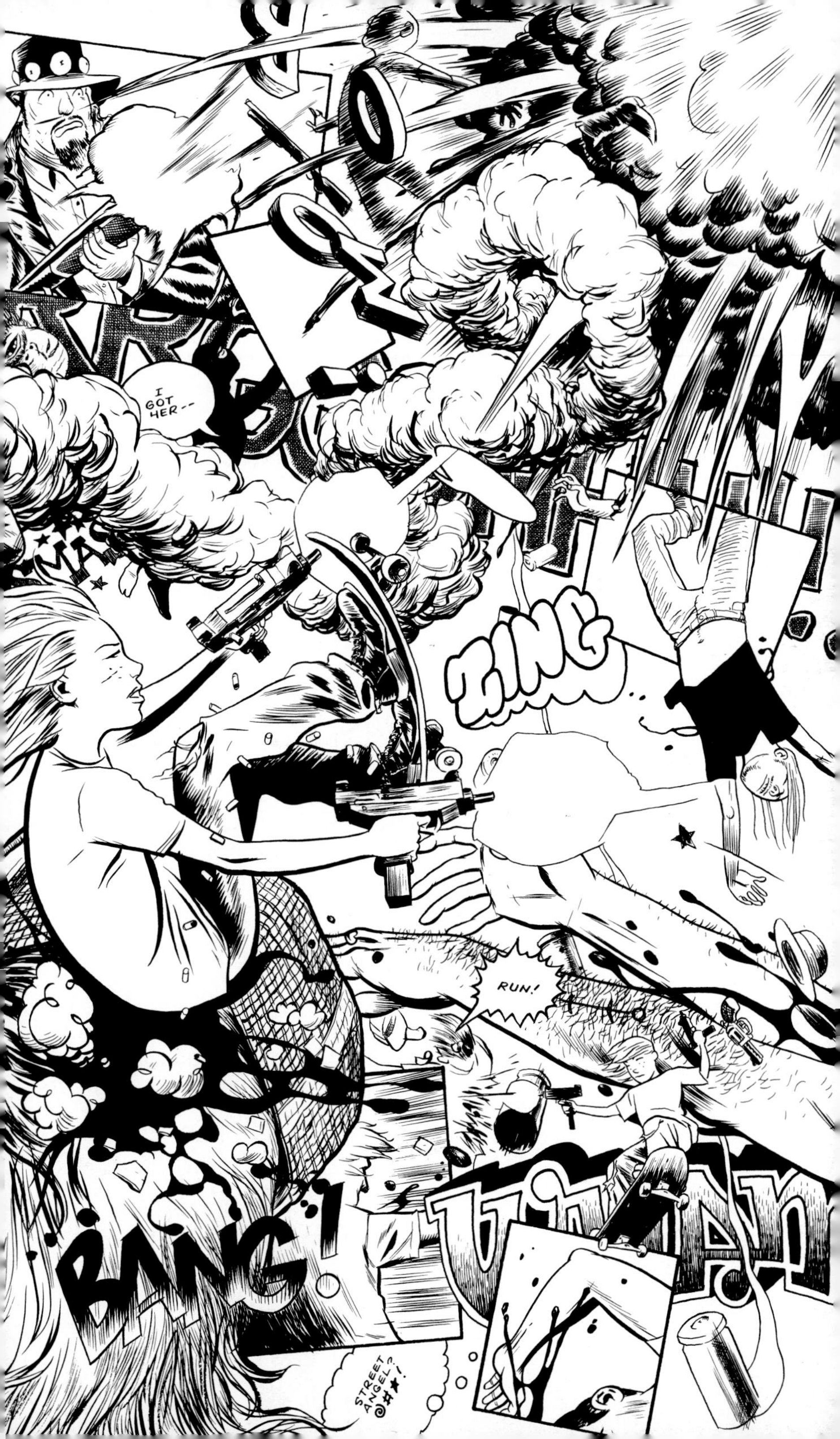
I GOT HER--
ZING
RUN!
BANG!
STREET ANGEL?
@#★!

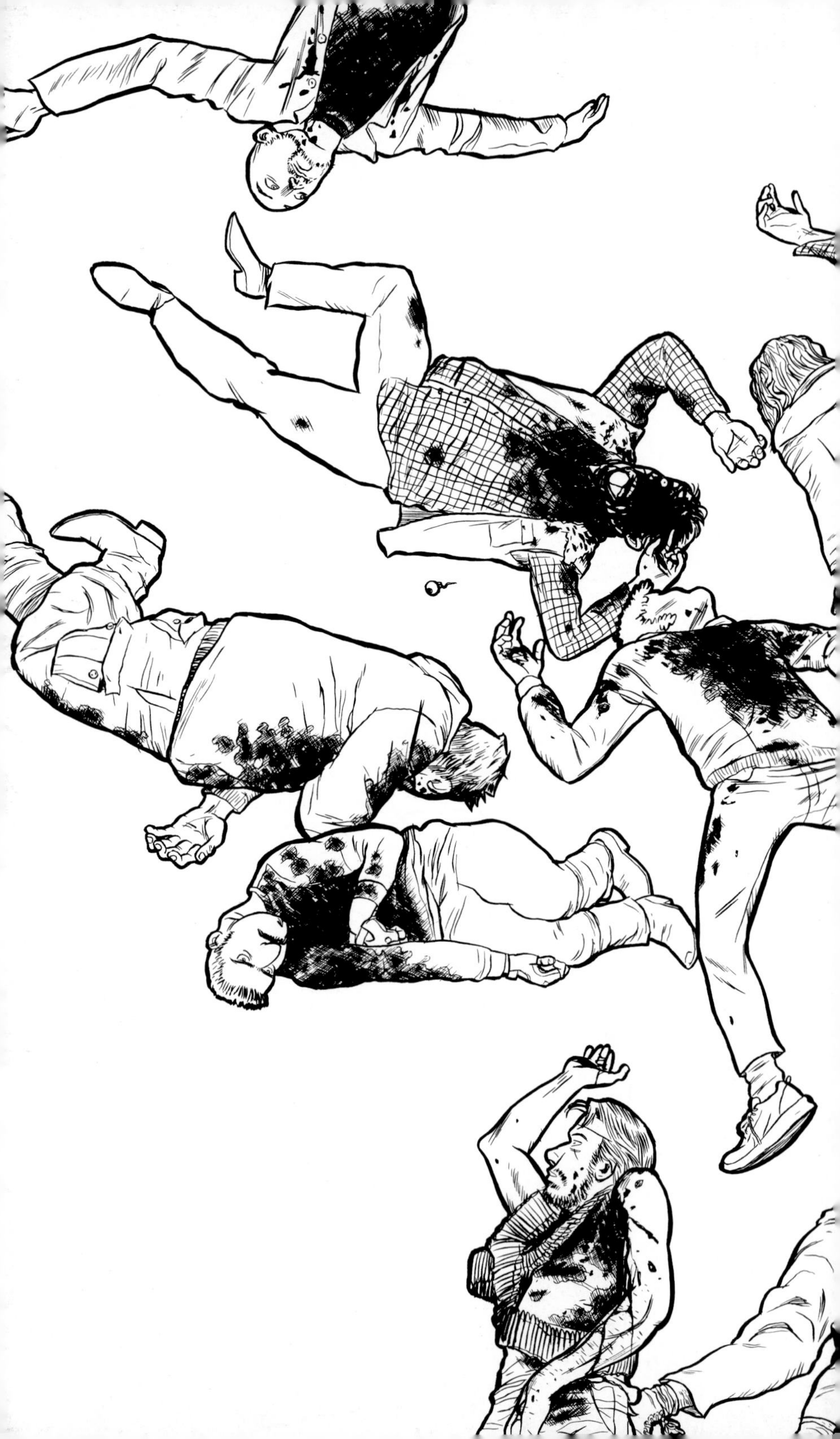

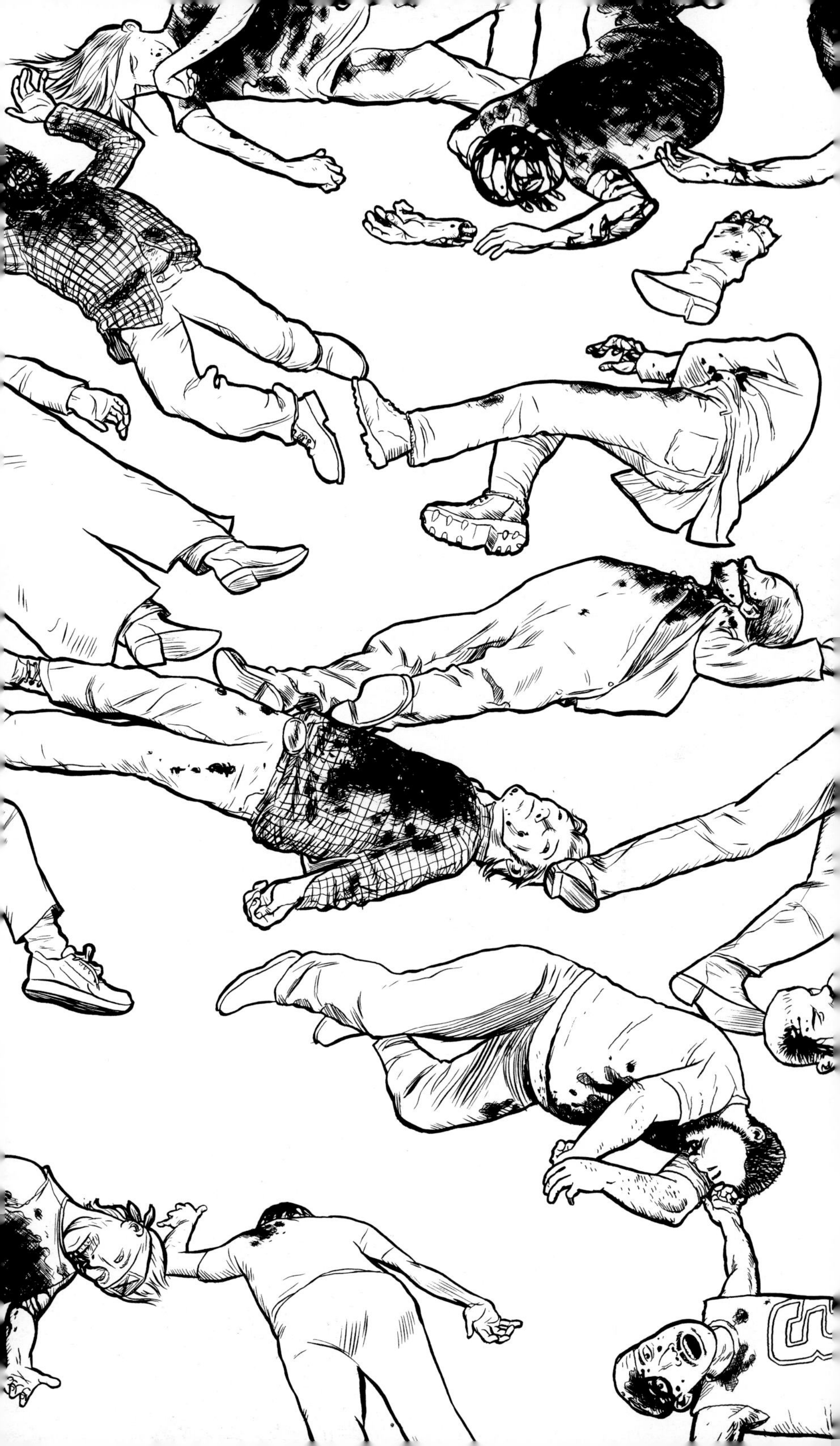

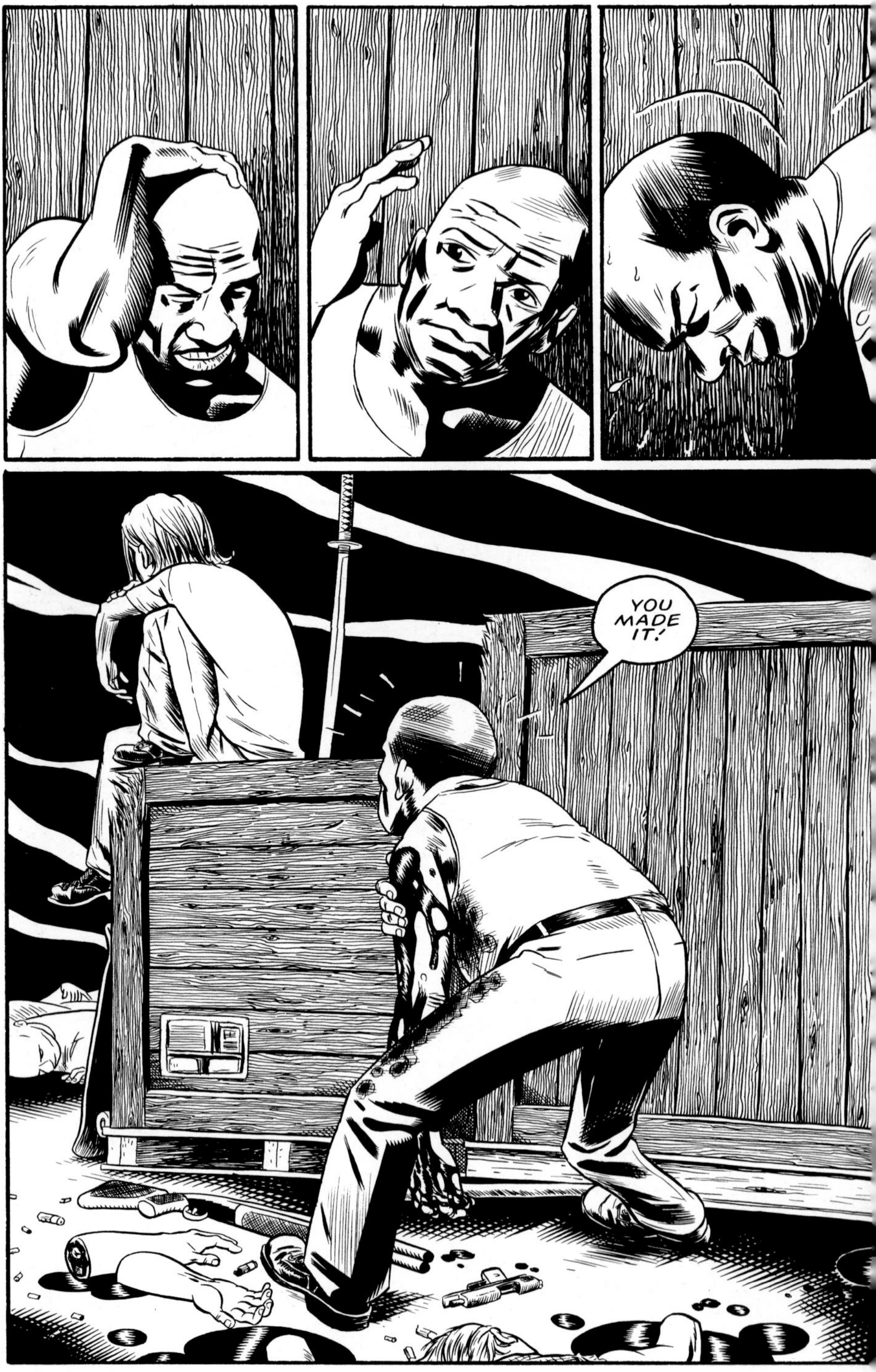
YOU MADE IT!

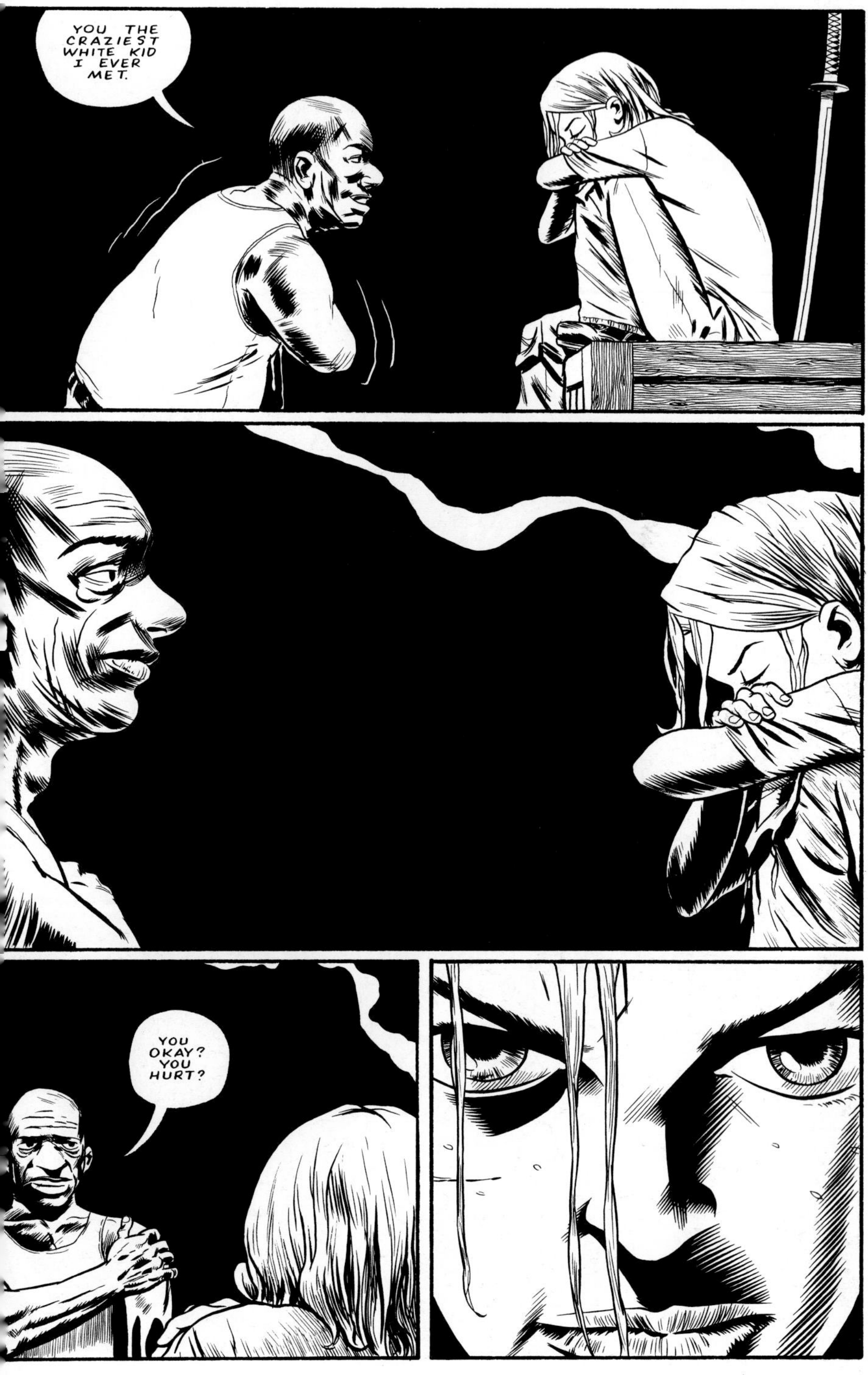
YOU THE CRAZIEST WHITE KID I EVER MET.
YOU OKAY? YOU HURT?

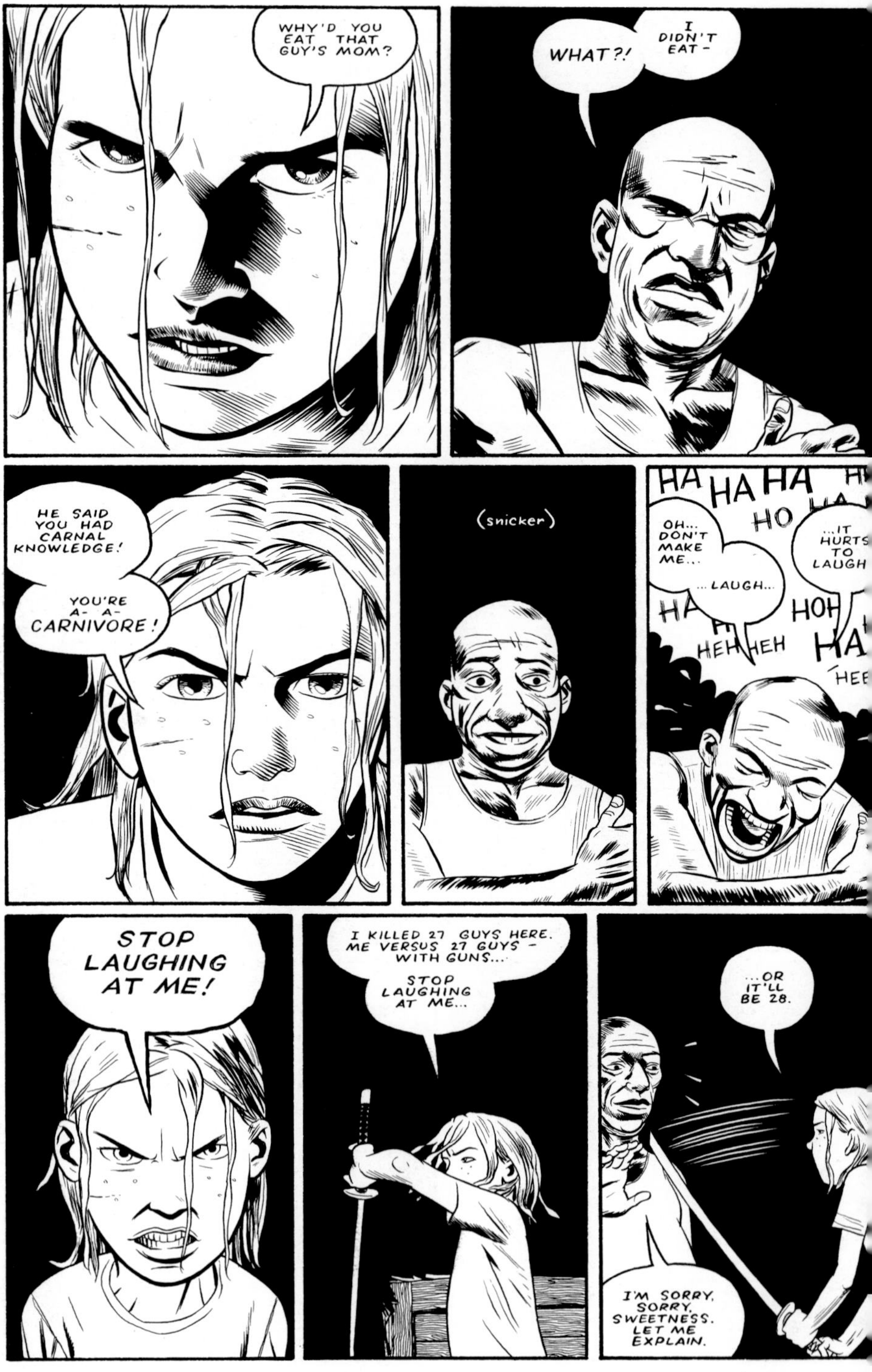
WHY'D YOU EAT THAT GUY'S MOM?
WHAT?!
I DIDN'T EAT -
HE SAID YOU HAD CARNAL KNOWLEDGE!
YOU'RE A- A- CARNIVORE!
(snicker)
HA HA HA
HO
OH... DON'T MAKE ME...
...LAUGH...
...IT HURTS TO LAUGH
HA HOH
HEH HEH
HA
STOP LAUGHING AT ME!
I KILLED 27 GUYS HERE. ME VERSUS 27 GUYS - WITH GUNS...
STOP LAUGHING AT ME...
...OR IT'LL BE 28.
I'M SORRY, SORRY, SWEETNESS. LET ME EXPLAIN.

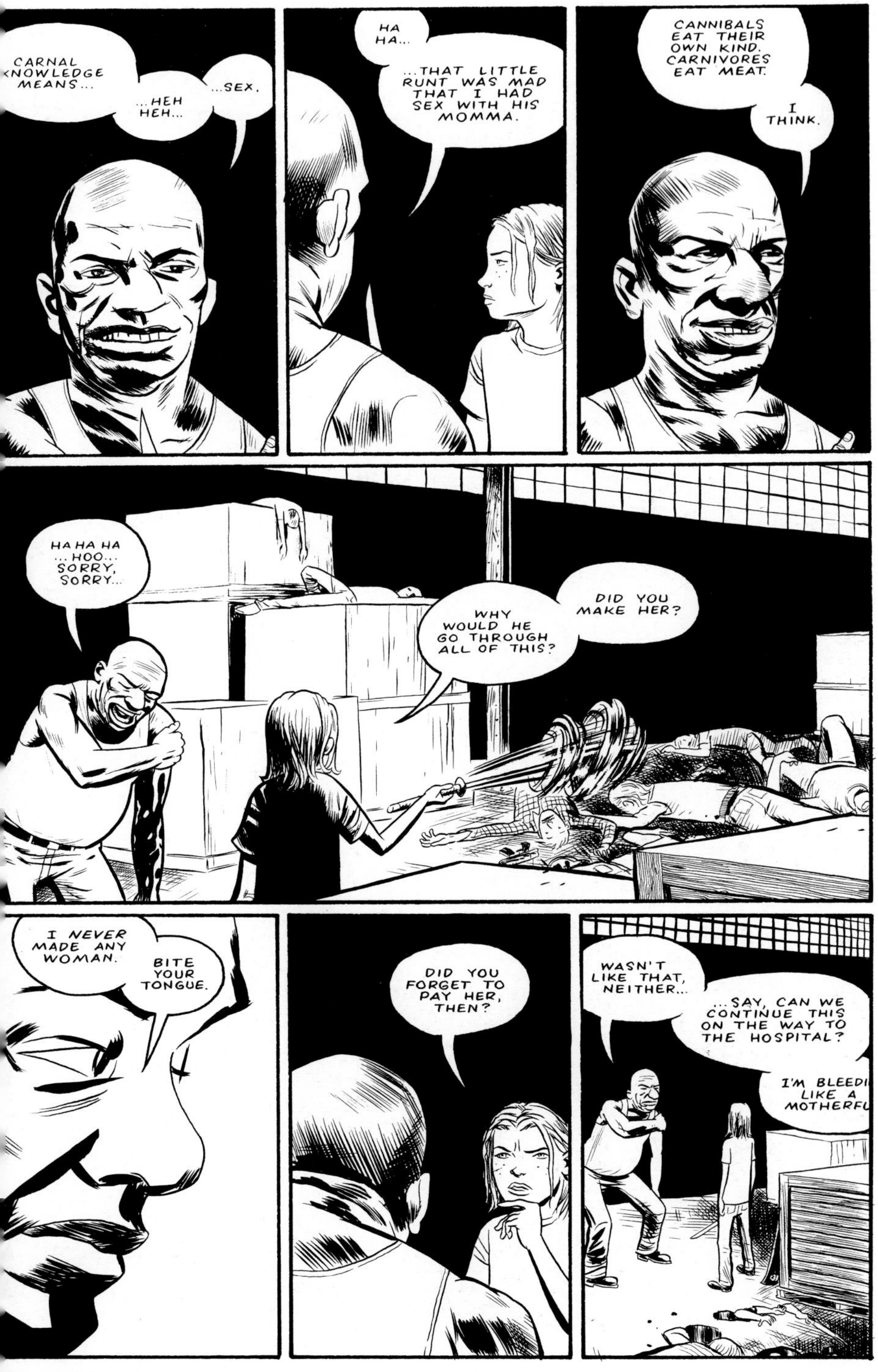
CARNAL KNOWLEDGE MEANS...
...HEH HEH...
...SEX.
HA HA...
...THAT LITTLE RUNT WAS MAD THAT I HAD SEX WITH HIS MOMMA.
CANNIBALS EAT THEIR OWN KIND. CARNIVORES EAT MEAT.
I THINK.
HA HA HA ...HOO... SORRY, SORRY...
DID YOU MAKE HER?
WHY WOULD HE GO THROUGH ALL OF THIS?
I NEVER MADE ANY WOMAN.
BITE YOUR TONGUE.
DID YOU FORGET TO PAY HER, THEN?
WASN'T LIKE THAT, NEITHER...
...SAY, CAN WE CONTINUE THIS ON THE WAY TO THE HOSPITAL?
I'M BLEEDI LIKE A MOTHERFU

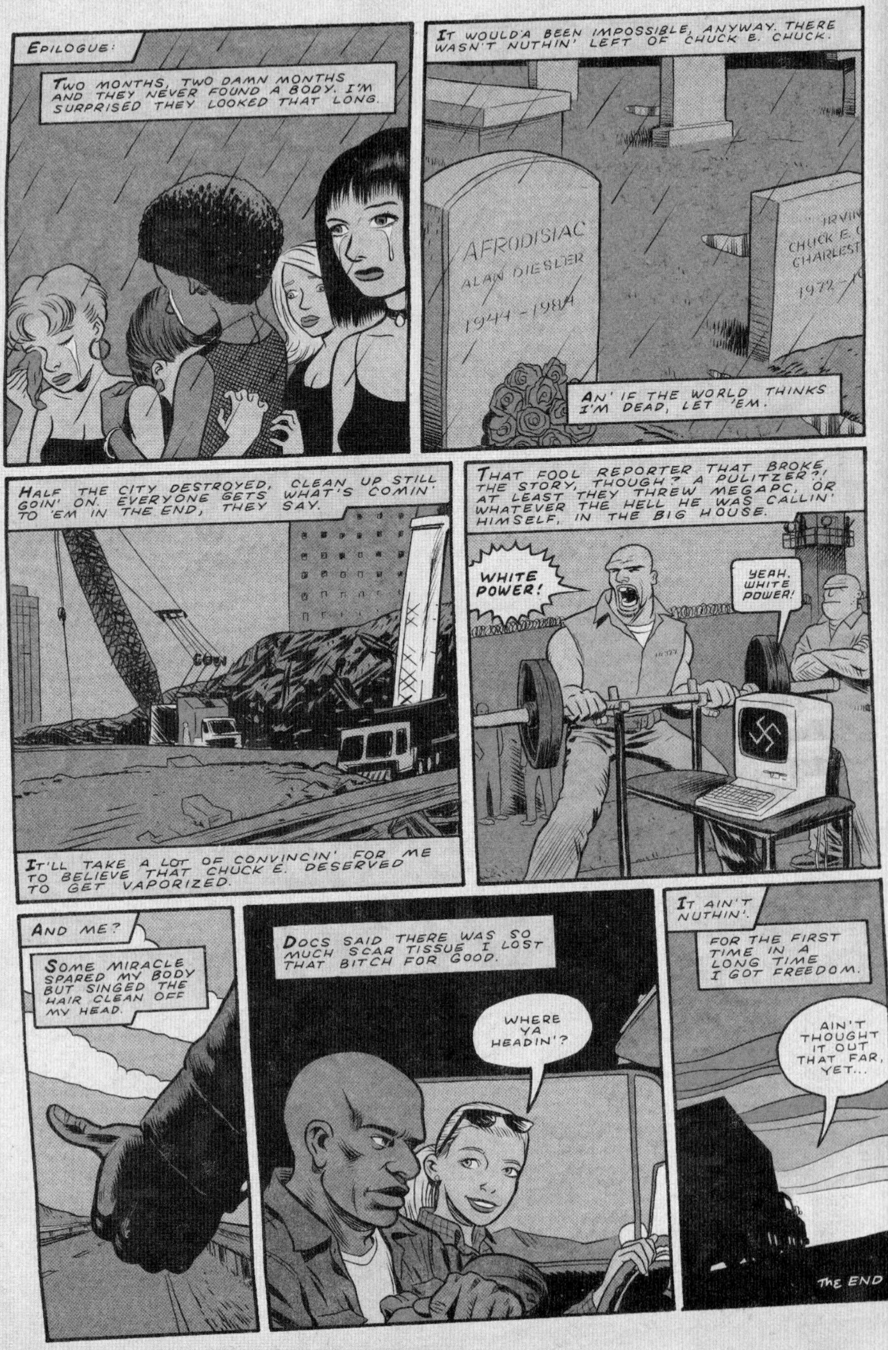

EPILOGUE:
TWO MONTHS, TWO DAMN MONTHS AND THEY NEVER FOUND A BODY. I'M SURPRISED THEY LOOKED THAT LONG.
IT WOULD'A BEEN IMPOSSIBLE, ANYWAY. THERE WASN'T NUTHIN' LEFT OF CHUCK E. CHUCK.
AFRODISIAC
ALAN DIESLER
1944 - 1984
IRVIN
CHUCK E. C
CHARLEST
1972 -
AN' IF THE WORLD THINKS I'M DEAD, LET 'EM.
HALF THE CITY DESTROYED, CLEAN UP STILL GOIN' ON. EVERYONE GETS WHAT'S COMIN' TO 'EM IN THE END, THEY SAY.
IT'LL TAKE A LOT OF CONVINCIN' FOR ME TO BELIEVE THAT CHUCK E. DESERVED TO GET VAPORIZED.
THAT FOOL REPORTER THAT BROKE THE STORY, THOUGH? A PULITZER?! AT LEAST THEY THREW MEGAPC, OR WHATEVER THE HELL HE WAS CALLIN' HIMSELF, IN THE BIG HOUSE.
WHITE POWER!
YEAH, WHITE POWER!
AND ME?
SOME MIRACLE SPARED MY BODY BUT SINGED THE HAIR CLEAN OFF MY HEAD.
DOCS SAID THERE WAS SO MUCH SCAR TISSUE I LOST THAT BITCH FOR GOOD.
WHERE YA HEADIN'?
IT AIN'T NUTHIN'.
FOR THE FIRST TIME IN A LONG TIME I GOT FREEDOM.
AIN'T THOUGHT IT OUT THAT FAR, YET...
THE END

MegaPute

Name: MegaPute, a.k.a.
MegaPute IIc, MC-PC,
AwesomePute 250 ii
Screensaver: Solar Eclipse
O/S: Windows ME

History:

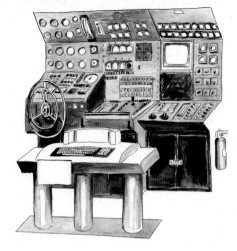

000000000000000000000000000000000000000000000000000000000000000000000000000000
000001000001111101111101111101111001111101111101111100000100000111110
000010100001000001000101000101000100010001100000010000001010000100000
000100010001111100101100100010100010001000000110000100000100001000100000
001111111001000001001101000101000100010000001100010000111111100100000
010000000010100000100010111110111100111110111110111110100000000101110
000000000000000000000000000000000000000000000000000000000000000000000000000000
001010100001100011010000101111101111100001111001111101111100001010100
001010100001010101010000101100000100000010001000100010000000001010100
001010100001001001010000100011000010000001000100010001110000001010100
000000000001000001010000100001100010000000100010001000100000000000000000
001010100001000001011111101111100010000001111001111101111100001010100
000000000000000000000000000000000000000000000000000000000000000000000000000000

Powers: 32 GB EXX SDRAMM memory; Dual 4.6 GHz Xeto Titanium processors, Up to 3 TB max internal storage; UL and CE approved; Accurate to 1nm; Wireless for on-the-go evil; Optional R/C motorized, gyroscopic cart (for mobility)

First Appearance: Afrodisiac #3

Abilities Matrix	0	1	2	3	4	5	6	7
Agility/Speed*								
Smarts								
Energy Protection								
Fight Skills								
Skate Skills								
Basketball Skills								
Strength								

* Can accelerate to and maintain speeds of 17 mph when outfitted with optional R/C cart

Untitled

Three Wishes

Paradox Lost

Shop Fu

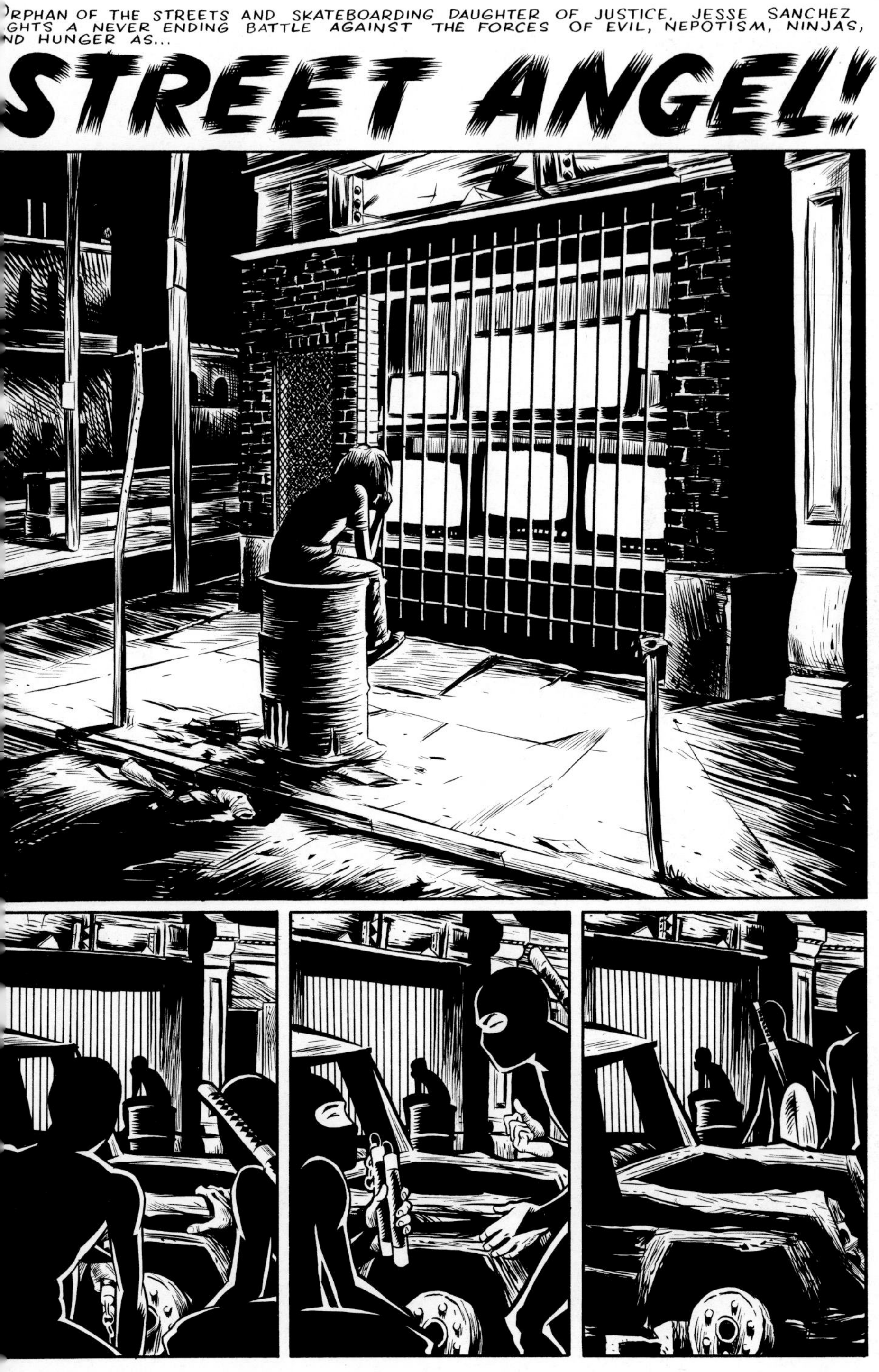
RPHAN OF THE STREETS AND SKATEBOARDING DAUGHTER OF JUSTICE, JESSE SANCHEZ
GHTS A NEVER ENDING BATTLE AGAINST THE FORCES OF EVIL, NEPOTISM, NINJAS,
ND HUNGER AS...
STREET ANGEL!

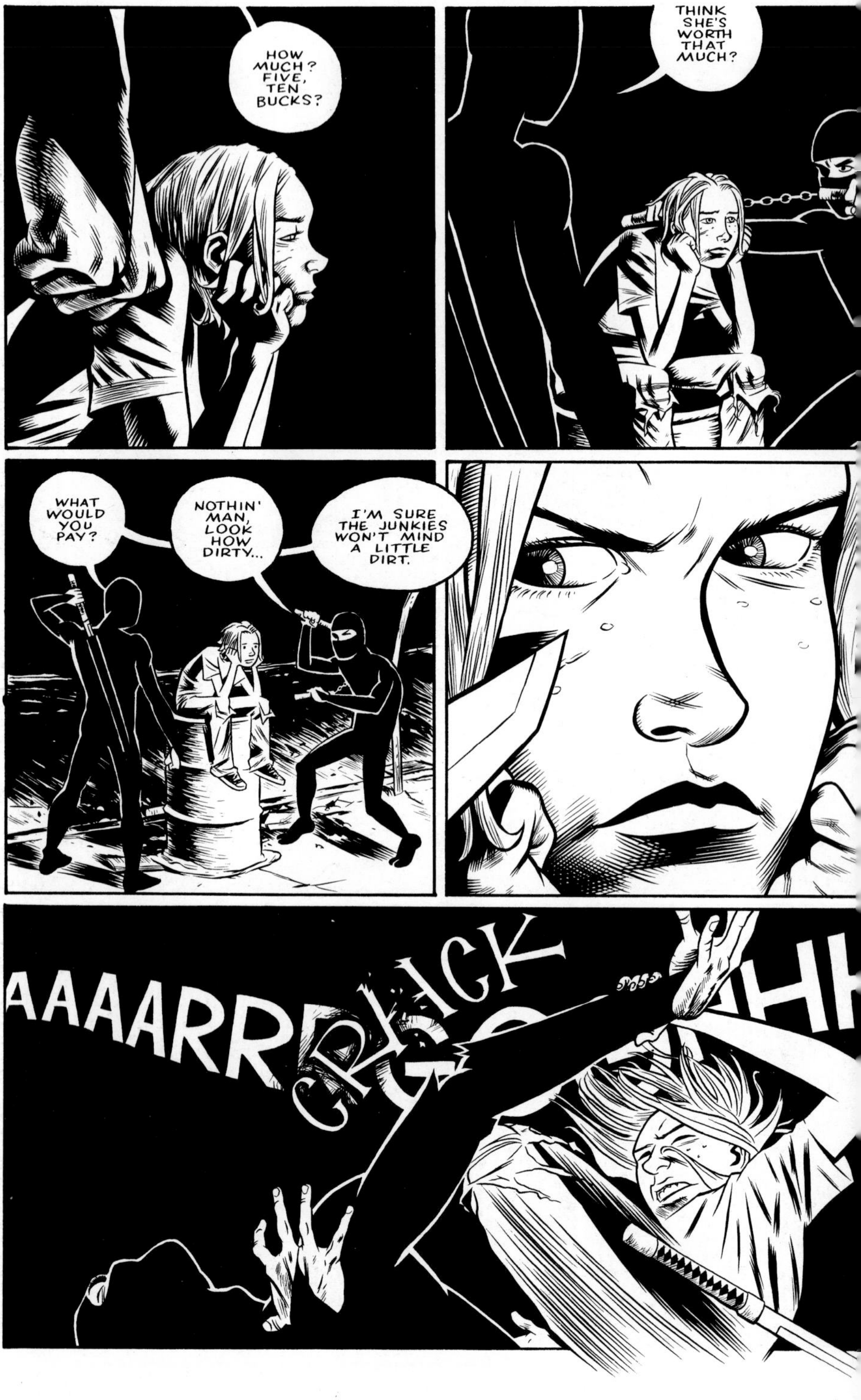
HOW MUCH? FIVE, TEN BUCKS?
THINK SHE'S WORTH THAT MUCH?
WHAT WOULD YOU PAY?
NOTHIN' MAN, LOOK HOW DIRTY...
I'M SURE THE JUNKIES WON'T MIND A LITTLE DIRT.
AAAARR
CRACK

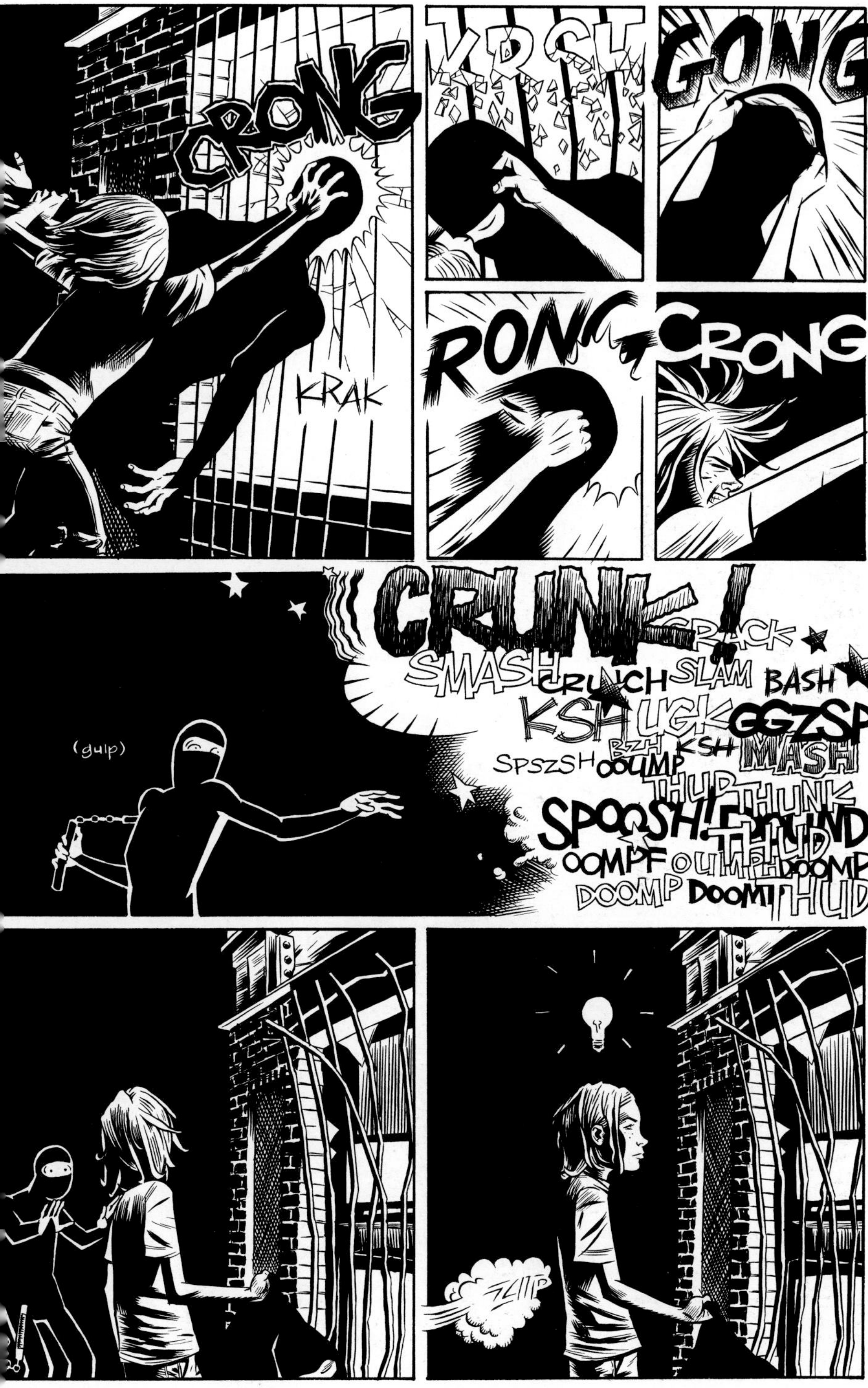
CRONG
KRAK
VRSH
GONG
RONG
CRONG
CRUNK!
CRACK
SMASH
CRUNCH
SLAM
BASH
KSH
UGK
GGZSP
BZH
KSH
SPSZSH
OOUMP
MASH
THUP
THUNK
SPOOSH!
THUD
OOMPF
OUMPH
DOOMP
DOOMP
DOOM
THUD
(gulp)
ZZIIP

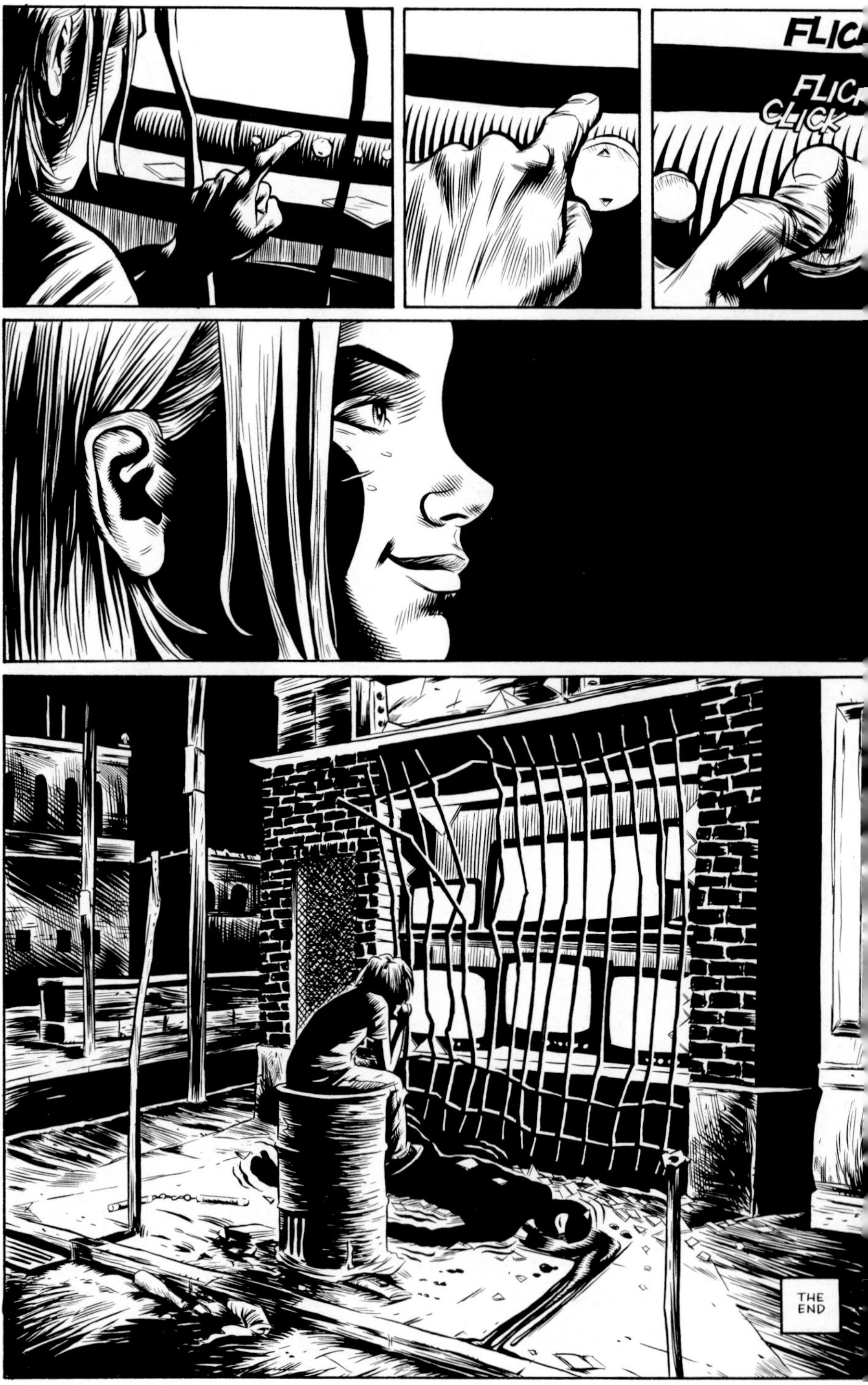
FLICK
FLICK
CLICK
THE END

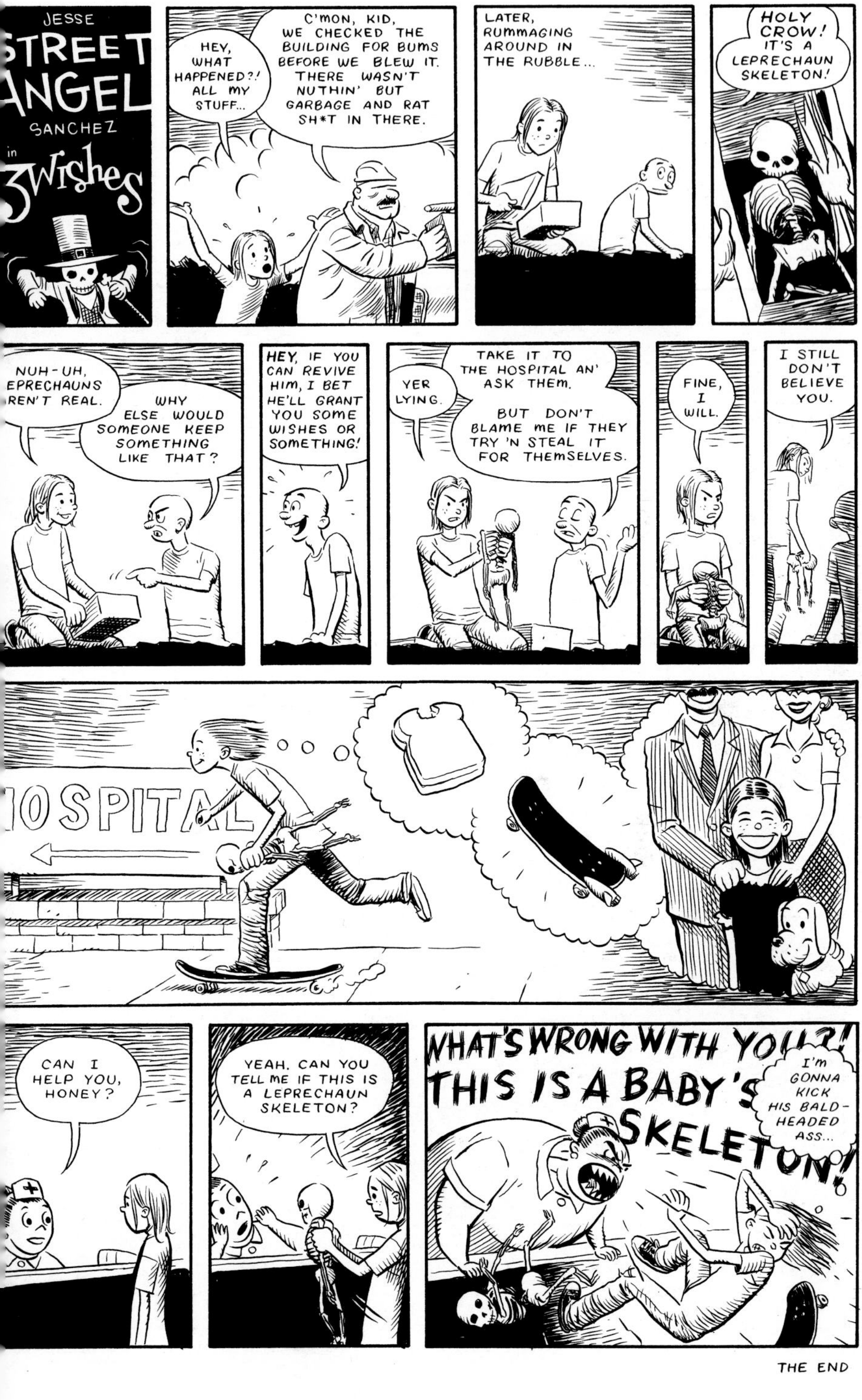
JESSE
STREET ANGEL
SANCHEZ
in
3 Wishes
HEY, WHAT HAPPENED?! ALL MY STUFF...
C'MON, KID, WE CHECKED THE BUILDING FOR BUMS BEFORE WE BLEW IT. THERE WASN'T NUTHIN' BUT GARBAGE AND RAT SH*T IN THERE.
LATER, RUMMAGING AROUND IN THE RUBBLE...
HOLY CROW! IT'S A LEPRECHAUN SKELETON!
NUH-UH, LEPRECHAUNS AREN'T REAL.
WHY ELSE WOULD SOMEONE KEEP SOMETHING LIKE THAT?
HEY, IF YOU CAN REVIVE HIM, I BET HE'LL GRANT YOU SOME WISHES OR SOMETHING!
YER LYING.
TAKE IT TO THE HOSPITAL AN' ASK THEM.
BUT DON'T BLAME ME IF THEY TRY 'N STEAL IT FOR THEMSELVES.
FINE, I WILL.
I STILL DON'T BELIEVE YOU.
HOSPITAL
CAN I HELP YOU, HONEY?
YEAH. CAN YOU TELL ME IF THIS IS A LEPRECHAUN SKELETON?
WHAT'S WRONG WITH YOU?! THIS IS A BABY'S SKELETON!
I'M GONNA KICK HIS BALD-HEADED ASS...

THE END

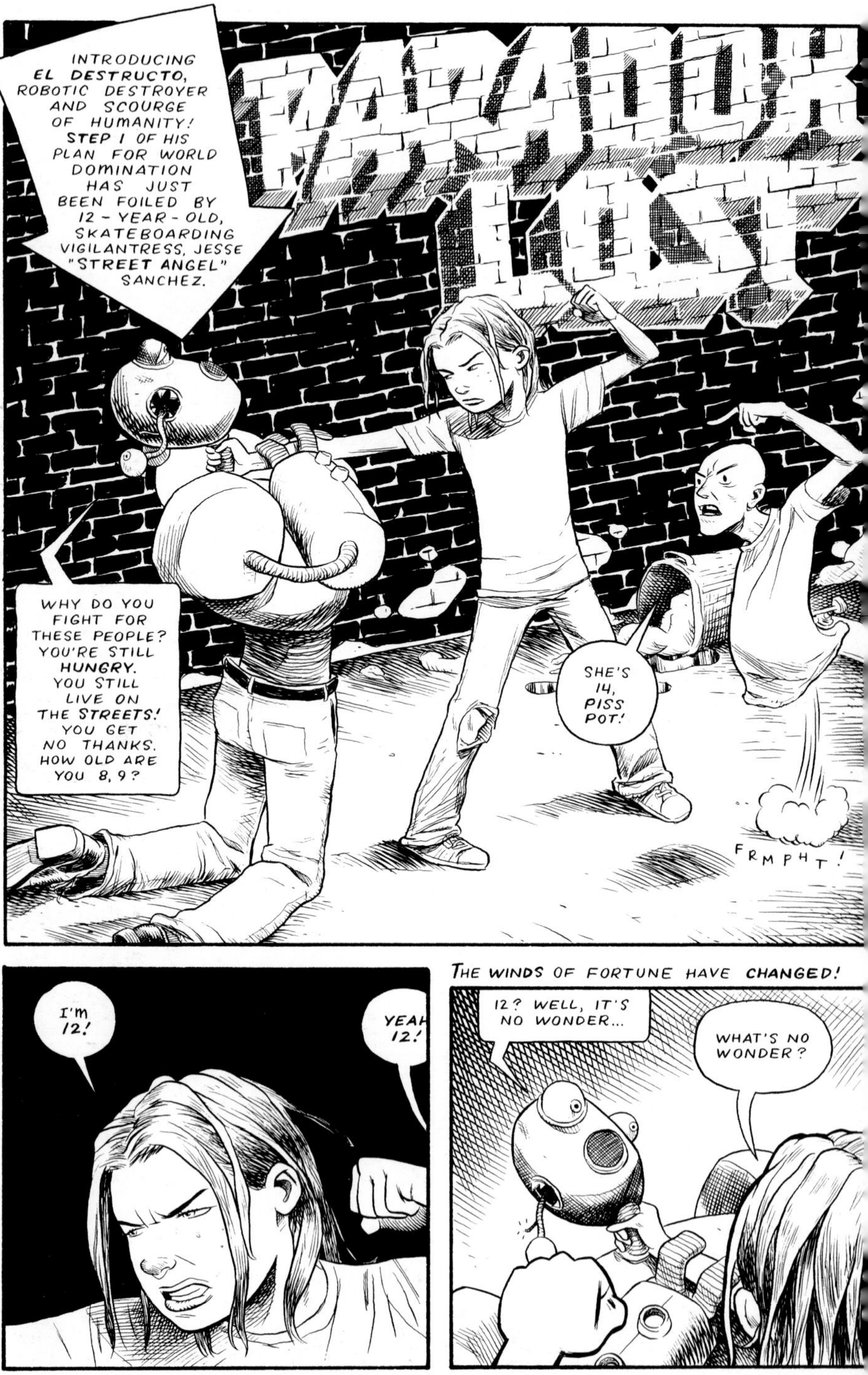

INTRODUCING **EL DESTRUCTO**, ROBOTIC DESTROYER AND SCOURGE OF HUMANITY! **STEP 1** OF HIS PLAN FOR WORLD DOMINATION HAS JUST BEEN FOILED BY 12 - YEAR - OLD, SKATEBOARDING VIGILANTRESS, JESSE "**STREET ANGEL**" SANCHEZ.
WHY DO YOU FIGHT FOR THESE PEOPLE? YOU'RE STILL **HUNGRY**. YOU STILL LIVE ON THE **STREETS**! YOU GET NO THANKS. HOW OLD ARE YOU 8, 9?
SHE'S 14, PISS POT!
FRMPHT!
I'M 12!
YEAH 12!
THE **WINDS** OF FORTUNE HAVE **CHANGED**!
12? WELL, IT'S NO WONDER...
WHAT'S NO WONDER?

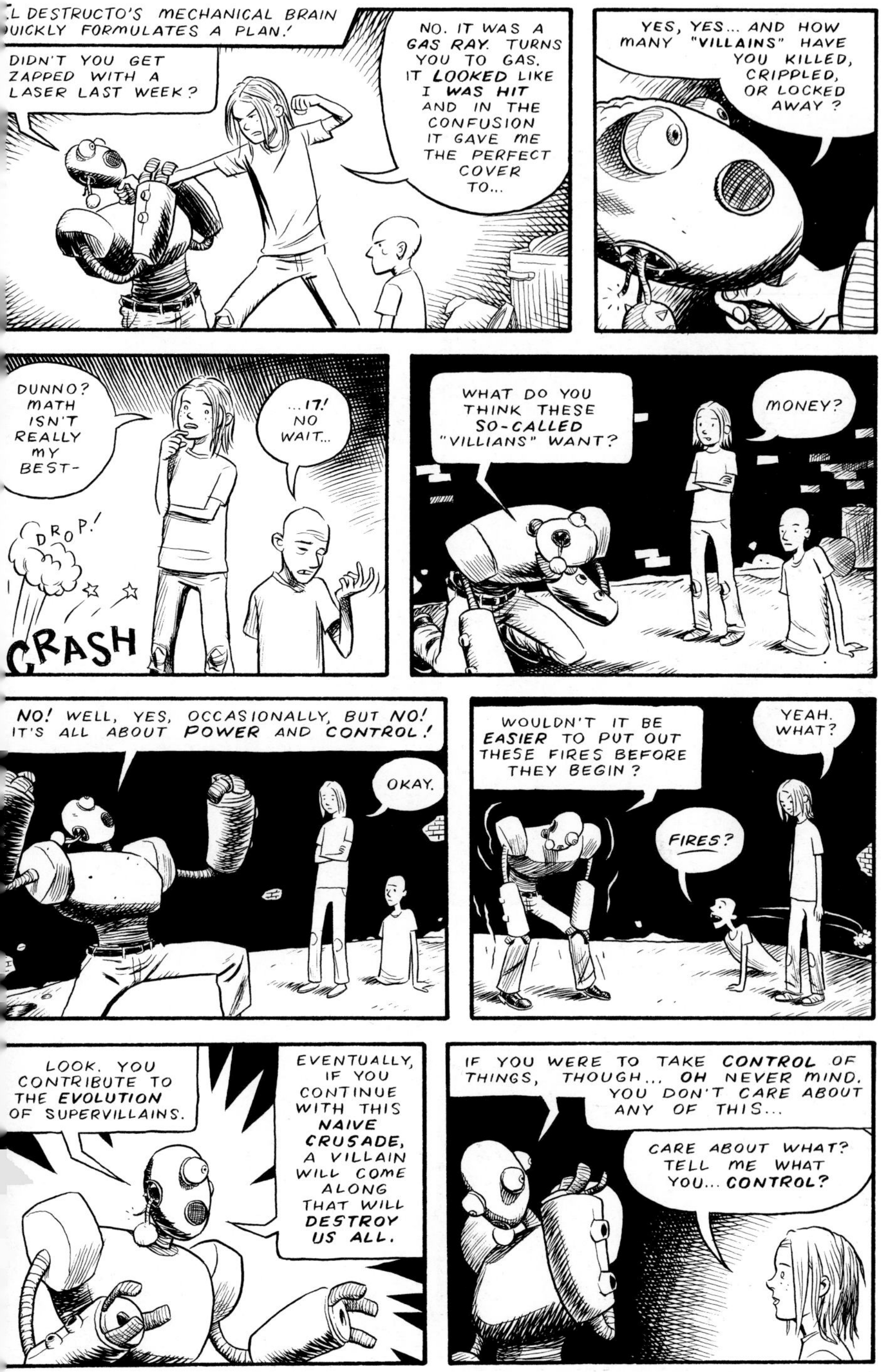

L DESTRUCTO'S MECHANICAL BRAIN
UICKLY FORMULATES A PLAN!
DIDN'T YOU GET ZAPPED WITH A LASER LAST WEEK?
NO. IT WAS A GAS RAY. TURNS YOU TO GAS. IT LOOKED LIKE I WAS HIT AND IN THE CONFUSION IT GAVE ME THE PERFECT COVER TO...
YES, YES... AND HOW MANY "VILLAINS" HAVE YOU KILLED, CRIPPLED, OR LOCKED AWAY?
DUNNO? MATH ISN'T REALLY MY BEST-
...IT! NO WAIT...
DROP!
CRASH
WHAT DO YOU THINK THESE SO-CALLED "VILLIANS" WANT?
MONEY?
NO! WELL, YES, OCCASIONALLY, BUT NO! IT'S ALL ABOUT POWER AND CONTROL!
OKAY.
WOULDN'T IT BE EASIER TO PUT OUT THESE FIRES BEFORE THEY BEGIN?
YEAH. WHAT?
FIRES?
LOOK. YOU CONTRIBUTE TO THE EVOLUTION OF SUPERVILLAINS.
EVENTUALLY, IF YOU CONTINUE WITH THIS NAIVE CRUSADE, A VILLAIN WILL COME ALONG THAT WILL DESTROY US ALL.
IF YOU WERE TO TAKE CONTROL OF THINGS, THOUGH... OH NEVER MIND. YOU DON'T CARE ABOUT ANY OF THIS...
CARE ABOUT WHAT? TELL ME WHAT YOU... CONTROL?

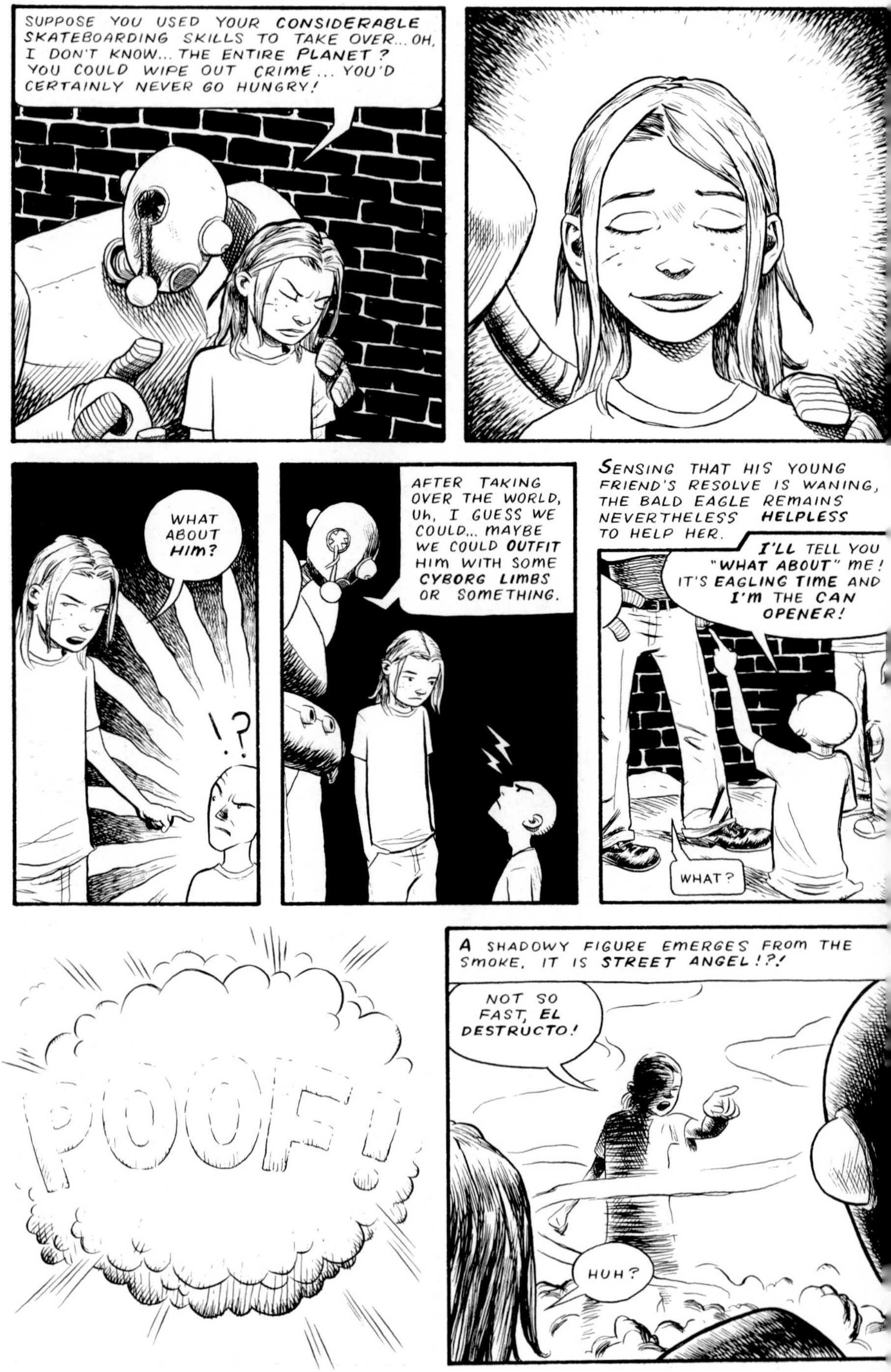
SUPPOSE YOU USED YOUR CONSIDERABLE SKATEBOARDING SKILLS TO TAKE OVER... OH, I DON'T KNOW... THE ENTIRE PLANET? YOU COULD WIPE OUT CRIME... YOU'D CERTAINLY NEVER GO HUNGRY!
WHAT ABOUT HIM?
!?
AFTER TAKING OVER THE WORLD, Uh, I GUESS WE COULD... MAYBE WE COULD OUTFIT HIM WITH SOME CYBORG LIMBS OR SOMETHING.
SENSING THAT HIS YOUNG FRIEND'S RESOLVE IS WANING, THE BALD EAGLE REMAINS NEVERTHELESS HELPLESS TO HELP HER.
I'LL TELL YOU "WHAT ABOUT" ME! IT'S EAGLING TIME AND I'M THE CAN OPENER!
WHAT?
POOF!
A SHADOWY FIGURE EMERGES FROM THE SMOKE, IT IS STREET ANGEL!?!
NOT SO FAST, EL DESTRUCTO!
HUH?

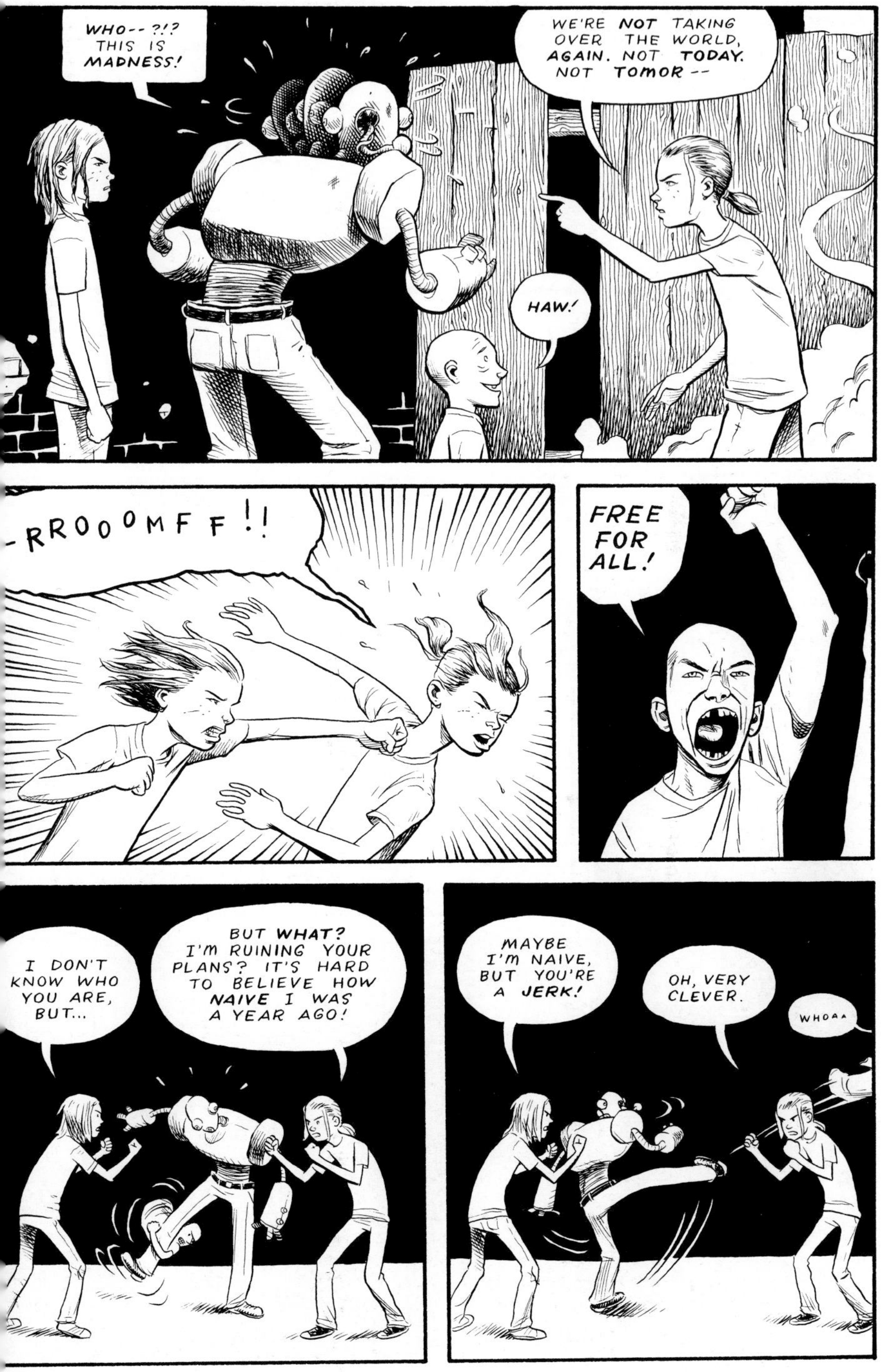
WHO--?!? THIS IS MADNESS!
WE'RE NOT TAKING OVER THE WORLD, AGAIN. NOT TODAY. NOT TOMOR--
HAW!
-RROOOMFF!!
FREE FOR ALL!
I DON'T KNOW WHO YOU ARE, BUT...
BUT WHAT? I'M RUINING YOUR PLANS? IT'S HARD TO BELIEVE HOW NAIVE I WAS A YEAR AGO!
MAYBE I'M NAIVE, BUT YOU'RE A JERK!
OH, VERY CLEVER.
WHOAA

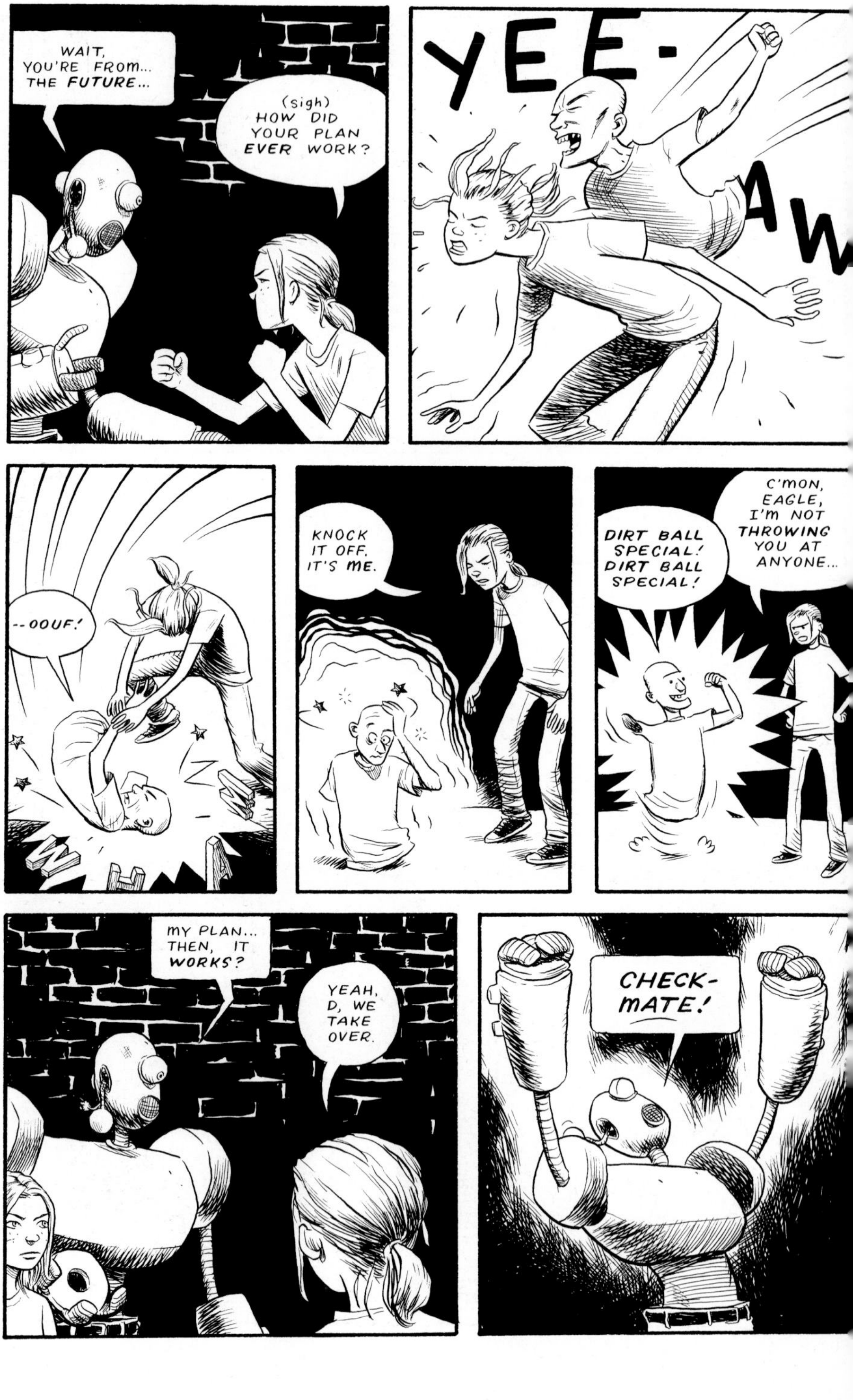
WAIT, YOU'RE FROM... THE FUTURE...
(sigh) HOW DID YOUR PLAN EVER WORK?
YEE-AW
--OOUF!
KNOCK IT OFF. IT'S ME.
DIRT BALL SPECIAL! DIRT BALL SPECIAL!
C'MON, EAGLE, I'M NOT THROWING YOU AT ANYONE...
MY PLAN... THEN, IT WORKS?
YEAH, D, WE TAKE OVER.
CHECK-MATE!

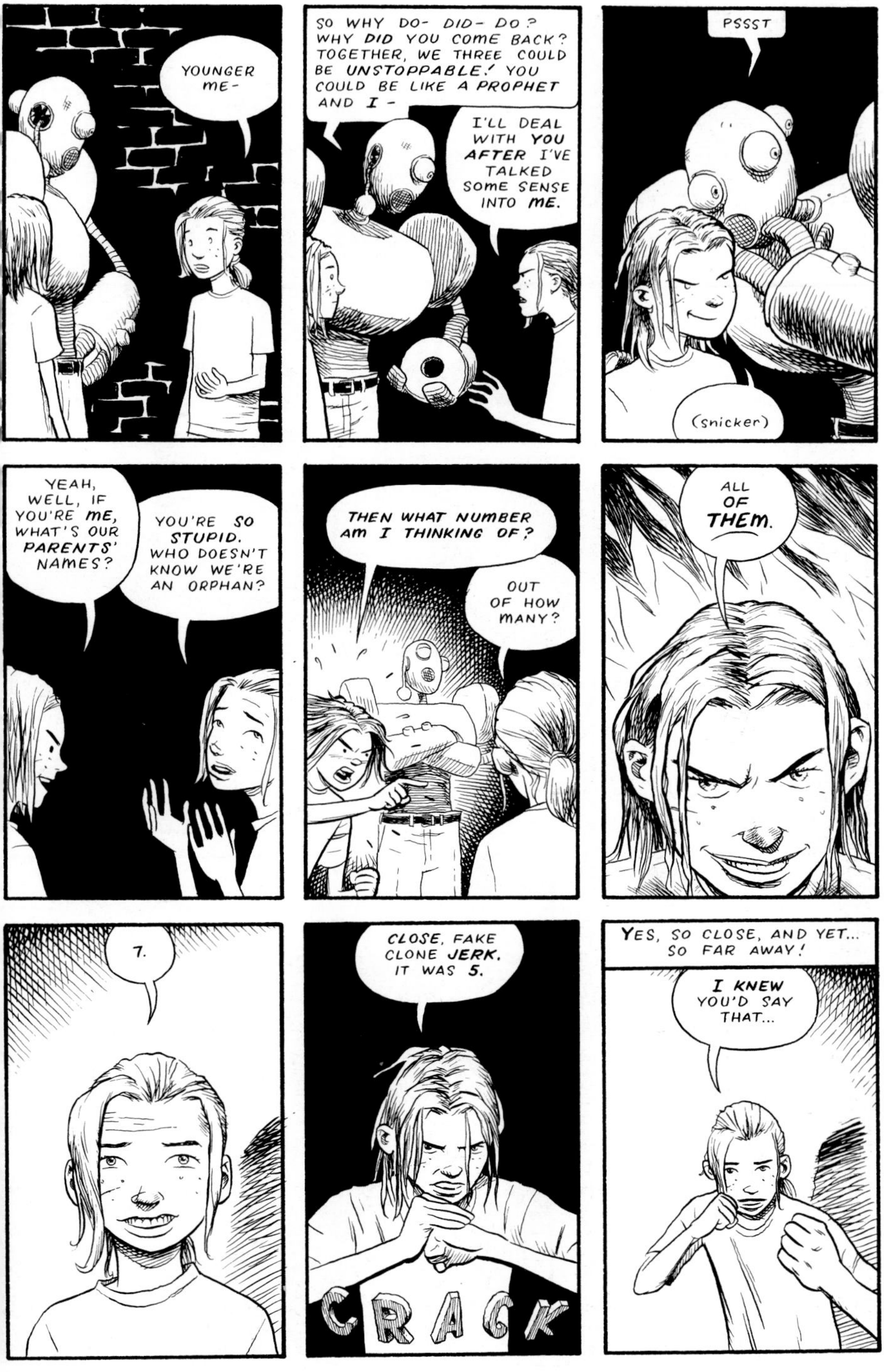
YOUNGER ME-
SO WHY DO- DID- DO? WHY DID YOU COME BACK? TOGETHER, WE THREE COULD BE UNSTOPPABLE! YOU COULD BE LIKE A PROPHET AND I -
I'LL DEAL WITH YOU AFTER I'VE TALKED SOME SENSE INTO ME.
PSSST
(snicker)
YEAH, WELL, IF YOU'RE ME, WHAT'S OUR PARENTS' NAMES?
YOU'RE SO STUPID. WHO DOESN'T KNOW WE'RE AN ORPHAN?
THEN WHAT NUMBER AM I THINKING OF?
OUT OF HOW MANY?
ALL OF THEM.
7.
CLOSE, FAKE CLONE JERK. IT WAS 5.
CRACK
YES, SO CLOSE, AND YET... SO FAR AWAY!
I KNEW YOU'D SAY THAT...

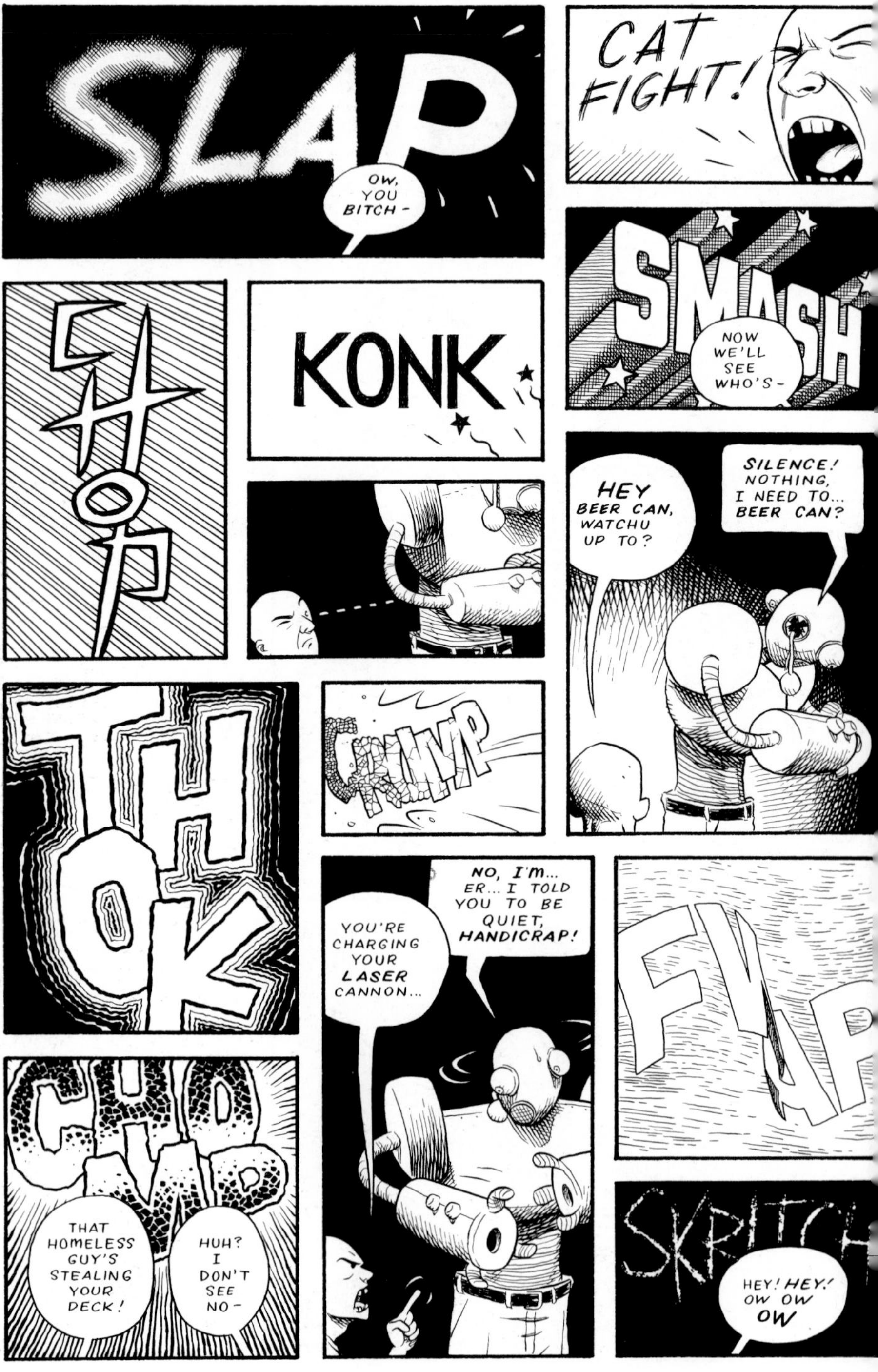
SLAP
OW, YOU BITCH -
CAT FIGHT!
SMASH
NOW WE'LL SEE WHO'S -
CHOP
KONK
HEY BEER CAN, WATCHU UP TO?
SILENCE! NOTHING, I NEED TO... BEER CAN?
THOOK
CRUMP
NO, I'M... ER... I TOLD YOU TO BE QUIET, HANDICRAP!
YOU'RE CHARGING YOUR LASER CANNON...
FWAP
CHOMP
THAT HOMELESS GUY'S STEALING YOUR DECK!
HUH? I DON'T SEE NO -
SKRITCH
HEY! HEY! OW OW OW

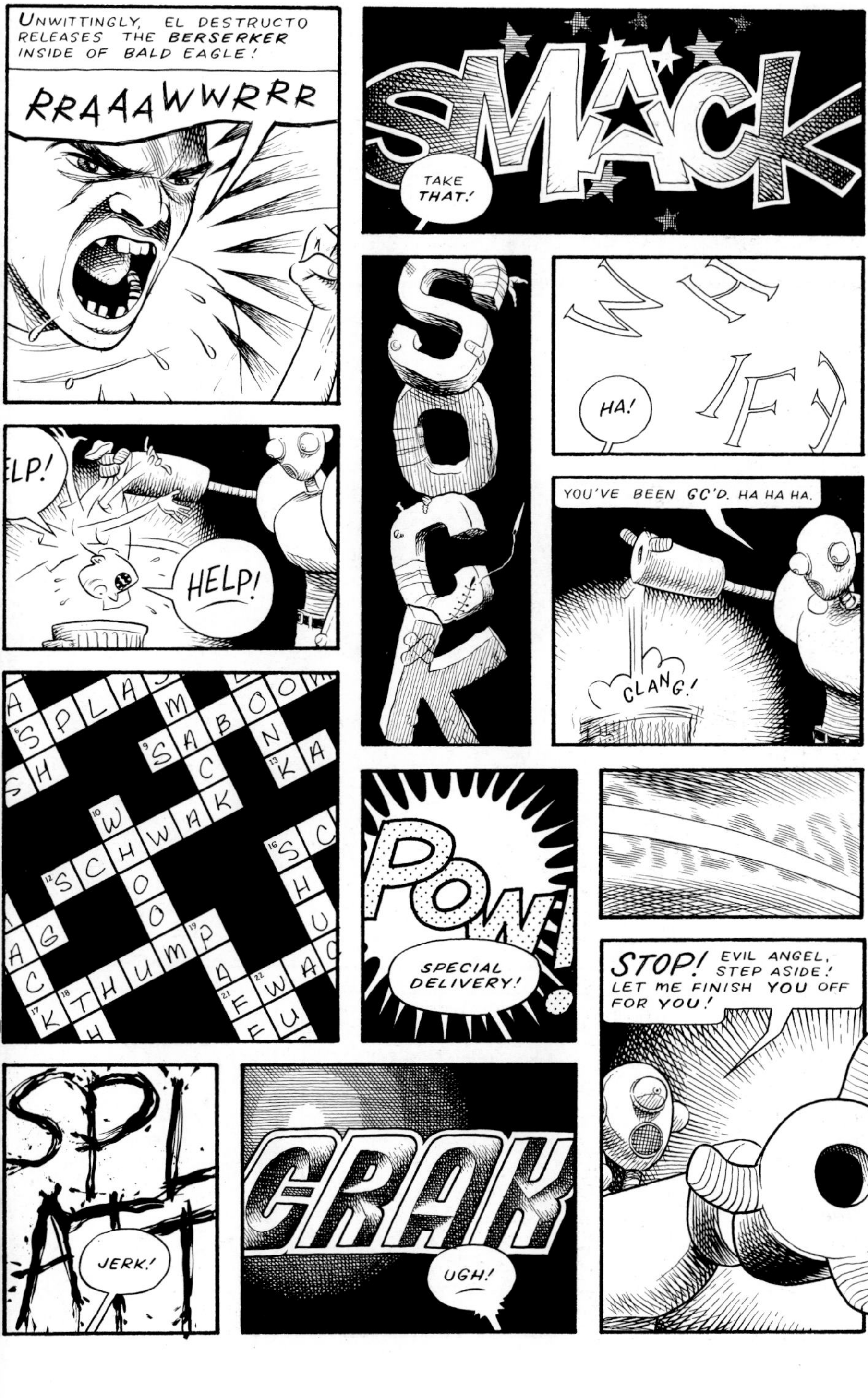

UNWITTINGLY, EL DESTRUCTO RELEASES THE BERSERKER INSIDE OF BALD EAGLE!
RRAAAWWRRR
SMACK
TAKE THAT!
SOCK
WHAMMY
HA!
YOU'VE BEEN GC'D. HA HA HA.
HELP!
HELP!
CLANG!
POW!
SPECIAL DELIVERY!
STOP! EVIL ANGEL, STEP ASIDE! LET ME FINISH YOU OFF FOR YOU!
SPLAT
JERK!
CRAK
UGH!

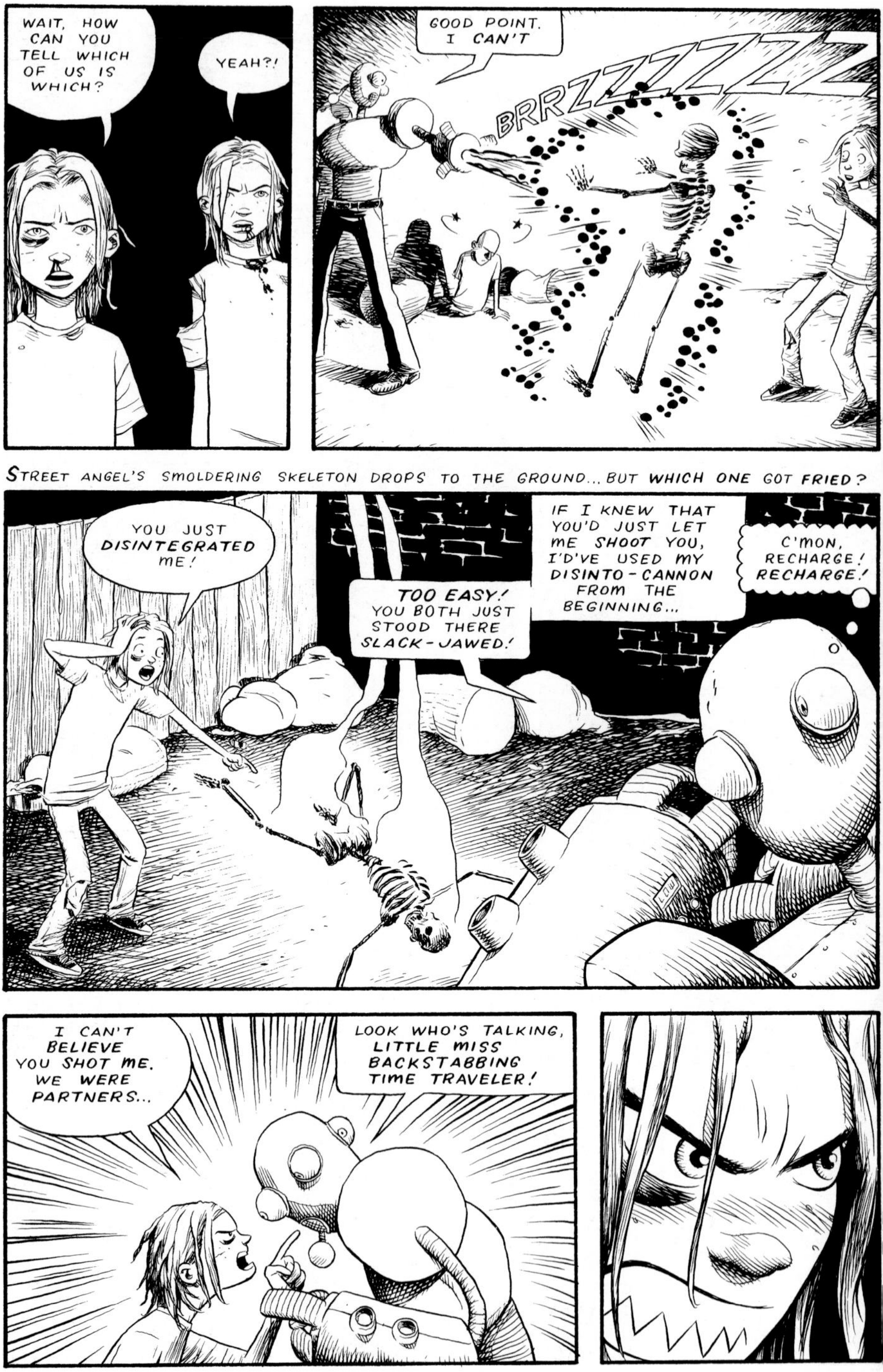
WAIT, HOW CAN YOU TELL WHICH OF US IS WHICH?
YEAH?!
GOOD POINT. I CAN'T
BRRZZZZZZZZ
STREET ANGEL'S SMOLDERING SKELETON DROPS TO THE GROUND... BUT WHICH ONE GOT FRIED?
YOU JUST DISINTEGRATED ME!
TOO EASY! YOU BOTH JUST STOOD THERE SLACK-JAWED!
IF I KNEW THAT YOU'D JUST LET ME SHOOT YOU, I'D'VE USED MY DISINTO-CANNON FROM THE BEGINNING...
C'MON, RECHARGE! RECHARGE!
I CAN'T BELIEVE YOU SHOT ME. WE WERE PARTNERS...
LOOK WHO'S TALKING, LITTLE MISS BACKSTABBING TIME TRAVELER!

BOOM!

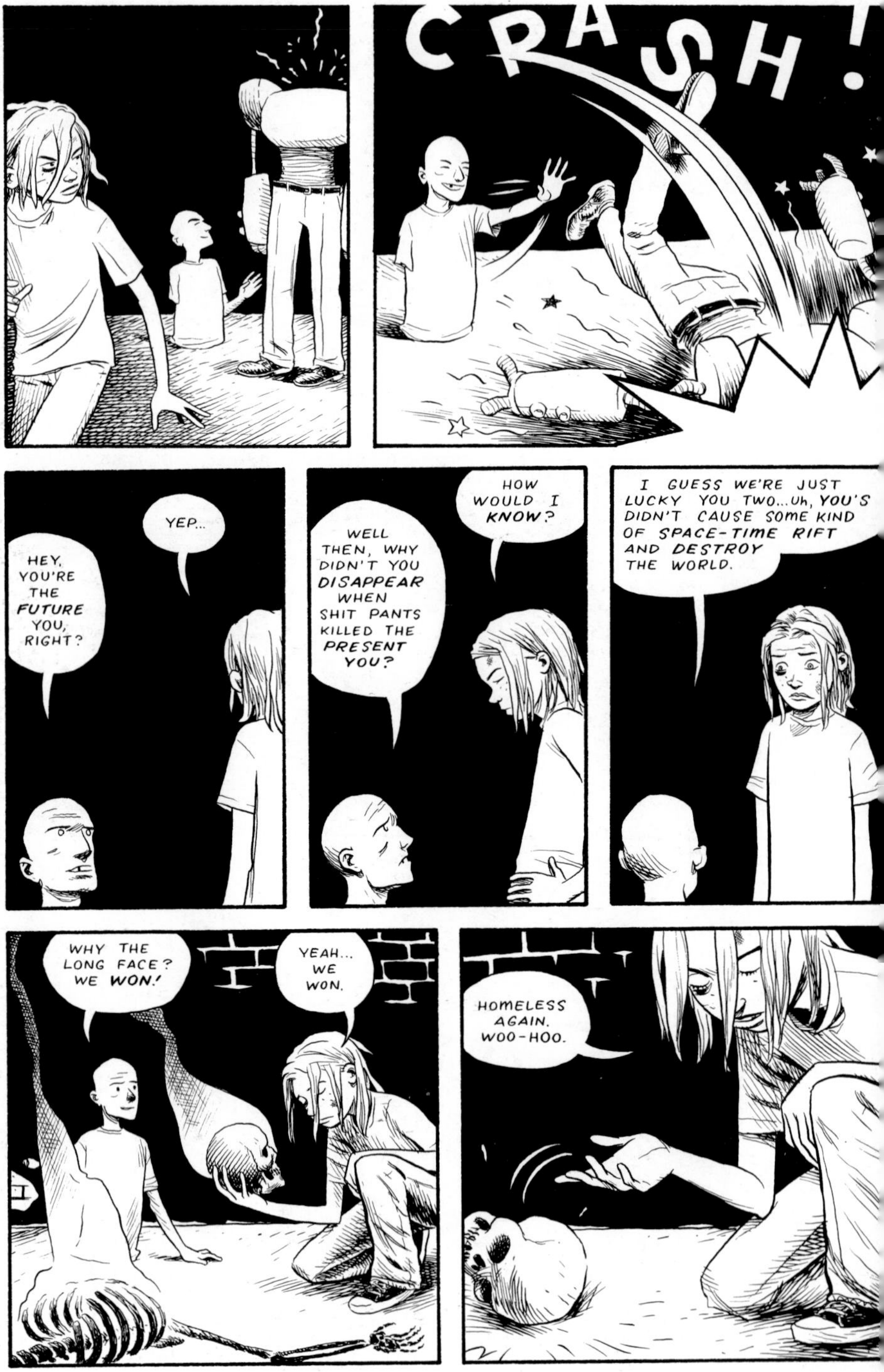
CRASH!
HEY, YOU'RE THE FUTURE YOU, RIGHT?
YEP...
WELL THEN, WHY DIDN'T YOU DISAPPEAR WHEN SHIT PANTS KILLED THE PRESENT YOU?
HOW WOULD I KNOW?
I GUESS WE'RE JUST LUCKY YOU TWO...Uh, YOU'S DIDN'T CAUSE SOME KIND OF SPACE-TIME RIFT AND DESTROY THE WORLD.
WHY THE LONG FACE? WE WON!
YEAH... WE WON.
HOMELESS AGAIN. WOO-HOO.

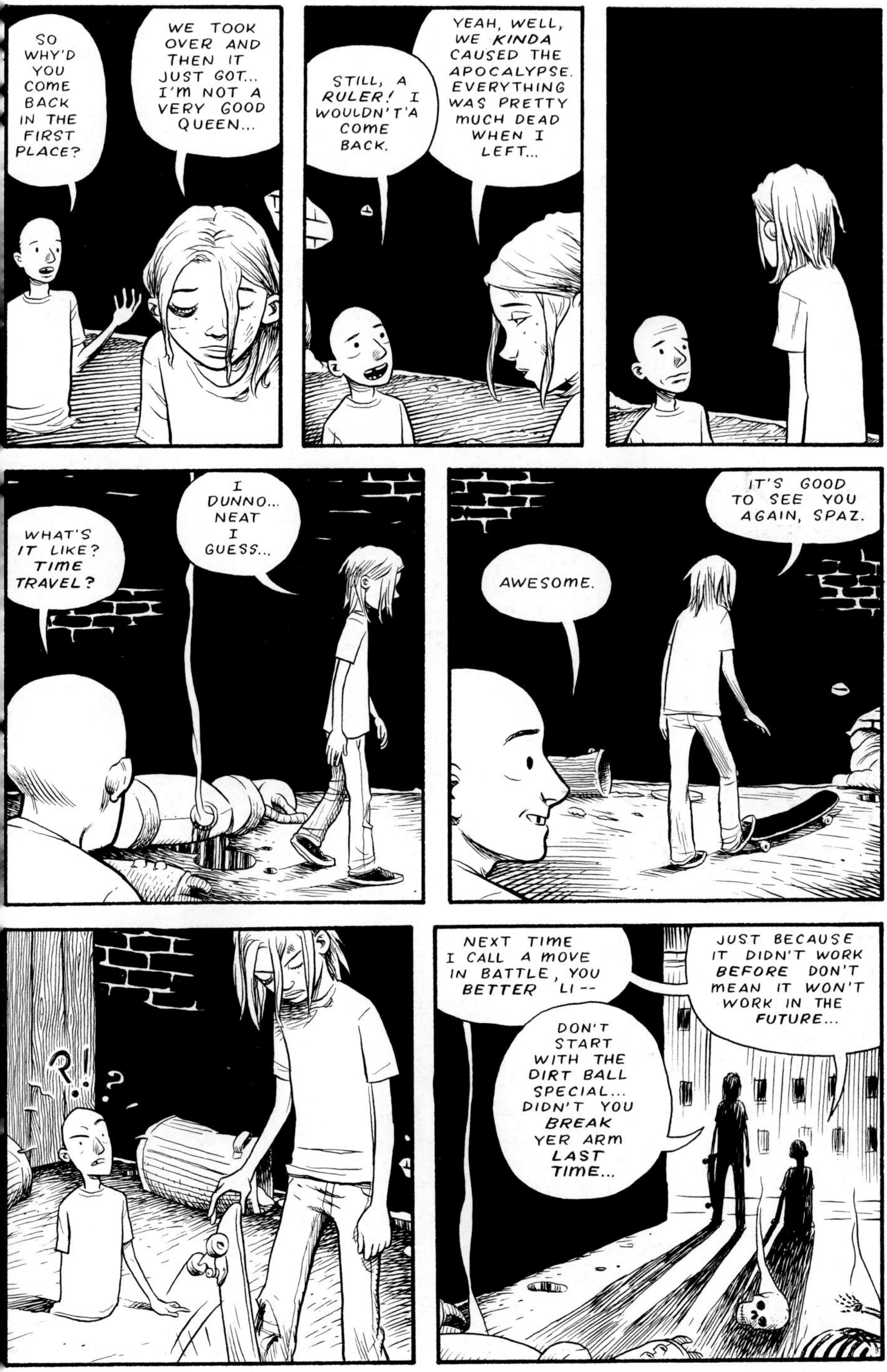
SO WHY'D YOU COME BACK IN THE FIRST PLACE?
WE TOOK OVER AND THEN IT JUST GOT... I'M NOT A VERY GOOD QUEEN...
STILL, A RULER! I WOULDN'T'A COME BACK.
YEAH, WELL, WE KINDA CAUSED THE APOCALYPSE. EVERYTHING WAS PRETTY MUCH DEAD WHEN I LEFT...
WHAT'S IT LIKE? TIME TRAVEL?
I DUNNO... NEAT I GUESS...
IT'S GOOD TO SEE YOU AGAIN, SPAZ.
AWESOME.
?!
?
NEXT TIME I CALL A MOVE IN BATTLE, YOU BETTER LI--
JUST BECAUSE IT DIDN'T WORK BEFORE DON'T MEAN IT WON'T WORK IN THE FUTURE...
DON'T START WITH THE DIRT BALL SPECIAL... DIDN'T YOU BREAK YER ARM LAST TIME...

THE END

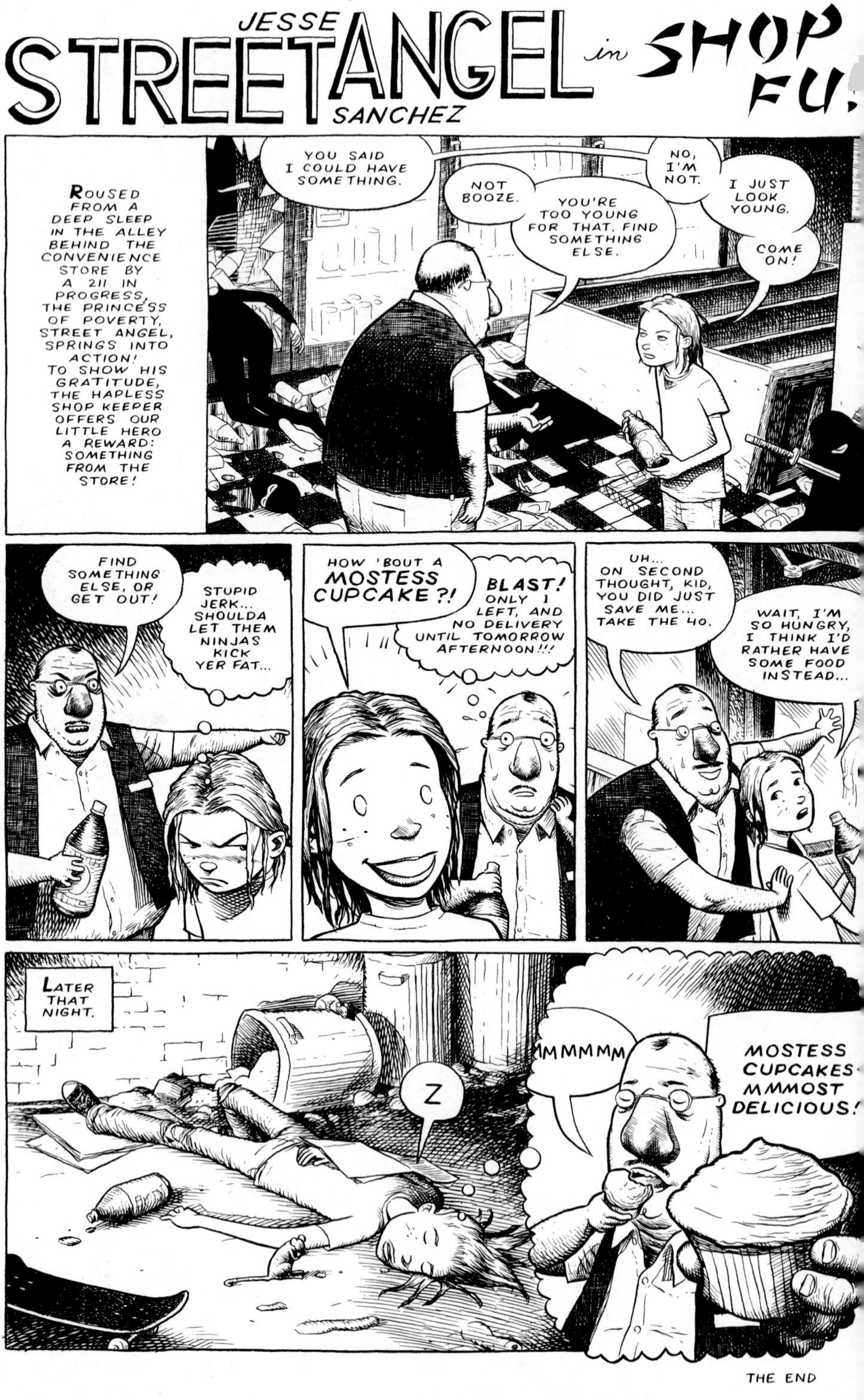
JESSE STREET ANGEL SANCHEZ in SHOP FU
ROUSED FROM A DEEP SLEEP IN THE ALLEY BEHIND THE CONVENIENCE STORE BY A 211 IN PROGRESS, THE PRINCESS OF POVERTY, STREET ANGEL, SPRINGS INTO ACTION! TO SHOW HIS GRATITUDE, THE HAPLESS SHOP KEEPER OFFERS OUR LITTLE HERO A REWARD: SOMETHING FROM THE STORE!
YOU SAID I COULD HAVE SOMETHING.
NOT BOOZE.
YOU'RE TOO YOUNG FOR THAT. FIND SOMETHING ELSE.
NO, I'M NOT.
I JUST LOOK YOUNG.
COME ON!
FIND SOMETHING ELSE, OR GET OUT!
STUPID JERK... SHOULDA LET THEM NINJAS KICK YER FAT...
HOW 'BOUT A MOSTESS CUPCAKE?!
BLAST! ONLY 1 LEFT, AND NO DELIVERY UNTIL TOMORROW AFTERNOON!!!
UH... ON SECOND THOUGHT, KID, YOU DID JUST SAVE ME... TAKE THE 40.
WAIT, I'M SO HUNGRY, I THINK I'D RATHER HAVE SOME FOOD INSTEAD...
LATER THAT NIGHT.
Z
MMMMMM
MOSTESS CUPCAKES MMMOST DELICIOUS!
THE END

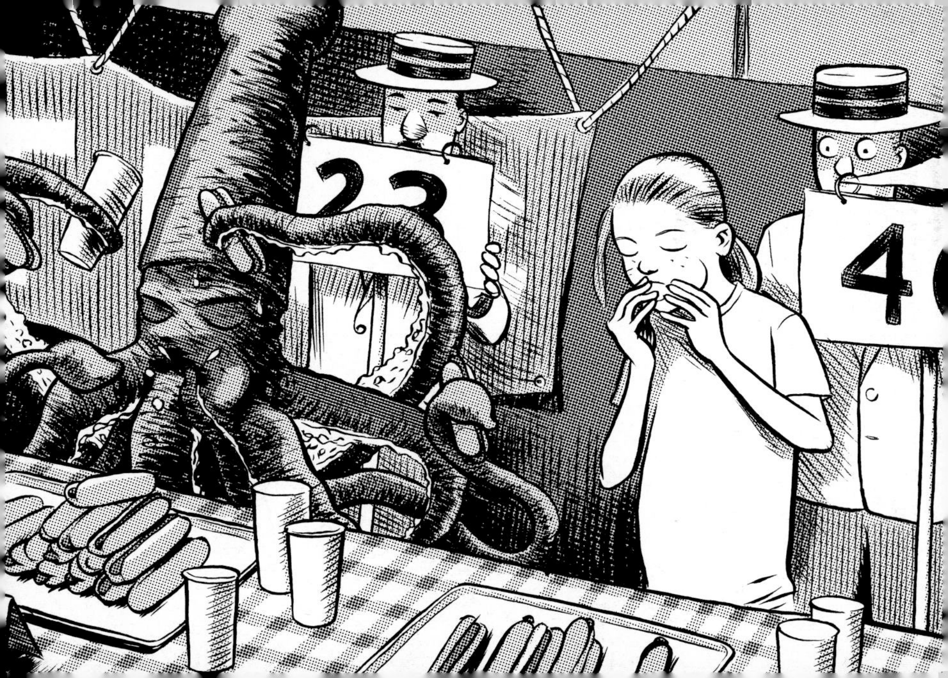
23
4

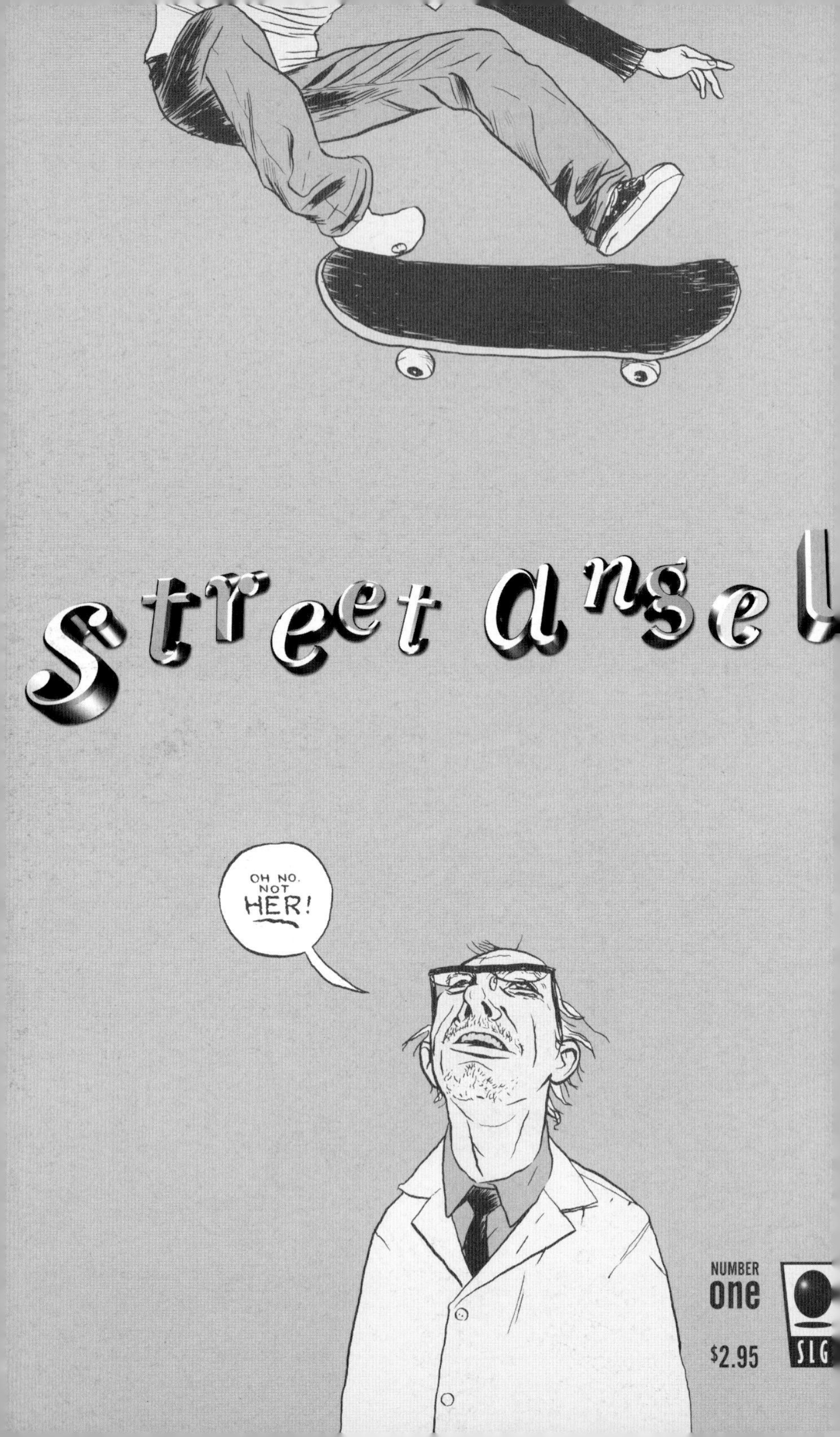
street angel
OH NO. NOT HER!
NUMBER one
$2.95
SLG

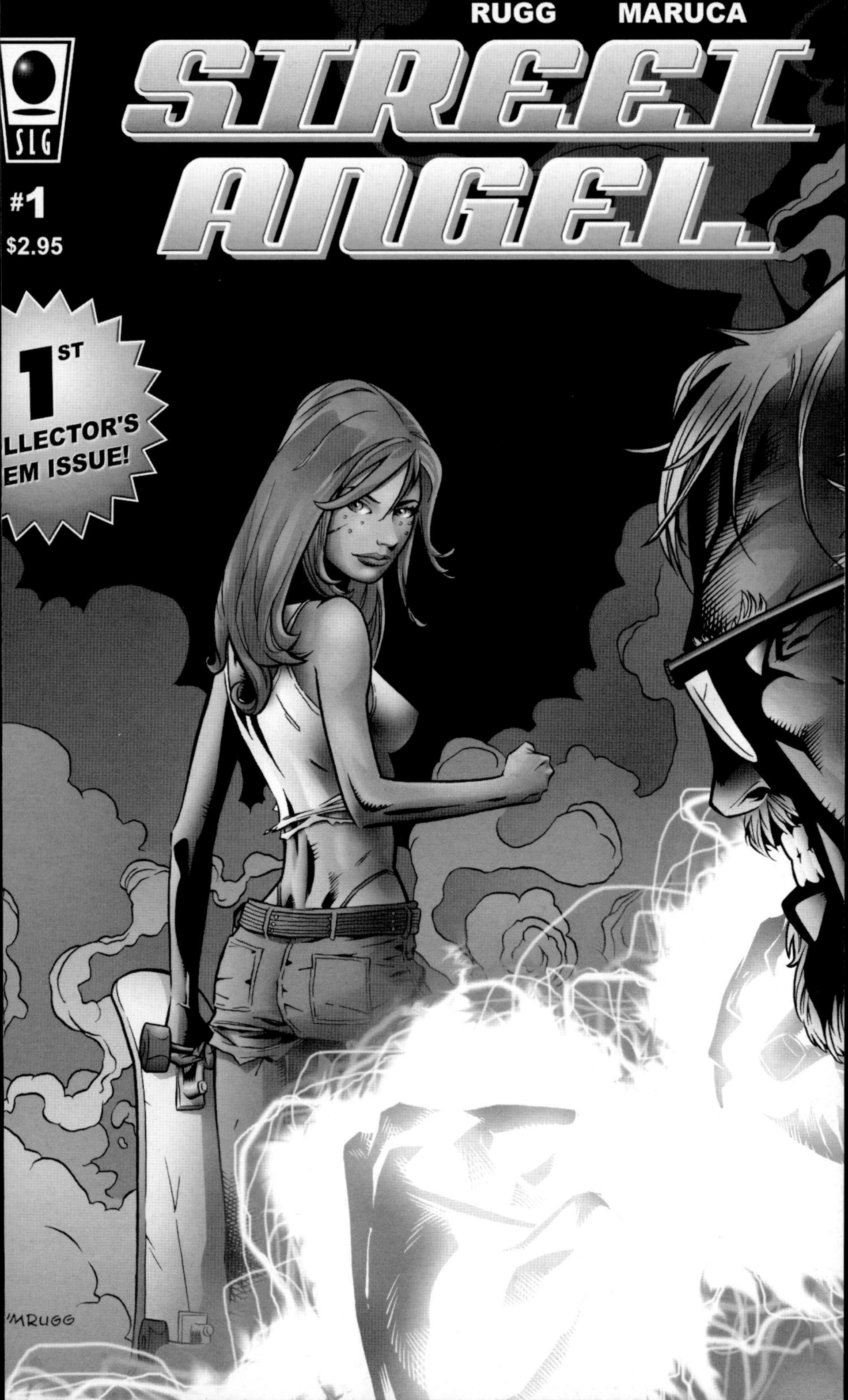
RUGG MARUCA
STREET ANGEL
SLG
#1
$2.95
1ST
LLECTOR'S
EM ISSUE!

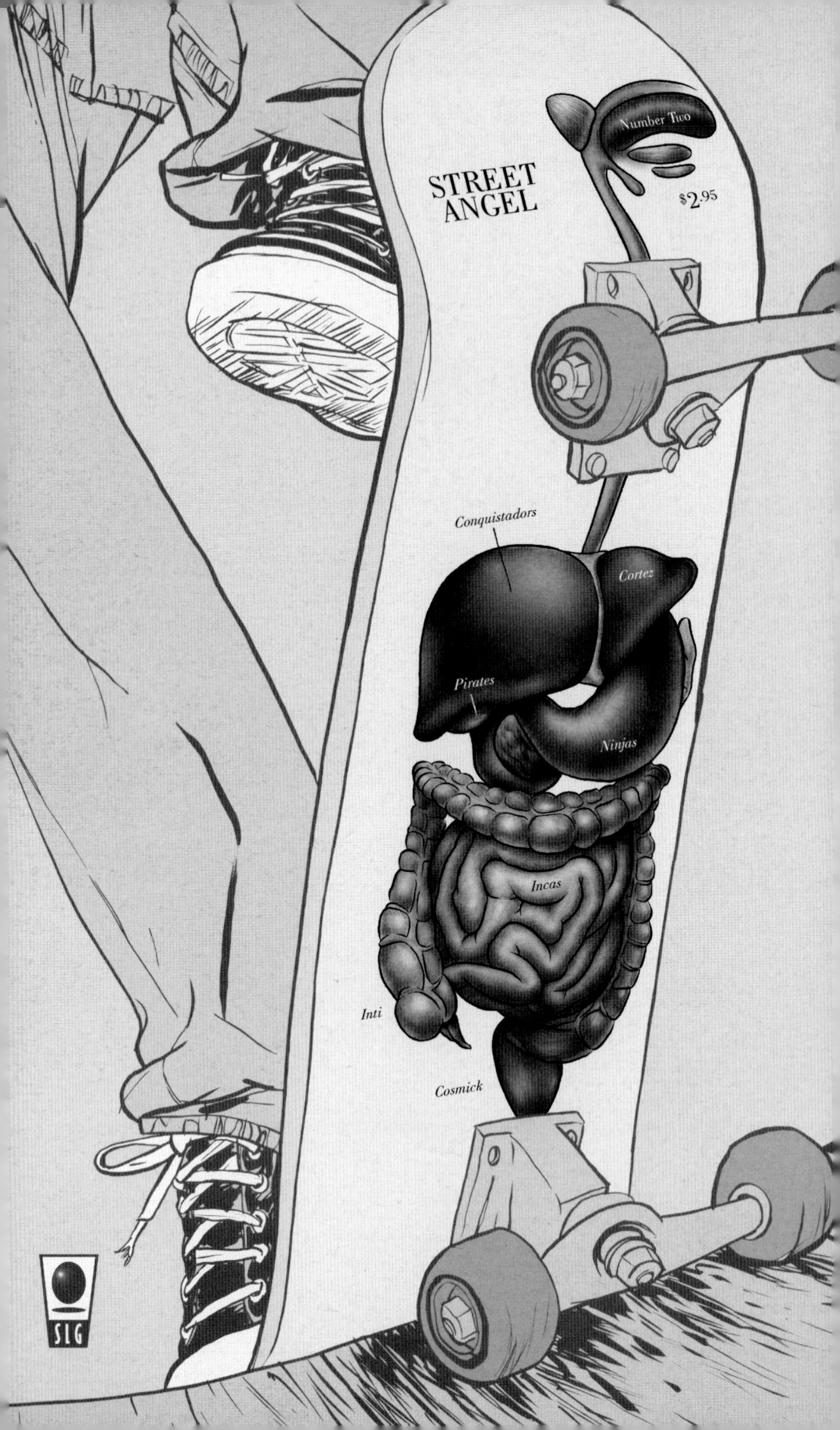
STREET ANGEL
Number Two
$2.95
Conquistadors
Cortez
Pirates
Ninjas
Incas
Inti
Cosmick
SLG

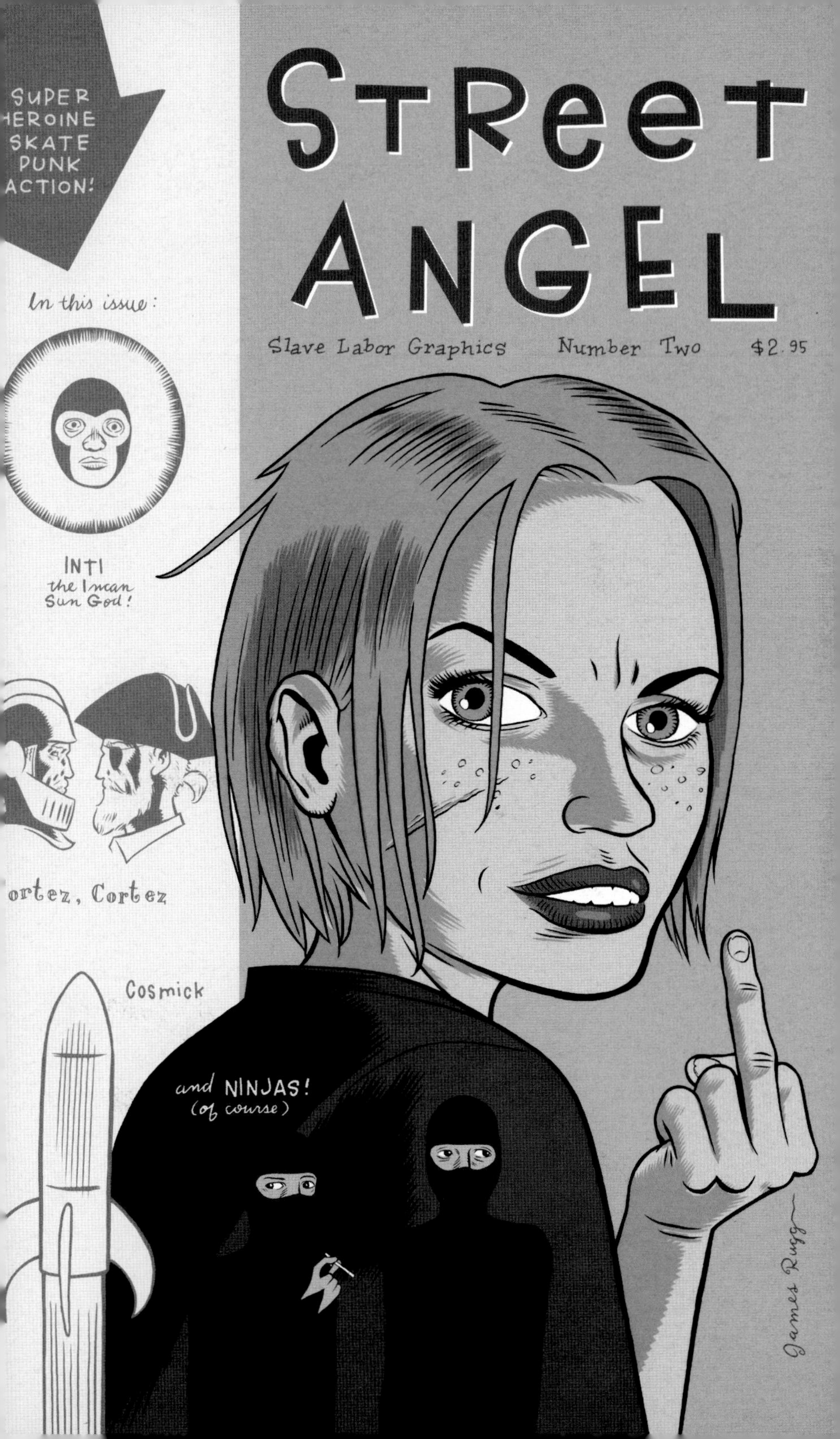
SUPER HEROINE SKATE PUNK ACTION!
STREET ANGEL
Slave Labor Graphics
Number Two
$2.95
In this issue:
INTI the Incan Sun God!
ortez, Cortez
Cosmick
and NINJAS! (of course)
James Rugg

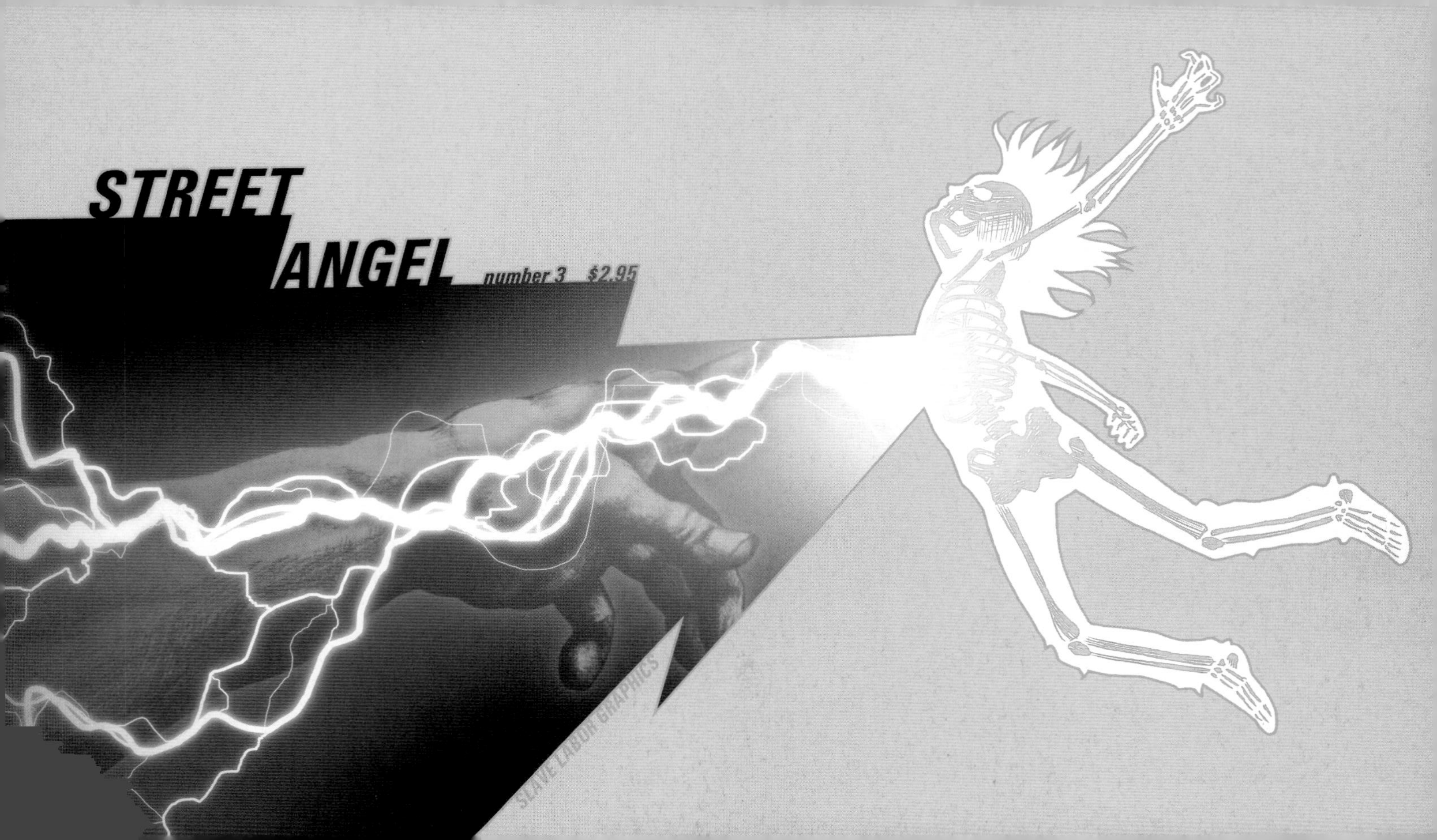
STREET
ANGEL
number 3 $2.95
SLAVE LABOR GRAPHICS

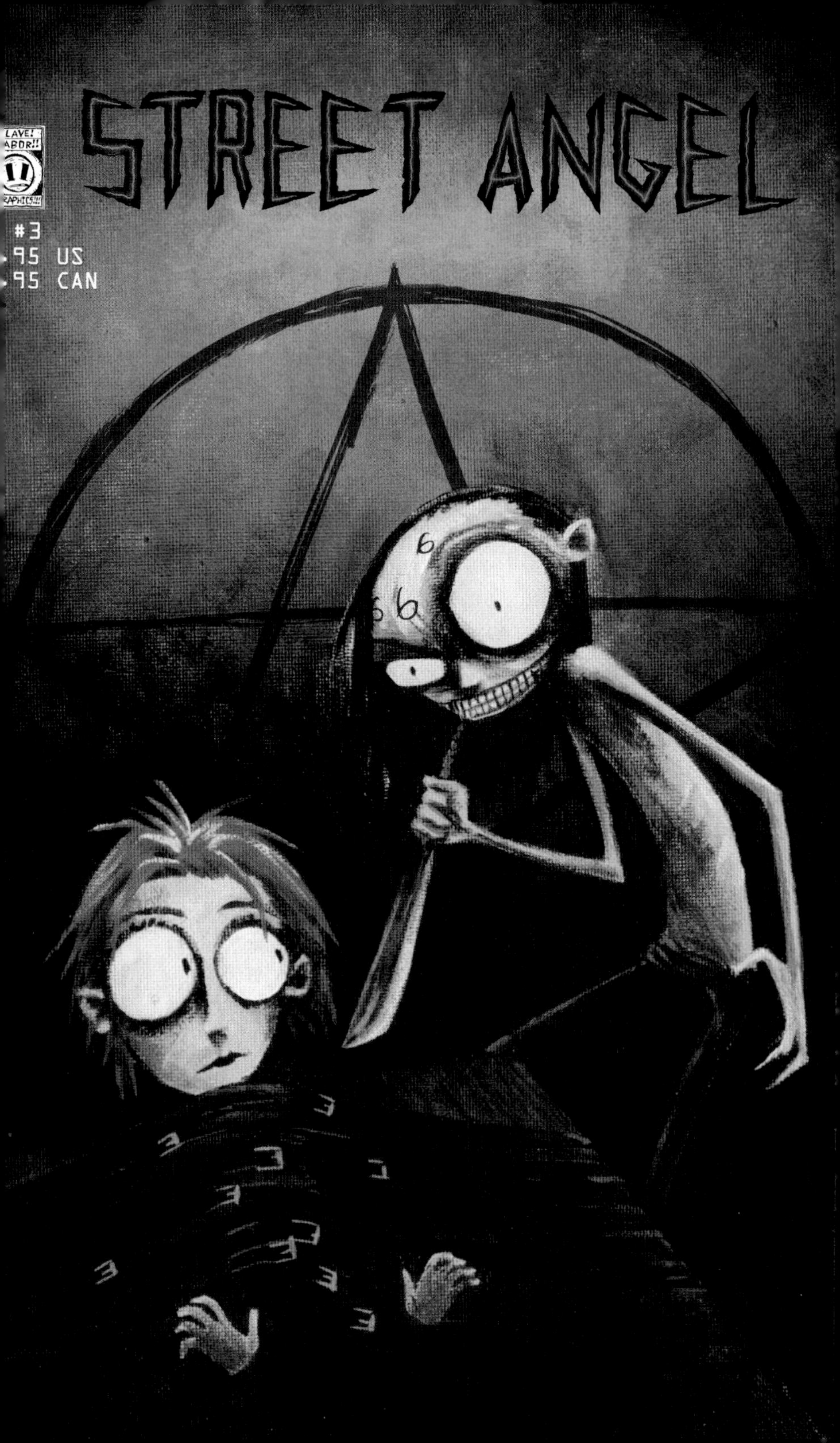
STREET ANGEL
#3
95 US
95 CAN
6
66

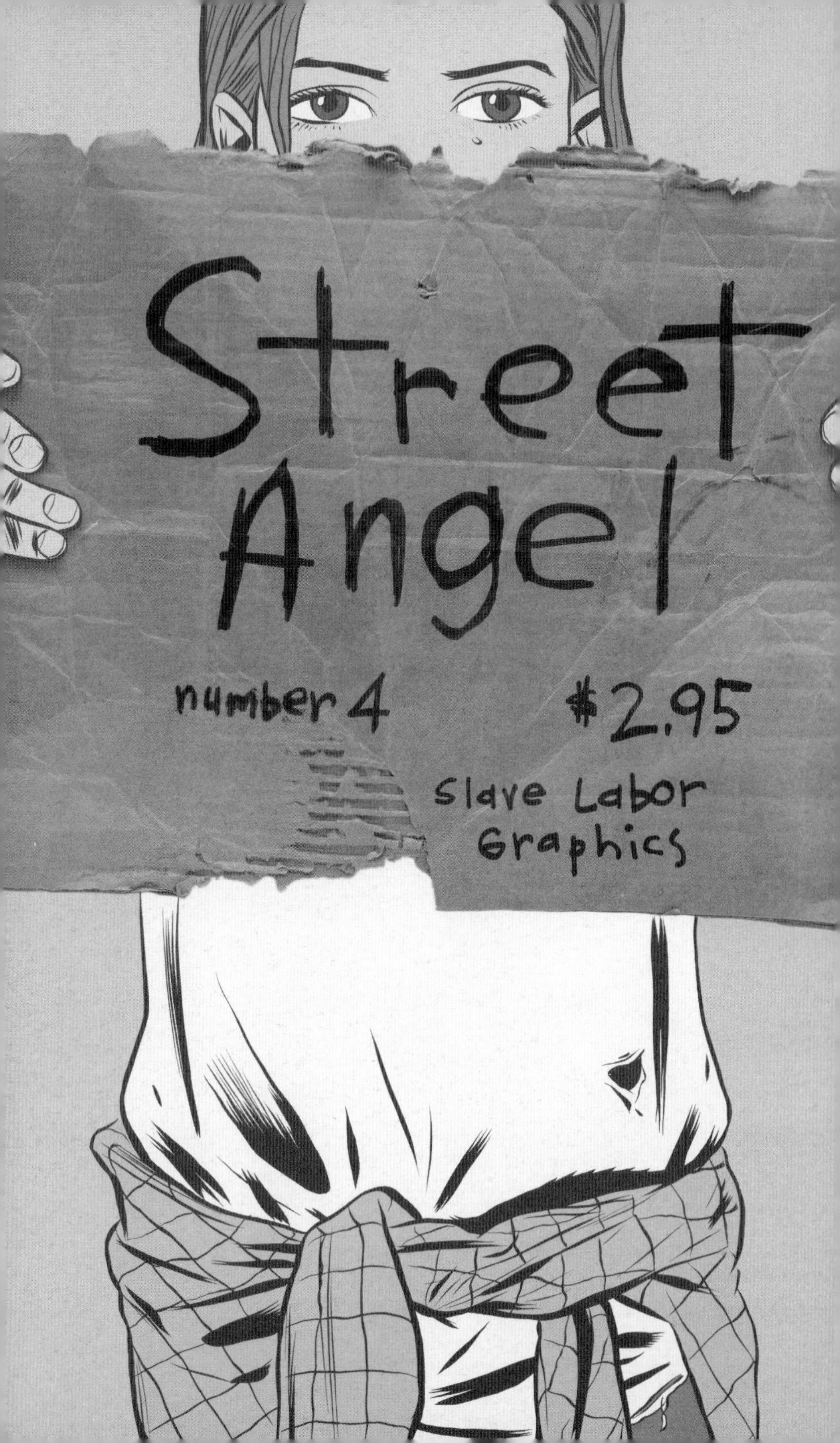
Street Angel
number 4
$2.95
Slave Labor Graphics

Street Angel

SHUX I'M HUNGRY. IF'N I DON'T FIND SOMETHIN' TO EAT SOON, I'M GONNA PASS OUT. THE WAR EFFORT'S GOT EVERYONE PINCHIN' PENNIES, AN' IT SURE BLOWS!

JAMES RUGG

Number 4. $2.95 Published by Slave Labor Graphics.

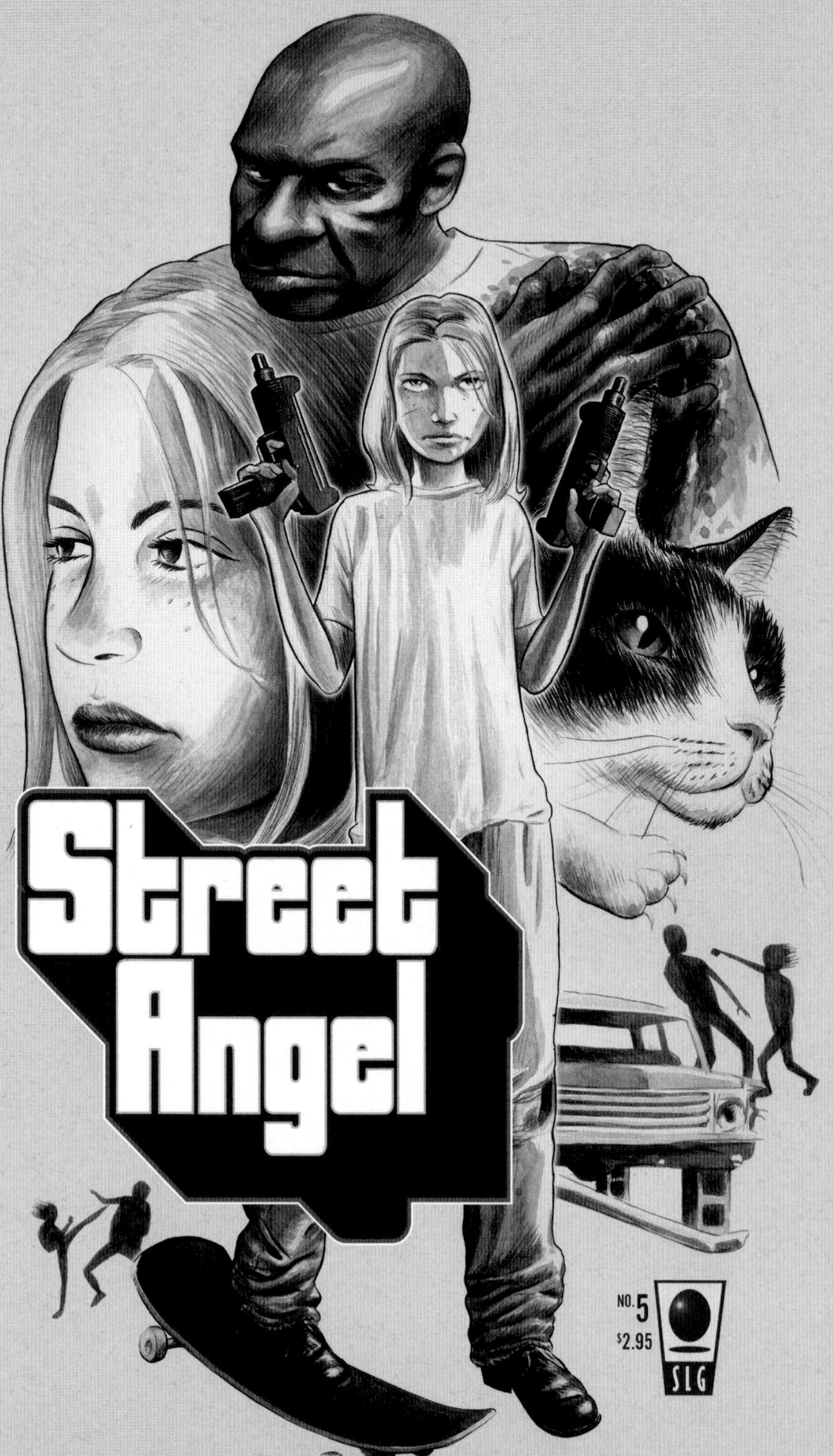

Street Angel
NO. 5
$2.95
SLG

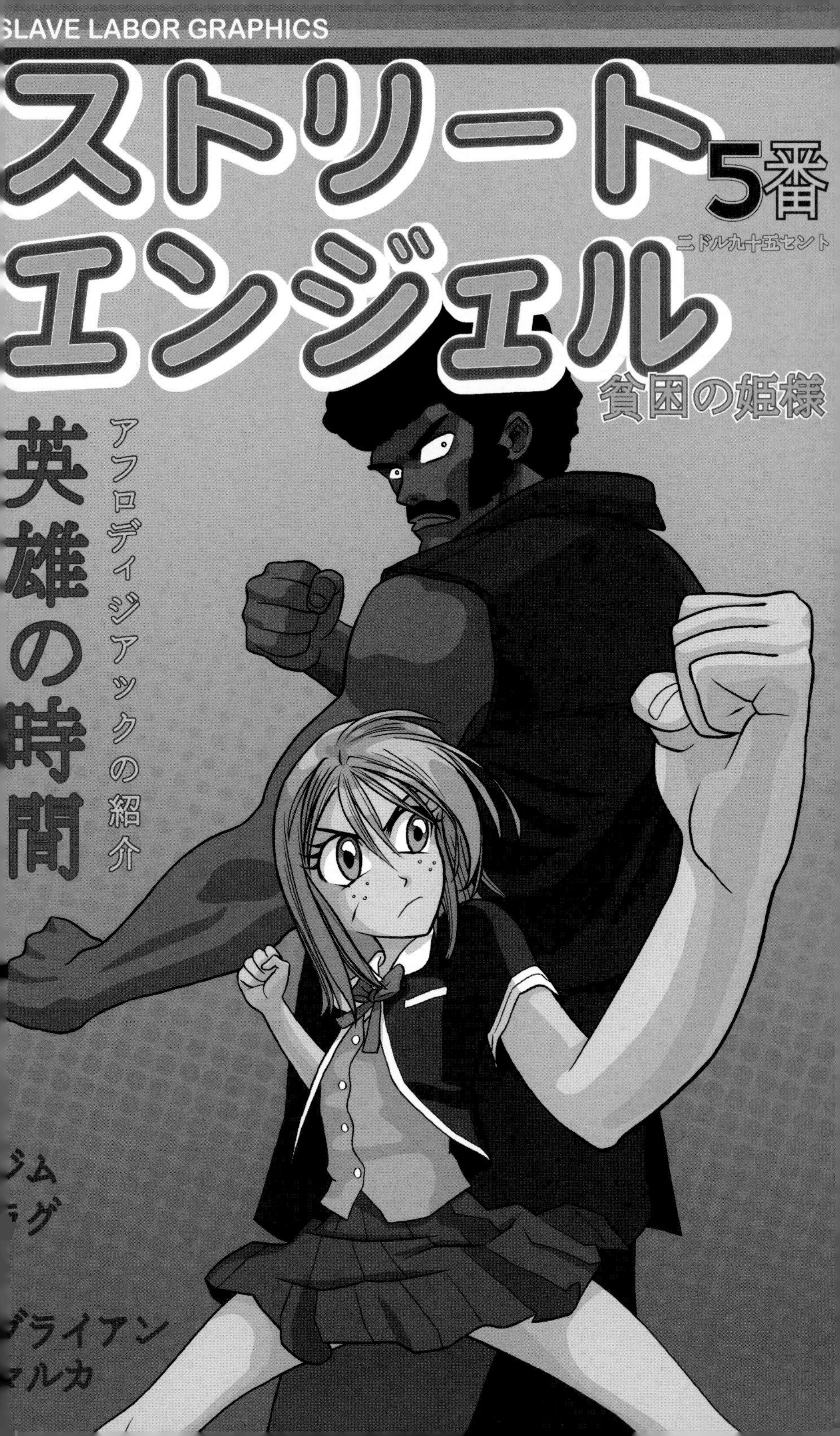
SLAVE LABOR GRAPHICS
ストリート
エンジェル
5番
二ドル九十五セント
貧困の姫様
英雄の時間
アフロディジアックの紹介
ム
グ
ライアン
ルカ

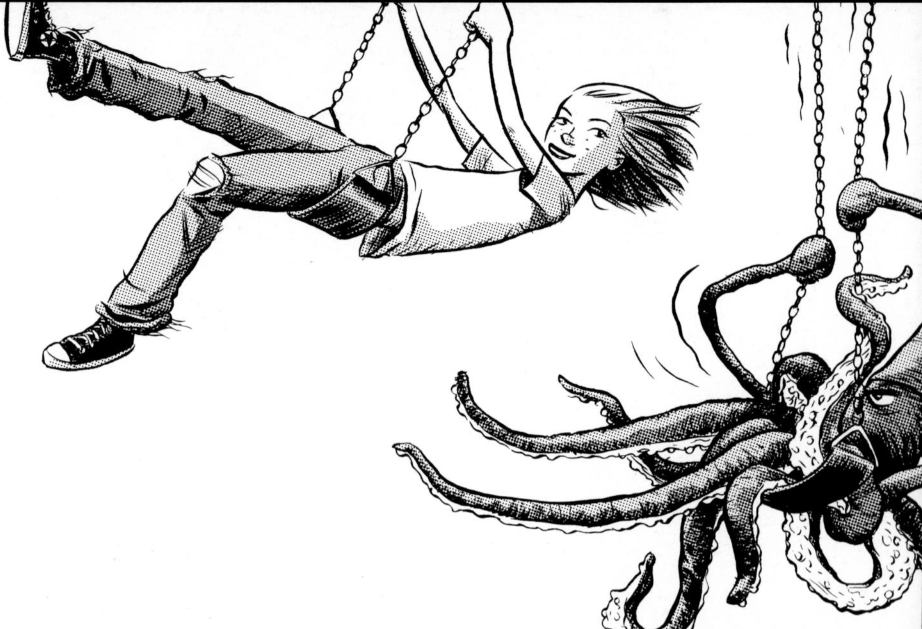

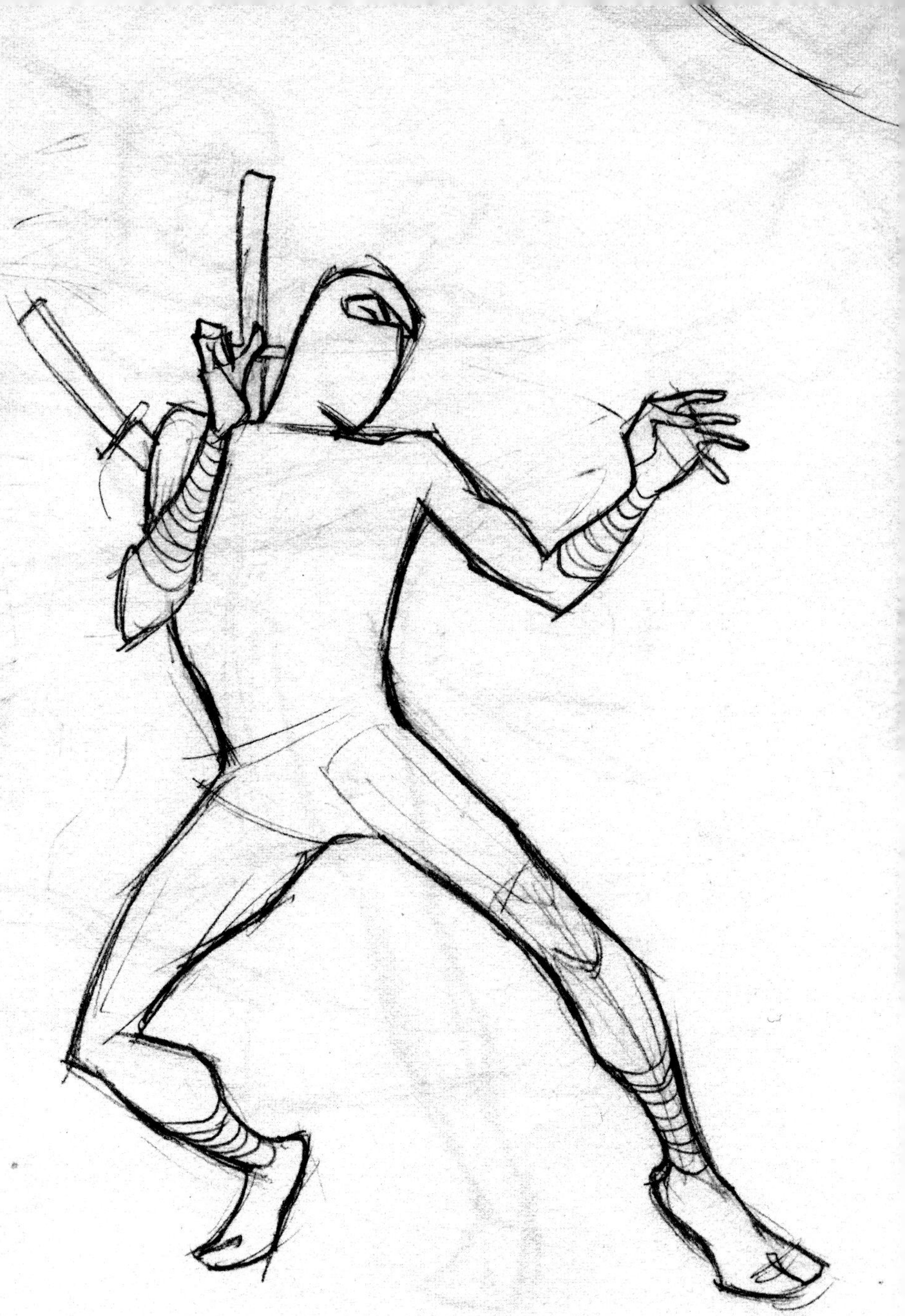

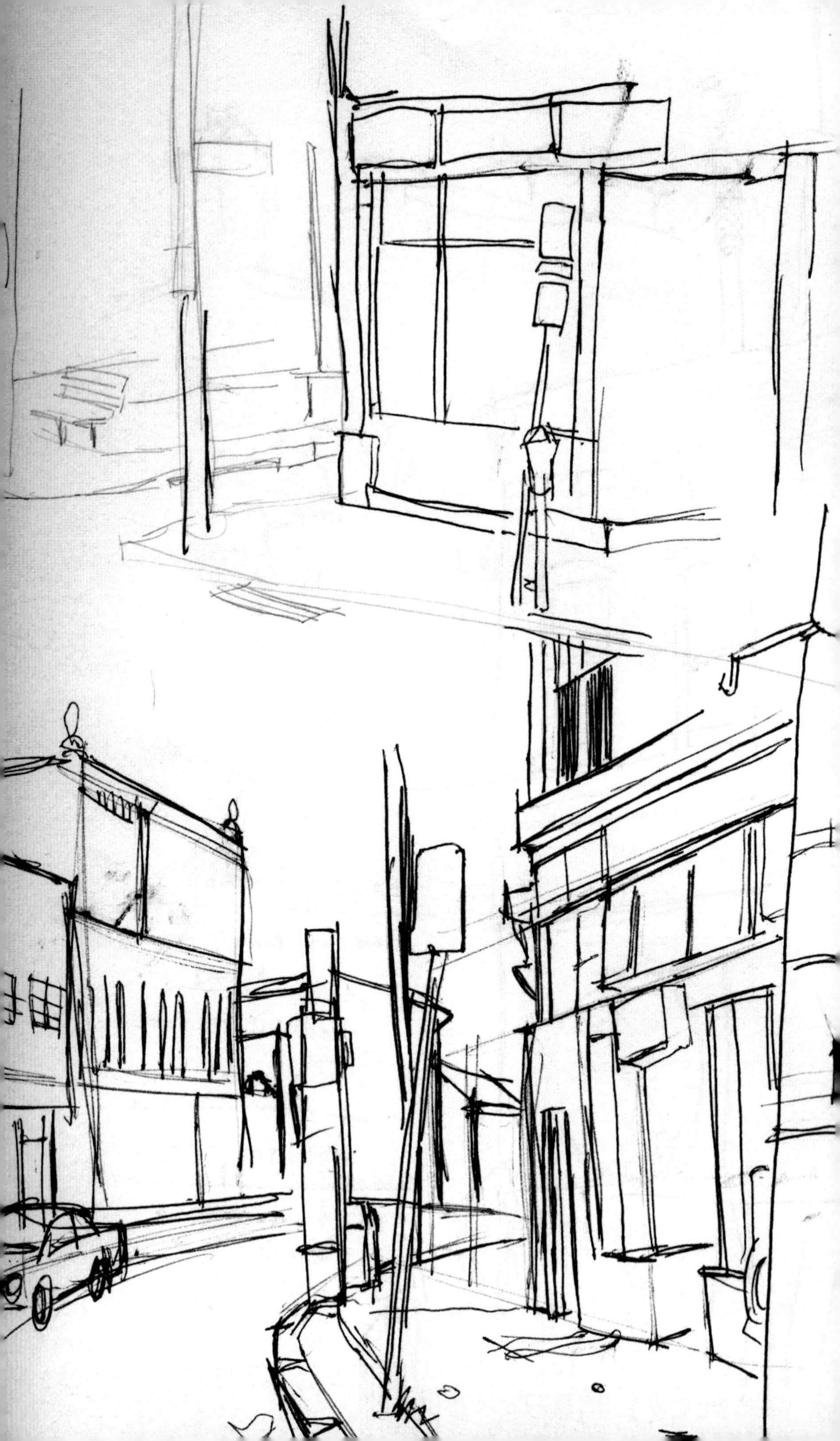

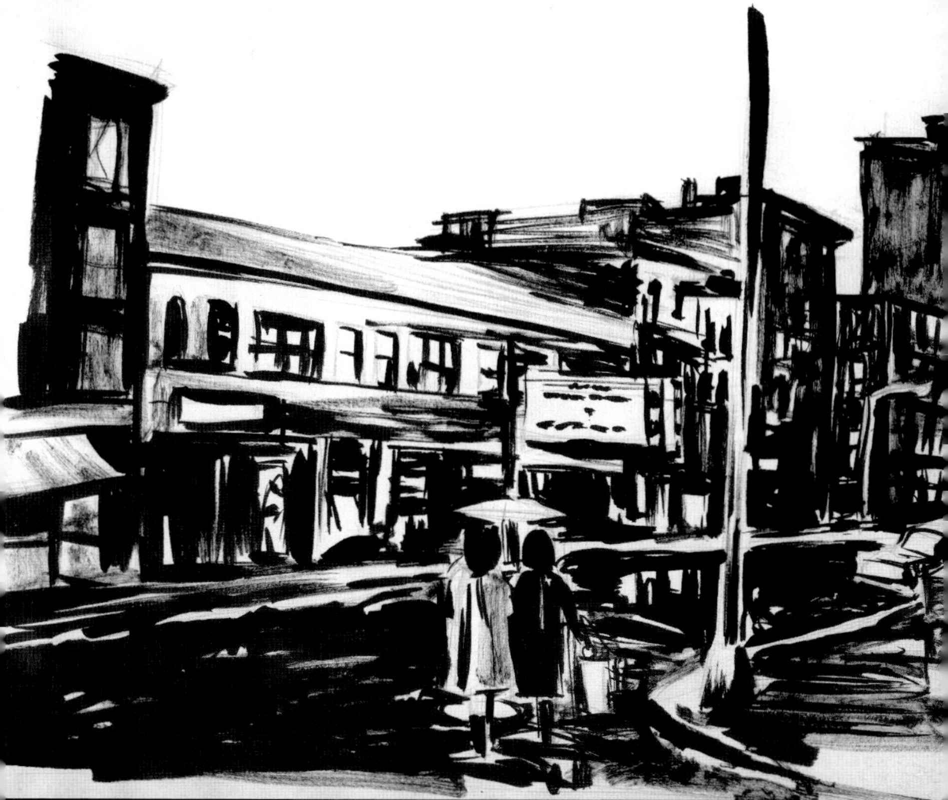

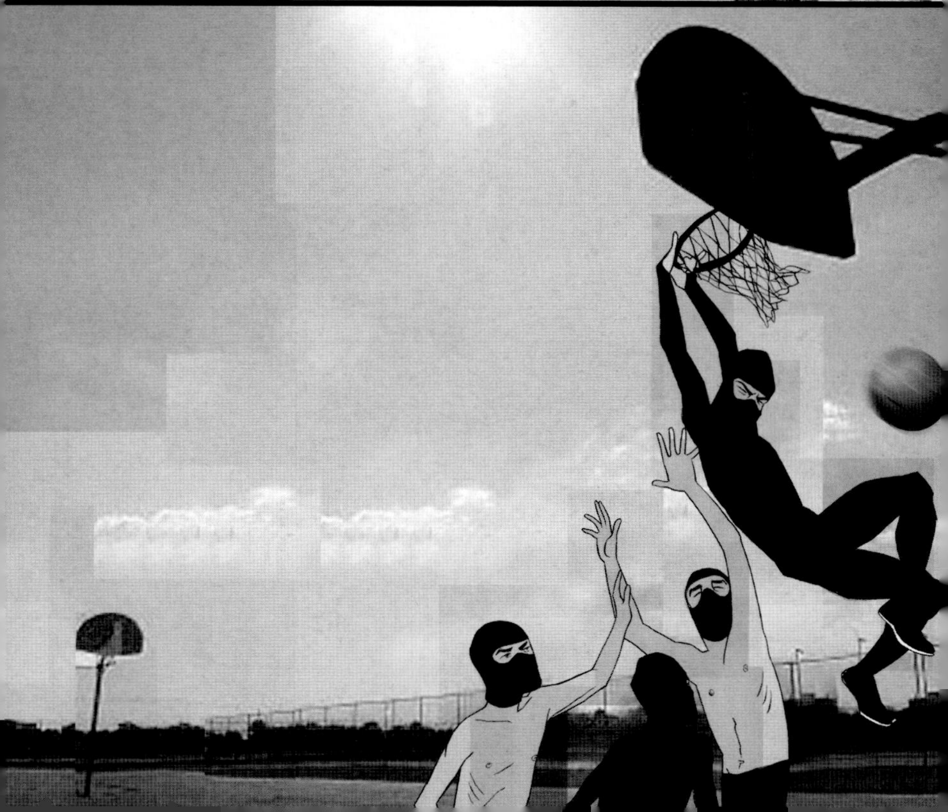

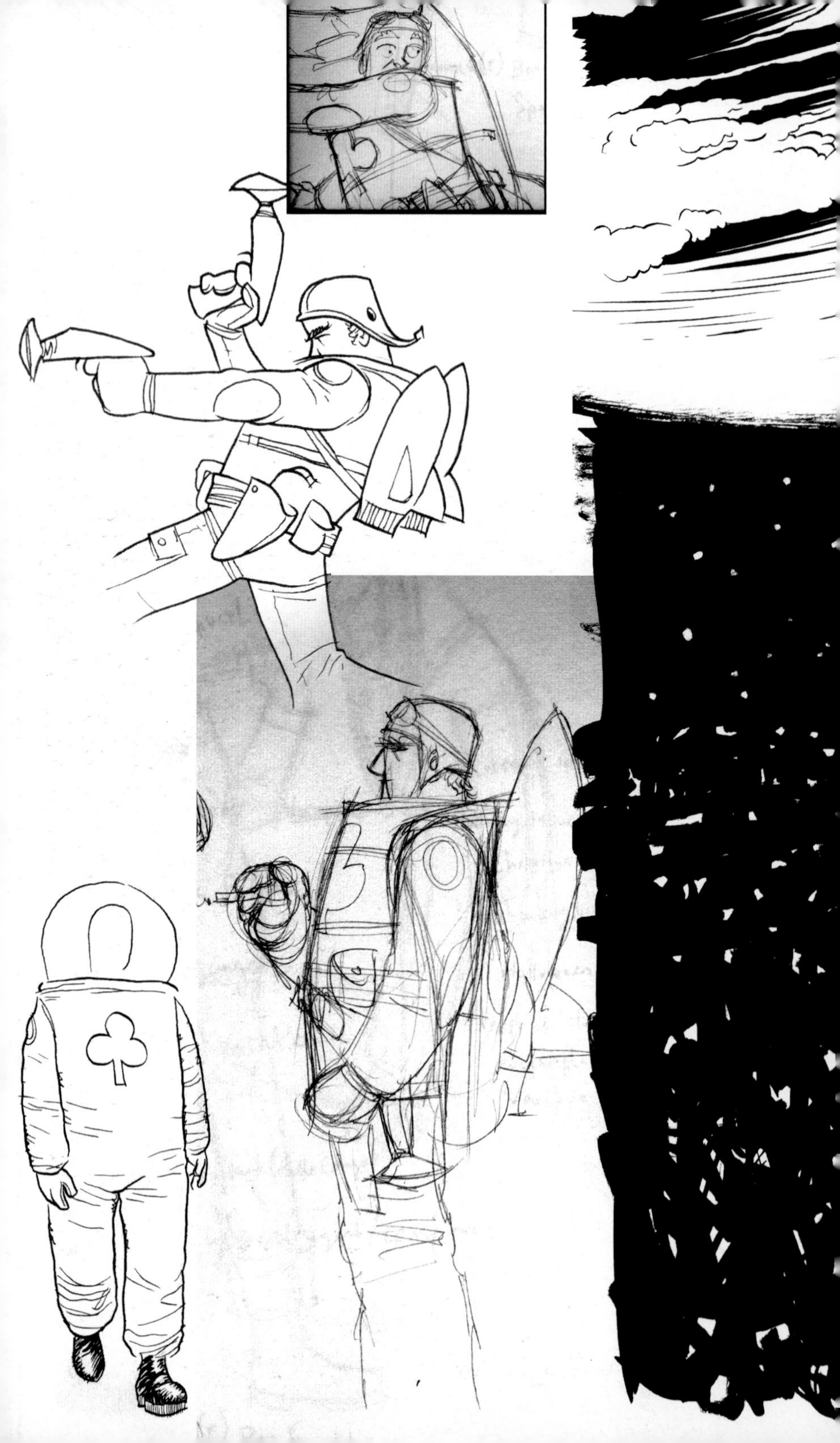

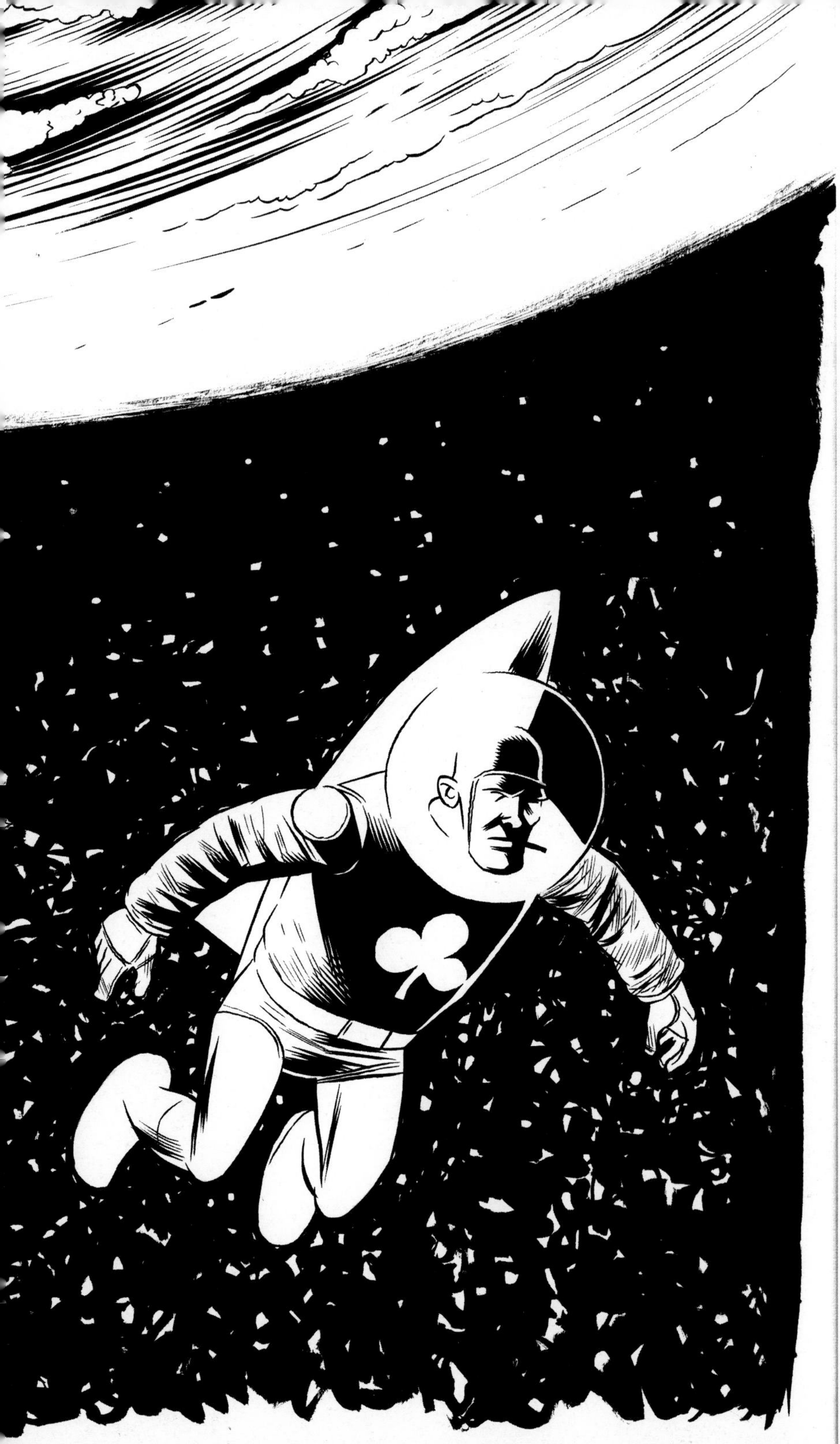

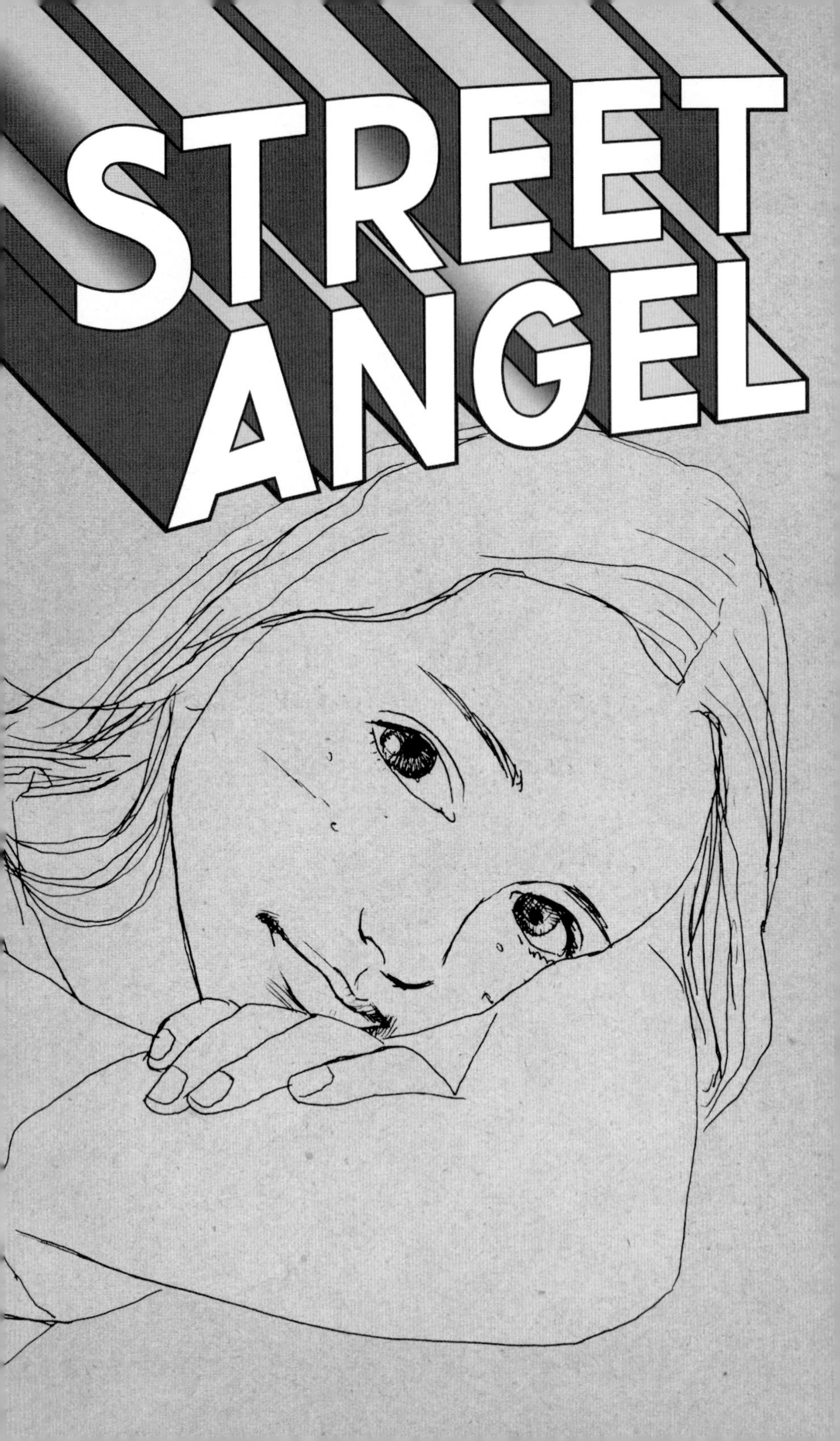
STREET
ANGEL

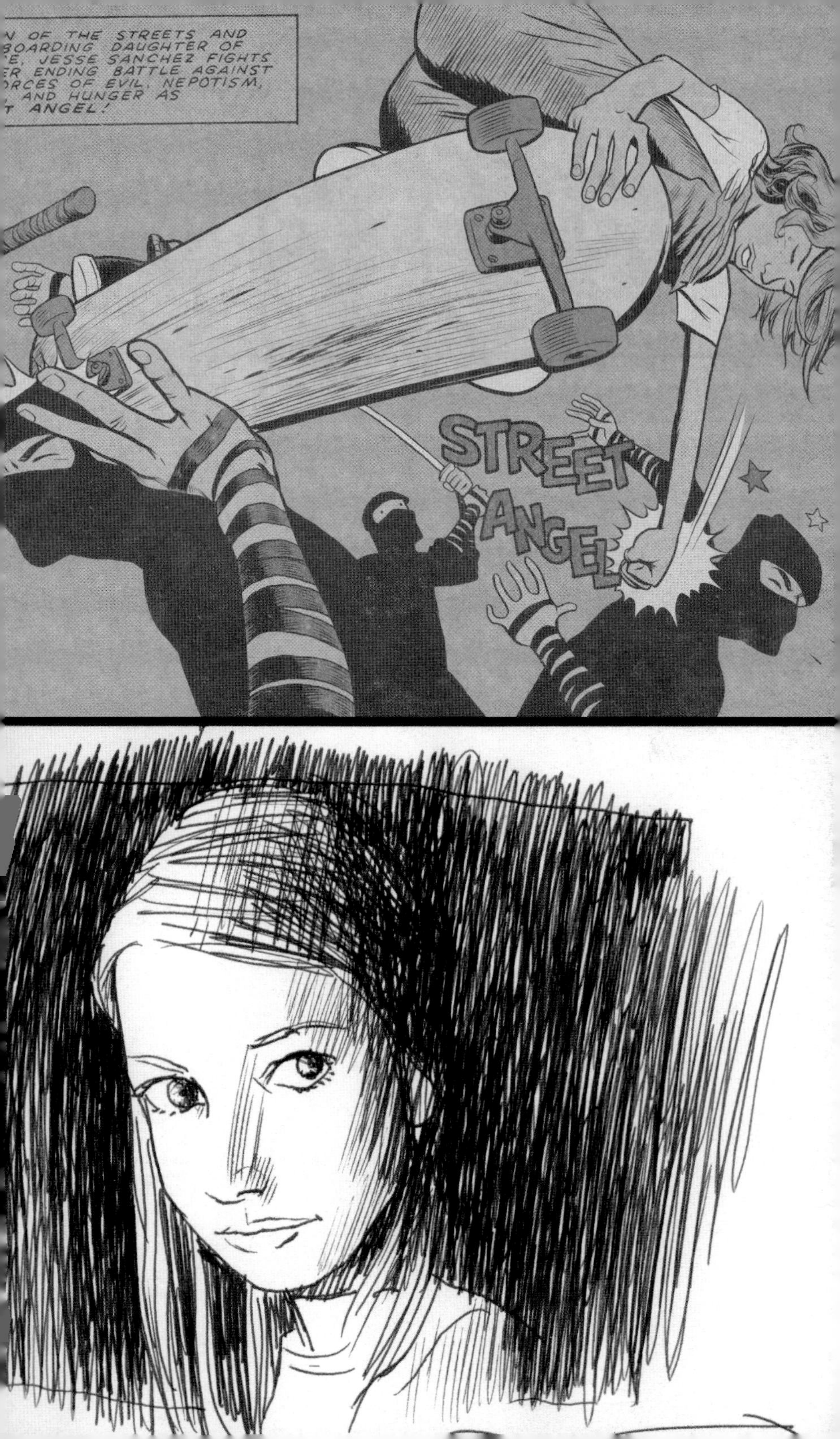
N OF THE STREETS AND
BOARDING DAUGHTER OF
E, JESSE SANCHEZ FIGHTS
ER ENDING BATTLE AGAINST
ORCES OF EVIL, NEPOTISM,
, AND HUNGER AS
T ANGEL!
STREET ANGEL

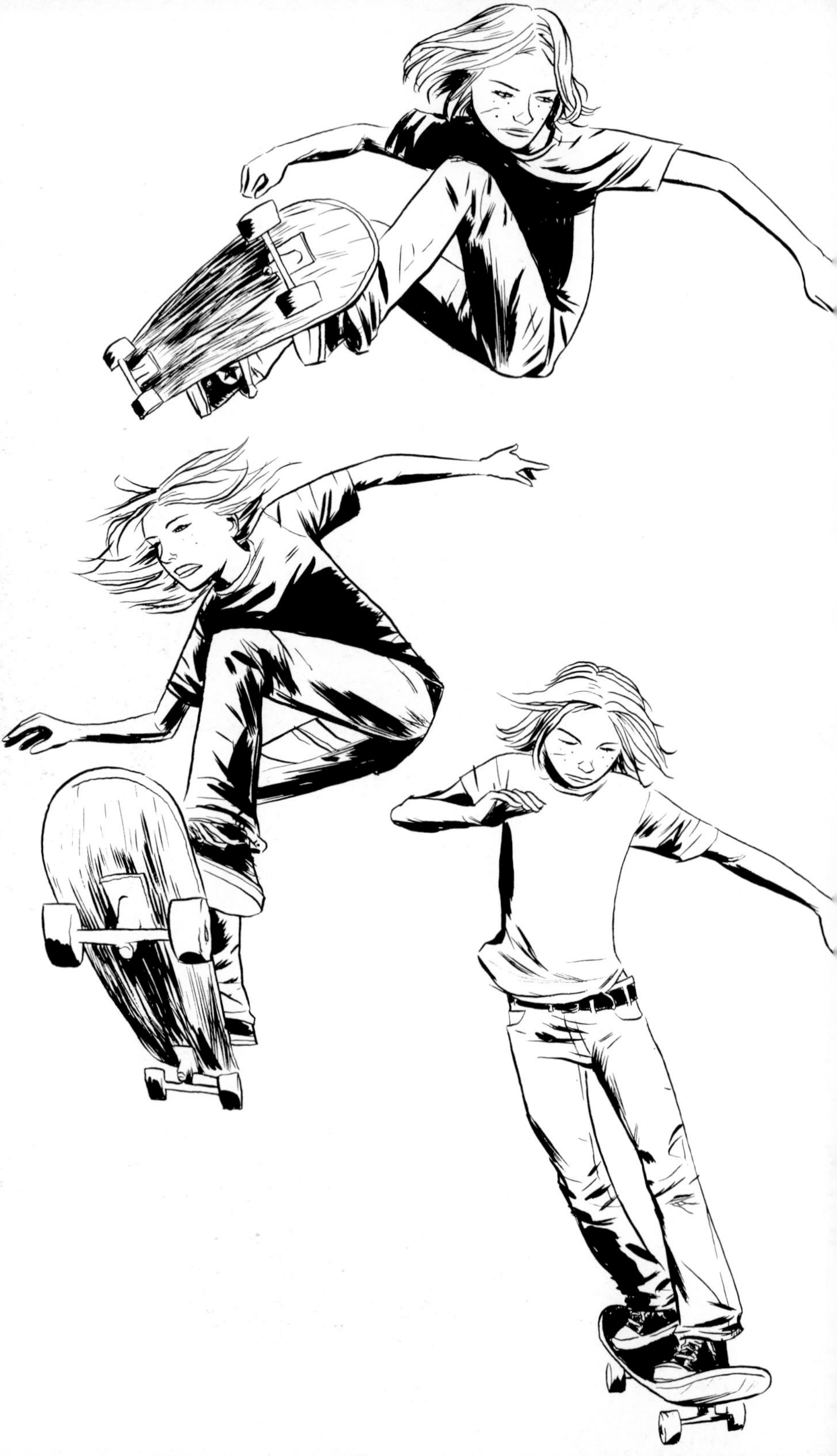

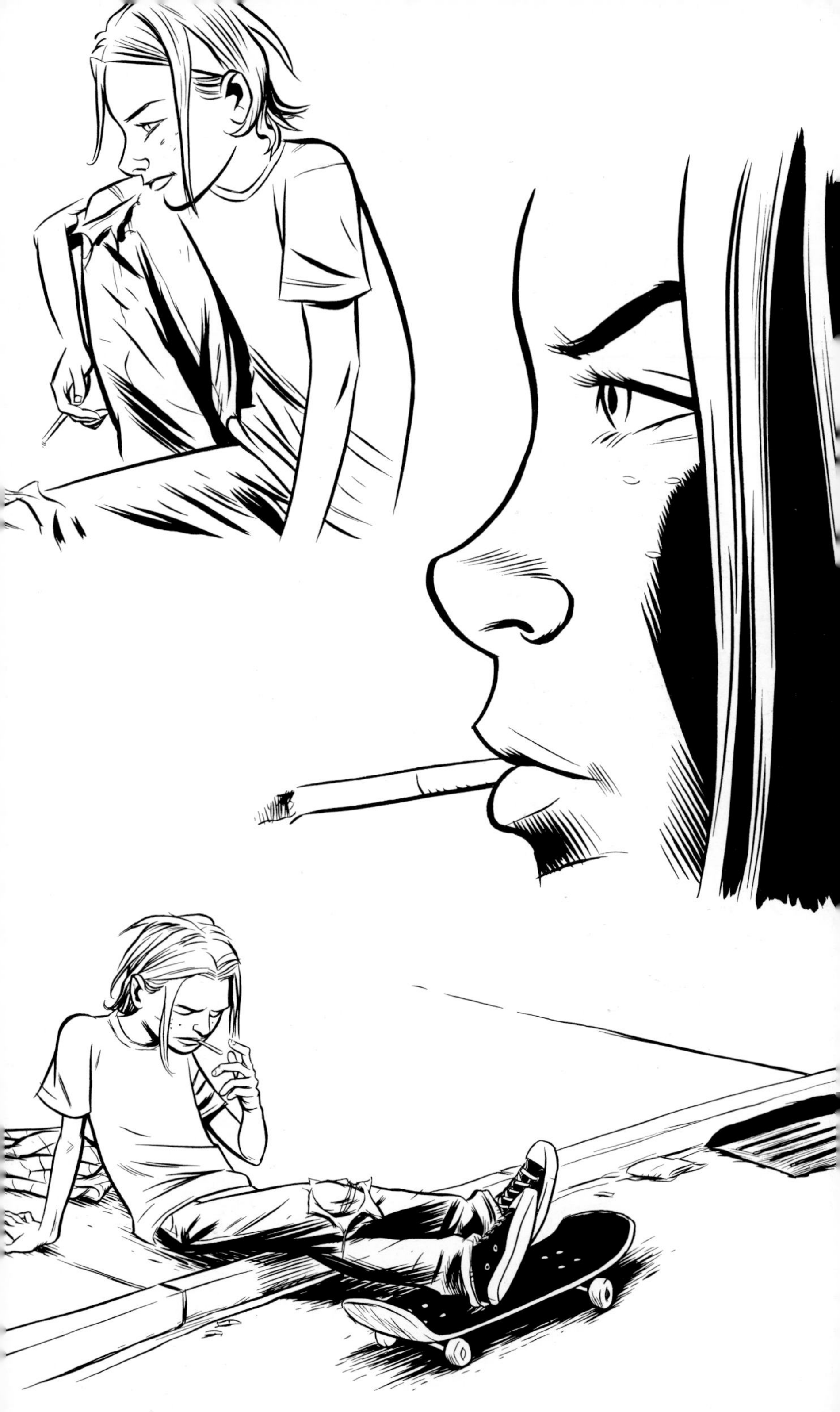

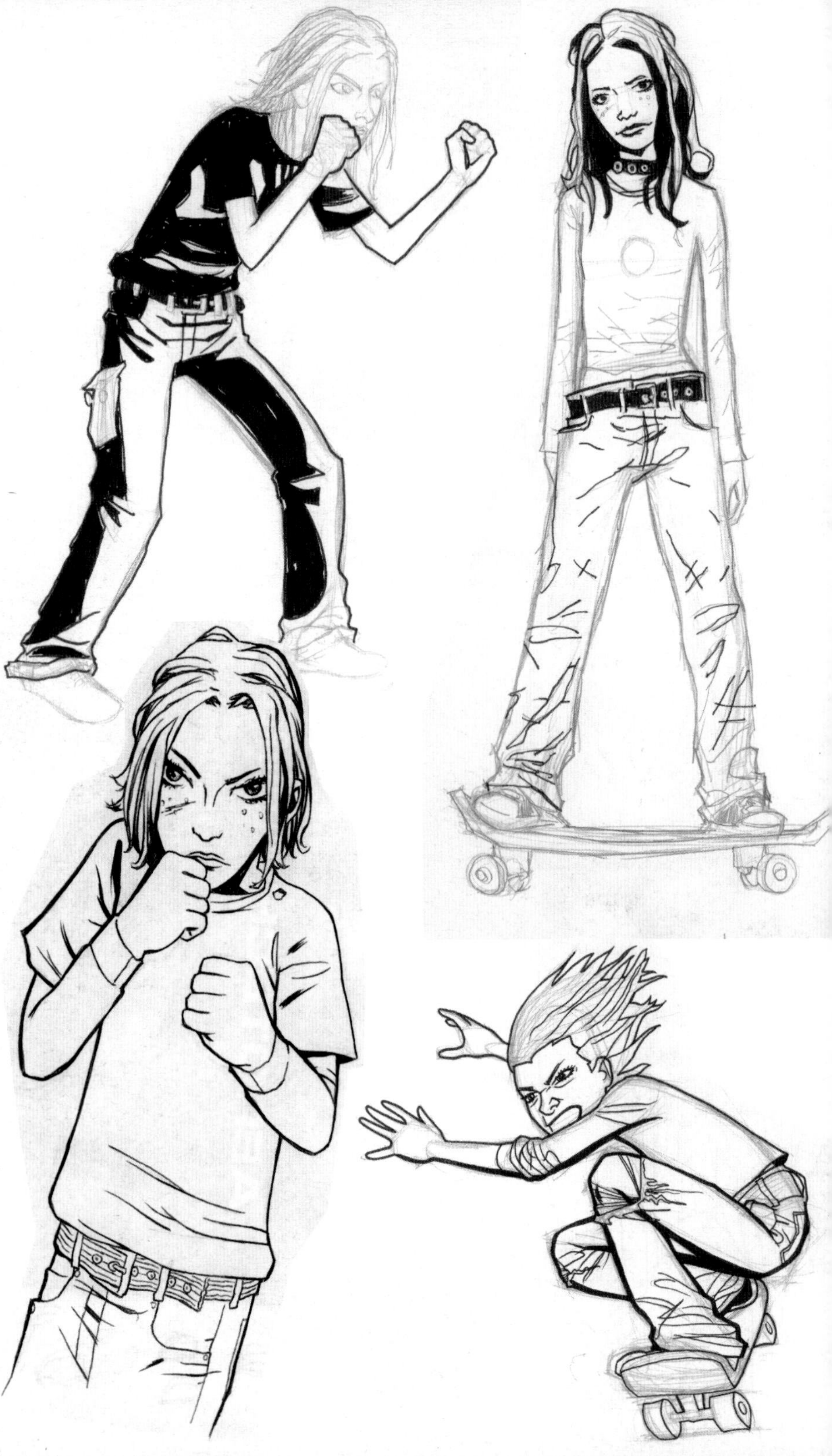

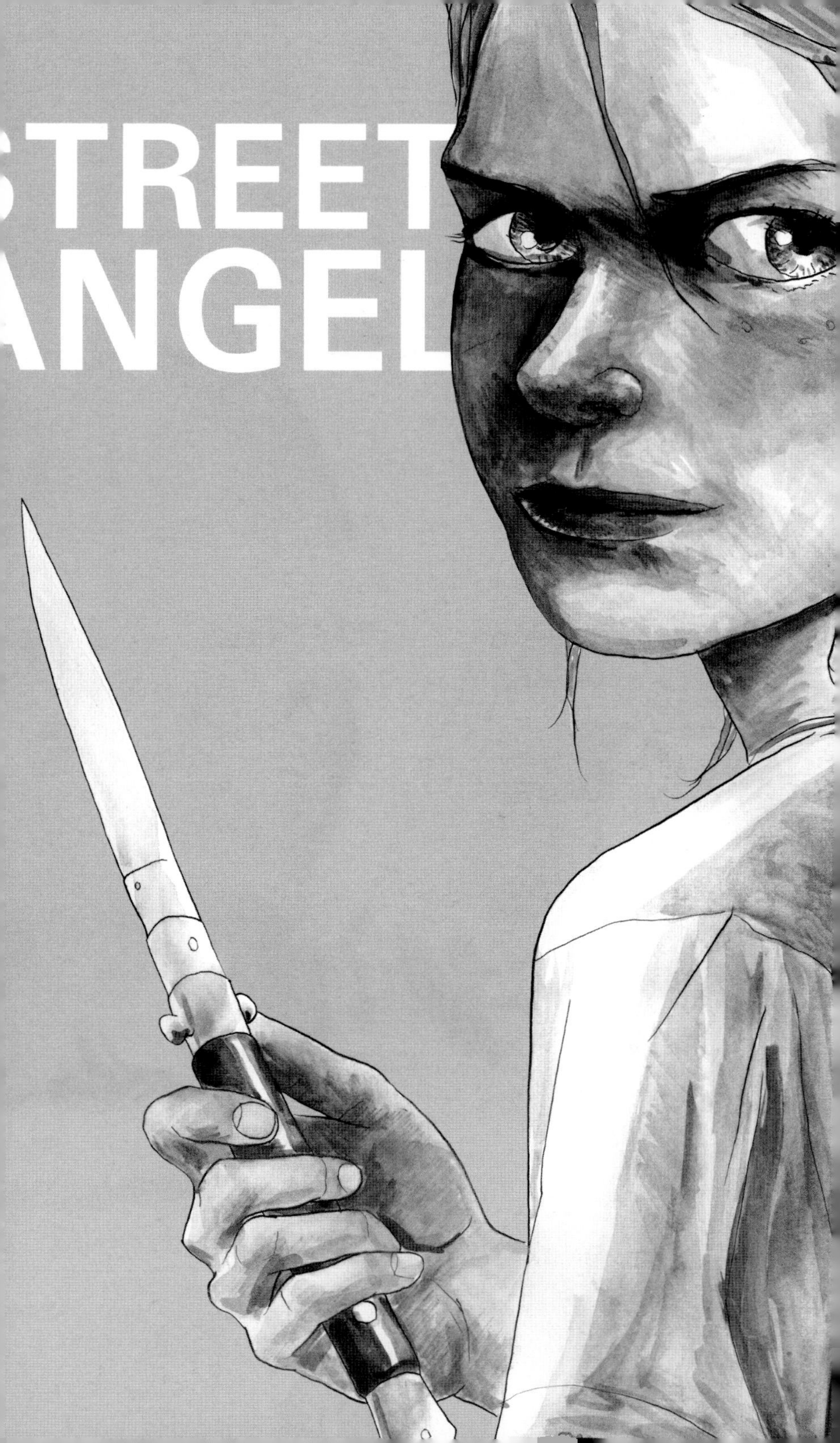
STREET
ANGEL

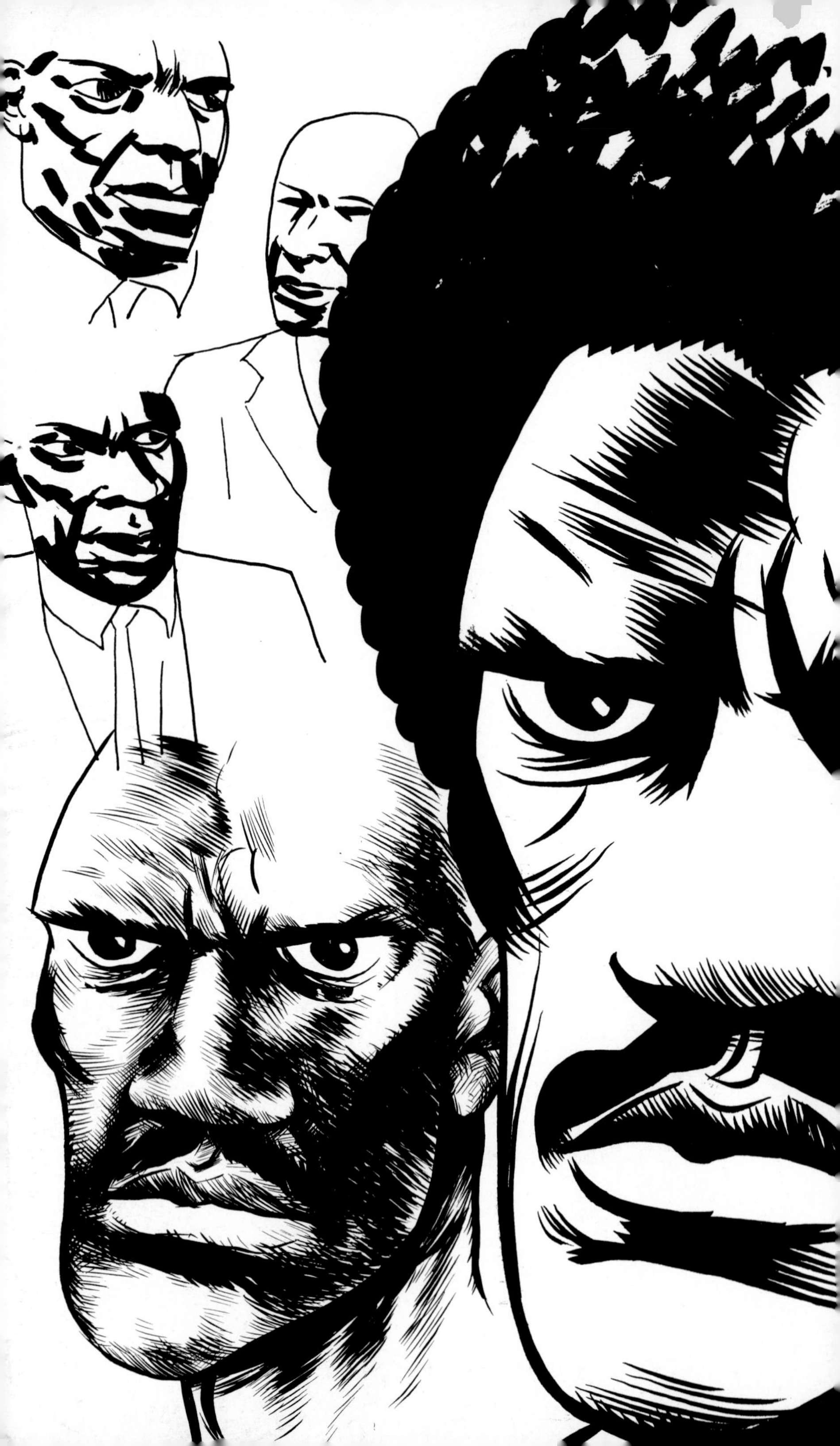

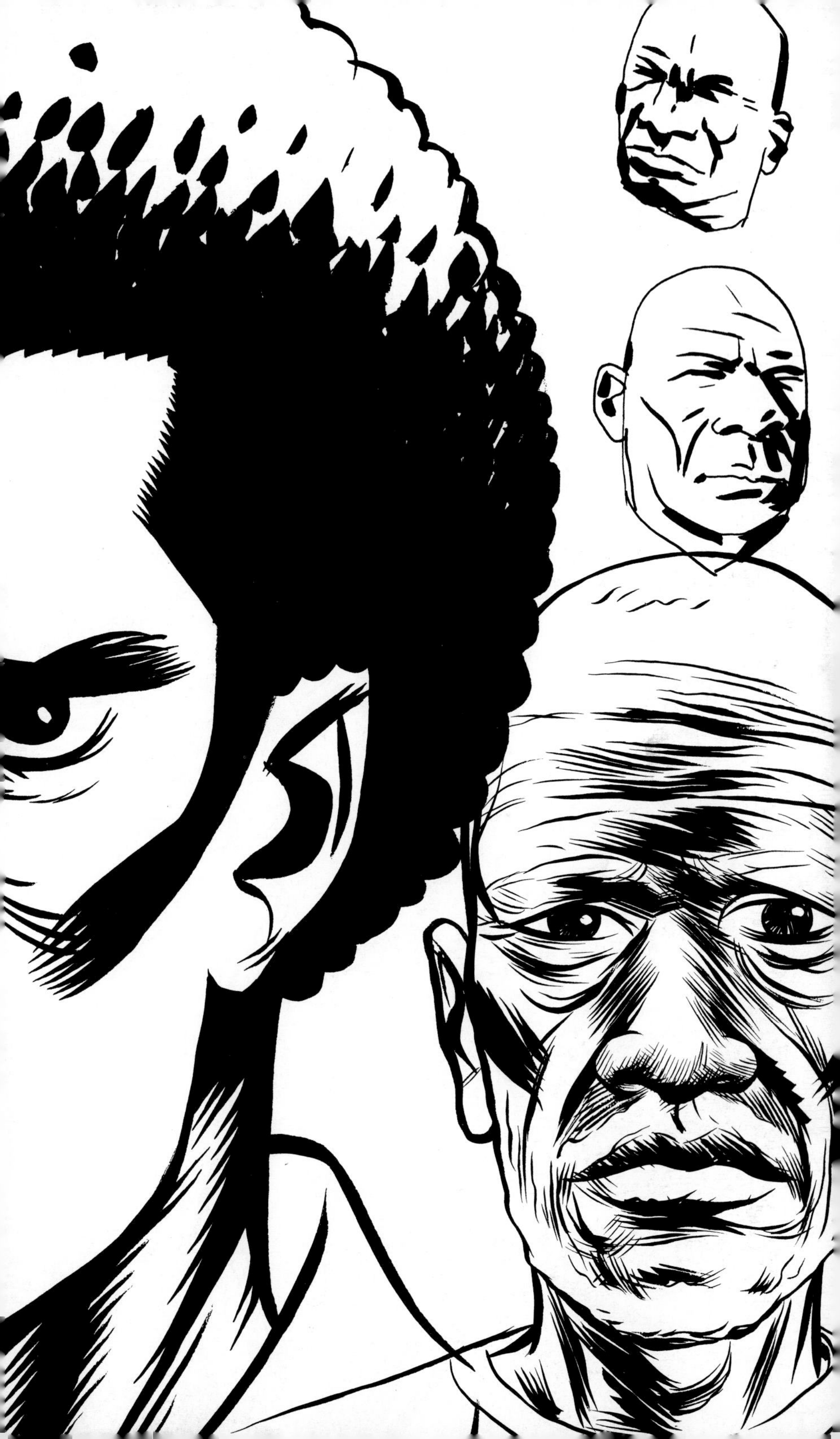

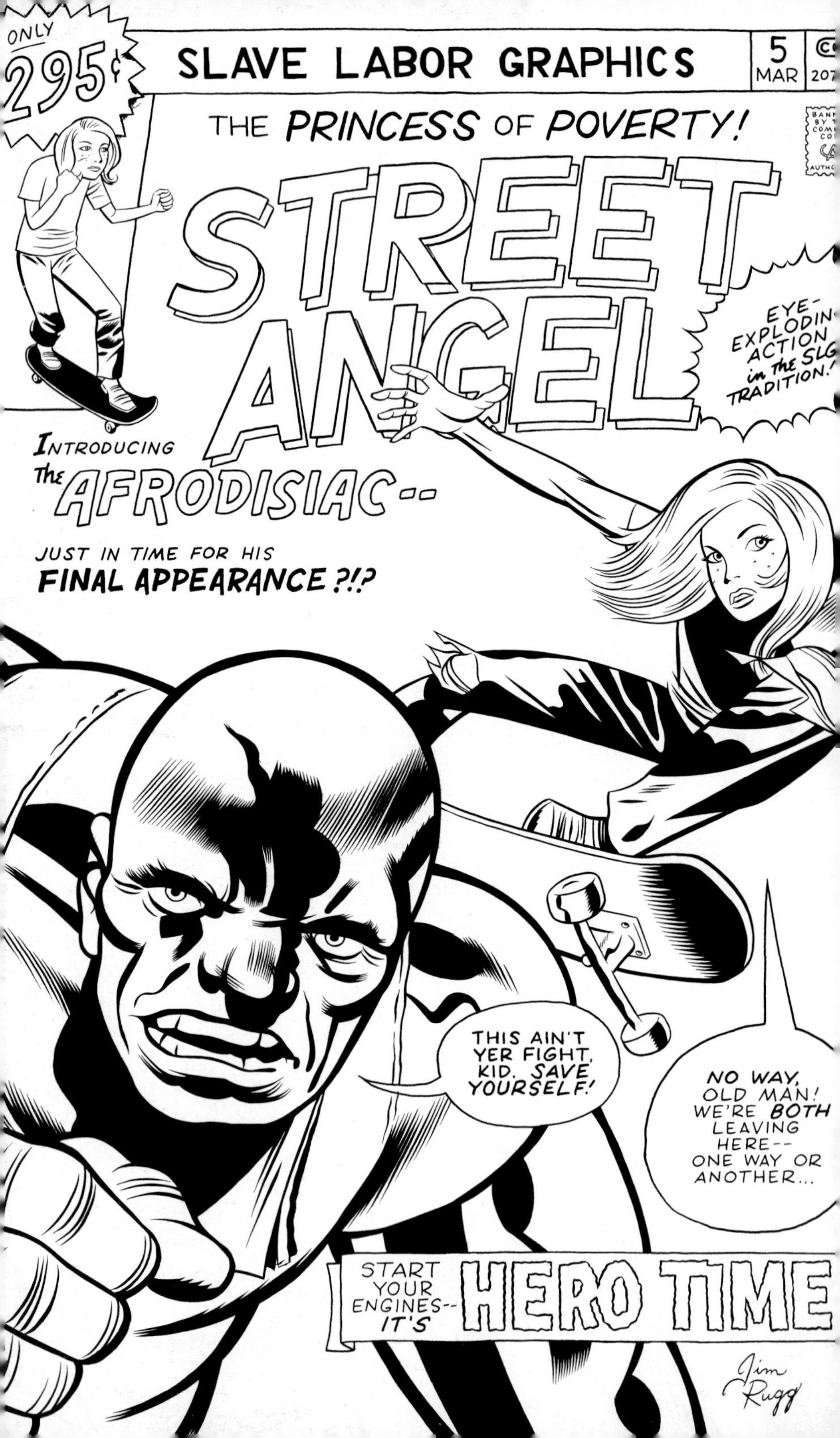
ONLY 295¢
SLAVE LABOR GRAPHICS
5
MAR
THE PRINCESS OF POVERTY!
STREET ANGEL
EYE-EXPLODIN
ACTION
in the SLG
TRADITION!
INTRODUCING
The AFRODISIAC--
JUST IN TIME FOR HIS
FINAL APPEARANCE ?!?
THIS AIN'T YER FIGHT, KID. SAVE YOURSELF!
NO WAY, OLD MAN! WE'RE BOTH LEAVING HERE-- ONE WAY OR ANOTHER...
START YOUR ENGINES-- IT'S
HERO TIME
Jim Rugg

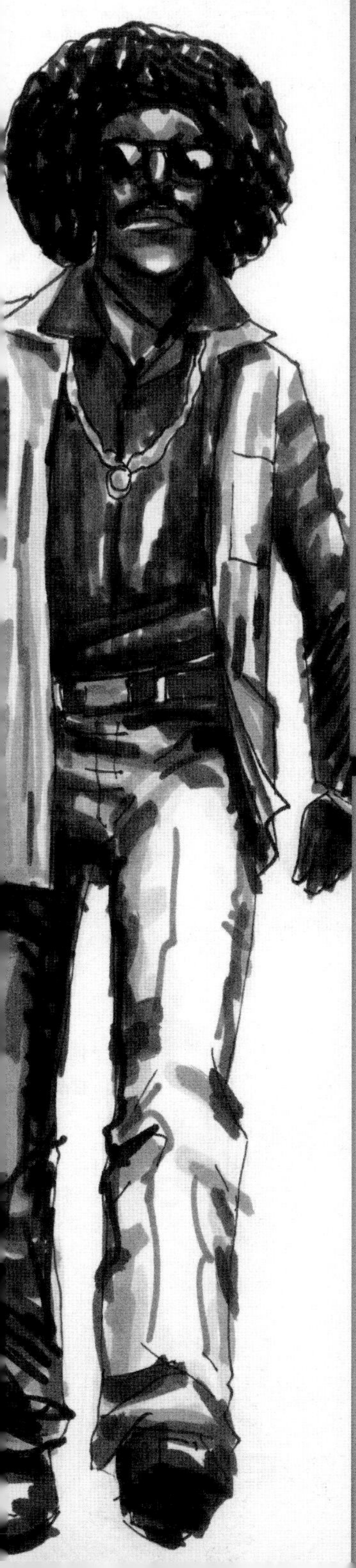

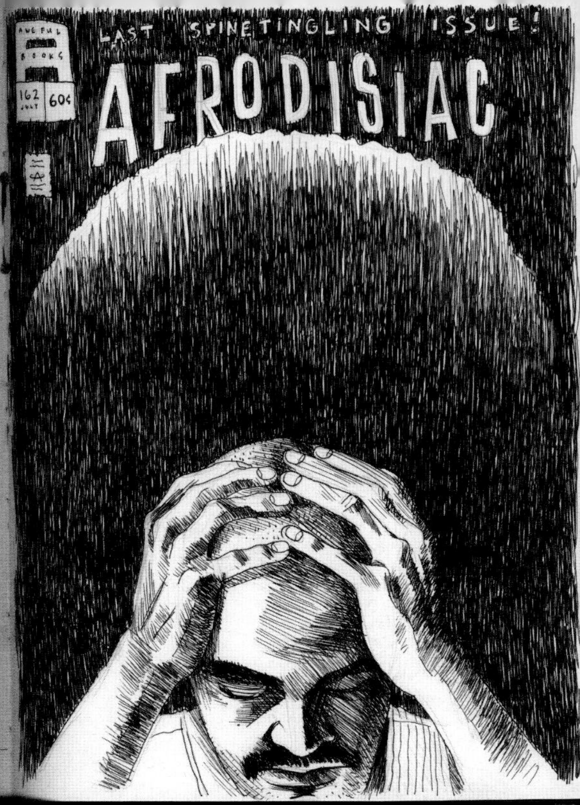
AWEFUL BOOKS
162 JULY
60¢
LAST SPINETINGLING ISSUE!
AFRODISIAC

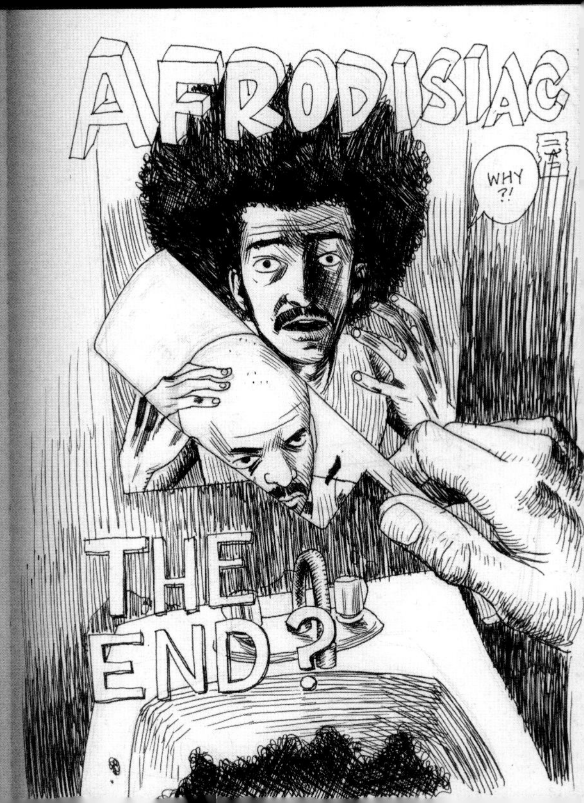
AFRODISIAC
WHY ?!
THE END?

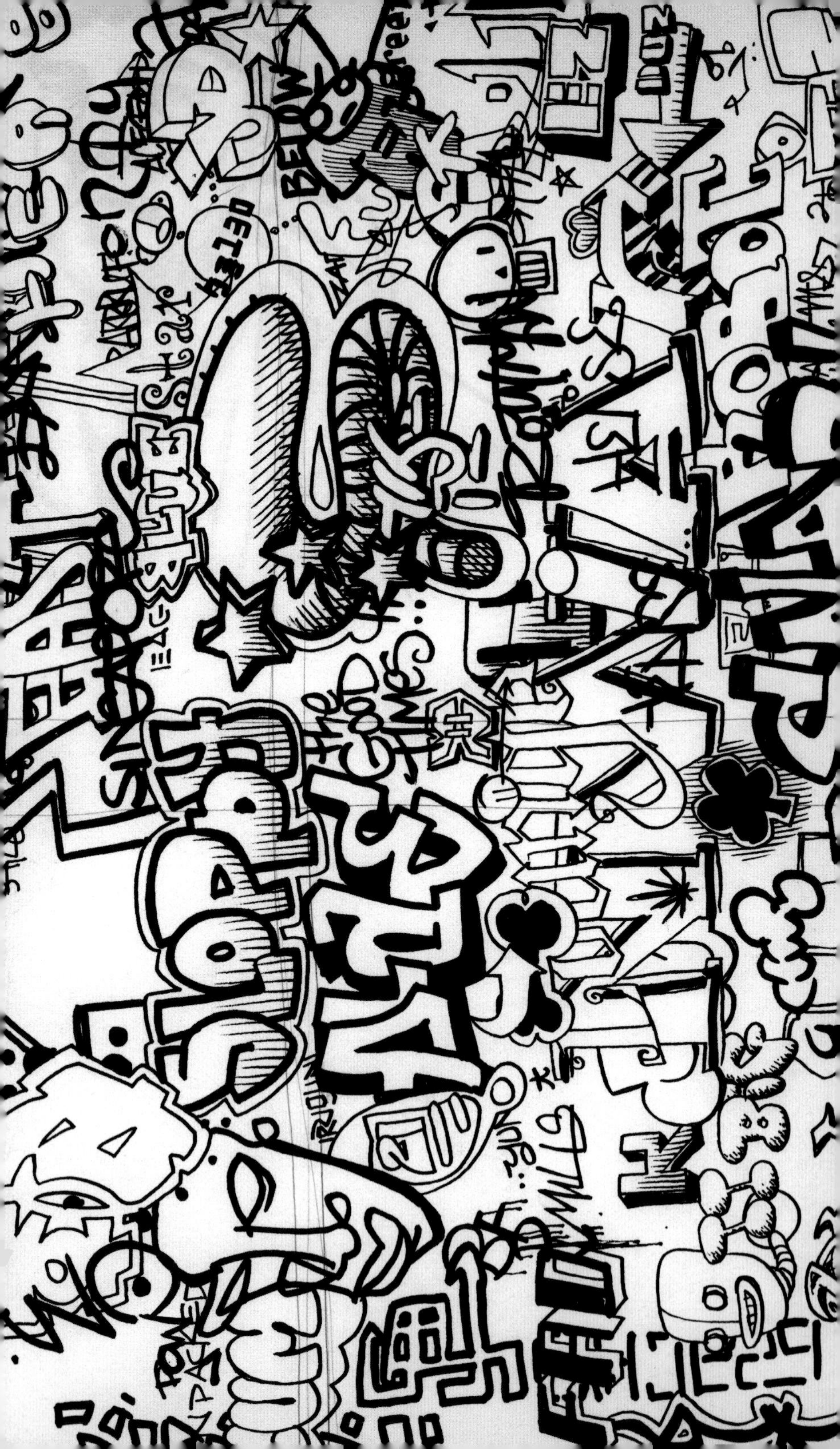

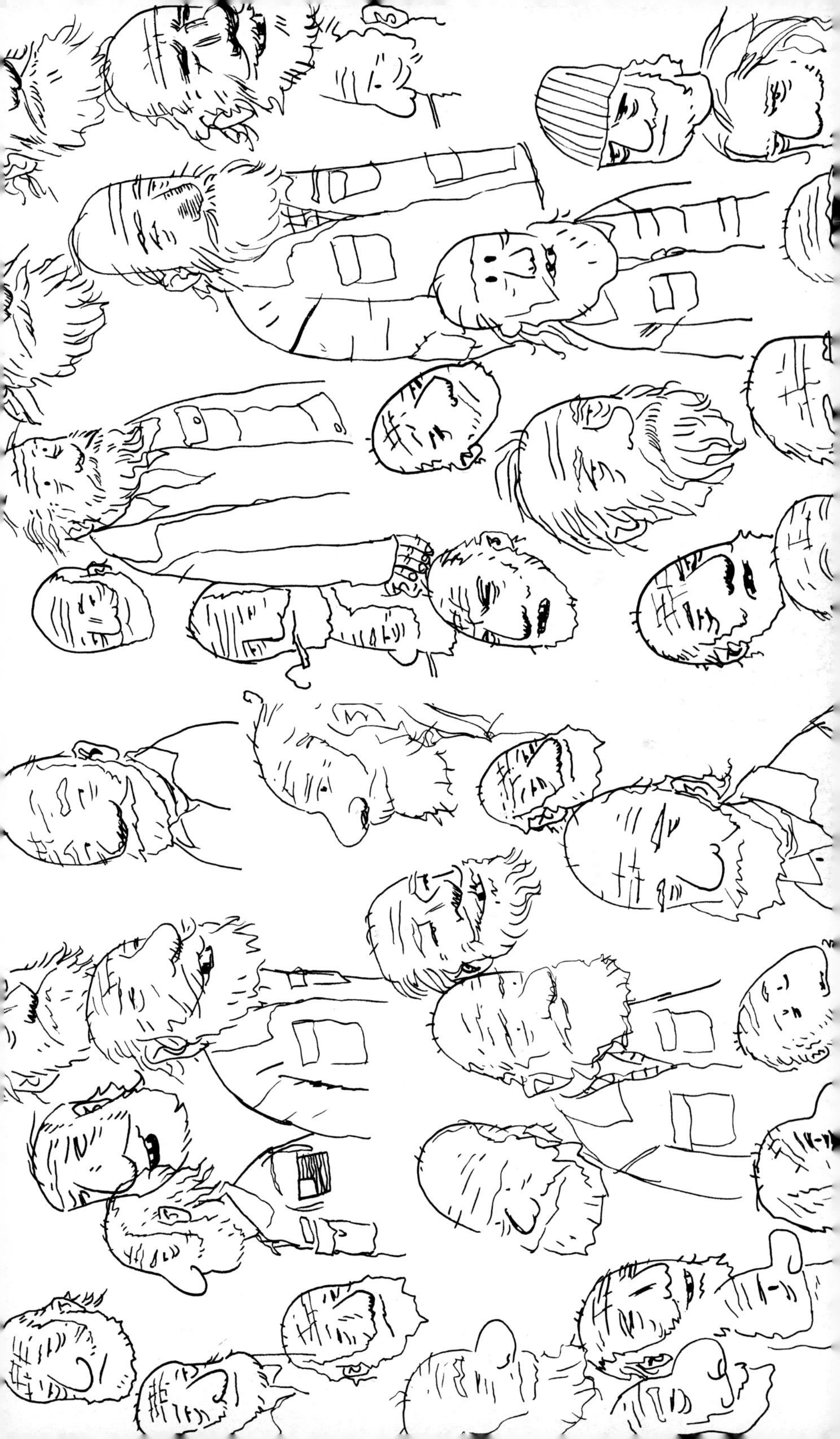

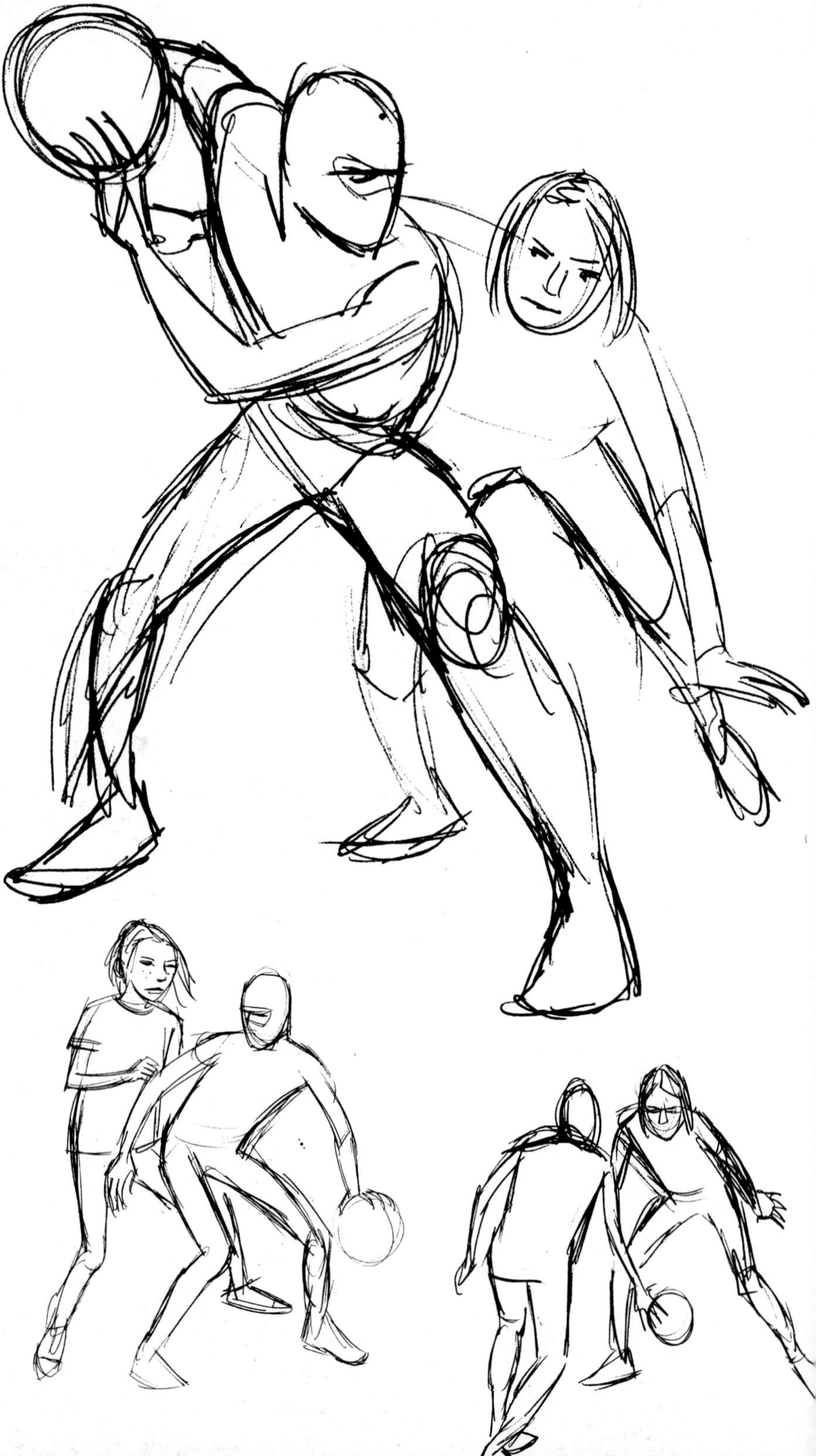

Pinups

Jeffrey Brown
Farel Dalrymple
Jesse Farrell
Richard Hahn
Dean Haspiel
Mike Hawthorne
Paul Hornschemeier
Dave Kiersh
Pat Lewis
Jasen Lex
Andy Macdonald
Jim Mahfood
Ted May
Scott Mills
Scott Morse
Bryan Lee O'Malley
Lark Pien
Ed Piskor
Brian Ralph
Zack Soto
Lauren Weinstein
Dan Zettwoch

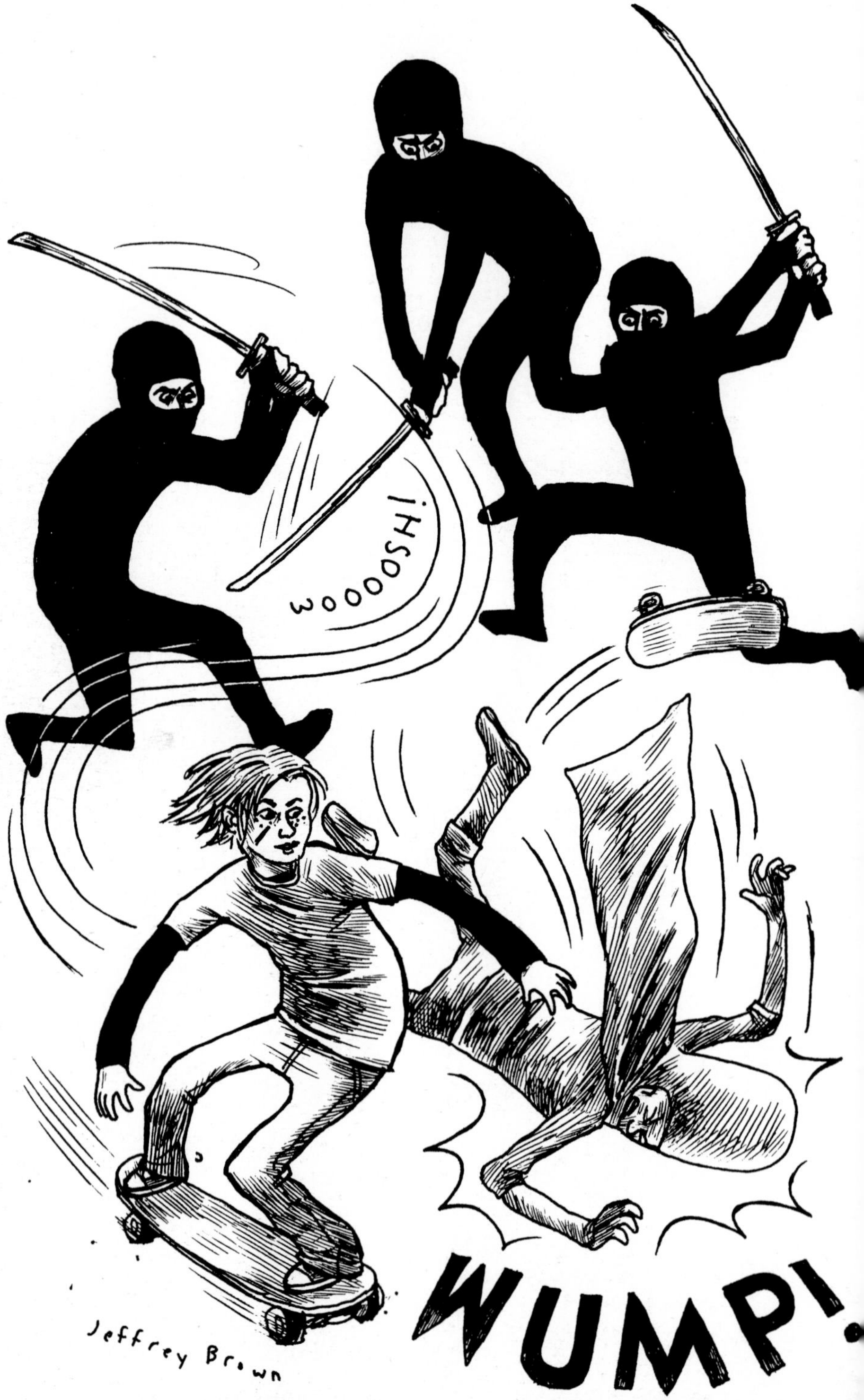
WOOOOSH!
WUMP!
Jeffrey Brown

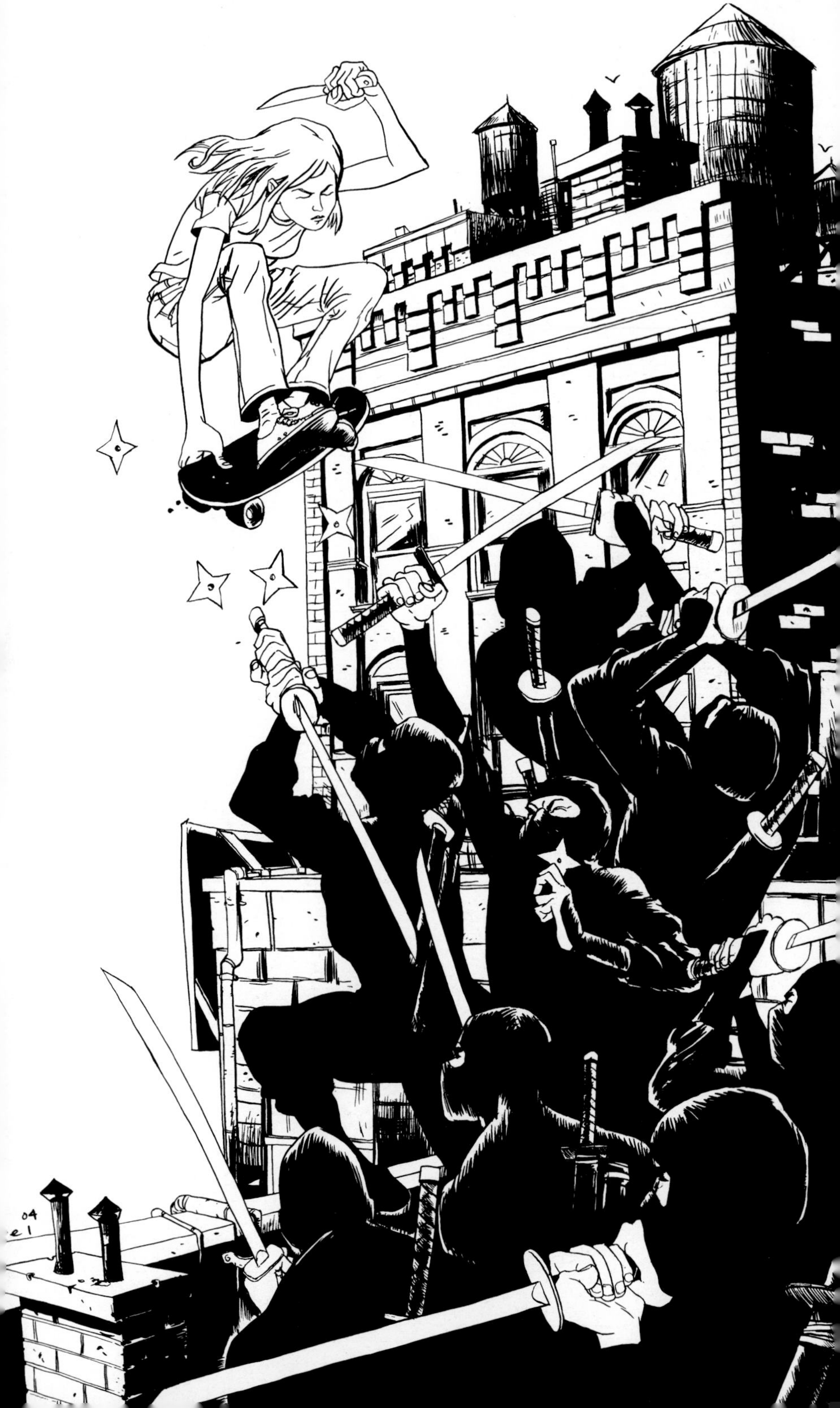

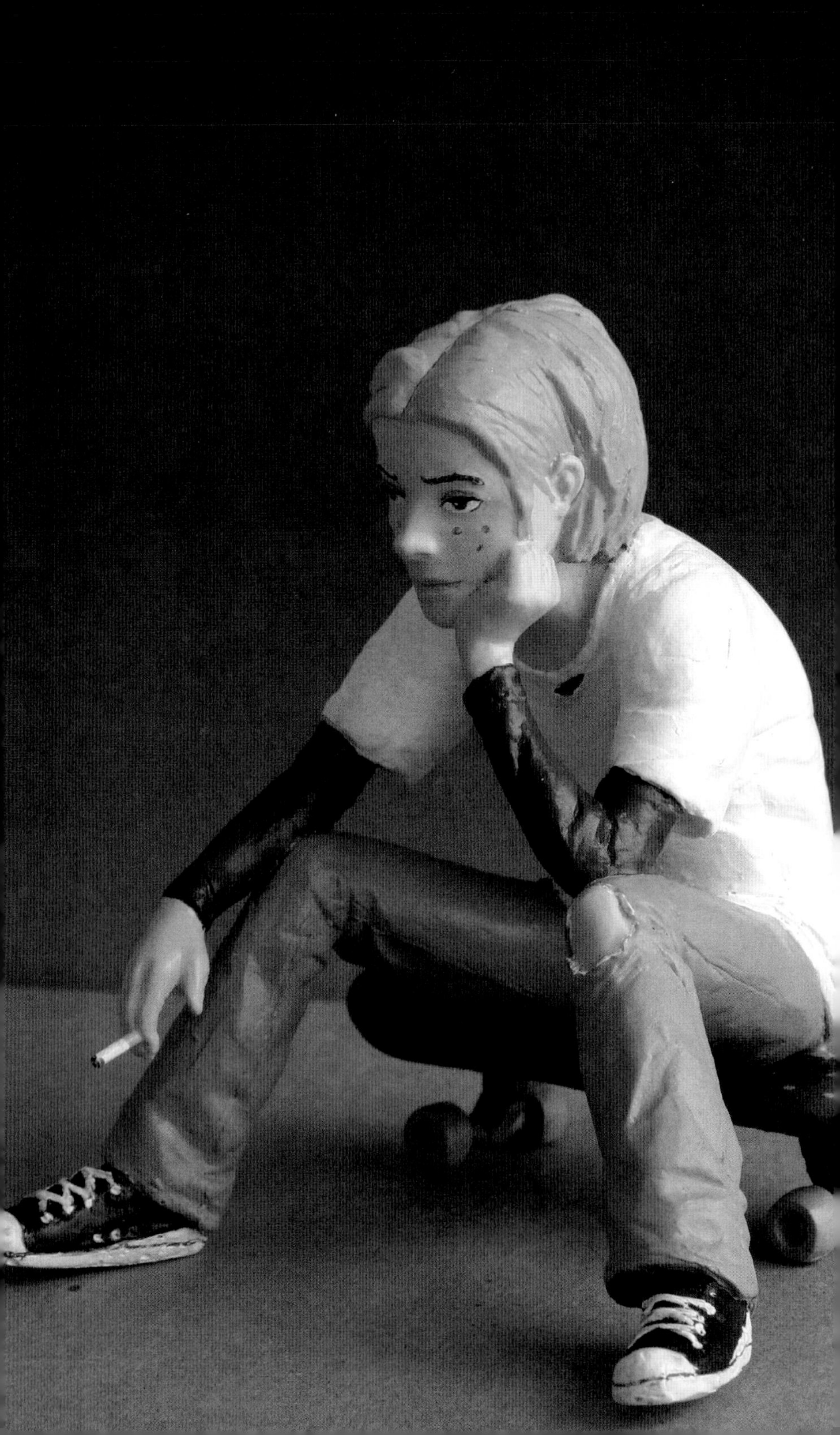

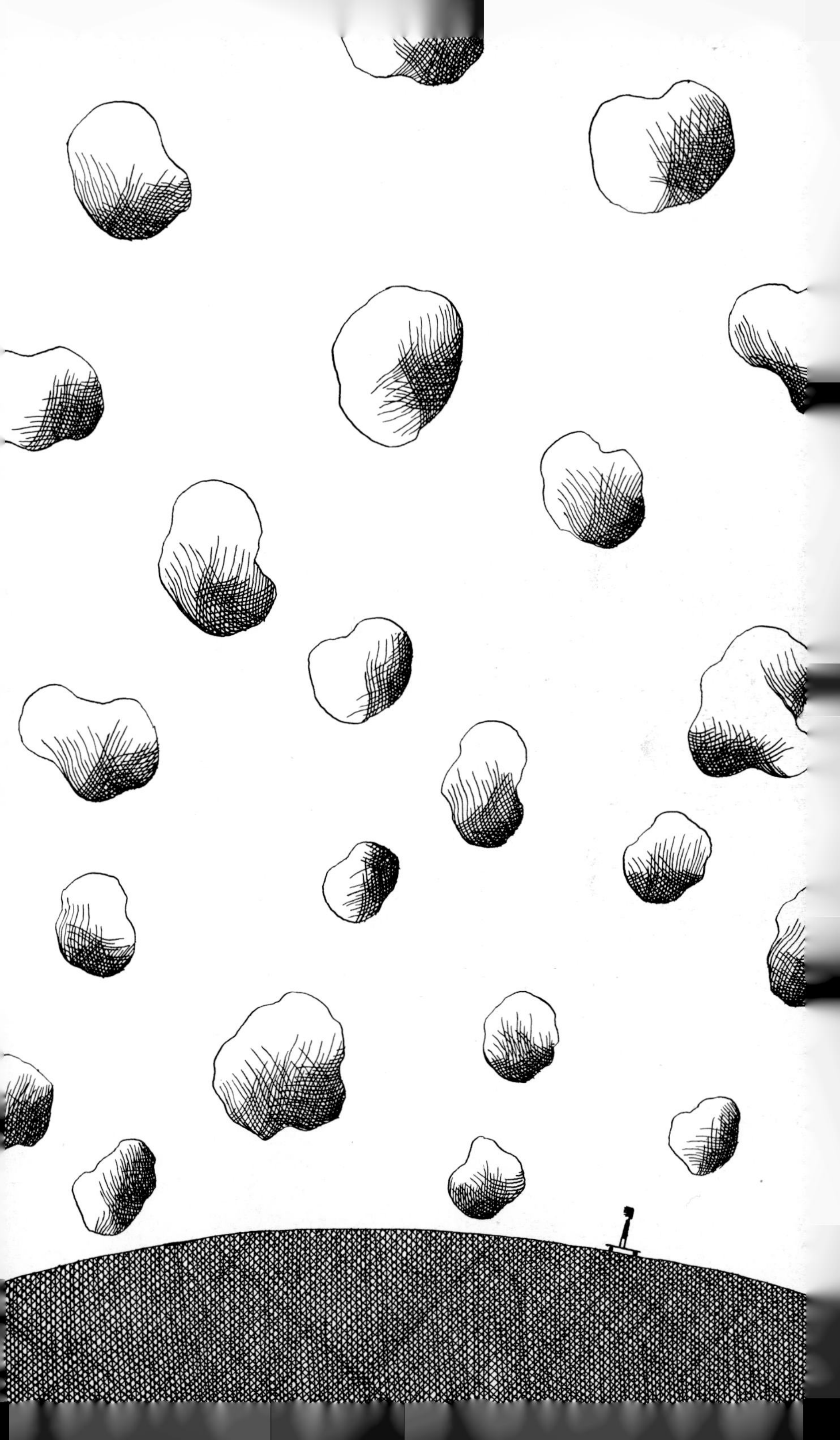

Billy Dogma meets Street Ange
in "Go Get A Late Pass!"

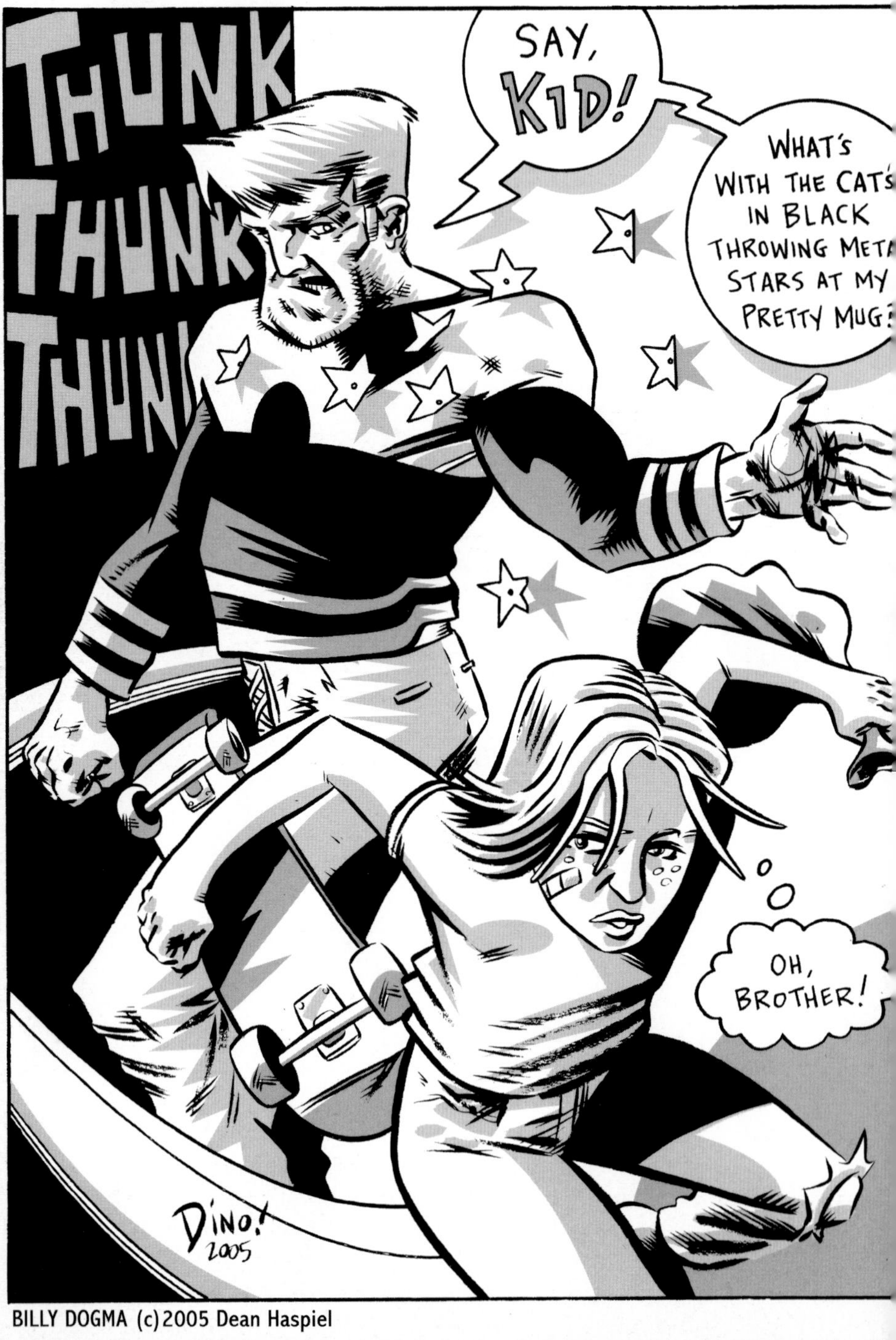
THUNK
THUNK
THUN
SAY, KID!
WHAT'S WITH THE CATS IN BLACK THROWING MET STARS AT MY PRETTY MUG
OH, BROTHER!
DINO! 2005

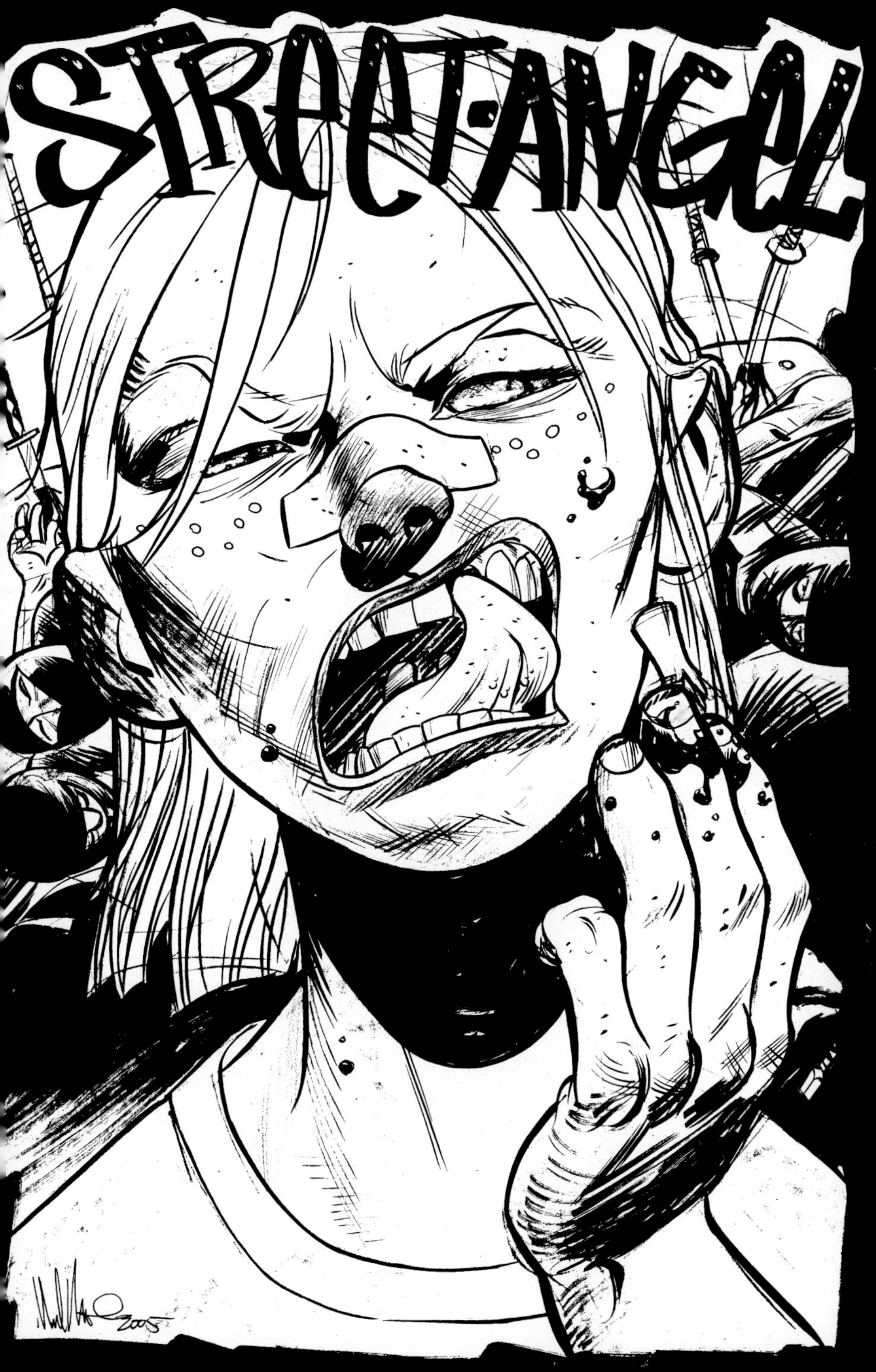
STREET ANGEL

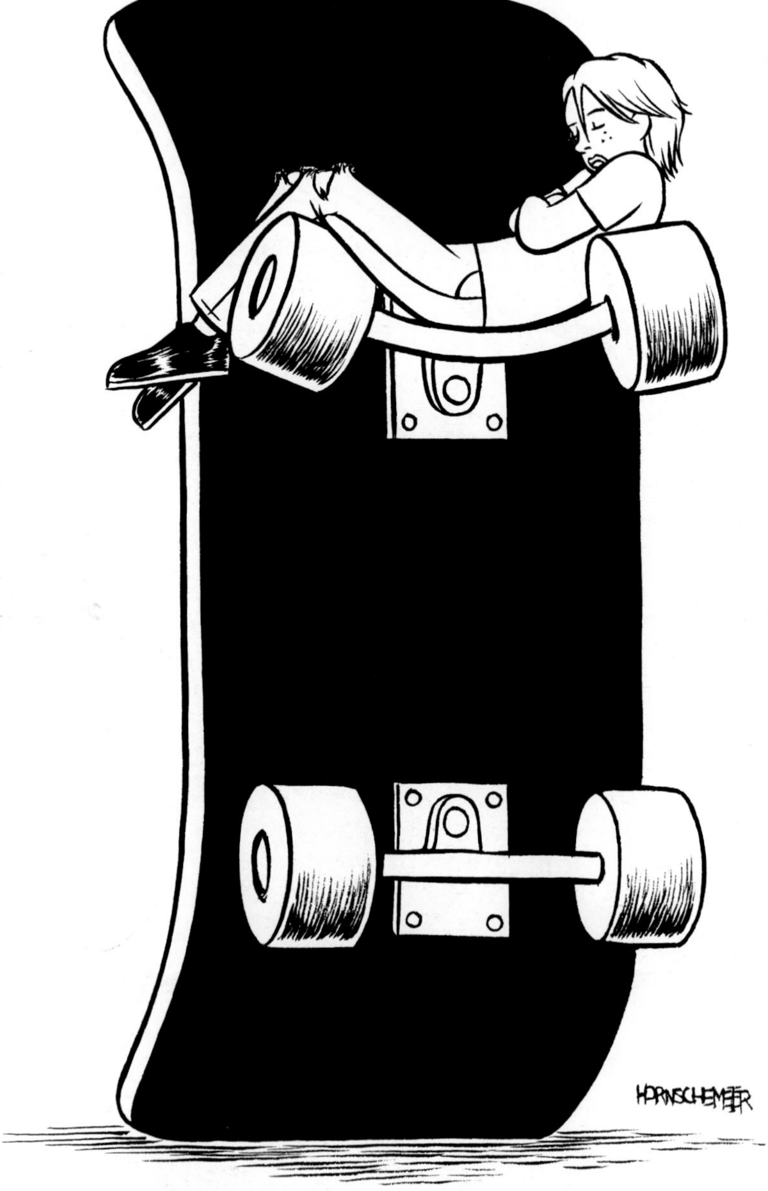
HORNSCHEMEIER

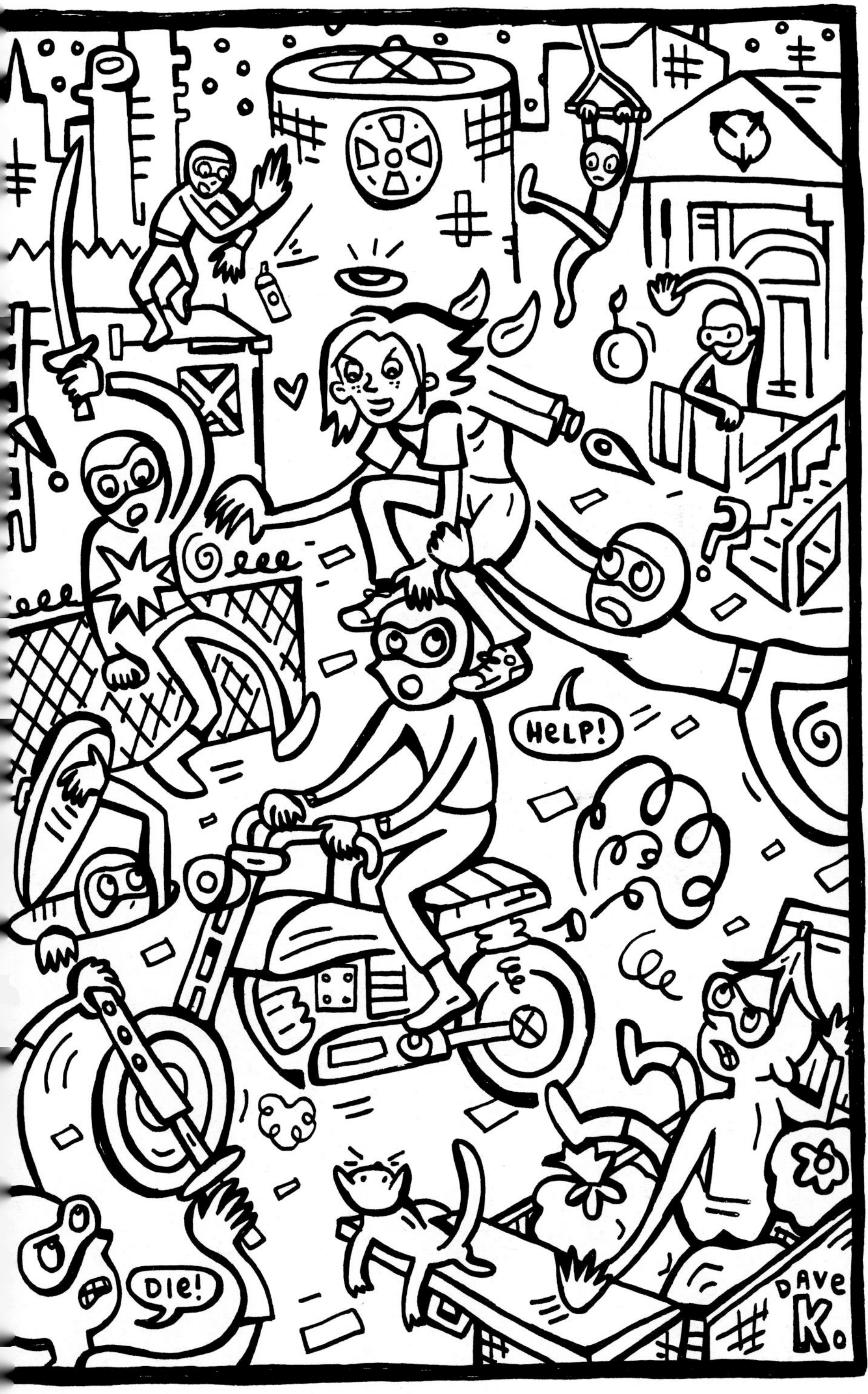
HELP!
DIE!
DAVE K.

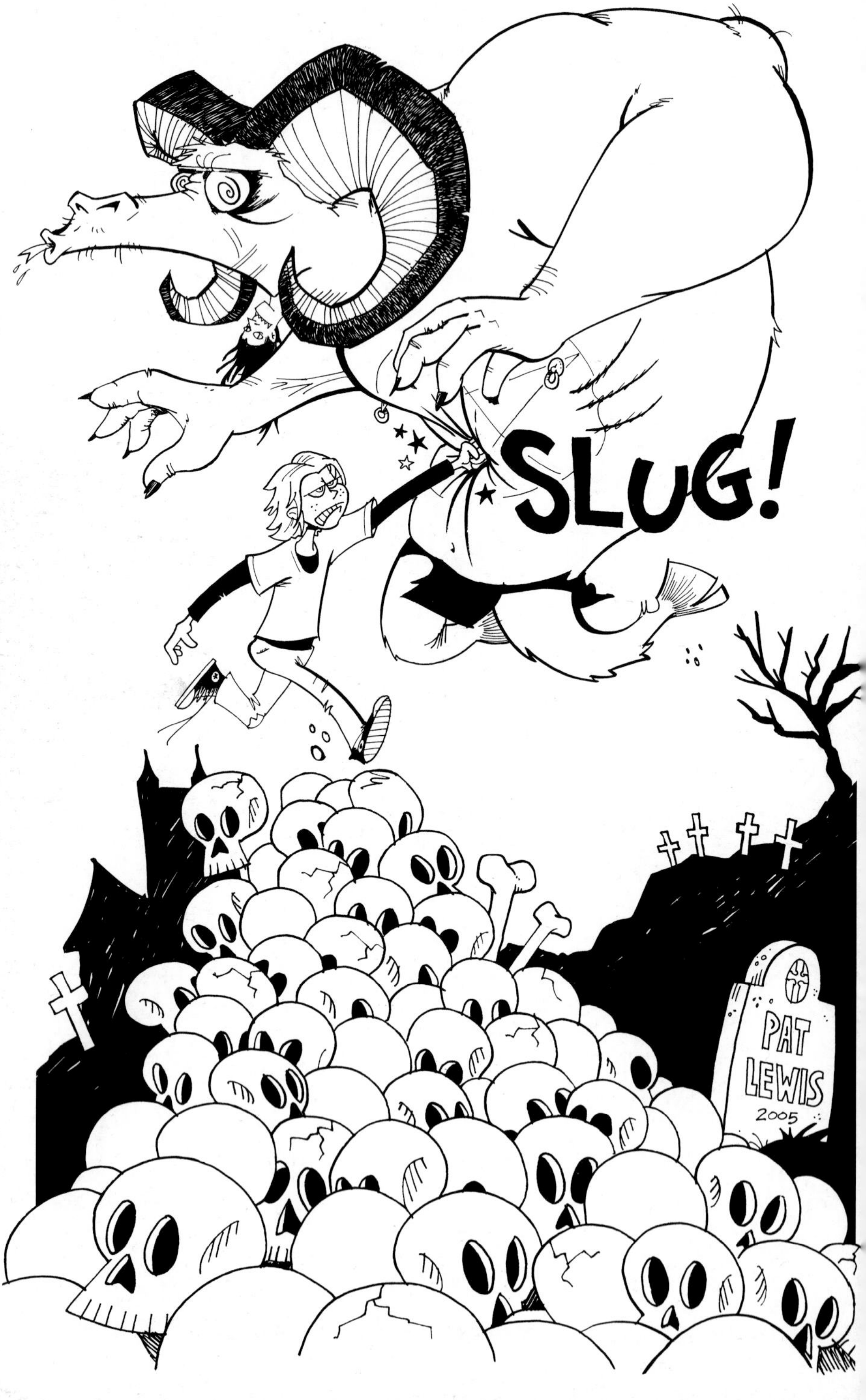
SLUG!
PAT LEWIS 2005

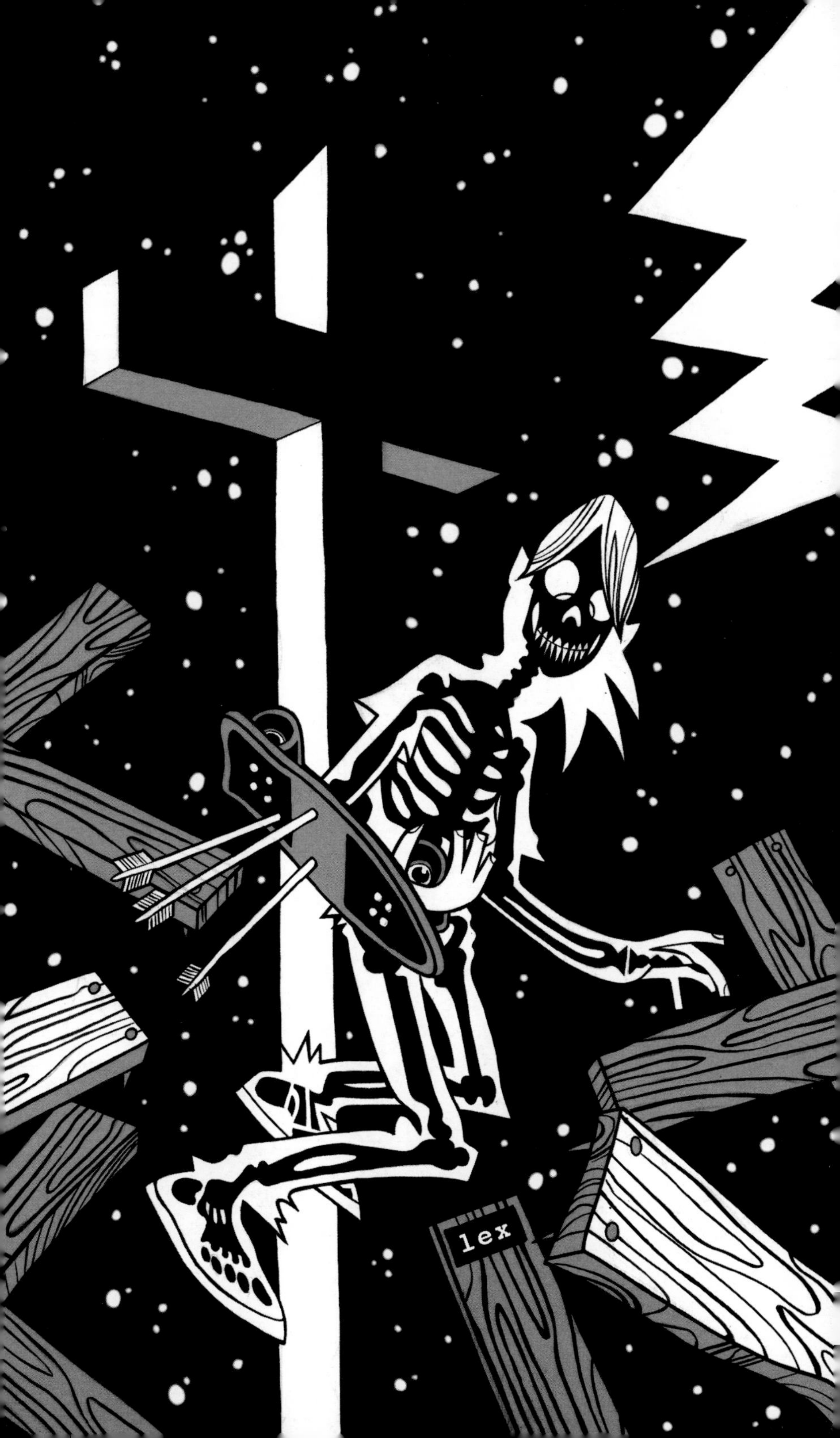
lex

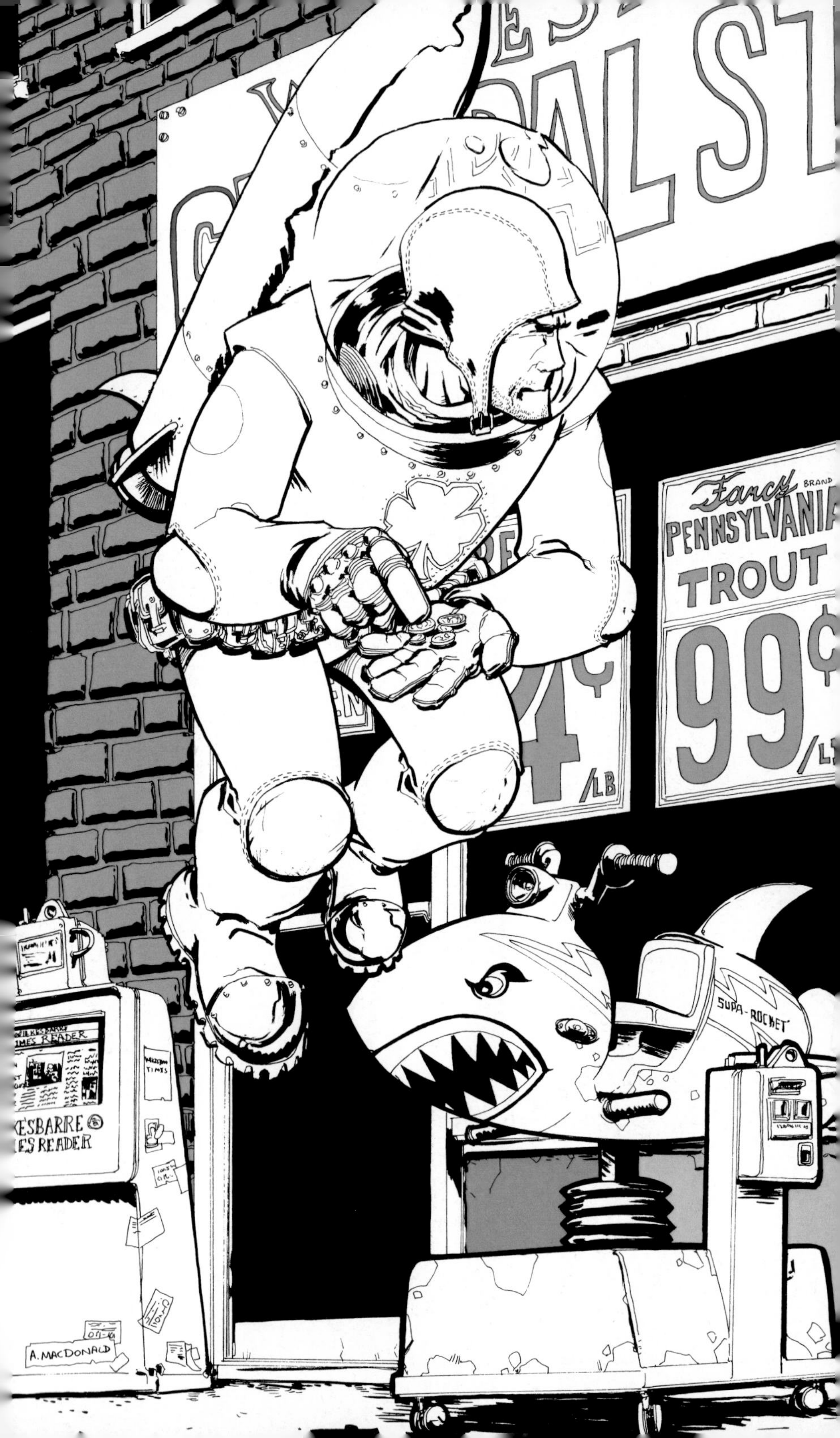
Fancy BRAND
PENNSYLVANIA
TROUT
99¢
/LB
/LB
SUPA-ROCKET
A. MACDONALD

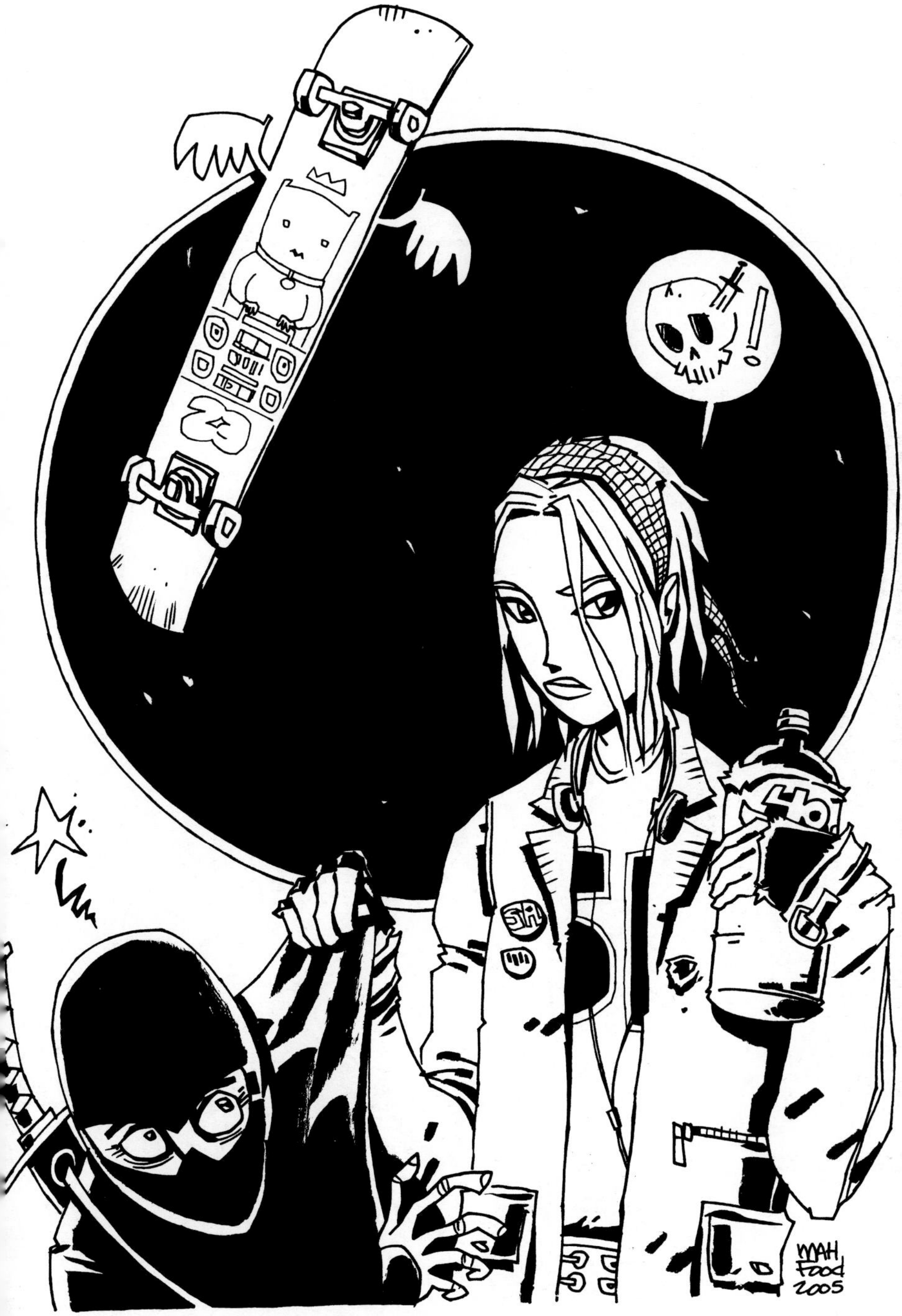
MAH Food 2005

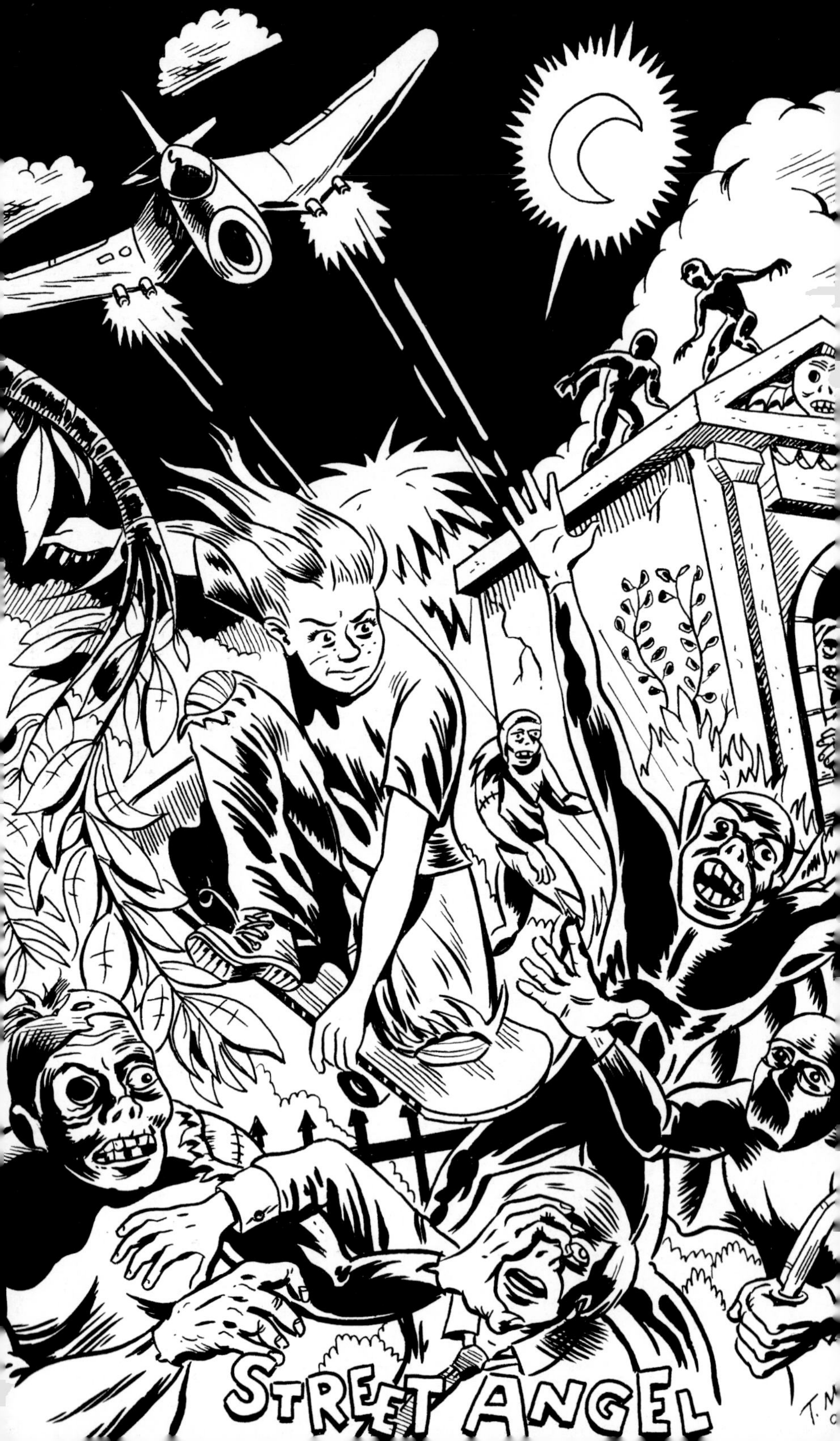
STREET ANGEL

The Magazine for Bad Mamma Jammas

PIMP HAND

In this issue:

KEEPIN' IT REAL
An In-Depth
How-To Guide

KICKIN' ASS & TAKIN' NAMES:
Do We Really Need
Their Names?

DOGGY STYLE:
The Best Way to
Hit That Shit?

And **AFRODISIAC**
The Definitive Interview
with the Definitive
Do-Gooder!

784555 137359802

3 Dollars, Bitch

Scott Mills H.N.I.C.

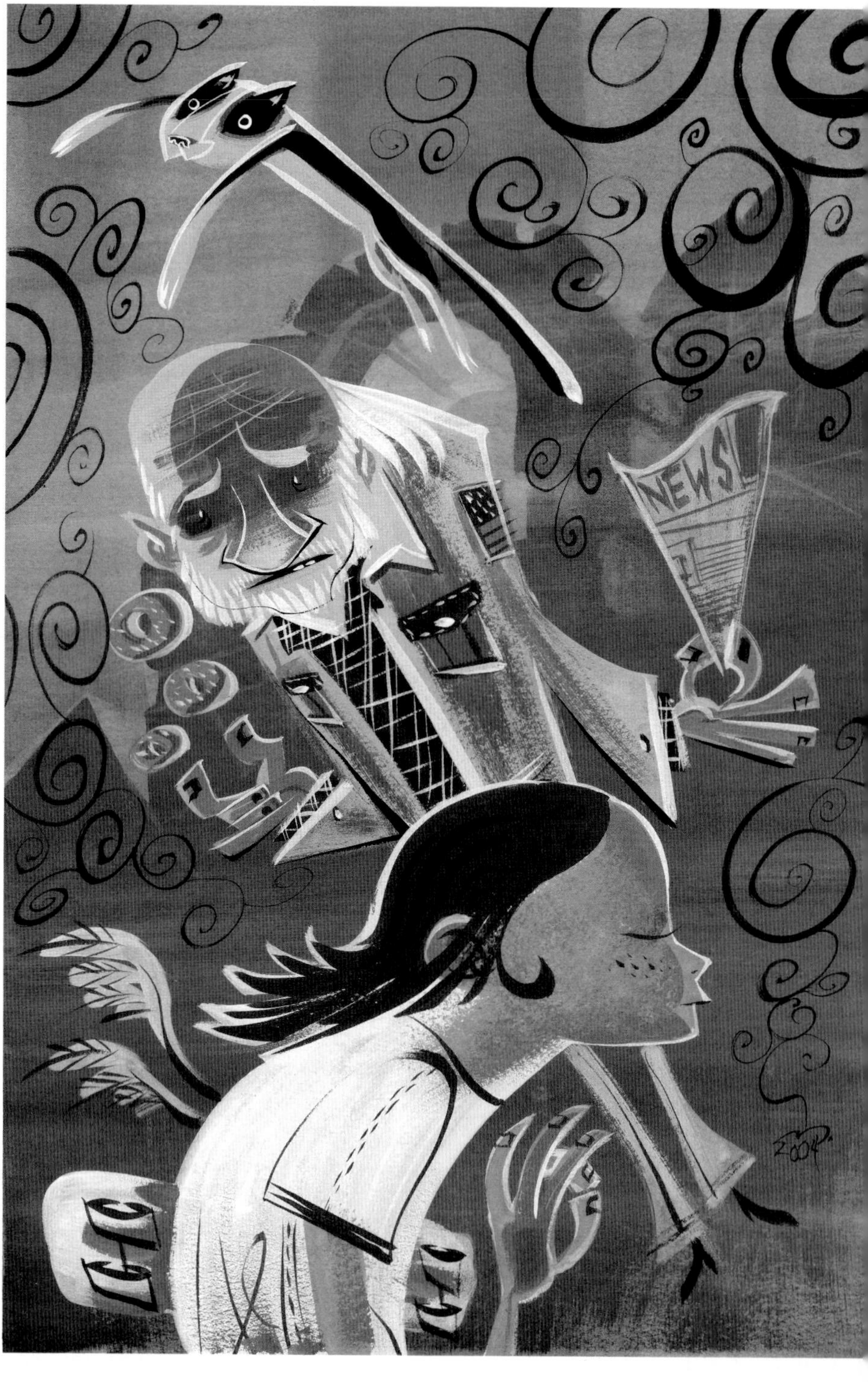
NEWS!

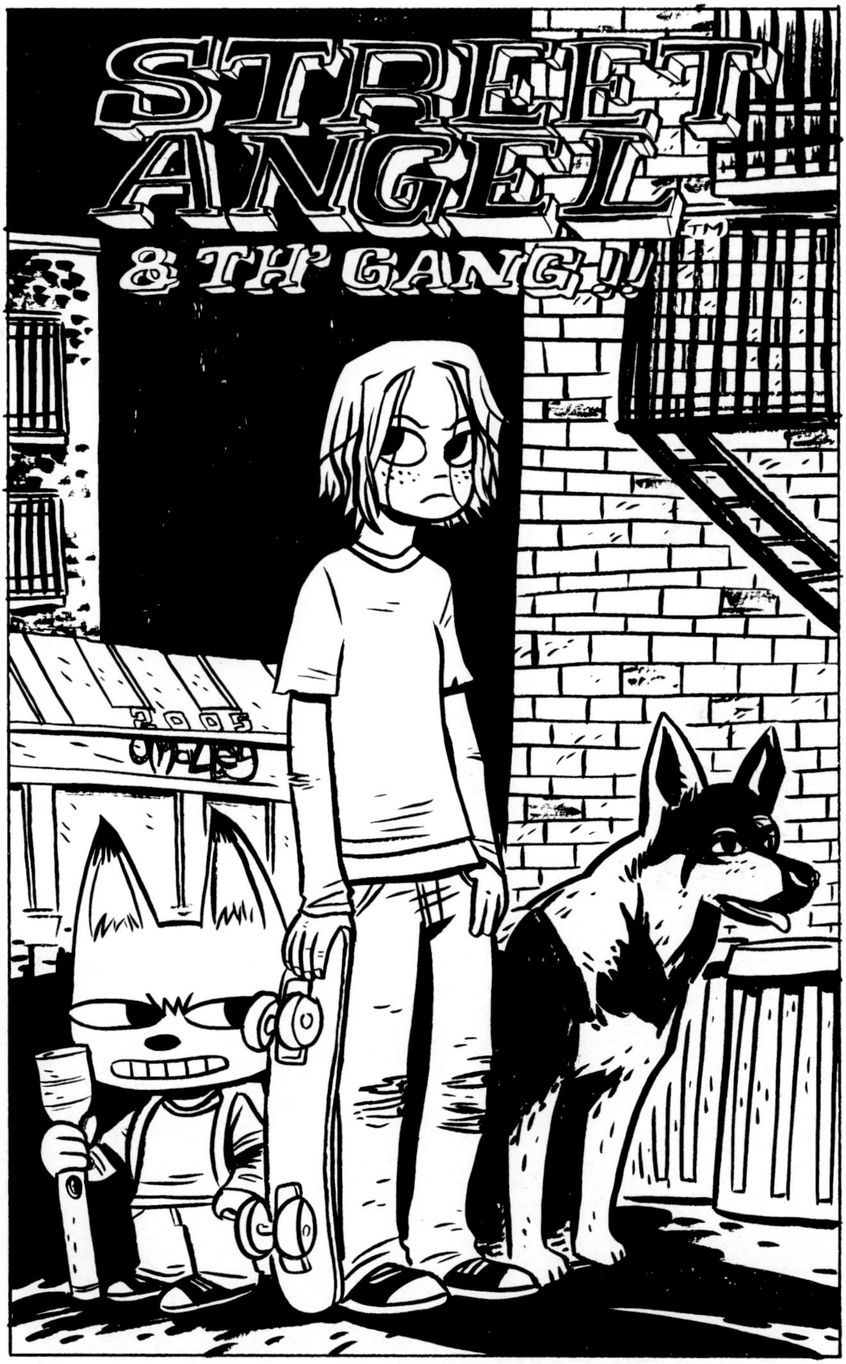
STREET ANGEL
& TH' GANG!!
TM

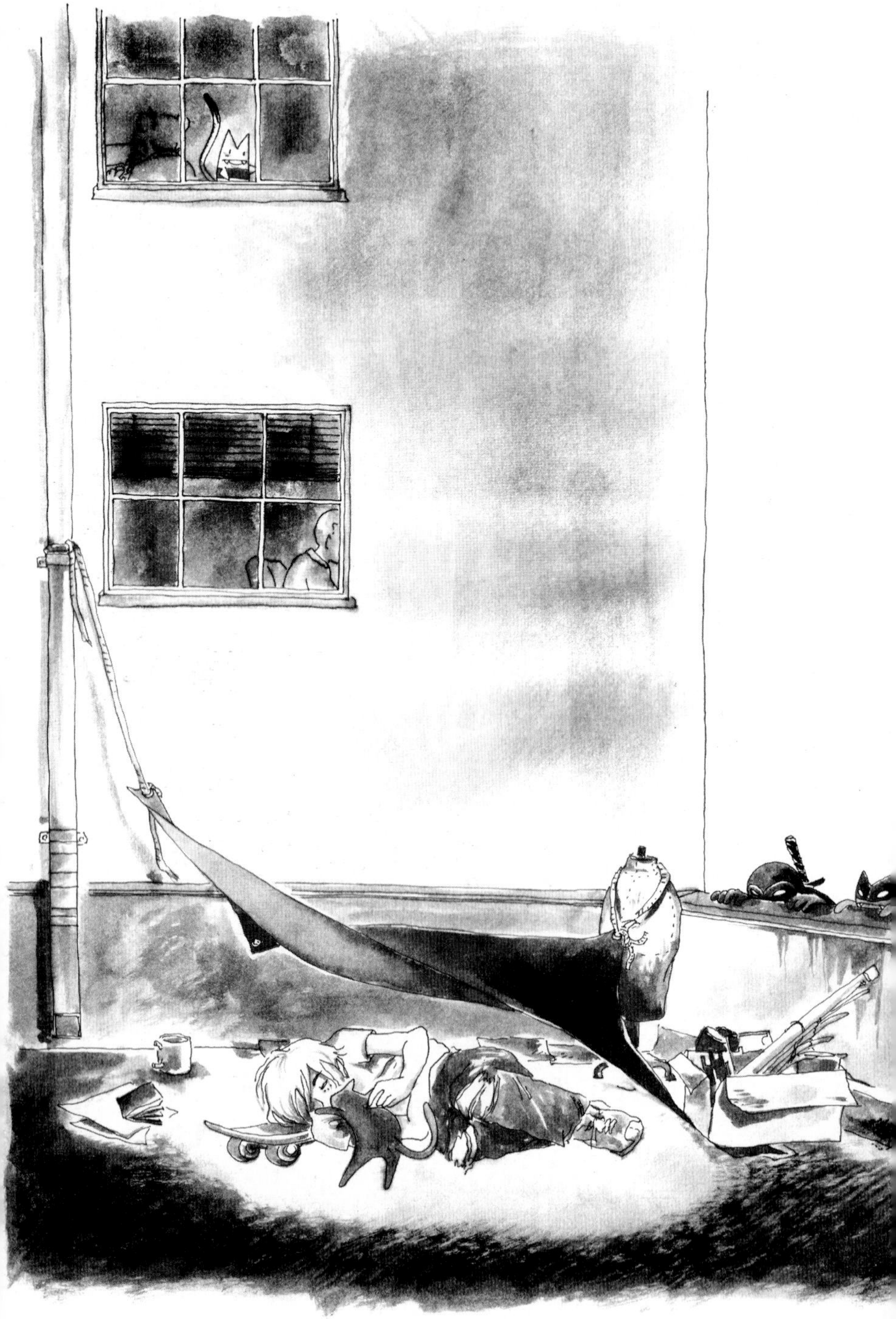

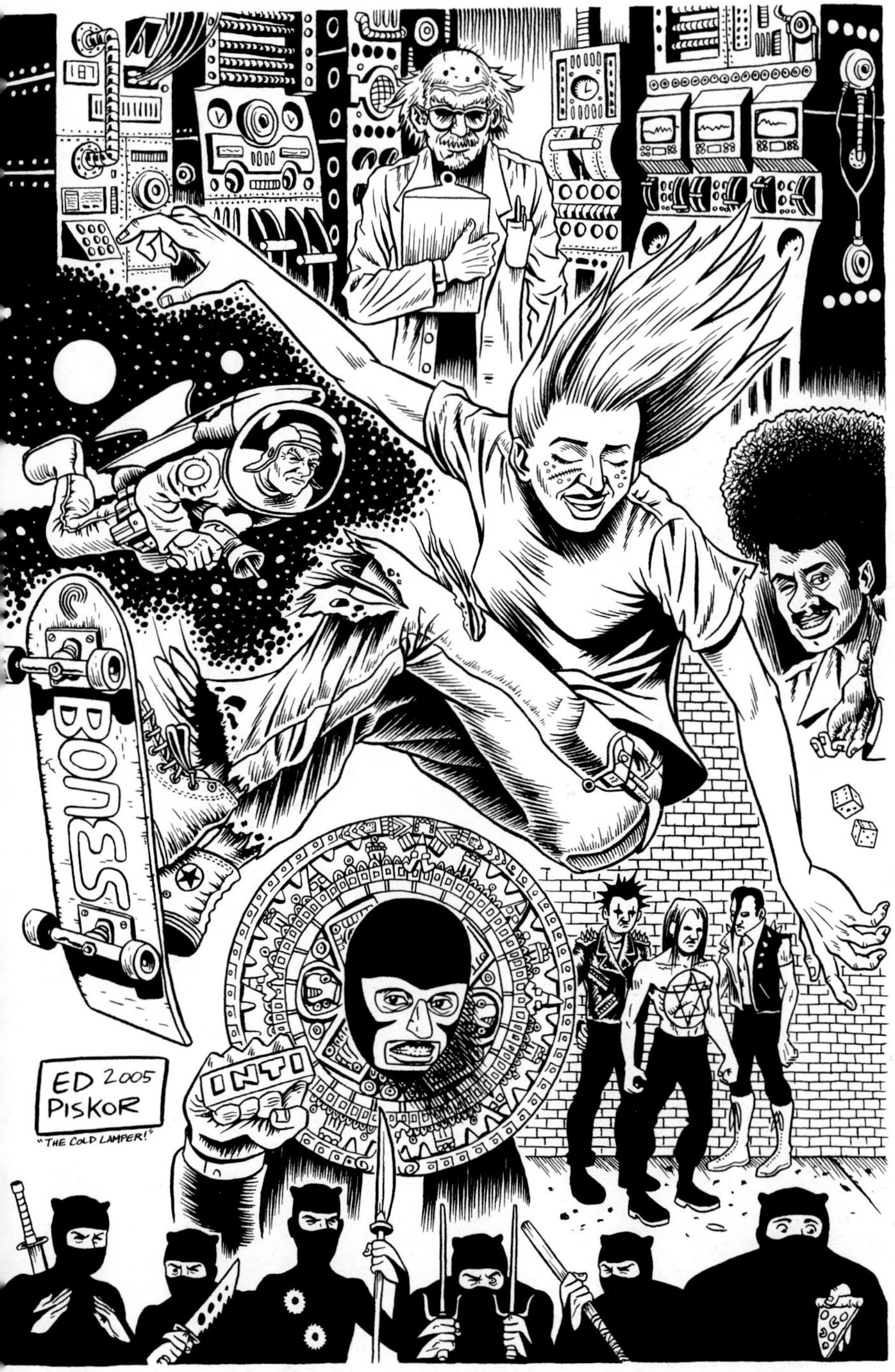

BONES
ED 2005
PISKOR
"THE COLD LAMPER!"
INTI

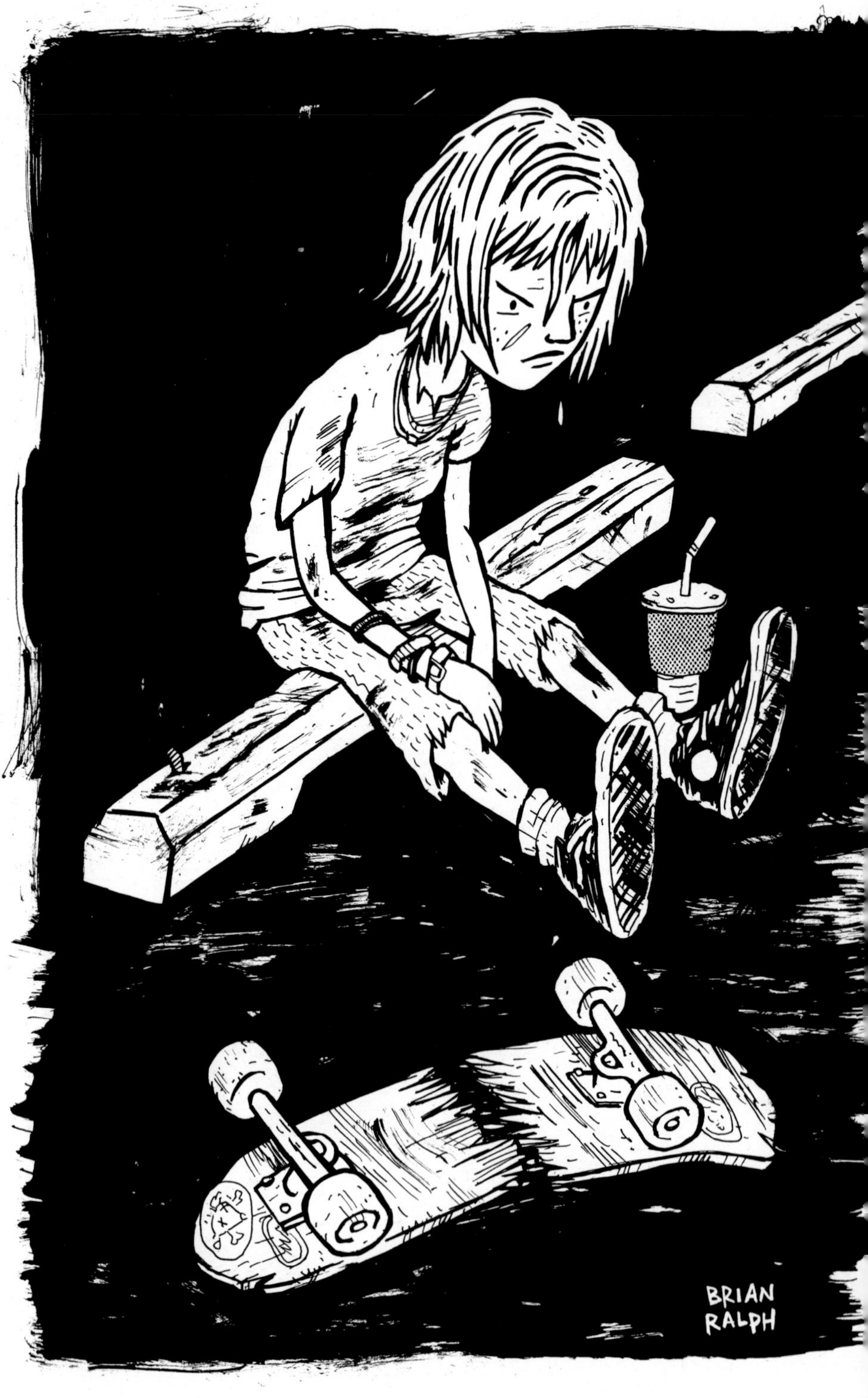
BRIAN
RALPH

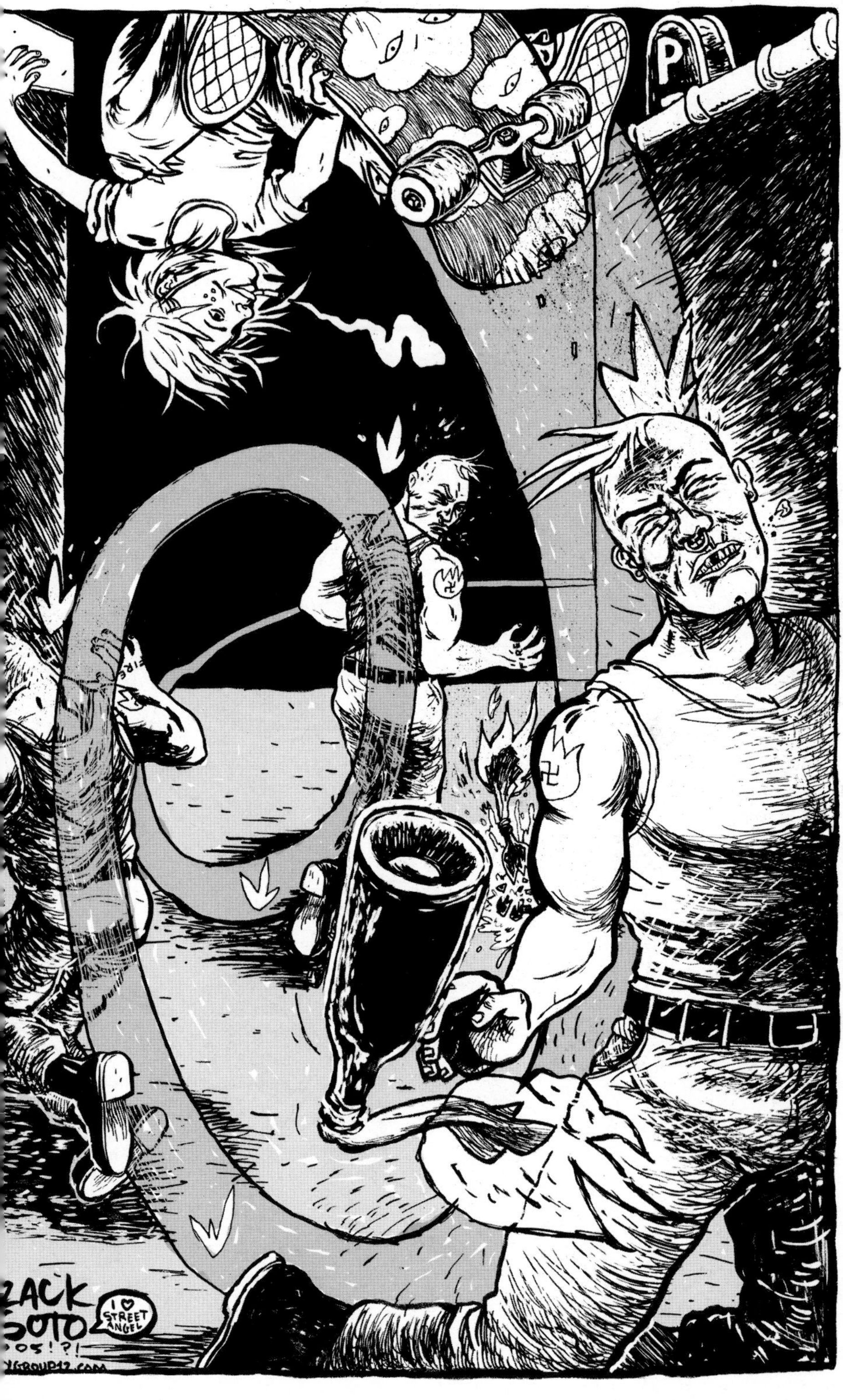
I ♥ STREET ANGEL
ZACK
SOTO
05!?!
YGROUP12.COM

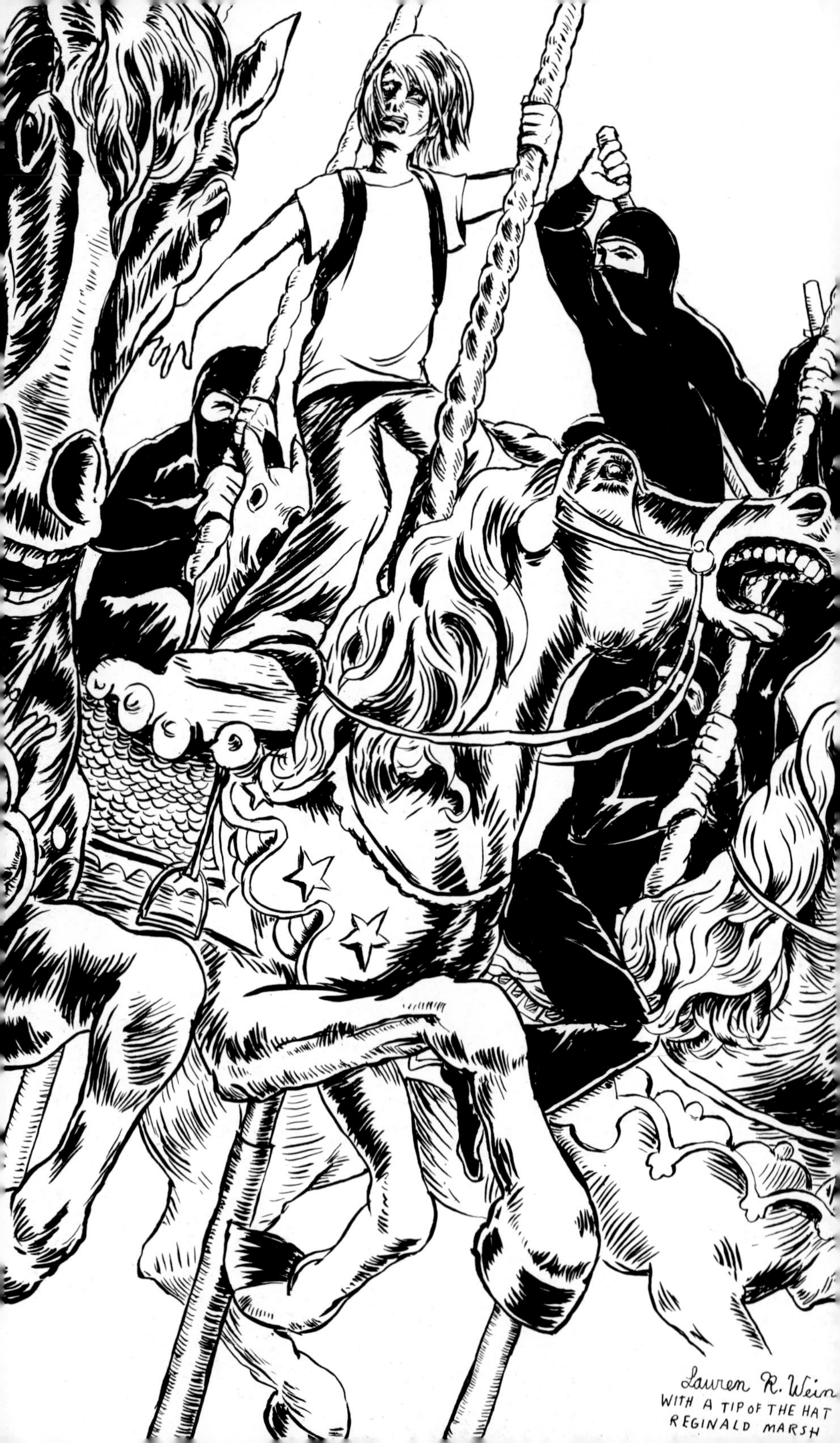
Lauren R. Wein
WITH A TIP OF THE HAT
REGINALD MARSH

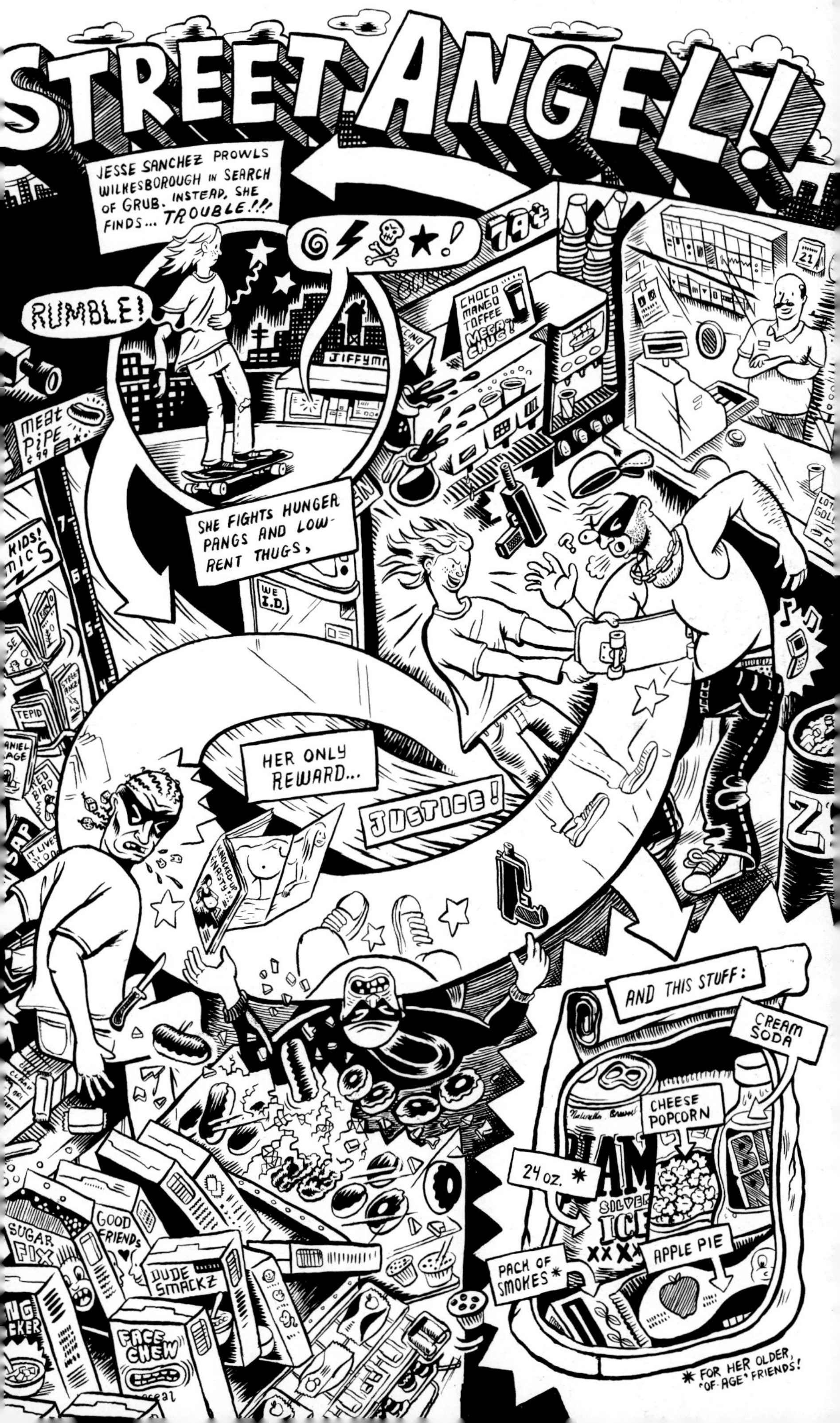
STREET ANGEL!
JESSE SANCHEZ PROWLS WILKESBOROUGH IN SEARCH OF GRUB. INSTEAD, SHE FINDS... TROUBLE!!!
RUMBLE!
79¢
CHOCO MANGO TOFFEE MEGA-CHUG!
meat PIPE $.99
SHE FIGHTS HUNGER PANGS AND LOW-RENT THUGS,
WE I.D.
TEPID
HER ONLY REWARD...
JUSTICE!
KNOCKED-UP & NASTY
IT LIVES
AND THIS STUFF:
CREAM SODA
CHEESE POPCORN
24 oz. *
PACK OF SMOKES *
APPLE PIE
SUGAR FIX
GOOD FRIENDS
DUDE SMACKZ
FACE CHEW
* FOR HER OLDER, "OF-AGE" FRIENDS!

Jim Rugg

I was born on February 1, 1977, and grew up in Connellsville, a post-industrial ghost town, about an hour south of Pittsburgh. After college I found a day job, moved to Pittsburgh, and made mini-comics until SLG began publishing Street Angel.

Thanks to everyone who generously gave his or her time and talent to create a pinup for this book.

Special thanks to Ron Mabon, Jasen Lex, Scott Mills, Farel Dalrymple, Evan Dorkin, Jennifer de Guzman, Dan Vado, Banjo, Brian Maruca, my family, and most of all, Natalie.

Thank you for reading.

Brian Maruca

Pittsburgh (1972-1984), Wilkes Barre (1984-1991), Pittsburgh (1991 -).

Special Thanks: Joey Leo, my wife (Kelly), my parents (mom and dad), my brother (Eric), Steve and Stacy Chbosky, Jim and Natalie (Rugg), Maki Nishimura-Russ, Mike Easler, Taco Bell, the good folks at SLG, Gloria Fan and Mosaic, Megatron, and all of the readers and reviewers.

Regular Thanks: Everyone else. You guys were good, just not special.